DATE DUE			

The Social Animal

A Series of Books in Psychology

EDITORS: Richard C. Atkinson
Jonathan Freedman
Gardner Lindzey
Richard F. Thompson

Second Edition

The Social Animal

Elliot Aronson
University of California, Santa Cruz

W. H. Freeman and Company
San Francisco

Library of Congress Cataloging in Publication Data

Aronson, Elliot.

   The social animal.

Includes bibliographical references and index.
   1. Social psychology.   I. Title.
[DNLM: 1. Psychology, Social.   HM251 A7691s]
HM251.A79 1976   301.1   75–35729
ISBN 0–7167–0552–4
ISBN 0–7167–0549–4 pbk.

Printed in the United States of America

10 9 8 7 6 5 4 3 2 1

to Vera, of Course

Acknowledgements

I am indicated on the title page as the sole author of this book, and it is certainly true that I wrote down all the words and did most of the thinking that produced them. Accordingly, if there are any stupidities in this book, they are mine, and if anything you read on these pages makes you angry, I'm the person you should yell at. At the same time, I want to confess that I never do anything entirely by myself: Many people contributed their knowledge and ideas to my word factory, and I would like to take this opportunity to thank them for their generous help.

Vera Aronson and Ellen Berscheid were particularly helpful. They painstakingly went over the original manuscript, page by page and line by line, making numerous suggestions and criticisms that had a significant impact on the final form of this book. Moreover, their enthusiasm for the project was infectious and helped me to climb out of frequent bouts of "writer's despair."

Several other people contributed valuable ideas and suggestions. I cannot possibly cite them all, but the most impactful contributors were Nancy Aston, Leonard Berkowitz, David Bradford, John Darley, Richard Easterlin, Jonathan Freedman, James Freel, Robert Helmreich, Michael Kahn, John Kaplan, Judson Mills, and Jev Sikes.

Thanks are also due to Judy Hilton and Faye Gibson, who typed and retyped various drafts of the manuscript as if they really enjoyed doing it; to Lyn Ellisor, who worked patiently on the bibliographical notes; and to William Ickes, who prepared the indexes. Most of this book was written while I was a Fellow at the Center for Advanced Study in the Behavioral Sciences at Stanford, California, and I am deeply grateful to the staff of that fine institution for providing me with the necessary leisure and facilities.

Finally, I am pleased to report that my friend and mentor, Leon Festinger, did not have anything to do with this manuscript—directly. He never read it, and, to my knowledge, he was not even aware that I was writing it. He is, however, responsible for its existence. I *could* say that he taught me all I know about social psychology, but that would be a lie. He taught me something much more valuable than that: he taught me how to find out the things that neither I nor anybody else knew.

March 1972

.   .   .

For the second edition of this book, I am happy to acknowledge the important contributions made by Pilar Gottlieb and Grace Schmidt, who typed, edited, xeroxed, indexed, and cajoled me into meeting my deadlines. I would also like to mention my students. While working on this manuscript, I had occasion to reexamine a good deal of my own research and many of my own ideas; and, in so doing, I was struck again (as I have been many times in the past) with how fortunate I've been to have worked with so many talented students. These people have taught me a great deal—all of them—from my very first research assistants in 1960, Merrill Carlsmith and John Darley, to the people who are currently collaborating with me. Indeed, one of my current research assistants, Diane Bridgeman, has made an important contribution to this revised edition—and I'm pleased to acknowledge my gratitude to her.

September 1975   ELLIOT ARONSON

Contents

Why I Wrote This Book   ix

1 What Is Social Psychology?   1

2 Conformity   11

3 Mass Communication, Propaganda, and Persuasion   45

4 Self-Justification   85

5 Human Aggression   141

6 Prejudice   173

7 Attraction: Why People Like Each Other   213

8 Communication in Sensitivity-Training Groups   247

9 Social Psychology as a Science   281

   Notes   303
   Name Index   327
   Subject Index   331

Why I Wrote This Book

In 1970–71, I was invited to spend the year in Stanford, California, at the Center for Advanced Study in the Behavioral Sciences. During that year, I was given all the support, encouragement, and freedom to do whatever I wanted, and I was assured that I was not responsible to anyone for anything. There, on a beautiful hill, roughly 30 miles from San Francisco (my favorite city), with a whole year in which to do anything my heart desired, I chose to write this book. Surrounded as I was by the beauty of the countryside, and close as I was to the excitement of San Francisco, why did I lock myself in a cubicle and write a book? It's not that I'm crazy and it's not that I needed the money. If there's any single reason why I wrote this book, it's that I once heard myself tell a large class of sophomores that social psychology is a young science—and it made me feel like a coward.

Let me explain: We social psychologists are fond of saying that social psychology is a young science—and it *is* a young science. Of course, astute observers have been making interesting pronounce-ments and proposing exciting hypotheses about social phenomena at least since the time of Aristotle, but these pronouncements and hypotheses were not seriously tested until well into the twentieth century. The first social psychological experiment (to my knowl-edge) was conducted by Triplett in 1897 (he measured the effect of competition on performance), but it wasn't until the late 1930s that experimental social psychology really took off, primarily under the inspiration of Kurt Lewin and his talented students. By the same token, it's interesting to note that, although Aristotle first asserted some of the basic principles of social influence and persuasion around 350 BC, it wasn't until the middle of the twentieth century that those principles were put to the experimental test by Carl Hovland and his associates.

In another sense, however, to claim that social psychology is a young science is to be guilty of a gigantic cop-out: It's a way of pleading with people not to expect too much from us. Specifically, it can be our way of dodging the responsibility for, and avoiding the risks inherent in, applying our findings to the problems of the world we live in. In this sense, protesting that social psychology is a young science is akin to claiming that we're not yet ready to say anything important, useful, or (if the reader will forgive me for using an overused word) relevant.

The purpose of this volume is unashamedly (but with some trepidation) to spell out the relevance that sociopsychological re-search might have for some of the problems besetting contemporary society. Most of the data discussed in this volume are based on experiments; most of the illustrations and examples, however, are derived from current social problems—including prejudice, propa-ganda, war, alienation, aggression, unrest, and political upheaval. This duality reflects two of my own biases—biases that I cherish. The first is that the experimental method is the best way to understand a complex phenomenon. It is a truism of science that the only way to really know the world is to reconstruct it: that is, in order to truly understand what causes what, we must do more than simply observe —rather, we must be responsible for *producing* the first "what" so that we can be sure that it really *caused* the second "what." My second bias is that the only way to be *certain* that the causal relations uncovered in experiments are valid is to bring them out of the laboratory and into the real world. Thus, as a scientist, I like to work in a laboratory; as a citizen, however, I like to have windows through which I can look out upon the world. Windows, of course, work in both directions: we often derive hypotheses from everyday life. We can best test these hypotheses under the sterile conditions of the laboratory; and, in order to try to keep our *ideas* from becoming sterile, we attempt to take our laboratory findings back out through the window to see if they hold up in the real world.

Implicit in all this is my belief that social psychology is extremely important—that social psychologists can play a vital role in making the world a better place in which to live. Indeed, in my more grandiose moments, I nurse the secret belief that social psychologists are in a unique position to have a profound and beneficial impact on our lives by providing an increased understanding of such important phenomena as conformity, persuasion, prejudice, love, and aggression. Now that my secret belief is no longer a secret, I can promise only to try not to force it down the reader's throat on the following pages. Rather, I'll leave it to the readers to decide, after they have finished this volume, whether social psychologists have discovered, or can *ever* discover, anything useful—much less anything uniquely important.

This is a slim volume, and purposely so. It is meant to be a brief introduction to the world of social psychology, not an encyclopedic catalogue of research and theory. Because I opted to make it brief, I had to be selective. This means both that there are some traditional topics that I chose not to cover and that I have not gone into exhaustive detail with those topics that I did choose to cover. Because of this, it was a difficult book to write. I have had to be more a "news analyst" than a "reporter." For example, there are many controversies that I did not fully describe. Rather, I exercised my own judgment; made an educated (and, I hope, honest) assessment of what is the most accurate description of the field, as of 1972; and stated it as clearly as I could.

This decision was made with the student in mind—this book was written for students, not for my colleagues. If I've learned nothing else in fifteen years of teaching, I *have* learned that, although a detailed presentation of all positions is useful (and sometimes even fascinating) to one's colleagues, it tends to leave students cold. Students, in effect, ask us what time it is, and we, in effect, present them with a chart showing the various time zones around the world, a history of time-telling from the sun dial to the Bulova Accutron, and a detailed description of the anatomy of the wrist watch. By the time we've finished, they've lost interest in the question. Nothing is safer than to state all sides of all issues, but few things are more boring. Although I have discussed controversial issues, I have not hesitated to draw conclusions. In short, I have attempted to be brief without being unfair, and I have tried to present complex material simply and clearly without *over*simplifying. Only the reader can determine how successful I have been in accomplishing either of these goals.

•   •   •

Early in 1975, I decided, with some reluctance, to revise this book. A lot has happened in three years. Not only have new things been discovered in the field of social psychology, but, even more important, the world has taken a few major turns since the winter of 1972, when I put the final scrawl on my yellow pad for the first edition. To name just a few of the major events: a brutal, draining, and divisive war came to an end, a vice-president and a president of the United States were forced to resign in humiliation, and the women's liberation movement was beginning to have a significant impact on the consciousness of the nation. These are sociopsychological events of the greatest significance. The indolent slob who lives inside of me began to acknowledge (with a long sigh) that any book that purports to be about us and our lives must stay abreast of the times. So, here it is, an updated *Social Animal*: slightly longer, slightly more complex, but, I hope, not different in tone and approach from the original.

The Social Animal

1

What Is Social Psychology?

As far as we know, Aristotle was the first person to formulate basic principles of social influence and persuasion; but, although he did say that man is a social animal, he was probably not the first person to make that observation. Moreover, chances are he was not the first person to marvel at the truth of that statement while simultaneously puzzling over its triteness and insubstantiality. Although it is certainly true that people are social animals, so are a host of other creatures, from ants and bees to monkeys and apes. What does it mean to say that humans are "social animals"? Let's look at some concrete examples:

> A college student named Sam and four of his acquaintances are watching a presidential candidate make a speech on television. Sam is favorably impressed; he likes him better than the opposing candidate because of his sincerity. After the speech, one of the other students asserts that he was turned off by the candidate—that he considered him to be a complete phony—and that he prefers the opposing candidate. All of the others are quick to agree with him. Sam looks puzzled and a trifle distressed. Finally, he mumbles to his acquaintances, "I guess he didn't come across as sincere as one might hope for him to be."

A second grade teacher stands before her class and asks, "What is the sum of six, nine, four, and eleven?" A girl in the third row puzzles over the question for several seconds, hesitates, raises her hand tentatively, and, when called on, haltingly answers, "Thirty?" The teacher nods, smiles at her, says, "Nice work, Peggy," and pastes a gold star on her forehead. She then asks the class, "What is the sum of seven, four, eight, three, and ten?" Without wasting a moment, Peggy leaps to her feet and shouts, "Thirty-two!"

A four-year-old boy is given a toy drum for his birthday. After pounding on it for a few minutes, he casts it aside and studiously ignores it for the next several weeks. One day, a friend comes to visit, picks up the drum, and is about to play with it. Suddenly the young "owner" tears the drum from his friend's grasp and proceeds to play with it as if it had always been his favorite toy.

A ten-year-old boy avidly consumes two bowls of Wheaties daily because an Olympic decathalon champion endorses the product and implies that he owes his athletic prowess, in part, to the consumption of that particular brand of cereal.

A housewife who has lived her entire life in a small town in Montana has never had any contact with real, live black people, but she "knows" that they are shiftless, lazy, and over-sexed.

Charlie, a high school senior, has recently moved to a new city. He used to be quite popular, but not any more: although the kids at school are civil to him, they have not been particularly friendly. He is feeling lonely, insecure, and unattractive. One day, during lunch period, he finds himself at a table with two of his female classmates. One of them is warm, attractive, brilliant and vivacious; he has been admiring her and day-dreaming about her. For several weeks he has been longing for an opportunity to talk to her. The other young woman is not nearly as appealing. Charlie ignores the vivacious woman of his dreams and begins an earnest conversation with her companion.

Following the 1970 tragedy at Kent State University, in which four students were shot and killed by Ohio National Guardsmen while demonstrating against the war in Southeast Asia, a high-school teacher from Kent, Ohio, asserted that the slain students deserved to die. She made this statement even though she was well aware of the fact that at least two of the victims were not participating in the demonstration but were peacefully walking across campus at the time of the shooting. Indeed, she went on to say, "Anyone who appears on the streets of a city like Kent with long hair, dirty clothes or barefooted deserves to be shot."[1]

Mary has just turned nine. For her birthday, she received a Suzie Homemaker baking and cooking set—complete with "her own little oven." Her parents chose this present because she seems very inter-ested in culinary things and is forever helping mommy set the table, prepare the meals, and clean the house. "Isn't it wonderful," says Mary's father, "how at age nine she is already interested in being a housewife? Little girls must have housewifery built into their genes. Those women's liberation people don't know what they're talking about."

George Woods is black. When he and I were growing up together in Massachusetts in the 1940s, he considered himself a "colored boy" and felt inferior to his white friends. There were many reasons for this feeling. That George was treated like an inferior by the white com-munity had a direct influence upon him, of course; and a number of other forces influenced him less directly. In those days, George could entertain himself by turning on the radio and listening to "Amos 'n Andy," a radio show in which black adults were portrayed as naive children, as stupid, lazy, and illiterate, but rather cute—not unlike friendly domesticated animals. The black characters were, of course, played by white actors. In films, George could see the stereotyped "colored man," usually a chauffeur or some other menial. A standard plot would have the "colored man" accompany the white hero into a haunted house, where they would hear a strange and ominous noise: The camera pans in on the "colored man's" face; his eyes grow large with fright; he screams, "Feet, do your stuff!" and dashes through the door, not taking the time to open it first. We can only guess what George experienced while viewing these films in the company of his white friends.

Most of George's adult acquaintances were blacks who "knew their place." They were obsequious to whites, used hair straightener in an attempt to look less black, and cared little about their African heritage. The idea was to be white, a goal which, of course, was un-attainable. I would be amazed if this climate did not lower George's self-concept because such changes in self-concept are not atypical: A famous study of black children in the forties by Kenneth and Mamie Clark showed that, as early as age three, many of the children had learned to feel inferior to whites.[2]

Things change. Although discrimination and unfairness are still very much a part of our society, George Woods' children, growing up in the seventies, need not face quite the same prospect as George himself did: the mass media now depict blacks in roles that are not exclusively menial; a new pride in blackness is emerging, along with an interest in, and enthusiasm about, Afro-American history and culture; and sales of hair straightener are down. The society is influencing George's children in a much different way than it influenced George.

Although things do change, we should not be complacent in the belief that all changes are in a humanistic direction. On August 30, 1936, during the Spanish Civil War, a single plane bombed Madrid. There were several casualties, but no one was killed. The world was profoundly shocked by the idea of a congested city being attacked from the air. Newspaper editorials around the world expressed the general horror and indignation of the citizenry.[3] Only nine years later, American planes dropped nuclear bombs on Hiroshima and Nagasaki. More than one hundred thousand people were killed and countless thousands suffered severe injuries. Shortly thereafter, a poll indicated that only 4.5 percent of the American population felt that we should not have used those weapons, and an astonishing 22.7 percent felt that we should have used many more of them before Japan had a chance to surrender. Clearly, something had happened during those nine years to influence opinion.

A Definition

What is social psychology? There are almost as many definitions of social psychology as there are social psychologists. Instead of listing some of these definitions, it might be more informative to let the subject matter define the field. The examples presented in the preceding pages are all illustrations of sociopsychological situations. As diverse as these situations may be, they do contain one common factor: social influence. The opinion of Sam's friends on the merits of the presidential candidate influenced Sam's judgment (or at least his public statement regarding that judgment). The rewards emanating from the teacher influenced the speed and vigor of Peggy's classroom responses. The four-year-old seemed to find his toy drum more attractive because of the inadvertent influence of his friend's interest. The Olympic athlete's influence on our Wheaties-eating youngster, on the other hand, was far from inadvertent; rather, it was intentionally designed to make him convince his mother to buy Wheaties. That Charlie ignored the woman of his dreams almost certainly has something to do with his fear of rejection, the way he was feeling about himself, and his implicit assumption about the relative likelihood of being rejected by either of the two women. The Montana housewife was certainly not born with an unflattering stereotype of black people in her head—somebody, somehow, put it there. Exactly how the high-school teacher in Kent, Ohio, came to believe that innocent people deserved to die is a fascinating and frighteningly current question; for now, let us simply say that this belief was probably influenced by her own indirect complicity in the tragic events on the campus. It is conceivable, as Mary's father says, that "housewifery" is genetic, but it is far more likely that, from infancy onward, Mary was rewarded and encouraged every time she expressed an interest in such "feminine" things as cooking, sewing, and dolls—to a greater extent than if she expressed an interest in football, boxing, and chemistry. It is also reasonable to assume that, if Mary's kid brother had shown an interest in "housewifery," he would *not* have received a Suzie Homemaker set for *his* birthday. Also, as with young George Woods, who felt inferior to his playmates, Mary's self-image could have been shaped by the mass media, which tend to depict women in roles that the culture encourages them to play: housewife, secretary, nurse, school teacher—the mass media rarely depict women as biochemists, college professors, or business executives. If we compare the young George Woods with his children, we will see that the self-images of minority-group members can change, and these changes can influence and be influenced by changes in the mass media and changes in the attitudes of the general population. This, of course, is graphically illustrated by the opinions of Americans about the use of nuclear weapons in 1945.

The key phrase in the preceding paragraph is "social influence." And this becomes our working definition of social psychology: the influences that people have upon the beliefs or behavior of others. Using this as our definition, we will attempt to understand many of the phenomena described in the preceding illustrations. How is a person influenced? Why does he accept influence—or, put another way, what's in it for him? What are the variables that increase or decrease the effectiveness of social influence? Does such influence have a permanent effect, or is it merely transitory? What are the variables that increase or decrease the permanence of the effects of social influence? Can the same principles be applied equally to the attitudes of the high-school teacher in Kent, Ohio, and to the toy preferences of young children? How does one person come to like another person? Is it through these same processes that he comes to like his new sports car or his box of Wheaties? How does a person develop prejudices against an ethnic or racial group? Is it akin to liking—but in reverse—or does it involve an entirely different set of psychological processes?

Most people are interested in questions of this sort; in a sense, therefore, most people are social psychologists. Because most of us spend a good deal of our time interacting with other people—being influenced by them, influencing them, being delighted, amused, and angered by them—it is natural that most of us develop hypotheses about social behavior. Although most amateur social psychologists test these hypotheses to their own satisfaction, these "tests" lack the rigor and impartiality of careful scientific investigation. Often, the results of scientific research are identical with what most people "know" to be true. This is not surprising; conventional wisdom is usually based upon shrewd observation that has stood the test of time. But it is important that social psychologists conduct research to test hypotheses—even those hypotheses that we all know are obviously true—because many things that we "know" to be true turn out to be false when carefully investigated. Although it seems reasonable, for example, to assume that people who are threatened with severe punishment for engaging in a certain behavior might eventually learn to despise that behavior, it turns out that when this question is studied scientifically we find that just the reverse is true: people who are threatened with mild punishment develop a dislike for the forbidden behavior; people who are severely threatened show, if anything, a slight *increase* in liking for the forbidden behavior. Likewise, most of us, from our own experience, would guess that, if we overheard someone saying nice things about us (behind our backs), we would tend to like that person—all other things being equal. This turns out to be true. But what is equally true is that we tend to like that person even more if some of the remarks we overhear him make about us are anything *but* nice. More will be said about these phenomena in the following chapters.

In his attempt to understand human social behavior, the professional social psychologist has a great advantage over most amateur social psychologists. Although, like the amateur, he usually begins with careful observation, he can go far beyond that. He does not need to wait for things to happen so that he can observe how people respond; he can, in fact, make things happen. That is, he can conduct an experiment in which scores of people are subjected to particular conditions (for example, a severe threat or a mild threat; overhearing nice things or overhearing a combination of nice and nasty things). Moreover, he can do this in situations in which everything can be held constant except for the particular conditions being investigated. He can, therefore, draw conclusions based on data far more precise and numerous than those available to the amateur social psychologist, who must depend upon observations of events that occur randomly and under complex circumstances.

Virtually all of the data presented in this book are based upon experimental evidence. It is important, for this reason, that the reader understand what constitutes an experiment in social psychology and that he understand the advantages, disadvantages, ethical problems, excitements, headaches, and heartaches that are associated with this kind of enterprise. Although an understanding of the experimental method is important, it is by no means essential to an understanding of the substantive material presented here. Therefore, the chapter "Social Psychology as a Science" is the final one in this book. The reader may peruse this chapter before reading on (if he prefers to understand the technicalities before delving into the substantive material), or he can read it at any point on his journey through the book—whenever his interest is piqued.

People Who Do Crazy Things Are Not Necessarily Crazy

The social psychologist studies social situations that affect people's behavior. Occasionally, these natural situations become focused into pressures so great that they cause people to behave in ways that can easily be classified as abnormal. When I say "people" I mean very large numbers of people. To my mind, it does not increase our understanding of human behavior to classify these people as psychotic. It is much more useful to try to understand the nature of the situation and the processes that were operating to produce the behavior. This leads us to Aronson's first law: "People who do crazy things are not necessarily crazy."

Let us take, as an illustration, the Ohio schoolteacher who asserted that the four Kent State students deserved to die. I don't think that she was alone in this belief—and, although all the people who hold this belief *may* be psychotic, I seriously doubt it, and I doubt that so classifying them does much to extend our knowledge. Similarly, in the aftermath of the Kent slayings, the rumor spread that the slain girls were pregnant anyway—so that it was a blessing that they died—and that all four of the students were filthy and so covered with lice that the mortuary attendants became nauseated while examining the bodies. These rumors, of course, were totally false. But, according to James Michener,[4] they spread like wild fire. Were all the people who believed and spread these rumors insane? Later in this book, we will examine the processes that produced this kind of behavior—processes to which most of us are susceptible, under the right sociopsychological conditions.

Ellen Berscheid[5] has observed that people have a tendency to explain unpleasant behavior by attaching a label to the perpetrator ("crazy," "sadistic," or whatever), thereby excluding him from the rest of "us nice people." In that way, we no longer have to worry about his behavior, because it has nothing to do with nice folks. According to Berscheid, the danger in this kind of thinking is that it tends to make us smug about our own susceptibility to the situational pressures that produce unpleasant behavior, and it leads to a rather simple-minded approach to the solution of social problems. Specifically, such a simple-minded solution might include the development of a set of diagnostic tests to determine who is a liar, who is a sadist, who is corrupt, who is a maniac; social action might then consist of identifying these people and relegating them to the appropriate institution. Of course, this is not to say that psychosis does not exist or that psychotics should never be institutionalized. Neither am I saying that all people are the same and respond exactly as crazily to the same intense social pressures. To repeat, what I *am* saying is that some situational variables can move a great proportion of us "normal" adults to behave in very unappetizing ways. It is of paramount importance that we attempt to understand these variables and the processes that produce unpleasant behavior.

An illustration might be useful. Think of a prison. Consider the guards. What are they like? Chances are, most people would imagine prison guards to be tough, callous, unfeeling people. Some might even consider them to be cruel, tyrannical, and sadistic. People who take this kind of *dispositional* view of the world might suggest that the reason people become guards is to have an opportunity to exercise their cruelty with relative impunity. Picture the prisoners. What are they like? Rebellious? Docile? No matter what specific pictures exist inside our heads, the point is that there *are* pictures there —and most of us believe that the prisoners and the guards are quite different from us in character and personality.

This *may* be true, but don't be too sure. In a dramatic piece of research, Philip Zimbardo created a simulated prison in the basement of the Psychology Department at Stanford University. Into this "prison" he brought a group of normal, mature, stable, intelligent young men. By flipping a coin, Zimbardo designated one-half of them prisoners and one-half of them guards, and they lived as such for six days. What happened? Let's allow Zimbardo to tell us in his own words:

> At the end of only six days we had to close down our mock prison because what we saw was frightening. It was no longer apparent to us or most of the subjects where they ended and their roles began. The majority had indeed become "prisoners" or "guards," no longer able to clearly differentiate between role-playing and self. There were dramatic changes in virtually every aspect of their behavior, thinking and feeling. In less than a week, the experience of imprisonment undid (temporarily) a lifetime of learning; human values were suspended, self-concepts were challenged, and the ugliest, most base, pathological side of human nature surfaced. We were horrified because we saw some boys ("guards") treat other boys as if they were despicable animals, taking pleasure in cruelty, while other boys ("prisoners") became servile, dehumanized robots who thought only of escape, of their own individual survival, and of their mounting hatred of the guards.[6]

2

Conformity

One consequence of the fact that we are social animals is that we live in a state of tension between values associated with individuality and values associated with conformity. James Thurber has captured the flavor of one kind of conformity in the following description:

> Suddenly somebody began to run. It may be that he had simply remembered, all of a moment, an engagement to meet his wife, for which he was now frightfully late. Whatever it was, he ran east on Broad Street (probably toward the Maramor Restaurant, a favorite place for a man to meet his wife). Somebody else began to run, perhaps a newsboy in high spirits. Another man, a portly gentleman of affairs, broke into a trot. Inside of ten minutes, everybody on High Street, from the Union Depot to the Courthouse was running. A loud mumble gradually crystalized into the dread word "dam." "The dam has broke!" The fear was put into words by a little old lady in an electric, or by a traffic cop, or by a small boy: nobody knows who, nor does it

now really matter. Two thousand people were abruptly in full flight. "Go east!" was the cry that arose—east away from the river, east to safety. "Go east! Go east!" . . .

. . . A tall spare woman with grim eyes and a determined chin ran past me down the middle of the street. I was still uncertain as to what was the matter, in spite of all the shouting. I drew up alongside the woman with some effort, for although she was in her late fifties, she had a beautiful easy running form and seemed to be in excellent condition. "What is it?" I puffed. She gave a quick glance and then looked ahead again, stepping up her pace a trifle. "Don't ask me, ask God!" she said.[1]

This passage from Thurber, although comical, is an apt illustration of people conforming. One or two individuals began running for their own reasons; before long, everyone was running. Why? Because others were running. According to Thurber's story, when the running people realized that the dam hadn't given way after all, they felt pretty foolish. And yet, how much more foolish would they have felt if they hadn't conformed, and the dam had, in fact, burst? Is conformity good or bad? In its simplest sense, this is an absurd question. But words do carry evaluative meaning—thus, to be called an individualist or a nonconformist is to be designated, by connotation, as a "good" person: the label evokes an image of Daniel Boone standing on a mountain top with a rifle slung over his shoulder, the breeze blowing through his hair, as the sun sets in the background. To be called a conformist is somehow to be designated as an "inadequate" person: it evokes an image of a row of Madison Avenue admen with grey flannel suits, porkpie hats, and attaché cases, looking as though they had been created by a cookie cutter, and all saying simultaneously, "Let's run it up the flagpole and see if anyone salutes."

But we can use synonymous words that convey very different images. For "individualist" or "nonconformist," we can substitute "deviate"; for "conformist," we can substitute "team player." Somehow, "deviate" does not evoke Daniel Boone on the mountain top, and "team player" does not evoke the cookie-cutter-produced Madison Avenue adman.

When we look a little closer, we see an inconsistency in the way our society seems to feel about conformity (team playing) and non-conformity (deviance). For example, one of the great best sellers of the 1950s was a book by John F. Kennedy called *Profiles in Courage*, wherein the author praised several politicians for their courage in resisting great pressure and refusing to conform. To put it another way, Kennedy was praising people who refused to be good team players, people who refused to vote or act as their parties or constituents expected them to. Although their actions earned Kennedy's praise long after the deeds were done, the immediate reactions of their colleagues were generally far from positive. Nonconformists may be praised by historians or idolized in films or literature long after the fact of their nonconformity, but they are usually not held in high esteem, at the time, by those people to whose demands they refuse to conform. This observation receives strong support from a number of experiments in social psychology, most notably from one by Stanley Schachter,[2] in which several groups of students participated. Each group met for a discussion of the case history of a juvenile delinquent named Johnny Rocco, which each member was given to read. After reading the case, each group was asked to discuss it and to suggest a treatment for Johnny on a scale that ranged from "very lenient treatment" on one end to "very hard treatment" on the other. A typical group consisted of approximately nine participants, six of whom were real students and three of whom were paid confederates of the experimenter. The confederates took turns playing one of three roles that they had carefully rehearsed in advance: the *modal* person, who took a position that conformed to the average position of the real students; the *deviate*, who took a position diametrically opposed to the general orientation of the group; and the *slider*, whose initial position was similar to the deviate's but who, in the course of the discussion, gradually "slid" into a modal, conforming position. The results clearly showed that the person who was liked most was the modal person who conformed to the group norm; the deviate was liked least.

Thus, the data indicate that the "establishment" or modal group tends to like conformists better than nonconformists. By reporting these results, we do not intend to suggest that conformity is always adaptive and nonconformity is always maladaptive. Clearly, there are situations wherein conformity is highly desirable and nonconformity would constitute an unmitigated disaster. Suppose, for example, that I were suddenly to decide that I was fed up with being a conformist. So I hop in my car and start driving down the *left*-hand side of the road—as a way of displaying my rugged individualism: not very adaptive, and not very fair to you, if you happen to be driving toward me (conformist-style) on the same street.

On the other hand, there are equally compelling situations in which conformity can be just as disastrous and just as tragic. One such example can be found in the memoirs of Albert Speer. Speer was one of Adolf Hitler's top advisors. In his memoirs, he describes the circle around Hitler as one of total conformity: deviation was not permitted. In such an atmosphere, even the most barbarous activities seemed reasonable, because the absence of dissent, which conveyed the illusion of unanimity, prevented any individual from entertaining the possibility that other options might exist.

> In normal circumstances people who turn their backs on reality are soon set straight by the mockery and criticism of those around them. In the Third Reich there were not such correctives. On the contrary, every self-deception was multiplied as in a hall of distorting mirrors, becoming a repeatedly confirmed picture of a fantastical dream world which no longer bore any relationship to the grim outside world. In those mirrors I could see nothing but my own face reproduced many times over.[3]

A more familiar but perhaps less dramatic example concerns some of the men involved with Richard Nixon and his "palace guard" in the Watergate cover-up. Here, men in high government office—many of whom were attorneys—perjured themselves, destroyed evidence, and offered bribes without an apparent second thought. This was due, at least in part, to the closed circle of single-mindedness that surrounded the president in the early 1970s. This single-mindedness made deviation virtually unthinkable—until after the circle had been broken. Once the circle was broken, several people (for example, Jeb Stuart Magruder, Herbert Porter, and Patrick Grey) seemed to view their illegal behavior with astonishment, as if it were performed during some sort of bad dream. John Dean put it this way:

Anyway, when you picked up the newspaper in the morning and read the new cover story that had replaced yesterday's cover story, you began to believe that today's news was the *truth*. This process created an atmosphere of unreality in the White House that prevailed to the very end. . . . If you said it often enough, it would become true. When the press learned of the wire taps on newsmen and White House staffers, for example, and flat denials failed, it was claimed that this was a national-security matter. I'm sure many people believed that the taps *were* for national security; they weren't. That was concocted as a justification after the fact. But when they said it, you understand, they really *believed* it.[4]

What Is Conformity?

Conformity can be defined as a change in a person's behavior or opinions as a result of real or imagined pressure from a person or group of people. Most situations are not as extreme as the examples cited above. We will attempt to zero in on the phenomenon of conformity by beginning with a less extreme (and perhaps simpler) illustration. Let's return to our friend Sam, the hypothetical college student we first encountered in Chapter 1. Recall that Sam watched a presidential candidate on television and was favorably impressed by his sincerity. However, in the face of the unanimous opinion of his friends that the candidate was insincere, Sam acceded—verbally, at least—to their opinion.

Several questions can be asked about this kind of situation: (1) What causes people to conform to group pressure? Specifically, what was in it for Sam? (2) What was the nature of the group pressure? Specifically, what were Sam's acquaintances doing to induce conformity? (3) Did Sam revise his opinion of the candidate during that brief but horrifying period when he learned that *all* of his fellow students disagreed with him? Or was it the case that Sam maintained his original opinion, but only modified what he *said* about the candidate? If there was a change in opinion, was it permanent or merely transient?

Unfortunately, we cannot say precisely and definitely what was going on in Sam's mind at the time, because there are many factors in the situation that we don't know about. For example, we don't know how confident Sam was in his initial opinion; we don't know how much he liked the people with whom he watched the candidate; we don't know whether Sam considered himself to be a good judge of sincerity or whether he considered the others to be good judges of sincerity; we don't know whether Sam is generally a strong person or a wishy-washy person; and so on. What we can do is construct an experimental situation that is somewhat like the one in which Sam found himself, and we can control and vary the factors that we think might be important. Such a basic situation was devised by Solomon Asch[5] in a classic set of experiments. Put yourself in the following scene: You have volunteered to participate in an experiment on perceptual judgment. You enter a room with four other participants. The experimenter shows all of you a straight line (line X). Simultaneously, he shows you three other lines for comparison (lines A, B, and C). Your job is to judge which of the three lines is closest in length to line X. The judgment strikes you as being a very easy one. It is perfectly clear to you that line B is the correct answer, and when your turn comes, you will clearly say that B is the one. But it's *not* your turn to respond. The person whose turn it is looks carefully at the lines and says "Line A." Your mouth drops open and you look at him quizically. "How can he believe it's A when any fool can see that it's B?" you ask yourself. "He must either blind or crazy." Now it's the second person's turn to respond. He also chooses line A. You begin to feel like Alice in Wonderland. "How can it be?" you ask yourself. "Are *both* of these people blind or crazy?" But then the next person responds, and he also says "Line A." You take another look at those lines. "Maybe *I'm* the only one who's losing his mind," you mutter inaudibly. Now it's the fourth person's turn, and he also judges the correct line to be line A. You break out in a cold sweat. Finally, it's your turn. "Why, it's line A, of course," you declare. "I knew it all the time."

This is the kind of conflict that the college students in Asch's experiment went through. As you might imagine, the individuals who answered first and gave the incorrect answer were in the employ of the experimenter and were instructed to agree on an incorrect answer. The perceptual judgment itself was an incredibly easy one. It was so easy that when individuals were not subjected to group pres-

sure, but were allowed to make a series of judgments of various sizes of lines while alone, there was almost a complete absence of errors. Indeed, the task was so easy, and physical reality was so clear-cut, that Asch himself firmly believed that there would be little, if any, yielding to group pressure. But he was wrong. When faced with a majority of their fellow students agreeing on the same incorrect responses in a series of twelve judgments, approximately one-quarter of the subjects conformed at least once by responding incorrectly. When we look at the entire spectrum of judgments, we find that an average of 35 percent of the overall responses conformed to the incorrect judgments rendered by Asch's accomplices.

The situation in the Asch experiment is intriguing inasmuch as, unlike many situations in which we may tend to conform, there were no explicit constraints against individuality. That is, the sanctions against nonconformity in many situations are clear and unequivocal. For example, I hate to wear a tie, and under most circumstances I can get away with this minor idiosyncracy. On occasion, however, I can't: I often find myself stopped at the entrance to a restaurant and politely (but firmly) informed that if I refuse to don the tie offered me by the headwaiter, I cannot dine in that restaurant. I can either put on the tie and eat in the restaurant, or leave, open-necked and comfortable, but hungry. The negative consequences of nonconformity are made very explicit.

But in Asch's experiment (and in the hypothetical example of Sam watching the candidate on television), the situations were much more subtle. In these situations, there were no explicit rewards for conformity and no explicit punishments for deviance. Why, then, did Sam and Asch's subjects conform? There seem to be two major possibilities; either they became convinced, in the face of the judgment of the unanimous majority, that their own opinions were wrong, or they "went along with the crowd" (while inwardly know-ing that their judgments were right) in order to be liked by the major-ity or to avoid being disliked by them for disagreeing.

In short, what we are suggesting is that these individuals had two important goals: the goal of being correct and the goal of staying in the good graces of other people by living up to their expectations. In many circumstances, both of these goals can be satisfied by a simple action. Driving on the right-hand side of the road is the correct thing to do and it satisfies other people's expectations. So, too, is sending flowers to your mother on Mother's Day, giving proper directions to a visitor in town, and studying hard to perform well on an exam. Similarly, if others agreed with your judgment of the lengths of the lines, you could satisfy both goals by being true to your own estimate. But, in Asch's experiment, these two goals were placed in conflict. If you were a subject in that experiment, and you initially believed that the correct answer was line *B*, then saying so might satisfy your desire to be correct—but it might also violate the expectations of your peers, and they might think you to be somewhat queer. On the other hand, choosing line *A* might win you the acceptance of the others, but, unless you became convinced that they were correct, it would violate your desire to be right.

Was Sam convinced by his fellow college students that his pre-ferred presidential candidate was a phony, or did he simply go along with their judgment in order to be accepted, while continuing to believe in the sincerity of the candidate? Again, I don't know; because Sam is a hypothetical person, we cannot answer that question de-finitively. Were the yielders in Asch's experiment convinced that their initial judgment was incorrect and the unamimous judgment of the others was right? We could ask them; indeed, in Asch's experi-ment, the yielders were asked afterward whether they really saw the lines differently or whether they merely said so. A few of the subjects insisted that they really saw it that way. But how can we be certain that the subjects were being truthful? Put yourself in a subject's place. Suppose you bowed to group pressure, even though you remained certain that your initial judgment was correct. This might be em-barrassing for you to admit, because it would make you appear weak and wishy-washy. Moreover, you would be admitting that you were not following the experimenter's instruction to present *your own* judgment. Thus, it is quite possible that subjects who said they actually saw it the way the group saw it might have been deceiving the experimenter in order to save face.

How, then, can we determine whether or not group pressure actually affects perceptual judgment? Let's speculate for a moment. Suppose we were to repeat the Asch experiment, but, although we would allow the real subjects to see the responses of the accomplices as before, we would *not* require them to make their judgments in the presence of the others. If the subjects' private choices were identical with their public ones, then we would see that the responses of the others in the original experiment actually did convince the subjects that their initial judgments were wrong. If, on the other hand, the subjects were going against their own best judgment only in order to mollify the group, then there would be significantly less yielding to the judgments of others in decisions made in private. This proposition has been tested experimentally on several occasions. The results are consistent: although assurance of total privacy has not been achieved in any of these studies, the greater the privacy, the less the conformity. This finding has consistently held up, whether the subjects were judging lengths of lines,[6] the numbers of metronome clicks,[7] or the esthetic value of a piece of modern art.[8] Thus, it appears that pressure to conform to the judgments of others has little (if any) effect on the *private* judgments of experimental subjects.

Variables That Increase or Decrease Conformity

In situations like the one investigated by Asch, one of the crucial factors that determines the likelihood that the subject's opinion will conform to that of the majority is whether or not the majority opinion is unanimous. If the subject is presented with only one ally, his tendency to conform to an erroneous judgment by the majority is reduced sharply.[9] Moreover, if there *is* unanimity, the actual size of the majority need not be very great in order for it to elicit maximum conformity from a person. In fact, the tendency for someone to conform to group pressure is about as great when the unanimous majority consists of only three other people as it is when the unanimous majority is sixteen.

One way that conformity to group pressure can be decreased is by inducing the individual to make some sort of commitment to his initial judgment. Picture yourself as an umpire at a major-league baseball game. There is a close play at first base and you call the runner out—in the presence of 50,000 fans. After the game, the three other umpires approach you and each says that he thought the runner was safe. How likely are you to alter your judgment? Compare this with a situation (like the Asch situation) in which each of the three umpires calls the runner safe and *then* it is your turn to make a judgment. Such a comparison was made in an experiment by Morton Deutsch and Harold Gerard, who used the Asch paradigm and found that, where there was no prior commitment (as in the Asch experiment), 24.7 percent of the responses conformed to the erroneous judgment of the majority. But, when the individuals had publicly committed themselves *before* hearing the judgment of the other "umpires," only 5.7 percent of their new responses were conformist.

Two other important factors are the kind of person the individual is and who constitutes the group. Individuals who have a generally low opinion of themselves are far more likely to yield to group pressure than those with high self-esteem. Furthermore, task-specific self-esteem can be influenced within a given situation. Thus, individuals who are allowed to have prior successes with such a task as judging the lengths of lines are far less likely to conform than those who walk into the situation cold. By the same token, if an individual believes that he has little or no ability for the task at hand, his tendency to conform increases.[10] There are also cultural differences. For example, it has been shown that Norwegians conform to a greater extent than Frenchmen and that Japanese students are more willing to take a minority position than American students.[11]

The other side of that coin, of course, has to do with the makeup of the group exerting the pressure. A group is more effective at inducing conformity if (1) it consists of experts, (2) the members (individually or collectively) are important to the individual, or (3) the members (individually or collectively) are comparable to the individual in some way. Thus, to go back to Sam, our hypothetical college student, I would speculate that it is more likely that Sam would conform to the pressure exerted by his acquaintances if he thought they were expert in politics and in making judgments about human relations. Similarly, he would be more likely to yield to those people if they were important potential friends than if they were of no consequence to him. And finally, their being fellow college students gives the judgment of Sam's acquaintances more impact on his behavior than, say, the judgment of a group of ten-year-old children, a group of hard-hats, or a group of Portuguese biochemists. There is at least one exception to the comparability phenomenon. It has been shown that, if the unanimous majority consists of white children, more conformity is induced in other children—both white *and* black.[12] It appears as though, among children, whites are seen as having more power than blacks.[13]

The results for the black children may be due in part to feelings of insecurity. For example, to return to our previous illustration, if Sam had felt sure that he was liked and accepted by his acquaintances, he would be more likely to voice disagreement than if he felt insecure in his relationship with them. This assertion receives strong support from an experiment by James Dittes and Harold Kelley,[14] in which college students were invited to join an attractive and prestigious group and were subsequently given information about how secure their position was in that group. Specifically, all members of the group were informed that, at any point during the lifetime of the group, the members could remove any member in the interests of efficiency. The group then engaged in a discussion of juvenile delinquency. Periodically, the discussion was interrupted and each member was asked to rate every other member on his value to the group. After the discussion, each member was shown how the others rated him; in actuality, the members were given prearranged false feedback. Some members were led to believe that they were well accepted, and others were led to believe that they were not terribly popular. Each member's conformity was measured by the opinions he subsequently expressed in the discussion of juvenile delinquency, and by his vulnerability to group pressure during the performance of a simple perceptual task. The results showed that, for the individuals who valued their membership in the group, those who were led to feel only moderately accepted were more likely to conform to the norms and standards set by the group than were those who were led to feel that they were totally accepted. In other words, it's easier for an individual who is securely esconced in a group to deviate from that group.

Rewards and Punishments versus Information

As I suggested earlier, there are two possible reasons why a person might conform. One is that the behavior of others might convince him that his initial judgment was erroneous. The other is that he may wish to avoid punishment (such as rejection or ridicule) or to gain a reward (such as love or acceptance) from the group. Furthermore, the behavior of the individuals in Asch's experiment and in similar other experiments seemed to be largely a matter of attempting to obtain a reward or to avoid punishment. This can be inferred from the fact that there was very little conformity when subjects were allowed to respond privately.

At the same time, there are many situations in which we conform to the behavior of others because their behavior is our only guide to appropriate action. In short, we often rely on other people as a means of determining reality. The quotation from Thurber at the beginning of this chapter gives an example of this type of conformity. According to Leon Festinger,[15] when physical reality becomes increasingly uncertain, people rely more and more on "social reality"—that is, they are more likely to conform to what other people are doing, not because they fear punishment from the group, but because the group's behavior supplies them with valuable information about what is expected of them. An example should help clarify this distinction: Suppose that you need to use the toilet in an unfamiliar classroom building. Under the sign "Rest Rooms" there are two doors, but, unfortunately, a vandal has removed the specific designations from the doors—that is, you cannot be certain which is the Men's room and which is the Women's room. Quite a dilemma—you are afraid to open either door for fear of being embarrassed or embarrassing others. As you stand there in dismay and discomfort, hopping from one foot to the other, the door on the left opens and out strolls a distinguished-looking gentleman. With a sigh of relief, you are now willing to forge ahead, reasonably secure in the knowledge that left is for men and right is for women. Why are you so confident? As we have seen, research has shown that, the more faith an individual has in the expertise and trustworthiness of the other person, the greater the tendency to follow his lead and conform to his behavior. Thus, the distinguished-looking gentleman would almost certainly be followed, to a greater extent, than, say, a seedy-looking fellow with wildly staring eyes.

Similarly, it is alleged that, in Turkey, it is considered gracious for a guest to belch after a meal as a way of showing his host that he enjoyed the meal. Suppose you didn't know this, and you were visiting the home of a Turkish dignitary in the company of some diplomats from the U.S. State Department. If, after the meal, these gentlemen began to belch, chances are you would belch also. They are providing you with valuable information. On the other hand, if you were in the same home in the company of a crew of behemoths from the Bulgarian Olympic wrestling team and these stalwarts belched after their meal, my guess is that you would avoid belching. That is, you would likely consider this an act of bad manners. However, if they glared at you for your failure to follow suit, you might indeed belch, too—not because of the information they supplied, but because you feared rejection or reprisals for refusing to be a good sport by going along with their boorish behavior.

I would suggest that conformity that results from the observation of others for the purpose of gaining information about proper behavior tends to have more powerful ramifications than conformity in the interest of being accepted or of avoiding punishment. I would argue that, if an individual finds himself in an ambiguous situation wherein he must use the behavior of other people as a template for his own behavior, it is likely he will repeat his newly learned behavior, without cue, on subsequent similar occasions. This would be the case unless, of course, he later received clear evidence that his actions were inappropriate or incorrect. Thus, to go back to our example, suppose you are reinvited to the home of the Turkish dignitary for dinner. But this time you are the only guest. The question is: Do you or don't you belch after the meal? A moment's reflection should make the answer perfectly clear: If you had belched after the first meal at his home because you realized that it was the proper thing to do (as would have been the case had you dined in the company of the diplomats), you would be quite likely to belch when dining alone with the dignitary. However, if you had belched the first time out of fear of rejection or punishment (as would have been the case had you dined in the company of the Bulgarian wrestlers), you would almost certainly *not* belch when you were the lone guest. To go back to Sam and the political candidate on television, you can now readily understand one of the major reasons why it would be so difficult for us to predict how Sam would actually vote in the election. If he had been merely going along with the group to avoid punishment or to gain acceptance, he would be likely, in the privacy of the polling booth, to vote in opposition to the view expressed by his acquaintances. If, on the other hand, Sam had been using the group as a source of information, he would almost certainly vote against the candidate that he had initially preferred.

To repeat: when reality is unclear, other people become a major source of information. The generality of this phenomenon is nicely illustrated by some research performed by Stanley Schachter and his students, who demonstrated that people conform to others even in assessing something as personal and idiosyncratic as the quality of their own emotions.[16] Before describing this research, we must first clarify what we mean by "emotions." According to William James,[17] an emotion has both a "feeling" content and a cognitive content. Specifically, if we are walking in the forest and bump into a hungry and ferocious bear, we undergo a physiological change. This change produces excitement—physiologically, this is a response of the sympathetic nervous system that is similar to one that might be produced by coming across a person with whom we are angry. We interpret this response as fear (rather than anger, say, or euphoria) only when we cognitively become aware that we are in the presence of a fear-producing stimulus (a ferocious bear). But what if we experienced physiological arousal in the absence of an appropriate stimulus? For example, what if someone surreptitiously slipped into our drink a chemical that produced the same physiological response? Would we experience fear? William James would probably say that we wouldn't—not unless there was an appropriate stimulus around.

Here is where Schachter enters the picture. In one experiment, subjects were injected either with epinephrine—a synthetic form of adrenalin, which causes physiological excitation—or with a harmless placebo. All the subjects were told that this chemical was a vitamin supplement called "suproxin." Some of the subjects who received epinephrine were informed that there would be side effects, including palpitation of the heart and hand tremors. These, indeed, are some of the effects of epinephrine. Accordingly, when these subjects experienced the epinephrine symptoms, they had an appropriate explanation. In effect, when the symptoms appeared, they would say to themselves, "My heart is pounding and my hands are shaking because of this injection I received and for no other reason." But other subjects were not forewarned about these symptoms. Thus, when their hearts started pounding and their hands started trembling, what were they to make of it? The answer is that they made of it whatever the people around them made of it. Specifically, a stooge was introduced into the situation and the subjects were informed that he had also received an injection of "suproxin." In one situation, the stooge was programmed to behave in a euphoric manner; in another, he was programmed to express a great deal of anger. Picture yourself in this situation: You are alone in this room with a person who supposedly has just been injected with the same drug you had received. He bounces around energetically, and happily wads up paper into balls and begins sinking hook shots into the waste basket. His euphoria is obvious. Gradually, the chemical you were given begins to take effect, and you begin to feel your heart pounding, your hands trembling, and so on. What emotion do you feel? Most subjects in this situation reported a feeling of euphoria—and behaved happily. On the other hand, imagine that instead of being placed in a room with a euphoric stooge you were placed in a room with a stooge programmed to behave in an angry manner: He complains about a questionnaire you both are filling out and eventually, in a fit of extreme annoyance, he rips the questionnaire up and angrily hurls it into the waste basket. Meanwhile, the symptoms of epinephrine are becoming apparent; you feel your own heart pounding, and your hands begin to tremble. How do you feel? In this situation, the vast majority of the subjects felt angry and behaved in an angry fashion.

It should be noted that, if subjects were given a placebo (that is, an injection of a benign solution that produces no symptoms), or if they were forewarned about the symptoms of the drug that they *had* been given, they were relatively unaffected by the antics of the stooge. To sum up this experiment: when physical reality was clear and explainable, the subjects' emotions were not greatly influenced by the behavior of other people—but when they were experiencing a strong physiological response, the origins of which were not clear, they interpreted their own feelings as either anger or euphoria, depending on the behavior of other people who supposedly were in the same chemical boat.

Responses to Social Influence

Thus far, we have been describing two kinds of conformity in more or less commonsensical terms. This distinction was based upon (1) whether the individual was being motivated by rewards or punishments or by a need to know, and on (2) the relative permanence of the conforming behavior. Let us move beyond this simple distinction to a more complex and more useful classification that applies not only to conformity, but to the entire spectrum of social influence. Instead of using the simple term conformity, I would like to distinguish between three kinds of responses to social influence: *compliance*, *identification*, and *internalization*.[18]

Compliance. This term best describes the mode of behavior of a person who is motivated by a desire to gain reward or avoid punishment. Typically, his behavior is only as long-lived as is the promise of the reward or the threat of punishment. Thus, one can induce a rat to run a maze efficiently by making him hungry and placing food at the end of the maze. One can also get a South Vietnamese peasant to recite the pledge of allegiance to the American flag by threatening him with pain if he doesn't comply or by promising to feed and enrich him if he does. Remove the food from the goal box and the rat will eventually stop running; remove the food or the threat of punishment and the Vietnamese will cease reciting the pledge of allegiance.

Identification. This is a response to social influence brought about by an individual's desire to be like the influencer. In identification, as in compliance, the individual does not behave in a particular way because such behavior is intrinsically satisfying; rather, he adopts a particular behavior because it puts him in a satisfying self-defining relationship to the person or persons with whom he is identifying. Identification differs from compliance in that the individual does come to believe in the opinions and values he adopts, although he does not believe in them very strongly. Thus, if an individual finds a person or a group attractive or appealing in some way, he will be inclined to accept influence from that person or group and adopt similar values and attitudes—not in order to obtain a reward or avoid a punishment (as in compliance), but simply to be like that person. I refer to this as the good-old-Uncle-Charlie phenomenon. Suppose you have an uncle named Charlie who happens to be a warm, dynamic, exciting person; and ever since you were a young child you loved him a lot and wanted to grow up to be like him. Uncle Charlie is a corporation executive who has a number of strong opinions, including a deep antipathy to social-welfare legislation—that is, he is convinced that anyone who really tries can earn a decent wage, and that, by handing money to people, the government only succeeds in eliminating their desire to work. As a young child, you heard Uncle Charlie announce this position on several occasions, and it has become part of your system of beliefs—neither because you thought it through and it seemed right to you, nor because Uncle Charlie rewarded you for adopting (or threatened to punish you for *not* adopting) this position. Rather, it has become part of your system because of your liking for Uncle Charlie, which has produced in you a tendency to incorporate into your life that which is his.

Internalization. The internalization of a value or belief is the most permanent, most deeply rooted response to social influence. The motivation to internalize a particular belief is the desire to be right. Thus, the reward for the belief is intrinsic. If the person who provides the influence is perceived to be trustworthy and of good judgment, we accept the belief he advocates and we integrate it into our own system of values. Once it is part of our own system, it becomes independent of its source and will become extremely resistant to change.

Let us discuss some of the important distinguishing characteristics of these three responses to social influence. Compliance is the least enduring and has the least effect on the individual, because people comply merely to gain reward or to avoid punishment. The complier understands the force of the circumstance and can easily change his behavior when the circumstance no longer prevails. At gunpoint, I could be made to say most anything; but with the threat of death removed, I could quickly shrug off those statements and their implications. If a child is kind and generous to his younger brother in order to obtain a cookie from his mother, he will not necessarily become a generous person because of it. He has not learned that generosity is a good thing in and of itself—what he *has* learned is that generosity is a good way to get cookies. When the cookie supply is exhausted, his generous behavior will eventually cease, unless that behavior is bolstered by some other reward (or punishment). Rewards and punishments are very important means, then, to get people to learn and to perform specific activities, but are very limited as techniques of social influence because they must be ever present to be effective—unless the individual discovers some additional reason for continuing to perform the rewarded behavior. This last point will be discussed shortly.

Continuous reward or punishment is not necessary for the response to social influence that we call identification. The person with whom the individual identifies need not be present at all; what is needed is only the individual's desire to be like that person. For example, if Uncle Charlie moves to a different city, and months (or even years) go by without your seeing him, you will continue to hold beliefs similar to his as long as (1) he remains important to you, (2) he still holds the same beliefs, and (3) these beliefs are not challenged by counteropinions that are more convincing. But, by the same token, these beliefs *can* be changed if Uncle Charlie has a change of heart, or if your love for Uncle Charlie begins to fade. They can also change if a person or group of people who are more important to you than Uncle Charlie profess a different set of beliefs. For example, suppose you are away at college and you find yourself a group of new, exciting friends who, unlike Uncle Charlie, are strongly in favor of social welfare. If you admire them as much (or more than) your uncle, you may change your beliefs in order to be more like them. Thus, a more important identification may supersede a previous identification.

The effect of social influence through identification can also be dissipated by a person's desire to be right. If a person has taken on a belief through identification, and is subsequently presented with a counterargument by an expert and trustworthy person, he will probably change his belief. Internalization is the most permanent response to social influence precisely because a person's motivation to be right is a powerful and self-sustaining force that does not depend upon constant surveillance in the form of agents of reward or punishment, as does compliance, or on his continued esteem for another person or group, as does identification.

It is important to realize that any specific action may be due to either compliance, identification, or internalization. For example, let us look at a simple piece of behavior: obedience of the laws pertaining to fast driving. Society pays a group of people called highway patrolmen to enforce these laws, and, as we all know, people tend to drive within the speed limit if they are forewarned that a certain stretch of highway is being carefully scrutinized by these patrolmen. This is compliance. It is a clear case of people obeying the law in order to avoid paying a penalty. Suppose you were to remove the patrolmen. As soon as people found out about it, many would increase their speed. But some people might continue to obey the speed limit; a person might continue to obey because his father (or his Uncle Charlie) always obeyed speed limits or always stressed the importance of obeying traffic laws. This, of course, is identification. Finally, a person might conform to the speed limit because he's convinced that speed laws are good, that obedience of such laws helps to prevent accidents, and that driving at moderate speed is a sane and reasonable form of behavior. This is internalization. And with internalization you would observe more flexibility in the behavior. For example, under certain conditions—at 6:00 AM, say, on a clear day with perfect visibility and with no traffic for miles around—the individual might exceed the speed limit. The compliant individual, however, might fear a radar trap, and the identifying individual might be identifying to a very rigid model—thus, both would be less responsive to important changes in the environment.

Let us look at the major component in each response to social influence. In compliance, the important component is *power*—the power of the influencer to dole out the reward for compliance and the punishment for noncompliance. Parents have the power to praise, give love, provide cookies, scream, give spankings, withhold allowances, and so on; teachers have the power to paste gold stars on our foreheads or flunk us out of college; and employers have the power to praise, promote, humiliate, or discharge us. The United States government has the power to increase or withhold economic and military aid from a dependent nation. Thus, our government can use this technique to influence, say, some country in Southeast Asia to hold a more or less democratic election. Rewards and punishments are effective means for producing this kind of compliance, but we might ask whether or not mere compliance is desirable: to induce a nation to hold a democratic election is easier than to induce the rulers of that nation to think and rule democratically.

In identification, the crucial component is attractiveness—the attractiveness of the person with whom the individual identifies. Because the individual identifies with the model, he wants to hold the same opinions that the model holds. Suppose you admire a person, and he takes a particular stand on an issue. Unless you have strong feelings or solid information to the contrary, there will be a tendency for you to adopt this position. Incidentally, it is interesting to note that the reverse is also true: If a person or group that you dislike announces a position, there will be a tendency for you to reject that position or adopt the opposite position. Suppose, for example, that you dislike some particular group (the John Birch Society, say, or the Weather Underground) and that group comes out against the draft. If you know nothing about the issue, your tendency will be to favor the draft—all other things being equal.

In internalization, the important component is credibility—the credibility of the person who supplies the information. For example, if you read a statement by a person who is highly credible—that is, someone who is both expert and truthful—you would tend to be influenced by it, because of your desire to be correct. Recall our earlier example of the diplomats at the Turkish dinner party. Your acceptance of their expertise made their behavior (belching after the meal) seem like the right thing to do. Accordingly, my guess is that this behavior (your tendency to belch after a meal at the home of a Turkish dignitary) would become internalized—you would do it, thereafter, because you believed it to be right.

Recall the experiment on conformity performed by Solomon Asch, in which social pressure induced many subjects to conform to the erroneous statements of a group. Recall further that when the subjects were allowed to respond in private, the incidence of conformity dropped considerably. Clearly, then, internalization or identification was not involved. It seems obvious that the subjects were *complying* to the unanimous opinion of the group in order to avoid the punishment of ridicule or rejection. If either identification or internalization had been involved, the conforming behavior would have persisted in private.

The trichotomy of compliance, identification, and internalization is a useful one. At the same time, it should be made clear that, like most ways of classifying the world, it is not perfect; there are some places where the categories overlap. Specifically, although it is true that compliance and identification are generally more temporary than internalization, there are circumstances that can increase their permanence. For example, permanence can be increased if an individual makes a firm commitment to continue to interact with the person or group of people that induced the original act of compliance. Thus, in an experiment by Charles Kiesler and his associates,[19] when subjects believed that they were going to continue interacting with an unattractive discussion group, they not only complied publicly, but they also seemed to internalize their conformity: that is, they changed their private opinions as well as their public behavior. This kind of situation will be discussed in greater detail in Chapter 4.

Permanence can also result if, while complying, an individual discovers something about his actions, or about the consequences of his actions, that makes it worthwhile for him to continue the behavior even after the reason for his original compliance (the reward or punishment) is no longer forthcoming. This is borne out by some of the research done on that aspect of social learning known as *behavior modification.* Typically, in behavior modification, an attempt is made to eliminate unwanted or maladaptive behavior by systematically punishing that behavior, by rewarding alternative behaviors, or both. For example, various attempts have been made to use this technique as a way of getting people to stop smoking cigarettes.[20] An individual might be given a series of painful electric shocks while performing the usual rituals of smoking—that is, while lighting a cigarette, bringing it up toward his lips, inhaling, and so on. After several trials, the individual will refuse to smoke. Unfortunately, it is fairly easy for a person to notice that there is a difference between the experimental situation and the world outside: He realizes that he will not be shocked when he is smoking outside of the experimental situation. Consequently, he may later experience a little residual anxiety when he begins to light a cigarette, but because electric shocks are clearly not forthcoming, his anxiety eventually fades. Thus, many people who temporarily cease smoking after this form of behavior modification will eventually return to cigarettes after electric shock is no longer a threat. How about those who stay off of cigarettes after behavior modification? Here is the point: Once an individual has been induced to comply, and therefore does not smoke for several days, it is possible for him to make a discovery: over the years, he may have come to believe that it was inevitable that his mouth feel hot, dry, and unpleasant upon waking every morning, but, after refraining from cigarettes for a few days, he may discover how delightful it feels to have a fresh, unparched mouth. This discovery may be enough to keep him from smoking again. Thus, although compliance, in and of itself, usually does not produce long-lasting behavior, it might set the stage for events that will lead to more permanent effects.

Obedience as a Form of Compliance

We have indicated that acts of compliance are, in general, ephemeral. This does not mean that they are trivial. Impermanent behavior can be extremely important. This fact has been demonstrated dramatically by Stanley Milgram in his studies of obedience.[21] Picture the scene: Subjects volunteer for an experiment. They are told that the experiment is a study of the effects of punishment on memory, but this is a lie. Actually, it is a study of the extent to which people will obey authority. In each trial, the experiment has two participants, one of whom is assigned the role of teacher, and the other, the role of learner. The teacher is instructed to present the learner with a series of stimuli. The learner, who is strapped to an electrified chair in a separate room, is supposed to respond appropriately to each stimulus by pressing one of four levers in front of him; this response activates one of the lights in front of the teacher. To assist in the learning process, the teacher is informed that he must deliver an electric shock, of increasing intensity, each time the learner responds incorrectly, or each time he fails to respond. In actuality, the learner or "victim," is an accomplice of the experimenter's, and is not really wired to the electricity, but the teacher (who *is* a real subject) firmly believes that the victim in the next room *is* wired to the electricity. Each time the victim fails to respond correctly, the subject is supposed to increase the voltage on the generator and press the shock button. The generator is calibrated from a low point of 15 volts to a high of 450 volts. At 75 volts, the victim begins to grunt and moan; at 150 volts, he asks to be let out of the experiment. At 180 volts, he cries out that he cannot stand the pain. The pointer moves beyond a place on the generator clearly labeled "Extreme Shock" and begins to approach a point labeled "Danger: Severe Shock." As the shock becomes more severe, the victim, instead of responding, begins to pound the wall and beg to be let out of the room. But this, of course, does not constitute a correct response, so the subject is instructed to increase the voltage and press the shock button again. A few trials later, the "learning" stimulus is presented to the victim, but nothing emanates from the room save an ominous silence. Of course, this does not constitute a correct response, so, once again, the experimenter instructs the subject to increase the voltage and press the shock button.

The participants in this experiment were a random sample of businessmen, professional men, white-collar workers and blue-collar workers. What percentage of these people continued to administer shocks to the very end of the experiment? How long would you have continued? Every year in my social psychology class, I pose these questions, and every year, some 99 percent of the four hundred students in the class indicate that they would not continue to administer shocks after the learners began to pound on the wall. The guesses made by my students are consistent with the results of Milgram's survey of forty psychiatrists at a leading medical school. The psychiatrists predicted that most subjects would quit at 150 volts, when the victim first asks to be freed. These psychiatrists also predicted that only about 4 percent of the subjects would continue to shock the victim after he refused to respond (at 300 volts), and that less than 1 percent would administer the highest shock on the generator.

How do subjects respond when they are actually in the situation? Interestingly enough, Milgram found that, in the typical study as described above, the great majority of his subjects—more than 62 percent—continued to administer shocks to the very end of the experiment, although some of them required a degree of prodding from the experimenter.

Milgram's results are provocative and somewhat dismaying in their implications: an astonishingly large proportion of people will cause pain to others in obedience to authority. The research may have important counterparts in the world outside of the experimental laboratory. For example, it is difficult to read these studies without noticing a loose kind of similarity between the behavior of Milgram's subjects and the blind obedience expressed by Adolf Eichmann, who attributed his responsibility for the murder of hundreds of thousands of innocent civilians to the fact that he was a good bureaucrat merely obeying orders issued by his superiors in the Nazi regime. Similarly, in our own decade, Lieutenant William Calley, who was convicted of the deliberate and unprovoked murder of women and children in My Lai, freely admitted to these acts, but said that he felt that this was justifiable obedience to the authority of his superior officers.

As provocative as these comparisons are, we should be cautious lest we overinterpret Milgram's results. Given the fact that 62 percent of the subjects in Milgram's experiment complied with the experimenter's command, some commentators have been tempted to suggest that perhaps most people would have behaved like Adolf

Eichmann or Lieutenant Calley if they found themselves in a similar situation. This *may* be true; but it should be emphasized that there are, in fact, some real and important differences between the situations encountered by Eichmann, by Calley, and by Milgram's subjects. In most of Milgram's studies, the authority figure issuing the orders was a scientist in a prestigious laboratory at Yale University. In this society, we have been conditioned to believe that scientists tend to be responsible, benevolent people of high integrity. This is especially true if the scientist is affiliated with a well-known and highly respected institution like Yale. The subjects might reasonably assume, then, that no scientist would issue orders that would result in the death or injury of a human as part of his experiment. This was clearly not true in either the Eichmann or the Calley examples.

Some evidence in support of this conjecture comes from further research by Milgram. He conducted a separate study[22] comparing the obedience of subjects to the commands of a scientist at Yale University with the obedience of subjects to the commands of a scientist working in a suite of offices in a rather rundown commercial building in the downtown shopping area of the industrial city of Bridgeport, Connecticut. In this study, the Yale scientist achieved an obedience rate of 65 percent, while only 48 percent of the subjects in Bridgeport were obedient. Thus, removing the prestige of Yale University did seem to reduce the degree of obedience somewhat. Of course, 48 percent is still a high figure. My guess is that, if the person conducting the study were not a scientist, even fewer people would have been obedient.

Another factor that reduces the extent of obedience is the physical absence of the authority figure. Milgram found that, when the experimenter was out of the room and issued his orders by telephone, the number of *fully* obedient subjects dropped to below 25 percent. Moreover, several of the subjects who did continue with the experiment "cheated"; specifically, they administered shocks of lower intensity than they were supposed to—and never bothered to tell the experimenter that they had deviated from the proper procedure. This last datum, I feel, represents a touching attempt by some individuals to be responsive to the demands of legitimate authority while, at the same time, minimizing the pain that they inflict on others. It is somewhat reminiscent of the behavior of Yossarian, the hero of Joseph Heller's novel *Catch 22*, who "accidentally" dropped his bombs over an empty field adjacent to the Italian village designated as his target.

The "Uninvolved" Bystander as Conformist

Several years ago, a young woman named Kitty Genovese was stabbed to death in New York City. This was a tragic event—but not, in itself, a particularly novel occurrence. After all, in a major population center, brutal murders are not uncommon. What was interesting about this event is the fact that no less than thirty-eight of her neighbors came to their windows at 3:00 AM in response to her screams of terror—and remained at their windows watching in helpless fascination for the 30 minutes it took her attacker to complete his grisly deed. Not one came to her assistance; not one so much as lifted the phone to call the police. Why?

Well, perhaps the onlookers were sleepy or dazed. After all, one is hardly in full control of his mental faculties at three o'clock in the morning. Perhaps. But it was in broad daylight that Eleanor Bradley, while shopping on Fifth Avenue in New York, tripped, fell, and broke her leg. She lay there for 40 minutes in a state of shock, while literally hundreds of passersby, in turn, paused momentarily to gawk at her, and then kept on walking.

Why did these bystanders fail to help? Are people in big cities impervious to the distress of others? Have they become so accustomed to disaster that they can be nonchalant in the face of pain and violence? Were the bystanders in these situations different from you or me in some way? The answer to all of these questions appears to be "No." Interviews conducted with the bystanders in the Genovese murder revealed that they were anything but nonchalant—they were horrified. Why, then, didn't they intervene? This is a difficult question to answer; subsequently, however, some clues about the reason these bystanders did nothing were suggested by the results of a series of ingenious experiments conducted by John Darley, Bibb Latané, and their colleagues.[23] These investigators hypothesized that the very number of people witnessing these tragedies mitigated against any-one helping—that is, a victim is less likely to get help if there are a large number of people watching his distress. Thus, nonintervention can be viewed as an act of conformity. In this case, it appears that, for each individual, the other people were defining the appropriateness and reasonableness of supportive or helping behavior. As we have seen, it is often reasonable to take one's cue from others. Occasion-ally, however, it can be misleading; and it tends to be particularly misleading in critical situations. In our society, it is considered gauche and uncool to reveal strong emotions in public. When we are not alone, most of us try to appear less fearful, less worried, less anxious, or less sexually aroused than we really are. For example, from the blasé looks on the faces of patrons of topless restaurants and strip joints, one would never guess that they were sexually aroused. Simi-larly, the proverbial visitor from Mars would never guess the fate in store for the patients in a dentist's waiting room by merely observing the impassive looks on their faces.

With these things in mind, let us consider the case of the woman who fell and broke her leg on Fifth Avenue. Suppose you arrived at the scene 10 minutes after she fell: You see a woman lying on the ground in apparent discomfort. What else do you see? You see scores of people walking past the woman, glancing at her, and continuing on their way. What will you conclude? It is conceivable that you may conclude that it's inappropriate for you to intervene. Perhaps it's not serious; perhaps she's intoxicated; perhaps she is playacting; perhaps the whole thing is being staged by Allen Funt, and you will make a public fool of yourself on "Candid Camera" if you intervene. "After all," you ask yourself, "If it's so damn important, why are none of these other people doing anything about it?" Thus, the fact that there are a lot of people around, rather than increasing the likelihood that *someone* will help, actually *decreases* the likelihood that any *one* of them will help.

This is an interesting conjecture, but is it true? To find out, Latané and Rodin[24] conducted an experiment constructed around "a lady in distress." In this experiment, a female experimenter asked college students to fill out a questionnaire. The experimenter then retired to the next room through an unlocked collapsible curtain, saying she would return when they finished the questionnaire. A few minutes later, she staged an "accident." What the students actually heard was the sound (from a hidden tape recording) of the young woman climbing a chair, followed by a loud scream and a crash, as if the chair had collapsed and she had fallen to the floor. They then heard moaning and crying and the anguished statement, "Oh, my God, my foot ... I ... I ... can't move it. Oh ... my ankle ... I can't get this thing off me." The cries continued for about a minute and gradually subsided.

The experimenters were interested in determining whether or not the subjects would come to the young woman's aid. The important variable in the experiment was whether or not the subjects were alone in the room. Of those who were alone, 70 percent offered to help the young woman; of those who were participating in pairs, only 20 percent offered help. Thus, it is clear that the presence of another bystander tends to inhibit action. When interviewed subsequently, each of the unhelpful subjects who had been in the room with another subject had concluded that it probably wasn't serious, partially because of the inactivity of their partner.

In the Genovese murder, there was probably an additional reason why the bystanders did not help. In such a situation, it may be that, if people are aware that an event is being witnessed by others (as were the bystanders in the Genovese case), there is a diffusion of responsibility. That is, each bystander may have felt that it wasn't solely his responsibility—others were watching, too. Accordingly, each bystander might have felt that someone else was calling the police or that it was someone else's duty to do so. To test this idea, Darley and Latané[25] arranged an experimental situation in which subjects were placed in separate rooms, but were able to communicate with each other by means of microphones and earphones. Thus, the subjects could hear one another but couldn't see one another. The investigators then staged a simulated epileptic attack: they played a tape recording that imitated an epileptic seizure on the part of one of the participants. In one experimental condition, each subject was led to believe that he was the only person whose microphone was tuned in during the seizure; in other conditions, each subject was led to believe that one or more people were tuned in also. The results showed that if the subject thought that he was the only listener, he was far more likely to leave his room and try to help than he was if he thought that others were listening, too. The greater the number of people he thought were listening, the less likely was he to help.

The behavior of the onlookers in the Genovese murder case and of the subjects in the Darley–Latané experiments projects a rather grim picture of the human condition. Is it true that people avoid helping each other if at all possible—that is, if someone provides a bad example by not intervening, or if the responsibility for action seems the least bit diffuse? Perhaps not. Perhaps there are situations in which people are inspired to come to the aid of their fellows. An incident in my own experience may shed some light on this issue. I was camping in Yosemite National Park a few years ago. It was late at night, and I was just dropping off to sleep when I heard a man's voice cry out. I couldn't be certain whether it was a cry of pain, surprise, or joy. I had no idea whether some people were just horsing around or whether one of my fellow campers was being attacked by a bear. I crawled out of my sleeping bag and looked around, trying to shake the cobwebs out of my head and trying to ascertain from where the scream had come, when I noticed a strange phenomenon. From all over the area, a myriad of flickering lights were converging on a single point. These were lanterns and flashlights being carried by dozens of campers running to the aid of the individual who had screamed. It turned out that his scream had been one of surprise caused by a relatively harmless flare-up in his gasoline stove. The other campers seemed almost disappointed when they learned that there was no help needed. They trudged back to their tents and, I assume, dropped off to sleep immediately. Not so with me, however: I tossed and turned, unable to get back to sleep. As a social psychologist with a great deal of faith in scientific data, I spent the night puzzling over the fact that my fellow campers had behaved in a totally different manner than the subjects in the Darley–Latané experiments.

Why had the campers behaved so differently? In what way were the situations different? There were at least two factors operating in the campground that were either not present or were present only to a very small degree in the situations previously discussed. One of these factors is reflected in my use, in the preceding paragraph, of the term "my fellow campers." Specifically, a feeling of "common fate" or mutuality may be engendered among people sharing the same interests, pleasures, hardships, and environmental conditions of a closed environment like a campground, a feeling of mutuality that is stronger than among people who are merely residents of the same planet, county, or city. A second, somewhat related factor is that there was no escape from the face-to-face aspect of the situation: the onlookers in the Genovese case could walk away from their windows into the relative protection and isolation of their own homes; the people on Fifth Avenue could walk past the woman lying on the sidewalk and keep on going, right out of her environment; the subjects in the Darley–Latané experiments were not in a face-to-face relationship with the victim, and they knew that they could escape from the environment in a very short time. In the campground, the events were occurring in a relatively restricted environment; whatever the campers allowed to happen that night they were going to have to face squarely the next morning. It seems that, under these circumstances, individuals are more willing to take responsibility for each other.

Of course, this is mere speculation. The behavior of the campers at Yosemite—while provocative—is not conclusive, because it was not part of a controlled experiment. One of the major problems with observational data like these is that the observer has no control over who the people in his situation are. Thus, differences between people always loom as a possible explanation for the differences in their behavior. For example, one might argue that individuals who go camping are—by nature or experience—kinder, gentler, more thoughtful, and more humane than New Yorkers. Perhaps they were Boy Scouts and Girl Scouts as children—hence the interest in camping—and, in scouting, they were taught to be helpful to other people. One of the reasons for doing experiments is to control this kind of uncertainty. Indeed, a recent experiment lends support to my speculation about my campground experience. This was an experiment performed by Irving Piliavin and his associates[26] in one of the cars of a train in the New York subway system. In this experiment, an accomplice of the experimenters staggered and collapsed in the pres-

ence of several individuals riding the subway. The "victim" remained stretched out on the floor of the train, staring at the ceiling.
This scene was repeated one hundred and three times under a variety
of conditions. The most striking result was that, a large part of the
time, people spontaneously rushed to the aid of the "stricken" individual. This was especially true when the victim was made to seem
obviously ill; in more than 95 percent of the trials, someone offered
help immediately. Even when the "victim" had been given a liquor
bottle to carry and was made to reek of alcohol, he received immediate help from someone on 50 percent of the trials. Unlike the
behavior of the subjects that Darley and Latané dealt with, the
helping behavior of the people on the subway train was not affected
by the number of bystanders. People helped just as often and just as
speedily on crowded trains (where there could be a diffusion of
responsibility) as they did on virtually empty trains. Although the
people doing the helping were New Yorkers (as in the Genovese
case, the Fifth Avenue case, and the Darley–Latané experiments),
they were also in an environment that, although very much unlike
Yosemite National Park, did have two things in common with the
campground: (1) people riding on the same subway car do have the
feeling of sharing a common fate, and (2) they were in a face-to-face
situation with the victim from which there was no immediate escape.

How can the tendency to help be increased further? There is a
good deal of evidence that people will help one another if they are
certain that the victim needs help and if they are certain that they can
do something helpful. For example, in one experiment, Robert
Baron[27] showed that, when an individual was in obvious pain—and
when the bystander knew that his or her response could alleviate the
suffering—then, the greater the apparent pain, the more quickly the
bystander responded. In the same experiment, it was shown that,
when the bystander did not believe that she or he could reduce the
victim's pain, there was an inverse relationship between pain and
speed of responding—that is, the greater the apparent pain, the more
slowly the bystander responded. To make sense out of these results,
we need to make use of the concept of *empathy*: in this case, our
tendency to experience unpleasant physiological responses at the
sight of another person in pain. The more the victim's pain, the

greater our unpleasant feeling. We can reduce this unpleasant feeling either by helping the victim or by psychologically removing ourselves from the situation. If there is clearly something we can do about it, we act quickly—especially when the victim is in great pain. If we believe that there is nothing we can do about it, the greater will be our tendency to turn away from it (in order to reduce our own feelings of unpleasantness), especially if the victim is in *great* pain.

A Note on Ethics

In their quest for knowledge, experimental social psychologists occasionally subject people to some fairly intense experiences. In this chapter alone we have discussed experiments in which people have been led into conflict between the evidence of their own eyes and the unanimous judgments of other people; in which they have been ordered to deliver intense electric shock to an apparently suffering victim; in which scores of innocent people riding a subway train have been forced to witness the apparent agony of a person in distress.

These procedures may raise serious ethical questions. A more complete treatment of ethics is presented in Chapter 9; here, let it suffice to make two general points: First, it is the responsibility of all experimenters in this field to protect the experimental subject from harm. The experimenter must take steps to insure that his subjects leave the experimental situation in a frame of mind that is at least as sound as it was when they entered the experimental situation. This frequently requires postexperimental "debriefing" procedures that require more time and effort than the main body of the experiment.

Given the ethical thin ice that experimenters must skate upon, why bother with these kinds of experiments at all? This brings me to the second point of ethics that I want to emphasize at this time: For a social psychologist, the ethical issue is not a one-sided affair. In a real sense, he is obligated to use his skills as a researcher to advance our knowledge and understanding of human behavior for the ultimate aim of human betterment. In short, the social psychologist has an ethical responsibility to the society as a whole; he would be remiss in fulfilling this responsibility if he failed to carry on his research to the best of his ability. He faces a dilemma when his general ethical responsibility to society conflicts with his more specific ethical responsibility to each individual subject in his experiment; and, to compound the situation, the conflict is greatest when he is investigating such important issues as conformity, obedience, helping, and the like, because, in general, the more important the issue, (1) the greater the potential benefit for society and (2) the more likely it is that an individual subject will experience discomfort, anxiety, or upset. Again, for a more complete treatment of this topic, the reader is directed to Chapter 9.

3

Mass Communication, Propaganda, and Persuasion

In November of 1974, the CBS television network aired a film called "Cry Rape." The film attracted the largest audience of any movie produced especially for TV. Essentially, the story made it clear that a rape victim who chooses to press charges against her attacker runs the risk of undergoing an ordeal that may be more harrowing than the rape itself. In this case, the rapist, exuding boyish innocence, presented a convincing argument to the effect that he had been seduced by the woman. During the next few weeks, there was a sharp decrease in the number of rapes reported by victims to police—apparently because victims, taking their cue from the TV movie, feared that the police would not believe them.[1]

It is a truism to say that we live in an age of mass communication; indeed, it can even be said that we live in an age characterized by attempts at mass persuasion. Every time we turn on the radio or TV set, every time we open a book, a magazine or a newspaper, someone is trying to educate us, to convince us to buy his product, to get us to vote for his candidate, or to subscribe to his version of what is right, true, or beautiful. This is most obvious in advertising: manufacturers of nearly identical products (aspirins, for example, or toothpastes, or detergents) spend vast amounts of money to persuade us to buy the product in *their* package. Influence through mass communication need not be blatant—it can be very subtle indeed. As the above illustration aptly illustrates, even when communicators are not making a direct attempt to sell us something, they can succeed in influencing the way we look at the world and the way we respond to important events in our lives.

Let's look at something supposedly objective—like the news. Are the newsmen trying to sell us anything? Probably not. But here, the mass media can exert a subtle influence on our opinions simply by determining which events are given exposure. Take television newscasts, for example: It has been said by no less an expert than the director of the British Broadcasting Corporation that television news is a form of *entertainment*. Accordingly, when those in charge of news programming make decisions about which news event to cover and which fraction of the miles of video tape and film that they use in a day is presented to the public, they make their decisions, at least in part, on the basis of the entertainment value of their material. Film footage of a flooded metropolis has much more entertainment value than footage devoted to a dam that was built in order to prevent such flooding: it is simply not very exciting to see a non-flood in action. And yet, the non-flood may be more important news. Just as such action events as football games are more entertaining on TV than such quiet events as chess matches, it is more likely that riots, bombings, earthquakes, massacres, and other violent acts will get more air time than stories about people helping each other, people working to prevent violence, and so on. Thus, news telecasts tend to focus on the violent behavior of individuals—college students, black militants, policemen—because "action" makes for more exciting viewing than does a portrayal of people behaving in a peaceful, orderly manner. This coverage does not present a balanced picture of what is happening in the nation—not because the people who run the news media are evil men who are trying to manipulate us, but simply because they are trying to entertain us. And, in trying to entertain us, they may, unwittingly, be influencing us toward the belief that most people behave violently, and that human behavior is different now than it was 25 years ago. This may cause us to be unhappy, and even depressed, about the temper of the times or the state of the nation. Ultimately, it might affect our vote, our tendency to contribute money to our alma mater, our desire to visit major urban centers, and so on. As we shall see, it may actually *cause* people to behave violently.

Such biased coverage was dramatically illustrated by the manner in which the media handled the non-riot that occurred in Austin, Texas, during the first week in May, 1970. The background of the story was a familiar one on college campuses during the war in Southeast Asia. Tensions were running high between University of Texas students and local police following a confrontation at an impromptu student demonstration against the invasion of Cambodia by U.S. troops. During the demonstration, some 6000 students marched on the state capitol, broke a few windows, and skirmished with police; the students were tear-gassed and several policemen and students were injured. But this was a mere preface—a minor event compared to what seemed to be coming. A few days later, students at the University of Texas were outraged at the wanton slaying of four students at Kent State University by members of the Ohio National Guard. To protest this event, the Texas students planned a gigantic march into downtown Austin—20,000 students were expected to turn out. The Austin City Council, fearing trouble, refused to issue a parade permit. In frustration and anger, the students decided to march anyway; their leaders opted to confine the march to the sidewalks, where, technically, it would not be illegal. Rumors spread that hundreds of armed rednecks and hooligans were descending on Austin from all over the state with the intention of assaulting the students. Other rumors abounded to the effect that state troopers and Texas Rangers (not known for their friendliness to students) had been called in and were determined to take strong and violent action against anyone disobeying the law by straying or falling off the sidewalk. In retrospect, it appears that these rumors were almost certainly untrue, but the important point is that they were widely believed. Because the probability of keeping a crowd of 20,000 people from pushing itself off the sidewalk was remote, the situation seemed certain to be a prelude to extreme violence. Sniffing an exciting story, news teams affiliated with the major television networks were alerted. As it turned out, however, the explosive situation was defused at the eleventh hour: a team of university psychologists, law professors, and law students succeeded, at the last moment, in convincing a federal judge to issue a temporary restraining order to prevent the city from enforcing the anti-parade ordinance. Moreover, it quickly became known that the testimony of several members of the police force, *in favor of allowing the students to march*, was instrumental in the judge's decision. This event—especially because of the role played in it by the police—resulted not only in the total absence of violence, but in a genuine explosion of good will and solidarity among various diverse elements of the community. Twenty thousand students did march, but they marched in a spirit of harmony. Co-eds offered cold drinks to the police officers who were diverting traffic away from the parade route; students and policemen exchanged friendly greetings, shook hands warmly, and so on. Interestingly enough, the national TV networks completely ignored this encouraging turn of events. Because most of us were aware of the fact that teams of nationally prominent newsmen from a variety of news media had descended on the city during the week, the lack of coverage seemed puzzling indeed. An unsettling explanation was provided by Philip Mann and Ira Iscoe who stated: "Since there was no violence, news media teams left town and there was no national publicity, a commentary whose implications are by now sadly self-evident."[2]

As we have said, this form of influence is probably unintentional; the networks are not *trying* to create the illusion that most people are violent. Let us look at a more conscious, more direct attempt to persuade people by the judicious selection of material to be presented in the media. Imagine the following hypothetical situation: Two individuals are running for President of the United States. One of the candidates has far less money to spend on his campaign than the other. Accordingly, in order to get maximum "free" exposure, he appears on many panel-type programs on television, such as "Meet the Press" or "Face the Nation." The interviewers on these panels are seasoned reporters who are not always sympathetic to the candidate. Frequently, they ask him difficult questions—occasionally, they ask him questions that are downright hostile. The candidate finds himself forever on the defensive. Sometimes, the camera catches him at an unflattering angle, or in the act of scratching his nose, or with his mouth hanging open, or yawning, or fidgeting. While viewing at home, his wife is surprised at the bags under his eyes and at how tired and old he looks. Sometimes, on these occasions, he has difficulty finding the right word; he hems and haws and sounds inarticulate.

His opponent with the well-stocked campaign chest does not need to appear on this kind of program. Instead, he spends vast amounts of money video-taping spot commercials. Because he pays the cameramen and the director, his countenance is captured only from the most flattering angles. His own personal make-up man works extra hard to remove the bags from under his eyes and to make him appear young and dynamic. His wife, watching at home, never saw him looking so well. The interviewer asks him questions that have been prepared and rehearsed in advance, so that his answers are reasonable, concise, and articulate. If the candidate does happen to stumble over a word or to draw a blank, the cameras are stopped and the scene is shot over and over again until it is letter-perfect.

The situation outlined above is no nightmarish projection into the future, but an approximation of what actually occurred during the 1968 presidential election. In an extraordinary behind-the-scenes account of Richard Nixon's campaign, journalist Joe McGinniss reported on the adeptness with which Nixon's advisors controlled the image of the candidate that was projected to the American people. In reporting these events, McGinniss suggests that TV may be a powerful means of seducing voters to vote for an image of a candidate rather than the candidate himself. Or, as one Nixon staffer put it: "This is the beginning of a whole new concept. . . . This is the way they'll be elected forevermore. The next guys up will have to be performers."[3] Specifically, what the staffer was referring to was a TV program in which the situation was arranged so that it looked as though candidate Nixon was spontaneously answering questions phoned in by voters. In reality, he was answering questions prepared by his staff and carefully rehearsed. When a voter asked a question on the telephone, Nixon's staff simply reworded it in the form of the prepared question, attributed the question to the voter, and allowed candidate Nixon to recite his prepared answer.

When McGinniss' book made its appearance, many people were shocked and appalled at what they considered to be unethical and dishonest behavior. On the other hand, the overwhelming majority of voters either didn't care or thought that Nixon's deceptiveness was merely an indication that he was a clever, shrewd politician. Richard Nixon's popularity remained high throughout his first term in office, and in 1972 he was reelected in one of the most lopsided landslides in our nation's history, despite the fact that, at the time, it was known that a group of individuals financed by the Committee to Reelect the President had been caught trying to break into the offices of the Democratic National Committee in a building called Watergate.

Nixon's large margin of victory in 1972 could be interpreted as indicating that such deceptive gimmickry was effective in spite of its blatant dishonesty. On the other hand, at least one astute observer, John Kenneth Galbraith, has commented that Nixon may have won in 1968 *in spite* of these devices.* Unfortunately, there is no way to assess how well this strategy actually worked in this specific campaign. No one studied it at the time. What we *can* do is look at this and other issues in a more general way. First, let us look at the broad issue of persuasion through the mass media. Subsequently, we will look at specific techniques of persuasion.

The broad question is this: How credible and effective are obvious attempts to package and sell products (toothpaste, aspirin, presidential candidates) through the mass media? The prima-facie evidence appears to suggest that it's extremely effective: Why else would corporations spend hundreds of millions of dollars a year trumpeting their products? We have all seen children being seduced by toy commercials that artfully depict the most drab toys in such a way that they are irresistible. The aim is to get kids to demand that their parents buy them the flashy-looking toys they've seen on TV, and it seems to work for a while. But kids catch on after a time; I've seen my own children, after several disappointments, develop a healthy skepticism (alas, even a certain degree of cynicism) about the truthfulness of these commercials. This kind of skepticism is common in adults. A recent public-opinion poll showed that 75 percent of the respondents believed that TV commercials contain untruthful argu-

---

*While legislation has been passed to curtail the amount of campaign spending, there is no current legislation effective against the kind of deception mentioned above.

ments. Moreover, the results indicate that the more educated the person, the more skeptical he is; and that people who are skeptical believe that their skepticism makes them immune to persuasion. This might lead us to conclude that the mere fact of knowing that a communicator is biased serves to protect us from being influenced by his message. This is probably not true, however. Simply because a person *thinks* that he is immune to persuasion does not necessarily mean that he *is* immune to persuasion. In the case of many consumer products, the public will tend to buy a specific brand for no other reason than the fact that it is heavily advertised.

Let's look at the headache-remedy business. Daryl Bem,[4] a social psychologist, provides us with an interesting analysis of our susceptibility to TV commercials even when we know that they are biased. According to Bem, a well known brand of aspirin (which we'll call "Brand A") advertises itself as 100 percent pure aspirin; the commercial goes on to say that government tests have shown that no other pain remedy is stronger or more effective than Brand A. What the makers didn't bother to mention is that the government test actually showed that no brand was any weaker or less effective than any of the others. In other words, all tested brands were equal—except in price, that is. For the privilege of gulping down Brand A, the buyer pays nearly $1.00 for one hundred tablets. According to Consumers Union, equally effective aspirin is available in some places for one-fifth the price (one hundred tablets for 19 cents). Or perhaps you prefer a buffered aspirin that "works twice as fact as regular aspirin," buffered so that it won't upset your stomach, as you've heard that plain aspirin may do. The same government test showed that this brand works no faster than regular aspirin, nor is there any difference between the two in the frequency of stomach upset. This well-known brand sells for around $1.50 for one hundred tablets. A lesser known buffered aspirin costs roughly 25 cents for the same quantity. Which brand sells better? Guess.

Two other major brands of pain reliever of a kind known generically as APC tablets have combined the main ingredient (aspirin) with phenacetin and caffeine. The worth of these expensive additives? Apparently nothing positive, and phenacetin in large doses is suspected as a cause of serious kidney damage. But it sounds great in the advertising: "Not one, not two, but a combination of medically proven ingredients." Though the tested effectiveness of these products was not greater than that of simple aspirin, the price certainly was, ranging from $1.40 to $1.60 for one hundred tablets. The only bonus the consumer might get with either of these brands is a greater frequency of stomach upsets (according to the same government-sponsored study).

Such blatant attempts at mass persuasion seem pitifully obvious. Yet the cash registers ring, and tremendous numbers of consumers apparently set aside their skepticism even though they know that the message is an obvious attempt to sell a product. Of course, there may be a basic difference between a person's susceptibility to aspirin commercials and his susceptibility to commercials for presidential candidates. When we are dealing with products that are identical or very similar, it may be that mere familiarity with the brand name makes a huge difference. Robert Zajonc[5] has shown that, all other things being equal, the more familiar an item is, the more attractive it is. Suppose I walk into a grocery store looking for a laundry detergent. I go to the detergent section and I am staggered by the wide array of brand names. Because it doesn't matter too much to me which one I buy, I may simply reach for one that is most familiar—and chances are it is familiar because I've heard and seen the name on TV commercials over and over and over again. If this is the case, then sudden increases in TV exposure should produce dramatic changes in familiarity and, perhaps, in sales. Let's look at the data. In 1972, the Northwestern Mutual Life Insurance Company conducted a nationwide poll to find out how well the public recognized its name. It came out thirty-fourth among insurance companies. Two weeks later the company repeated the poll. This time it came out third in name familiarity. What caused this amazing leap from obscurity to fame? Two weeks and one million dollars worth of advertising on television. Of course familiarity does not necessarily mean sales, but the two are frequently linked. Thus, A & W root beer boosted its share of the market from 15 percent to 50 percent after six months of television advertising. In the early 1970s, Grapenuts was a venerable but nearly forgotten cereal. Suddenly, a natural-foods enthusiast named Euell Gibbons began plugging it in a series of commercials, which increased the sales of this rather bland cereal by 30 percent in just a few months.

But is voting for a presidential candidate the same kind of decision as choosing a soft drink or a breakfast cereal? The data on this issue are not entirely clear at this point, but it's my guess that the influence due merely to familiarity becomes less important as issues become more important. Thus, it may be fallacious to assume that people voted for Nixon in 1968 because he became a household word like "Tide," "Gleem," and "Bayer." We will say more about this toward the end of this chapter.

Education or Propaganda

Aspirin commercials are obvious attempts to sell something at a high price by intentionally misleading the audience. They can be considered propaganda. "Selling" a presidential candidate, however, is much more complicated. Thus, the devices used by Nixon's staff to display him in a favorable and forceful manner could conceivably be considered as education; an attempt to educate the public on the policies and virtues of the candidate by allowing him to present his views as clearly, efficiently, and articulately as possible. What is the difference between propaganda and education? My dictionary (*The American Heritage Dictionary of the English Language*, 1969) defines "propaganda" as "the systematic propagation of a given doctrine . . ." and "education" as "the act or process of imparting knowledge or skill." Again, we could all agree that aspirin ads are propaganda, but what about the American film and television industries, which, until recently, depicted blacks in almost exclusively stereotyped roles? Or, more subtly, what about the vast majority of high-school textbooks in American history that ignore the contribution of blacks and Jews to the American scene? Is this merely imparting knowledge?

The problem of differentiating education and propaganda can be more subtle still. Let us look at arithmetic as taught in the public schools. What could be more educational? By that I mean, what could be more pure, objective, factual, untainted by doctrine? Watch out. Think back to your elementary-school days. Do you remember the examples used in your arithmetic text? Most of the examples dealt with buying, selling, renting, working for wages, and computing interest. As Zimbardo and Ebbeson[6] point out, these examples do more than simply reflect the capitalistic system in which the education is occurring: they systematically endorse the system, legitimize it, and, by implication, suggest that it is the natural and normal way. As a way of illustrating multiplication and percentages, the textbook has Mr. Jones borrowing $4000 at 9½ percent interest from a bank in order to purchase a new car. Would this example be used in a society that felt that it was sinful to charge interest, as early Christian societies believed? Would this example be used in a society that believed that a person shouldn't seek possessions that he can't afford? I am not suggesting that it's wrong or evil to use these kinds of illustrations in arithmetic books; I am merely pointing out that they are a form of propaganda and that we should recognize them as such.

In practice, whether a person regards a particular course of instruction as educational or propagandistic depends, to a large extent, on his values. Reflect, for a moment, on a film about drug abuse that my children were required to see in their high school: at one point, the film mentioned the fact that many hard-core addicts began by sampling marijuana. I'm certain that most school officials would regard the presentation of this piece of factual information as a case of "imparting knowledge," and that most marijuana enthusiasts would probably regard it as "the systematic propagation of a given doctrine"—that is, the implication that marijuana leads to the use of addictive drugs. By the same token, the reader might reflect on sex education in the schools as viewed by a member of the John Birch Society or by the editor of *Playboy* magazine; or he might recall that a process that the Chinese communists call re-education would be referred to as "brainwashing" by most Americans. This is not to say that all communications are drastically slanted and one-sided. Rather, when we are dealing with an emotionally charged issue about which people's opinions differ greatly, it is probably impossible to construct a communication that people on both sides of the issue would agree was fair and impartial. We will present a more detailed discussion of communication as viewed through "the eye of the beholder" in the next chapter. For now, it is important to note that, whether we call it propaganda or education, persuasion is a reality. It won't go away if we ignore it. We should therefore attempt to understand it by analyzing the experimental literature on persuasion.

What factors increase the effectiveness of a communication?

Basically, there are three classes of variables that are important: (1) the source of the communication (who says it), (2) the nature of the communication (how he says it), and (3) the characteristics of the audience (to whom he says it).

The Source of the Communication

Credibility. Picture the following scene: Your doorbell rings, and, when you answer it, you find a middle-aged man in a rather loud, checkered sports jacket. His tie is loose, his collar is frayed, his pants need ironing, he needs a shave, and his eyes keep looking off to the side and over your head as he talks to you. He is carrying a small can in his hand with a slot on the top and he's trying to convince you to contribute a few dollars to a charitable organization that you've never heard of. Although his actual pitch sounds fairly reasonable, what are the possibilities of his succeeding in prying you loose from your money? Let's turn the clock back a few minutes: You open your door in response to the ringing of the doorbell, and standing there is a middle-aged man in a conservative business suit, well-tailored and well-pressed. He looks you squarely in the eye, introduces himself as a vice-president of the City National Bank, and asks you if you would contribute a few dollars to a charitable organization (that you've never heard of), using exactly the same words as the fellow in the loud, checkered jacket. Would you be more likely to contribute some money?

I was struck by this phenomenon a few years ago when I saw the poet Allen Ginsberg on one of the late-night talk shows. Ginsberg was among the most popular of the poets of the so-called beat generation; his poem "Howl" had shocked and stimulated the literary establishment in the fifties. On the talk show, Ginsberg was at it again: having just finished boasting about his homosexuality, he was talking about the generation gap. The camera panned in. He was fat, bearded, and looked a trifle wild-eyed (was he stoned?); long hair grew in unruly patches from the sides of his otherwise bald head; he was wearing a tie-dyed T-shirt with a hole in it, and a few strands of beads. Although he was talking earnestly—and, in my opinion, very sensibly—about the problems of the young, the studio audience was laughing. They seemed to be treating him like a clown. It dawned on me that, in all probability, the vast majority of the people at home, lying in bed watching the poet from between their feet, could not possibly take him seriously—no matter how sensible his message, and no matter how earnestly he delivered it. His appearance and his reputation were, in all probability, overdetermining the audience's reaction. The scientist in me longed to substitute the conservative-looking banker in the neatly pressed business suit for the wild-eyed poet and have him move his lips while Ginsberg said the same words off camera. My guess is that, under these circumstances, Ginsberg's message would have been well received.

No need. Similar experiments have already been done. Indeed, speculations about the effects of prestige on persuasion are ancient. More than 300 years before Christ, Aristotle, the world's first published social psychologist, wrote:

> We believe good men more fully and more readily than others: this is true generally whatever the question is, and absolutely true where exact certainty is impossible and opinions are divided. . . . It is not true, as some writers assume in their treatises on rhetoric, that the personal goodness revealed by the speaker contributes nothing to his power of persuasion; on the contrary, his character may almost be called the most effective means of persuasion he possesses.[7]

It required some 2300 years for Aristotle's observation to be put to a rigorous scientific test. This was accomplished by Carl Hovland and Walter Weiss.[8] What these investigators did was very simple: They presented large numbers of people with a communication that argued a particular point of view—for example, that building atomic-powered submarines was a feasible undertaking (this experiment was performed in 1951, when harnessing atomic energy for such purposes was merely a dream). Some of the people were informed that the argument was made by a person possessing a great deal of credibility; for others, the same argument was attributed to a source with low credibility. Specifically, the argument that atomic-powered submarines could be built in the near future was attributed to either J. Robert Oppenheimer, a nationally known and highly respected atomic physicist, or to *Pravda*, the official newspaper of the Communist Party in the Soviet Union—a publication not famous in the United States for its objectivity and truthfulness. Before reading the arguments, the members of the audience were asked to fill out some rating scales that revealed their opinions on the topic. They then read the communication. A large percentage of those people who believed that the communication came from J. Robert Oppenheimer changed their opinions—they then believed more strongly in the feasibility of atomic submarines. Very few of those who read an identical communication attributed to *Pravda* shifted their opinions in the direction of the communication.

This same phenomenon has received repeated confirmations by several different investigators using a wide variety of topics and attributing the communications to a wide variety of communicators. Careful experiments have shown that a judge of the juvenile court is better than most people at swaying opinion about juvenile delinquency, that the Surgeon General of the United States can sway opinion about health insurance, and that a medical journal can sway opinion about whether or not antihistamines should be dispensed without a prescription. What do Robert Oppenheimer, the judge, the Surgeon General, and the medical journal have that *Pravda* doesn't have? That is, what is the difference that makes the difference in their effectiveness? Aristotle said that we believe "good" men, by which he meant men of high moral calibre. Hovland and Weiss use the term "credible," which removes the moral connotations that are present in the Aristotelian definition. Oppenheimer, a juvenile court judge, and the Surgeon General are all credible—that is not to say that they are necessarily "good," but that they are both *expert* and *trustworthy*. It makes sense to allow yourself to be influenced by someone who is trustworthy and who knows what he's talking about. It makes sense for people to be influenced by J. Robert Oppenheimer when he is voicing an opinion about atomic power, and it makes sense for people to be influenced by the Surgeon General when he is talking about health insurance. These are expert, trustworthy men. But not all people are equally influenced by the same communicator. Indeed, the same communicator may be regarded by some members of an audience as possessing high credibility, and by others as possessing low credibility. Moreover, certain "peripheral" attributes of the communicator may loom large for some members of the audience; such attributes can serve to make a given communicator either remarkably effective or remarkably ineffective.

This phenomenon was forcefully demonstrated in an experiment that I performed in collaboration with Burton Golden,[9] in which we presented sixth graders with a speech extolling the usefulness and importance of arithmetic. The communicator was introduced either as a prize-winning engineer from a prestigious university, or as a man who washed dishes for a living. As one might expect, the engineer was far more effective at influencing the kids' opinions about arithmetic than the dishwasher. This finding is consistent with previous research; in and of itself, it is obvious and not very interesting. But, in addition, we varied the race of the communicator: in some of the trials he was white, and in others, black. Several weeks prior to the experiment, the children had filled out a questionnaire designed to measure the degree of their prejudice against black people. The results were striking: Among those children who were most prejudiced against blacks, the black engineer was *less* influential than the white engineer, although both men delivered the same speech. Moreover, among those children who were the least prejudiced against blacks, the black engineer was *more* influential than the white engineer. It seems unreasonable that such a peripheral attribute as skin color would affect a person's credibility to an audience. It might be argued that, in a purely rational world, a prestigious engineer should be able to influence sixth graders about the importance of arithmetic regardless of the color of his skin, but apparently this is not a purely rational world: depending upon the individual listener's attitude toward blacks, he was either *more* influenced or *less* influenced by a black communicator than by an otherwise identical white communicator.

This kind of behavior is not very adaptive. If the quality of your life depended on the extent to which you were to allow a communication about arithmetic to influence your opinion, the expertise and trustworthiness of the communicator would seem to be the most reasonable factors to heed. To the extent that other factors (such as skin color) decrease or increase your susceptibility to persuasion on an issue irrelevant to such factors, you are behaving in a maladaptive manner. But, although such behavior is maladaptive, it should not be very astonishing to anyone who has ever watched commercials on

TV. Here, not only are various peripheral aspects of the communicator emphasized, but frequently the *only* aspects of the communicator that the viewer is able to perceive are totally peripheral and irrelevant to the communication. Who is an expert on the topic of razor blades or shaving cream? Well, perhaps a barber; maybe a dermatologist or a chemist. Who is it that tells us what blades or lather we should use? Most often, it's some mountainous professional football player who must squint hard at the cue-card in order to make out the name of the sponsor's product. Throughout the 1950s and 1960s, one of the most persistent peddlers of breakfast food has been a former Olympic decathlon champion, who is probably far more effective at selling "Wheaties" than some learned professor of nutrition would be, even if the professor were acknowledged to be far more expert on the subject. How effective *are* these guys? Ask yourself: Would you buy a certain brand of shaving cream because Broadway Joe Namath receives a facial massage from a pretty blonde? Can he interest you in a popcorn popper or a pair of pantyhose? Do you want to phone your aging mother long distance because Bill Russell sinks a basketball shot while sitting in a swivel chair? Do you want to change razors because Mark Spitz, who won seven gold medals in swimming at the Munich Olympics, uses a certain brand? Can old George Blanda sell you an auto tire? Can Arnold Palmer put you into friendlier skies on your next airplane trip?

People recognize athletes. D. E. Hutchins, director of advertising for AT&T, said: "We have discovered through various surveys that the sports star enjoys a tremendous recognition factor—superior to that of Hollywood movie stars and nameless models picked on looks. But believability is something else. Will people be influenced by an ad just because a prominent sports personality is involved?"[10] Recently, a survey was conducted in which 2500 heads of households were asked whether they could be influenced by such sports personalities as Joe Namath and Muhammad Ali. The overwhelming majority said that they didn't think they could be—that they didn't trust these athletes. Can people predict their own behavior? Before answering, let's take a closer look at the factor of "trust."

Increasing Trustworthiness. Clearly, trust is an important factor in determining whether or not a communicator will be effective. It may be that the crucial reason why the relatively more prejudiced sixth graders in the Aronson–Golden experiment were less influenced by the black engineer than by the white engineer was that they simply did not trust blacks. If this is true, then if we could offer the audience clear independent evidence that a person is trustworthy, that person should be a very effective communicator, even though he is otherwise unattractive.

How does a person make himself seem clearly trustworthy to us? One way is for him to argue against his own self-interest. If a person has nothing to gain (and perhaps something to lose) by convincing us, we will trust him and he will be more effective. An illustration may be helpful: Suppose that Joe "The Shoulder" Napolitano, a habitual criminal recently convicted as a smuggler and peddler of heroin, was delivering a communication on the abuses of the American judiciary system. Would he influence you? Probably not. Most people would probably regard him as unattractive and untrustworthy: he seems to fit clearly outside of the Aristotelian definition of a "good man." But suppose he was arguing that criminal justice was too *lenient*—that a criminal could almost always beat the rap if he had a smart lawyer, and that even if a criminal *were* convicted, the sentences normally meted out are too soft. Would he influence you? I'm quite certain he would; in fact, a few years ago, I performed this very experiment in collaboration with Elaine Walster and Darcy Abrahams,[11] and it confirmed that hypothesis. In the actual experiment, we presented our subjects with a newspaper clipping of an interview between a news reporter and Joe "The Shoulder" Napolitano, who was identified just as I have identified him here. In one experimental condition, Joe "The Shoulder" argued for stricter courts and more severe sentences. In another condition, he argued that the courts should be more lenient and the sentences less severe. We also ran a parallel set of conditions in which the same statements were attributed to a respected public official. When Joe "The Shoulder" argued for more lenient courts, he was totally ineffective; indeed, he actually caused the subjects' opinions to change slightly in the opposite direction. But when he was arguing for stricter, more powerful courts, he was extremely effective—as effective as the respected public official delivering the same argument. This study demonstrates that Aristotle was not completely correct—a communicator can be an unattractive, immoral person and still be effective, as long as it is clear that he has nothing to gain (and perhaps something to lose) by persuading us.

The trustworthiness of a person who is not particularly attractive can also be increased if his audience is absolutely certain that he is not *trying* to influence them. Suppose a stockbroker calls you up and gives you a hot tip on a particular stock. Will you buy? It's hard to be sure. On the one hand, the broker is probably an expert, and this might influence you to buy. On the other hand, the stockbroker has something to gain by giving you this tip (a commission), and this could lower his effectiveness. But suppose you happened to overhear him telling his wife that a particular stock was about to rise. Because he was obviously not *trying* to influence you, you might be more readily influenced. This is exactly what was discovered in an experiment by Elaine Walster and Leon Festinger.[12] In this study, a conversation was staged between two graduate students in which one of them expressed his opinion on an issue. The situation was arranged so that an undergraduate subject was allowed to overhear this conversation. In one experimental condition, it was clear to the subject that the graduate students were well aware of his presence in the next room; therefore, the subject knew that anything being said could conceivably be directed at him with the intention of influencing his opinion. In the other condition, the situation was arranged so that the subject believed that the graduate students were unaware of his presence in the next room. In this condition, the subject's opinion changed significantly more in the direction of the opinion expressed by the graduate students.

Attractiveness

Where do these findings leave our friend the football player holding up his can of shaving cream? Clearly he is *trying* to influence us—the shaving cream company is not paying him all that money *not* to sell shaving cream. Moreover, he seems to be operating in his own self-interest; if we were to take a good look at the situation, it would be clear to us that the only reason he's up there with the shaving cream is to make a buck. These factors should make him less trustworthy. And apparently they do—as indicated by the results of the research I've just described. But does this make him less effective? Not necessarily. Although the majority of the heads of household said they didn't trust Joe Namath, that doesn't necessarily mean that they didn't buy the shaving cream or the panty hose. Another crucial factor that determines the effectiveness of the communicator is how attractive or likable he is—regardless of his overall expertise or trustworthiness. Several years ago, Judson Mills and I did a simple laboratory experiment that demonstrated that a beautiful woman—simply because she was beautiful—could have a major impact on the opinions of an audience on a topic wholly irrelevant to her beauty, and, furthermore, that her impact was greatest when she openly expressed a desire to influence the audience.[13] Thus, we seem to be influenced by people we like. Where our liking for a communicator is involved (rather than his expertise), we seem to behave as though we were trying to please him. Accordingly, the more that communicator wants us to change our opinions, the more we change them—but *only about trivial issues.* That is, it is true that football players can get us to use a particular shaving cream and beautiful women can get us to agree with them on an abstract topic whether or not we are willing to admit it. At the same time, it is unlikely that they could influence us to vote for their presidential candidate or to adopt their position on the legalization of marijuana.

To summarize this section we might list these phenomena:

1. Our opinions are influenced by individuals who are both expert and trustworthy.
2. A communicator's trustworthiness (and effectiveness) can be increased if he argues a position apparently opposed to his own self-interest.
3. A communicator's trustworthiness (and effectiveness) can be increased if he does not seem to be trying to influence our opinion.
4. At least where trivial opinions and behaviors are concerned, if we like a person and can identify with him, his opinions and behaviors will be more influential upon our own than their content would ordinarily warrant.
5. Again, where trivial opinions and behaviors are concerned, if we like a person, we will tend to be influenced by him even if it is clear that he is trying to influence us and that he stands to profit by doing so.

The Nature of the Communication

The manner in which a communication is stated plays an important role in determining its effectiveness. There are several ways in which communications can differ from one another. I have selected four that I consider to be among the most important: (1) Is a communication more persuasive if it is designed to appeal to the audience's reasoning ability, or is it more persuasive if it is aimed at arousing the audience's emotions? (2) Should the communication present only one side of the argument, or should it also include an attempt to refute the opposing view? (3) If two sides are presented, as in a debate, does the order in which they are presented affect the relative impact on either side? (4) What is the relationship between the effectiveness of the communication and the discrepancy that exists between the audience's original opinion and the opinion advocated by the communication?

Logical versus Emotional Appeals. Several years ago, I was living in a community that was about to vote on whether or not to fluoridate the water supply as a means of combating tooth decay. An information campaign that seemed quite logical and reasonable was launched by the proponents of fluoridation. It consisted largely of statements by noted dentists describing the benefits of fluorides and discussing the evidence on the reduction of tooth decay in areas with fluoridated water, as well as statements by physicians and other health authorities to the effect that fluoridation has no harmful effects. The opponents used an appeal that was much more emotional in flavor. For example, one leaflet consisted of a huge picture of a rather ugly rat, along with the inscription "Don't let them put rat-poison in your drinking water." The referendum to fluoridate the water supply was soundly defeated. Of course, this incident doesn't prove conclusively that emotional appeals are superior, mainly because the incident was not a scientifically controlled study; we have no idea how the people would have voted on fluoridation if *no* publicity were circulated, nor do we know whether the antifluoridation circular reached more people, whether it was easier to read than the proponents' literature, and so forth. Although the actual research in this area is far from conclusive, there does appear to be some evidence favoring an appeal that is primarily emotional. In one early study, for example, George W.

Hartmann[14] tried to measure the extent to which he could induce people to vote for a particular political candidate as a function of what kind of appeal he used. He demonstrated that individuals who received a message that was *primarily* emotional in tenor voted for the candidates endorsed by the message to a greater extent than did people who received a message that was *primarily* logical.

The word *primarily* is italicized for a good reason—it seems to define the major problem with research in this area. Namely, there are no foolproof, mutually exclusive definitions of "emotional" and "rational." In the fluoridation illustration, for example, most people would probably agree that the antifluoridation pamphlet was designed to arouse fear; yet, it is not entirely illogical, because it is indeed true that the fluoride that is used in minute concentrations to prevent tooth decay is used in massive concentrations as a rat poison. On the other side, to present the views of professional men is not entirely free from emotional appeal: it may be comforting (on an emotional level) to know that physicians and dentists endorse the use of fluorides.

Because, in practice, operational distinctions between "logical" and "emotional" are difficult to draw, some researchers have turned to an equally interesting and far more researchable problem: the problem of the effect of various levels of a specific emotion on opinion change. Suppose you wish to arouse fear in the hearts of your audience as a way of inducing opinion change. Would it be more effective to arouse just a little fear, or should you try to scare the hell out of them? For example, if your goal is to convince people to drive more carefully, would you be more effective if you showed them gory technicolor films of the broken and bloody bodies of the victims of highway accidents, or would you be more effective if you soft-pedaled your communication—showing crumpled fenders, discussing increased insurance rates due to careless driving, and pointing out the possibility that people who drive carelessly may have their driver's licenses suspended? Common sense argues on both sides of this street. On the one hand, it suggests that a good scare will motivate people to action; on the other hand, it argues that too much fear can be debilitating—that is, it might interfere with a person's ability to pay attention to the message, to comprehend it, and to act upon it. We've all believed, at one time or another, that "it only happens to the other guy—it can't happen to me." Thus, people continue to drive at very high speeds, and to insist on driving after they've had a few drinks, even though they should know better. Perhaps this is because the possible negative consequences of these actions are so great that we try not to think about them. Thus, it has been argued that, if a communication arouses a great deal of fear, we tend *not* to pay close attention to it.

What does the evidence tell us? The overwhelming weight of experimental data suggests that, all other things being equal, the more frightened a person is by a communication the more likely he is to take positive preventive action. The most prolific researchers in this area have been Howard Leventhal and his associates.[15] In one experiment, they tried to induce people to stop smoking and to take chest X-rays. Some subjects were exposed to a low-fear treatment: they were simply presented with the recommendation to stop smoking and get their chests X-rayed. Others were subjected to moderate fear: they were shown a film depicting a young man whose chest X-rays revealed that he had lung cancer. The people subjected to the high-fear condition saw the same film that the "moderate-fear" people saw—and, in addition, they were treated to a rather gory color film of a lung-cancer operation. The results showed that those people who were most frightened were also most eager to stop smoking and most likely to take chest X-rays.

Is this true for all people? It is not. There is a reason why common sense leads some people to believe that a great deal of fear leads to inaction: it does—for certain people, under certain conditions. What Leventhal and his colleagues discovered is that people who have a reasonably good opinion of themselves (high self-esteem) are the ones who are most likely to be moved by high degrees of fear arousal. People with low opinions of themselves were the least likely to take immediate action when confronted with a communication that aroused a great deal of fear—but (and here is the interesting part) after a delay, they behaved very much like the subjects with high self-esteem. That is, if immediate action was not required, but action could be taken later, people with low self-esteem were more likely to take that action if they were exposed to a communication that aroused a great deal of fear. The reason for this may be that people who have a low opinion of themselves have a great deal of difficulty coping with the world. A high-fear communication overwhelms them and makes them feel like crawling into bed and pulling the covers up over their heads. Low or moderate fear is something that they can more easily deal with at the moment they experience it. But if given time—that is, if it's not essential that they act immediately—they will be more likely to act if the message truly scared the hell out of them.

Subsequent research by Leventhal and his co-workers lends support to this analysis. In one study, subjects were shown films of serious automobile accidents. Some subjects watched the films on a large screen from up close; others watched them from far away on a much smaller screen. Among those subjects with high or moderate self-esteem, the ones who saw the films on the large screen were much more likely to take protective action, subsequently, than were the ones who saw the films on the small screen. Subjects with low self-esteem were more likely to take action when they saw the films on a small screen; those subjects with low self-esteem who saw the films on a large screen reported a great deal of fatigue and stated that they had a great deal of difficulty even thinking of themselves as victims of automobile accidents. Thus, it does seem that people with low self-esteem are overwhelmed by fear, if an immediate response is necessary.

It should be relatively easy to make a person with high self-esteem behave like a person with low self-esteem. We can overwhelm him by making him feel that there is nothing he can do to prevent or discover a threatening situation. This will lead most people to bury their heads in the sand—even those who have high self-esteem. Conversely, suppose you wanted to reduce the automobile accident rate, or to help people give up smoking, and you were faced with low self-esteem people. How would you proceed? If you construct a message that contains clear, specific, and optimistic instructions, it might increase the feeling among the members of your audience that they can cope with the danger. Experiments by Leventhal and his associates show that fear-arousing messages that contain specific instructions about how, when, and where to take action are much more effective than recommendations that do not include such instructions. For example, a campaign conducted on a college campus urging students to take tetanus shots included specific instructions about where and when they were available. The campaign materials included a map showing the location of the student health service and a suggestion that each student set aside a convenient time to stop by. The results showed that high-fear appeals were more effective than low-fear appeals in producing favorable *attitudes* toward tetanus shots among the students, and that they also increased the students' stated intentions to take the shots. The highly specific instructions about how to go about getting the shots did not in any way effect these opinions and intentions, but the instructions did have a big effect on the *actual behavior*: Of those subjects who were instructed about how to proceed, 28 percent actually got the tetanus shots, but of those who received no specific instructions, only 3 percent actually went down to get them. In a control group exposed only to the action instructions—no fear-arousing message—there was no shot taking. Thus, specific instructions alone are not enough to produce action—fear is a necessary component for action in such situations.

Very similar results were uncovered in Leventhal's cigarette experiment. In attempting to help people give up smoking cigarettes, Leventhal found that a high-fear communication produced a much greater *intention* to stop smoking. Unless it was accompanied by recommendations for specific behavior, however, it produced little results. Similarly, specific instructions ("buy a magazine instead of a pack of cigarettes; drink plenty of water when you have the urge to smoke," and so on) without a fear-arousing communication were relatively ineffective. The combination of fear arousal and specific instructions produced the best results; the students in this condition were still smoking less four months after they were subjected to the experimental procedure.

One-sided versus Two-sided Arguments. Suppose you are trying to persuade your audience that capital punishment is necessary. Would you persuade more people if you simply stated your view and ignored the arguments against capital punishment, or would you be more persuasive if you discussed the opposing arguments and attempted to refute them? Before trying to answer this question, let us try to understand what is involved. If a communicator mentions the opposition's arguments, it might indicate that he is an objective, fair-minded person; this could enhance his effectiveness. On the other hand, if a communicator so much as mentions the arguments on the other side of the issue, it might suggest to the audience that the issue is a controversial one; this could confuse the audience, make them equivocate, and it might ultimately reduce the persuasiveness of the communication. With these possibilities in mind, it should not come as a surprise to the reader that there is no simple relation between one-sided arguments and the effectiveness of the communication. It depends to some extent upon the intelligence of the audience: the more intelligent the members of the audience are, the less likely they are to be persuaded by a one-sided argument and the more likely they are to be persuaded by an argument that brings out the important opposing arguments and then proceeds to refute them. This makes sense: an intelligent person is more likely to know some of the counterarguments—when the communicator avoids mentioning these, the intelligent members of the audience are likely to conclude that the communicator is either unfair or is unable to refute such arguments. On the other hand, an unintelligent person is less apt to know of the existence of opposing arguments. If the counterargument is ignored, he is persuaded; if the counterargument is presented, he may get confused.

Another factor that plays a vital role is the initial position of the audience. As we might expect, if a member of the audience is already predisposed to believe the communicator's argument, a one-sided presentation has a greater impact on his opinion than a two-sided presentation. If, however, a member of the audience is leaning in the opposite direction, then a two-sided refutational argument is more persuasive.[16] Most politicians seem to be well aware of this phenomenon; they tend to present vastly different kinds of speeches, depending upon who constitutes the audience. When talking to the party faithful, they almost invariably deliver a hell-raising set of arguments favoring their own party platform and candidacy. If they do mention the opposition, it is in a derisive, mocking tone. On the other hand, when appearing on network TV or when speaking to any audience of mixed loyalties, they tend to take a more statesman-like position, giving the opposing view a reasonably accurate airing before proceeding to demolish it.

The Order of Presentation. Imagine that you are running for the city council. You and your opponent are invited to address a large audience in the civic auditorium. It is a close election—many members of the audience are as yet undecided—and the outcome may hinge on your speech. You have worked hard on writing and rehearsing it. As you take your seat on the stage, the master of ceremonies asks you whether you would prefer to lead off or speak last. You ponder this for a moment. You think, *Speaking first may have an advantage, because first impressions are lasting; if I can get the audience on my side early, then my opponent will not only have to sell himself, but he'll also have to unsell the audience on me—he'll be bucking a trend. On the other hand, if I speak last, I may have an advantage, because when the people leave the auditorium, they may remember the last thing they heard. The early statements made by my opponent, no matter how powerful, will be buried by my rhetoric simply because being last my speech will be more vivid, more memorable.* You stammer: "I'd like to speak first . . . no, last . . . no first . . . no, wait a minute." In confusion, you race off the stage, find a phone booth, and phone your friend the social psychologist. Surely, he must know which order has an advantage.

I'm afraid that if you expect a one-word answer, you are in for a disappointment. Moreover, if you wait to hear all of the social psychologist's elaborations and qualifying remarks, you might miss the opportunity of ever delivering your speech at all. Indeed, you might even miss the election itself.

Needless to say, the issue is a complex one involving both learning and retention. I'll try to state it as simply as possible. The issues are similar to the common-sense issues that you, as our hypothetical politician, pondered alone. It is true that, all other things being equal, the audience's memory should be better for the speech that was made last, simply because it is closer in time to the election. On the other hand, the actual learning of the second material will not be as thorough as the learning of the first material, simply because the very existence of the first material inhibits the learning process. Thus, from our knowledge of the phenomena of learning, it would appear that, all other things being equal, the first argument will be more effective; we'll call this the *primacy effect*. But from our knowledge of the phenomena of retention, on the other hand, it would appear that, all other things being equal, the last argument will be more effective; we'll call this the *recency effect*.

The fact that these two approaches seemingly make for opposite predictions does not mean that it doesn't matter which argument comes first; nor does it mean that it is hopeless to attempt to make a definitive prediction. What it does mean is that, by knowing something about the way both inhibition and retention work, we can predict the conditions under which either the primacy effect or the recency effect will prevail. The crucial variable is *time*—that is, the amount of time that separates the events in the situation: (1) the amount of time between the first communication and the second communication and (2) the amount of time between the end of the second communication and the moment when the members of the audience must finally make up their minds. Here are the crucial points: (1) Inhibition (interference) is greatest if very little time elapses between the two communications; here, the first communication produces maximum interference with the learning of the second communication, and a primacy effect will occur—the first speaker will have the advantage. (2) Retention is greatest, and recency effects will therefore prevail, when the audience must make up its mind immediately after hearing the second communication.

Okay. Is the candidate for city council still on the phone? Here's the plan: If the two speakers present their arguments back to back, and if the election is still several days away, you should speak first. The primacy of your speech will interfere with the audience's ability to learn your opponent's arguments; with the election several days away, differential effects due to memory are negligible. But if the election is going to be held immediately after the second speech, and there is going to be a prolonged coffee break between the two speeches, you would do well to speak last. Because of the coffee break between speeches, the interference of the first speech with the learning of the second speech will be minimal; because the audience must make up its mind right after the second speech, the second speaker has retention working for him. Therefore, the recency effect would predominate: all other things being equal, the last speech will be the more persuasive.

These speculations were confirmed in a clever experiment by Norman Miller and Donald Campbell.[17] In this experiment, a simulated jury trial was arranged, in which the subjects were presented with a condensed version of the transcript of an actual jury trial of a suit for damages brought against the manufacturers of an allegedly defective vaporizer. The *pro* side of the argument consisted of the testimony of witnesses for the plaintiff, cross-examination of defense witnesses by the plaintiff's lawyer, and the opening and closing speeches of the plaintiff's lawyer. The *con* side of the argument consisted of the testimony of witnesses for the defense, the defense lawyer's cross-examinations, and his opening and closing statements. The condensed version of this transcript was arranged so that all of the *pro* arguments were placed in one block and all of the *con* arguments were placed in another block. The investigators varied the time that intervened between the reading of the two arguments and between the reading of the last argument and the announcement of the verdict. A recency effect was obtained when there was a large gap between the first and second arguments and a small gap between the second argument and the verdict. A primacy effect was obtained when there was a small gap between the first and second arguments and a large gap between the second argument and the verdict. The topic of this experiment (a jury trial) serves to underscore the immense practical significance that these phenomena may have. If it is true that the order of presentation has an effect on such things as whether a jury finds a defendant guilty or innocent, then our trial procedures should be examined and steps should be taken to prevent any possible miscarriages of justice due to primacy or recency effects.

The Size of the Discrepancy. If a communicator is talking to an audience that strongly disagrees with his point of view, will presenting his position in its most extreme form be more effective, or will modulating his position by presenting it in such a way that it does not seem terribly different from the audience's position? For example, suppose you believe that, in order to stay healthy, people should exercise vigorously every day; any vigorous exercise would be helpful, but an hour's worth would be preferable. Your audience consists of a group of college professors who seem to believe that turning the pages of a book is sufficient exercise for the average person. Would you change their opinion to a greater extent by arguing that people should exercise for a full hour every day, or by suggesting a briefer, less taxing regimen? In short, what is the most effective level of discrepancy between the opinion of the audience and the recommendation of the communicator? This is a vital issue for any propagandist or educator.

Let us look at this situation from the point of view of the audience. As I mentioned in Chapter 2, most of us have a strong desire to be correct—to have "correct" opinions and to perform reasonable actions. When someone comes along and disagrees with us, it makes us feel uncomfortable because it suggests that our opinions or actions may be wrong or based on misinformation. The greater the disagreement, the greater is our discomfort. How can we reduce this discomfort? Simply by changing our opinions or actions. The greater the disagreement, the greater our opinion change will be. This line of reasoning, then, would suggest that the communicator should argue for one hour per day of rigorous exercise; the greater the discrepancy, the more the opinion change: indeed, several investigators have found that this "linear" relation holds true. A good example of this relation was provided by an experiment by Philip Zimbardo.[18] Each of the college women recruited as subjects for the experiment was asked to bring a close friend with her to the laboratory. Each pair of friends was then presented with a case study of juvenile delinquency, and then each of the subjects was asked, separately and in private, to indicate her recommendations on the matter. Each subject was led to believe that her close friend disagreed with her—either by a small margin or by an extremely large margin. Zimbardo found that the greater the apparent margin between the friends' judgments, the more they changed their opinions toward what they supposed were the opinions of their friends.

However, a careful look at the research literature also turns up several experiments that disconfirm the line of reasoning presented above. For example, Carl Hovland, O. J. Harvey, and Muzafer Sherif[19] argued that, if a particular communication differs considerably from a person's own position, it is, in effect, outside of his "latitude of acceptance," and he will *not* be much influenced by it. They conducted an experiment and found a *curvilinear* relation between discrepancy and opinion change. By "curvilinear," I mean that, as a small discrepancy increased somewhat, so did the degree of opinion change; but as the discrepancy continued to increase, opinion change began to slacken; and finally, as the discrepancy became large, the amount of opinion change became very small. When the discrepancy was very large, almost no opinion change was observed at all. Let's take a closer look at this experiment. The communication was based on a red-hot issue—one that the subjects felt strongly about: whether their state should remain "dry" or "go wet"—that is, whether or not to change the law prohibiting the distribution and sale of alcoholic beverages. The voters of the state were virtually equally divided on this issue, and the subjects were a representative sample: some of the subjects felt strongly that the state should remain dry, others felt strongly that it should go wet, and yet others took a moderate position. The subjects were then divided into groups in which all three opinions were represented. Each group was presented with a different communication, so that in each group, there were subjects who found the communication close to their own position, some who found it moderately discrepant from their own position, and some who found it extremely discrepant from their own position. Specifically, one group was presented with a "wet" message, which argued for the unlimited and unrestricted sale of liquor; another group was presented with a "dry" message, which argued for complete prohibition; and a third group was presented with a moderately "wet" message, which argued to allow some drinking but with certain controls and restrictions. The greatest opinion changes occurred when there was a moderate discrepancy between the actual message and the opinions of individual members of the audience.

What an exciting state of affairs! When there exist a substantial number of research findings that point in one direction and a similarly substantial number of research findings that point in a different direction, it doesn't necessarily mean that someone has to be wrong; rather, it suggests that there is a significant factor that hasn't been accounted for—and this is indeed exciting, for it gives the scientist an opportunity to play detective. I beg the readers' indulgence here, for I would like to dwell on this issue—not only for its substantive value, but also because it provides us with an opportunity to analyze one of the more adventurous aspects of social psychology as a science. Basically, there are two ways of proceeding with this game of detective. We can begin by assembling all of the experiments that show one result and all of those that show the other result and (imaginary magnifying glass in hand) painstakingly scrutinize them, looking for the one factor common to the experiments in group *A* and lacking in those in group *B*; then we can try to determine, *conceptually*, why this factor should make a difference. Or, conversely, we can begin by speculating conceptually about what factor or factors might make a difference; then we can glance through the existing literature, with this conceptual lantern in hand, to see if the experiments in group *A* differ from the experiments in group *B* in this dimension.

My own personal preference is for the second mode. Accordingly, with two of my students—J. Merrill Carlsmith and Judith Turner—I began to speculate about what factor or factors might make such a difference. We began by accepting the notion discussed above: the greater the discrepancy, the greater the discomfort for the members of the audience. But we reasoned that this does not necessarily mean that the members of an audience will change their opinion. There are at least four ways in which members of an audience can reduce their discomfort: (1) they can change their opinion; (2) they can induce the communicator to change *his* opinion; (3) they can seek support for their original opinion by finding other people who share their views, in spite of what the communicator says; or (4) they can derogate the communicator—convince themselves that the communicator is stupid, or immoral, or a Commie—and thereby invalidate that person's opinion.

In a great many communication situations, including those that pertain in these experiments, the message is delivered either as a written statement (as a newspaper or magazine article, for example) or by a communicator who is not approachable by the audience (as on TV, on the lecture platform, and so on). Also, the subject is often alone, or part of an audience whose members have no opportunity to interact with each other. Thus, under these circumstances, it is virtually impossible for the recipients of the communication either to have immediate impact on the communicator's opinion or to seek immediate social support. This leaves the recipients two major ways of reducing this discomfort—they can change their opinion, or they can derogate the communicator.

Under what circumstances would an individual find it easy or difficult to derogate the communicator? It would be very difficult to derogate a liked and respected personal friend; it would also be difficult to derogate someone who is a highly trustworthy expert on the issue under discussion. But if the communicator's credibility were ambiguous, it would *not* be difficult to derogate him. Following this line of reasoning, we suggested that, if a communicator's credibility were high, the greater the discrepancy between his views and the audience's views, the greater the impact he would have on the opinions of the audience. However, if the communicator's credibility were not very high, he would be, by definition, subject to derogation. This is not to say that he couldn't influence the opinions of the audience. He probably would be able to influence people to change their opinions, if his opinions were not too different from theirs. But the more discrepant such a communicator's position is from those of his audience, the more the audience might begin to question his wisdom, intelligence, and sanity. The more they question his wisdom, intelligence, and sanity, the less likely they are to be influenced by him. Let's return to our example involving physical exercise: Imagine a 73-year-old man, with the body of a man half his age, who had just won the 26-mile Boston Marathon. If he told me that a good way to stay in condition and live a long healthy life was to exercise vigorously for one hour every day, I would believe him. Boy, would I believe him! He would get much more exercise out of me than if he suggested that I should exercise for only ten minutes a day. But suppose that a person somewhat less credible, such as a high-school track coach, were delivering the communication. If he suggested that I exercise ten minutes a day, his suggestion would be within my own latitude of acceptance, and he might influence my opinion and behavior. But if he advised me to exercise vigorously for an hour a day, I would be inclined to write him off as a quack, a health freak, a monomaniac—and I could comfortably continue being indolent. Thus, I would agree with Hovland, Harvey, and Sherif: a person will consider an extremely discrepant communication to be outside of his latitude of acceptance—but only if the communicator is not highly credible.

Armed with these speculations, my colleagues and I scrutinized the existing experiments on this issue, paying special attention to the ways in which the communicator was described. Lo and behold, we discovered that each of the experiments that showed a direct linear relation between discrepancy and opinion change happened to describe the source of the communication as more credible than did those whose results showed a curvilinear relation. This confirmed our speculations about the role of credibility. But we didn't stop there: we constructed an experiment in which we systematically investigated the size of the discrepancy and the credibility of the communicator in one research design.[20] In this experiment, college women were asked to read several stanzas from obscure modern poetry and to rank them in terms of how good they were. Then each woman was given an essay to read purporting to be a criticism of modern poetry that specifically mentioned a stanza that she had rated poorly. For some subjects, the essayist described this particular stanza in glowing terms—this created a large discrepancy between the opinion of the communicator and the opinion voiced by the students in this experimental condition. For some subjects, the essayist was only mildly favorable in the way that he described the stanza—this set up a moderate discrepancy between the essayist and the students in this condition. In a third condition, the essayist was mildly scornful in his treatment of the stanza—which placed the recipients of this communication in a "mild-discrepancy" situation. Finally, to one-half of the women in the experiment, the writer of the essay was identified as the poet T. S. Eliot, a highly credible communicator; to the rest of the subjects, the essay writer was identified as a college student. The subjects were subsequently allowed to rank the stanzas once again. When T. S. Eliot was ostensibly the communicator, the essay had the most influence on the students when its evaluation of the stanza was most discrepant from theirs; when a fellow student of medium credibility was identified as the essayist, the essay produced a little opinion change when it was slightly discrepant from the opinion of the students, a great deal of change when it was moderately discrepant, and only a little opinion change when it was extremely discrepant.

To sum up this section, the conflicting results seem to be accounted for: when a communicator has high credibility, the greater the discrepancy between the view he advocates and the view of the audience, the more the audience will be persuaded; on the other hand, when a communicator's credibility is doubtful or slim, he will produce maximum opinion change at moderate discrepancies.

Characteristics of the Audience

Self-esteem. All listeners, readers, or viewers are not alike. Some people are more difficult to persuade. In addition, as we have seen, the kind of communication that appeals to one person may not appeal to another. For example, recall that the intelligence of a member of the audience and his prior opinion will play major roles in determining whether a two-sided communication will be more effective than a one-sided communication.

What effect does an individual's personality have on his persuasibility? The one personality variable that is most consistently related to persuasibility is self-esteem. An individual who feels inadequate as a person is more easily influenced by a persuasive communication than an individual who thinks highly of himself. This seems reasonable enough; after all, if a person doesn't like himself, then it follows that he doesn't place a very high premium on his own ideas. Consequently, if his ideas are challenged, he may not be very reluctant to give them up. Recall that people want to be right. If a person who has high self-esteem listens to a communication that is at variance with his own opinion, he must make up his mind whether he stands a better chance of being right if he changes his opinion or if he stands pat. A person with high self-esteem may experience some conflict when he finds himself in disagreement with a highly credible communicator. For a person with low self-esteem, there is little or no conflict—because he doesn't think very highly of himself, he probably believes that he stands a better chance of being right if he goes along with the recommendations of the communicator.

Prior Experience of the Audience. Another audience-related factor of considerable importance is the frame of mind that the audience is in just prior to the communication. An audience can be made receptive to a communication if it has been well fed and is relaxed and happy. Indeed, as Irving Janis and his associates have discovered, people who are allowed to eat desirable food while reading a persuasive communication are more influenced by what they read than are people in a control (noneating) group.[21]

Conversely, members of an audience can be made less receptive and less persuasible. One way of accomplishing this is by forewarn-

ing the individuals that an attempt is going to be made to persuade
them. This is especially true if the content of the message differs from
their own beliefs. I would argue that the phrase, "And now, a message
from our sponsor . . . " renders that message less persuasive than it
would have been if the communicator had simply glided into it
without prologue. The forewarning seems to say "Watch out, I'm
going to try to persuade you . . . " and people tend to respond by
marshalling defenses against the message. This phenomenon was
demonstrated in an experiment by Jonathan Freedman and David
Sears.[22] Teenagers were told that they would be hearing a talk
entitled "Why Teenagers Should Not Be Allowed to Drive." Ten
minutes later, the speaker presented them with his communication. In
a control condition, the same talk was given without the ten-minute
forewarning. The subjects in the control condition were more thoroughly convinced by the communication than were those who had
been forewarned.

A more elaborate audience-preparation phenomenon has been
developed by William McGuire and his associates, and has been
appropriately dubbed the *inoculation effect*. We have already seen that
a two-sided (refutational) presentation is more effective for convincing most audiences than a one-sided presentation. Expanding on
this phenomenon, McGuire suggested that, if a person receives prior
exposure to a brief communication that he is then able to refute, he
tends to be "immunized" against a subsequent full-blown presentation of the same argument, in much the same way that a small amount
of an attenuated virus immunizes a person against a full-blown attack
by that virus. In an experiment by William McGuire and Dimitri
Papageorgis,[23] a group of people stated their opinions; these opinions
were then subjected to a mild attack—and the attack was refuted.
These people were subsequently subjected to a *powerful* argument
against their initial opinions. Members of this group showed a much
smaller tendency to change their opinions than did the members of a
control group whose opinions had not been previously subjected to
the mild attack. In effect, they had been inoculated against opinion
change and made relatively immune. Thus, not only is it often more
effective as a propaganda technique to use a two-sided refutational
presentation, but, if it is used skillfully, such a presentation tends to
increase the audience's resistance to subsequent counterpropaganda.

How does the inoculation effect work? Prior exposure, in the form of a watered-down attack on a person's beliefs, produces resistance to later persuasion because (1) the person becomes motivated to defend his beliefs and (2) he gains some practice in doing so. Often, beliefs that we hold are never called into question; when they are not, it is relatively easy for us to lose sight of why we hold them. Thus, if subjected to a severe attack, such beliefs may crumble. In order to motivate a person to bolster his beliefs, he must be made aware of their vulnerability, and the best way to do this is to attack them mildly. The person is then better equipped to resist a more serious attack.

This is an important point that is frequently ignored or misunderstood by people who make important decisions. For example, in the aftermath of the Korean War, when several of our prisoners of war were supposedly brainwashed by the Chinese Communists, a Senate committee recommended that, in order to build resistance among the people to brainwashing and other forms of Communist propaganda, courses on "patriotism and Americanism" should be instituted in our public school system. But William McGuire's results suggest that the best way to help our GIs resist anti-American propaganda would be to challenge their belief in the American way of life, and that the best way to build resistance to pro-Communist propaganda would be to teach courses on Communism, presenting both sides of the argument. If such an idea had been proposed in the 1950s, when the cold war was in full swing and Senator Joseph McCarthy was conducting his witch hunt, this idea would probably have been considered to be part of the Communist conspiracy. It is hoped that the day of the ostrich is over; we cannot resist propaganda by burying our heads in the sand. The person who is easiest to "brainwash" is the person whose ideas about Americanism are based upon slogans that have never been seriously challenged.

How Well Do the Principles Work?

Suppose you inherited a television station. Here is a golden opportunity to change people's opinions on important issues. You have just finished reading this chapter (so you know how to do it) and you're in control of a very powerful medium of communication. You choose your favorite issue: Let's say that you are in favor of free health care, and you would like to persuade others to agree with you. How do you set about doing it? That's simple. You choose a time slot following a highly intellectual program (in order to be certain that intelligent people are watching) and, accordingly, you present a two-sided argument (because two-sided arguments work best on intelligent people). You arrange your arguments in such a manner that the argument in favor of free medical care is stronger and appears first (in order to take advantage of the primacy effect). You describe the plight of the poor, how they get sick and die for lack of adequate medical care, and you do it in a manner that inspires a great deal of fear; at the same time you offer a specific plan of action, because this combination produces the most opinion change and the most action in the most people. You present some of the arguments against your position and offer strong refutation of these arguments. You arrange things so that the speaker is an expert, is trustworthy, and is extremely likeable. You make your argument as strongly positive as you are able, in order to maximize the discrepancy between the argument presented and the initial attitude of the audience. And then you sit back, relax, and wait for those opinions to start changing.

It's not that simple. Imagine a typical viewer: Let's say that she is a 45-year-old middle-class housewife who is strongly opposed to government intervention. She feels that any form of social legislation is a plot to undermine the democratic way. She stumbles across your program while looking for an evening's entertainment. She begins to hear your arguments in favor of free health care. As she listens, she becomes slightly less confident in her original convictions. She is not quite as certain as she had been that the government shouldn't intervene in matters of health. What does she do? If she is anything like the subjects in Lance Canon's[24] experiment, she would reach over, twist the dial on her TV set, and begin to watch "All in the Family." Canon found that, as a person's confidence is weakened, he becomes less prone to listen to arguments against his own beliefs. Thus, the very people who might be most susceptible to having their opinions changed are the ones least likely to continue to expose themselves to a communication designed for that purpose.

Suppose you can get a captive audience and force them to listen.

That's not as difficult as it seems; for example, you may be able to get permission to show your TV program to a classroom full of high-school students or army recruits. In such situations, the viewers cannot walk over and change the channel. Will your program have an effect on the opinions of your audience? Not necessarily. We can force people to listen to a communication; we can even force people to pay close attention to the content (by giving an exam afterwards in a classroom situation, for example, offering high rewards for good performance and severe punishments for poor performance); but we cannot be certain that their opinions will change. When faced with information that runs counter to their beliefs, people have a tendency either to distort its meaning or to invent counterarguments on the spot. In this way, they are able to avoid changing their opinions.

It is possible to overcome some of this resistance. Leon Festinger and Nathan Maccoby[25] conducted an experiment in which they attempted to prevent members of their audience from inventing arguments in refutation of the message being presented to them. This was accomplished by simply distracting the audience somewhat while the communication was being presented. Two groups of students who belonged to a college fraternity were required to listen to a tape-recorded argument about the evils of college fraternities. The argument was erudite, powerful, and, as you might imagine, widely discrepant from the beliefs of the members of the audience. During the presentation of the communication, one of the groups was distracted. Specifically, they were shown a highly entertaining silent film. Festinger and Maccoby reasoned that, because this group was engaged in two tasks simultaneously—listening to the tape-recorded argument against fraternities and watching an entertaining film—their minds would be so occupied that they would have little or no opportunity to think up arguments in refutation of the tape-recorded message. The members of the control group, on the other hand, were not distracted by a film; therefore, they would be better able to devote some of their thoughts to resisting the communication by thinking up counterarguments. The results of the experiment confirmed this reasoning. The students who were distracted by watching the film underwent substantially more opinion change against fraternities than did the students who were not distracted.

Although this experiment suggests one way of overcoming audience resistance, the effects of such techniques are of short duration and, hence, of limited value. In general, beliefs that people hold important are difficult to change through direct communication. On the face of it, there appears to be a basic difference between an issue like free medical care, on the one hand, and issues like the feasibility of atomic-powered submarines, whether antihistimines should be sold without a prescription, and the practical importance of arithmetic, on the other. What is the difference? One difference is that the medical-care issue is more important. Who cares about atomic-powered submarines, anyway? It's of trivial importance. But what are the components of "important" or "trivial"?

In order to provide an answer to this question, we must first examine what we mean by the term "opinion," which we've been using throughout this chapter. On the simplest level, an opinion is what a person believes to be factually true. Thus, it is my opinion that there are more than 40,000 students enrolled at The University of Texas, that wearing seat belts reduces traffic fatalities, and that New York City is hot in the summer. Such opinions are primarily cognitive—that is, they are unemotional, they take place in the head rather than in the gut. They are also transient—that is, they can be changed by good, clear evidence to the contrary. Thus, if Ralph Nader (whom I regard as a highly credible source on the traffic issue) presented me with data indicating that seat belts, as they are currently constructed, do not reduce fatalities significantly, I would change my opinion on that issue.

On the other hand, suppose that a person holds the opinion that Jews engage in "sharp" business practices, or that Orientals are sneaky, or that people under twenty-five have a special wisdom, or that the United States of America is the greatest (or most awful) country in the history of the world, or that New York City is a jungle. How do these opinions differ from the ones stated in the preceding paragraph? For one thing, they are evaluative—that is, they imply likes or dislikes. For a person to believe that Orientals are sneaky implies strongly that he doesn't like Orientals. The opinion that New York City is a jungle is different from the opinion that New York City is hot in the summer. The opinion that New York City is a jungle is not simply cognitive—it is also highly evaluative and highly emotional. An opinion that includes an evaluative and an emotional component is called an *attitude*. Compared to opinions, attitudes are extremely difficult to change.

Suppose that Sam is an ardent liberal and humanist who swears by Ralph Nader. Accordingly, Sam is influenced by everything that Nader uncovers about cars, safety, government abuse, the military–industrial complex, and so on. But suppose, for example, that Nader conducted an exhaustive study that indicated that, in terms of intelligence, blacks were genetically inferior to whites. Would this be likely to affect Sam's opinion? Because the issue is rooted in an emotional complex, it is likely that such a statement by Nader would not influence Sam as easily or as thoroughly as a statement by Nader about cars, sealing wax, cabbages, or kings. Individuals resist having their attitudes changed; thus, direct communications that challenge existing attitudes tend to be less influential. In order to change attitudes, it is essential first to understand what motivates this resistance. Why do people distort messages that differ from their own attitudes? Why do they invent counterarguments? Why is it important for them to avoid changing their attitudes? These are important and complex questions, and I will attempt to answer them in the next chapter.

4

Self-Justification

Picture the following scene: A young man is being hypnotized. The hypnotist places him under a posthypnotic suggestion and tells him that, when the clock strikes four, he will: (1) go to the closet, get his raincoat and galoshes, and put them on; (2) grab an umbrella; (3) walk eight blocks to the A&P supermarket and purchase six cartons of cigarettes; and (4) return home. He is told that, as soon as he reenters his apartment, he will "snap out of it" and will be himself again.

When the clock strikes four, the young man immediately heads for the closet, dons his raincoat and galoshes, grabs his umbrella, and trudges out the door on his quest for cigarettes. There are a few strange things about his errand: (1) it is a clear, sunshiny day—there isn't a cloud in the sky; (2) there is a drugstore half a block away that sells cigarettes for the same price as the A&P eight blocks away; and (3) the young man doesn't smoke.

He arrives home, opens the door, reenters his apartment, snaps out of his "trance," and discovers himself standing there in his rain-coat and galoshes, with his umbrella in one hand and a huge sack of cigarette cartons in the other. He looks momentarily confused. His friend, the hypnotist, says,

"Hey, Sam, where've you been?"

"Oh, just down to the store."

"What did you buy?"

"Um . . . um . . . it seems that I bought these cigarettes."

"But you don't smoke, do you?"

"No, but . . . um . . . um . . . I'm going to do a lot of entertaining during the next several weeks, and some of my friends smoke."

"How come you're wearing all that rain gear on such a sunny day?"

"Well . . . actually, the weather is quite changeable this time of year, and I didn't want to take any chances."

"But there isn't a cloud in the sky."

"Well, you never can tell."

"By the way, where did you buy the cigarettes?"

"Oh, heh, heh. Well, um . . . down at the A&P."

"How come you went that far?"

"Well, um . . . um . . . it was such a nice day, I thought it might be fun to take a long walk."

Most people are motivated to justify their own actions, beliefs, and feelings. When a person does something, he will try, if at all possible, to convince himself (and others) that it was a logical, reasonable thing to do. There *was* a good reason why Sam performed those silly actions—he was hypnotized. But because Sam didn't know that he had been hypnotized, and because it was apparently difficult for him to accept the fact that he was capable of behaving in a totally nonsensical manner, he went to great lengths to convince himself (and his friend) that there was a method to his madness, that his actions were actually quite sensible.

The experiment by Stanley Schachter and Jerry Singer discussed in Chapter 2 (pp. 24–25) can also be undertood in these terms. Recall that these investigators injected people with epinephrine. Those who were forewarned about the symptoms caused by this drug (palpitations of the heart, sweaty palms, and hand tremors) had a sensible explanation for the symptoms when they appeared: "Oh, yeah, that's just the drug affecting me." Those who were misled about the aftereffects of the drug, however, had no such handy, logical explanation for their symptoms. But they couldn't leave the symptoms unjustified—they tried to account for them by convincing themselves that they were either deliriously happy or angry, depending upon the social stimuli in the environment.

The concept of self-justification can be applied more broadly still. Suppose you are in the midst of a great natural disaster, such as an earthquake. All around you, buildings are toppling and people are getting killed and injured. Needless to say, you are frightened. Is there any need to seek justification for this fear? Certainly not, the evidence is all around you: the injured people and the devastated buildings are ample justifications for your fear. But suppose, instead, that there is an earthquake in a neighboring town. You can feel the tremors, and you hear stories of the damage done to the other town. You are terribly frightened—but you are not in the midst of the devastated area: neither you nor the people around you have been hurt, and no buildings in your town have been damaged. Would you need to justify this fear? Yes. Much like the people in the Schacter–Singer experiment experiencing strong physiological reactions to epinephrine but not knowing why, and much like our hypnotized friend in the raincoat and galoshes, you would be inclined to justify your own actions or feelings. In this situation, you would be inclined to justify the fact that you're scared out of your wits, but there is nothing to be afraid of immediately. These disaster situations are not hypothetical examples—they actually occurred several years ago in India. In the aftermath of an earthquake, investigators collected and analyzed the rumors that were being spread. What they discovered was rather startling: Jamuna Prasad,[1] an Indian psychologist, found that, when the disaster occurred in a neighboring town such that the residents of the village in question could feel the tremors but were not in immediate danger, there was an abundance of rumors forecasting impending doom. Specifically, the residents of this village believed and helped spread rumors to the effect that (1) a flood was rushing toward them; (2) February 26 would be a day of deluge and destruction; (3) there would be another severe earthquake on the day of the lunar eclipse; (4) there would be a cyclone within a few days; and (5) unforeseeable calamities were on the horizon.

Why in the world would people invent, believe, and communicate such stories? Were these people masochists? Certainly, these rumors would not help the people to feel calm and serene. One rather compelling explanation for this phenomenon is that the people were terribly frightened and, because there was not ample justification for this fear, they invented their own. Thus, they were not compelled to feel foolish. After all, if a cyclone is on the way, isn't it perfectly reasonable that I be wild-eyed with fear? This explanation is bolstered by Durganand Sinha's study of rumors.[2] Sinha investigated the rumors being spread in an Indian village following a disaster of similar magnitude. The major difference between the situation in Prasad's study and the one in Sinha's study was that the people being investigated by Sinha had actually suffered the destruction and witnessed the damage. They were scared, but they had good reasons to be scared—they had no need to seek additional justification for their fears. Thus, their rumors contained no prediction of impending disaster and no serious exaggeration. Indeed, if anything, the rumors were comforting. For example, one rumor predicted (falsely) that the water supply would be restored within a very short time.

The kind of process we have been discussing here has been encapsulated into a theory of human cognition by Leon Festinger.[3] Called the theory of *cognitive dissonance*, it is, as theories go, remarkably simple; but—as we shall see—the range of its application is enormous. First, we will discuss the formal aspects of the theory, and then we will discuss its ramifications. Basically, cognitive dissonance is a state of tension that occurs whenever an individual simultaneously holds two cognitions (ideas, attitudes, beliefs, opinions) that are psychologically inconsistent. Stated differently, two cognitions are dissonant if, considering these two cognitions alone, the opposite of one follows from the other. Because the occurrence of cognitive dissonance is unpleasant, people are motivated to reduce it; this is roughly analagous to the processes involved in the induction and reduction of such drives as hunger or thirst—except that, here, the driving force is cognitive discomfort rather than physiological discomfort. To hold two ideas that contradict each other is to flirt with absurdity, and —as Albert Camus, the existentialist philosopher, has observed—man is a creature who spends his entire life in an attempt to convince himself that his existence is not absurd.

How do we convince ourselves that our lives are not absurd—that is, how do we reduce cognitive dissonance? By changing one or both cognitions in such a way so as to render them more compatible (more consonant) with each other, or by adding new cognitions that help bridge the gap between the original cognitions. Let us cite an example that is, alas, all too familiar to many people. Suppose a person smokes cigarettes and then reads the Surgeon General's report linking cigarette smoking to lung cancer and other respiratory diseases. He experiences dissonance. His cognition "I smoke cigarettes" is dissonant with his cognition "cigarette smoking produces cancer." Clearly, the most efficient way to reduce dissonance in such a situation is to give up smoking. The cognition "cigarette smoking produces cancer" is *consonant* with the cognition "I do not smoke." But, for most people, it is not easy to give up smoking. Suppose a person tried to stop smoking and failed. What does he do to reduce dissonance? In all probability, he will try to work on the other cognition: "Cigarette smoking produces cancer." He might attempt to make light of the evidence linking cigarette smoking to cancer. For example, he might try to convince himself that the experimental evidence is inconclusive. In addition, he might seek out intelligent people who smoke and, by so doing, convince himself, in effect, that, if Sam, Jack, and Harry smoke, it can't be all that dangerous. He might switch to a filter-tipped brand and delude himself into believing that the filter traps the cancer-producing materials. Finally, he might add cognitions that are consonant with smoking in an attempt to make his behavior less absurd in spite of its danger. Thus, he might enhance the value he places on smoking; that is, he might come to believe that smoking is an important and highly enjoyable activity that is essential to his sanity: "I may lead a shorter life, but it will be a more enjoyable one." Similarly, he might actually try to make a virtue out of smoking by developing a romantic, devil-may-care image of himself, flouting danger by smoking cigarettes. All such behavior reduces dissonance by reducing the absurdity of the notion of going out of one's way to contract cancer. The individual justifies his behavior by cognitively minimizing the danger or by exaggerating the importance of the action. In effect, the individual has succeeded either in building himself an attitude or in changing an existing attitude.

Imagine a 16-year-old girl who has not begun to smoke. After reading the Surgeon General's report, is she apt to believe it? Of course. The evidence is objectively sound, the source is expert and trustworthy, and there is no reason not to believe the report. And this is the crux of the matter: Earlier in this book, I made the point that people strive to be right, and the values and beliefs become internalized when they appear to be correct. It is this striving to be right that motivates people to pay close attention to what other people are doing and to heed the advice of expert, trustworthy communicators. This is extremely rational behavior. There are forces, however, that can work against this rational behavior. The theory of cognitive dissonance does not picture people as rational animals; rather, it pictures them as rational*izing* animals. According to the underlying assumptions of the theory, people are motivated not so much to *be* right— rather, they are motivated to *believe* that they are right (and wise, and decent, and good). Sometimes, a person's motivation to be right and his motivation to *believe* that he is right are working in the same direction. This is what is happening with the young lady who doesn't smoke and, therefore, finds it easy to accept the notion that smoking causes lung cancer. This would also be true for a smoker who encounters the evidence linking cigarette smoking to cancer and *does* succeed in giving up cigarettes. Occasionally, however, the need to reduce dissonance (the need to convince oneself that one *is* right) leads to behavior that is maladaptive and therefore irrational. For example, psychologists who have tried to help people give up smoking have reported the incidental finding that people who try to give up smoking and *fail* will come, in time, to develop a less intense attitude toward the dangers of smoking than those who have not yet made a concerted effort to give it up. The key to this apparent paradox is a person's degree of commitment to a particular action. The more a person is committed to an action or belief, the more resistant he will be to information that threatens that belief, and the more he will attempt to bolster his action or belief. If he has tried to quit smoking and has failed, he is committed to smoke. Thus, he becomes less intense in his belief that smoking is dangerous. By the same token, I would argue that a person who had recently built a magnificent new $100,000 house smack on the San Andreas fault near San Francisco would be less receptive to the arguments predicting an imminent earthquake than would a person who was only renting the house for a few months. The new homeowner is committed; he doesn't want to believe that he has done an absurd thing.

Let us stay with cigarette smoking for a moment and present an extreme example: Suppose you were the vice-president of a major cigarette company—you are in a situation of maximum commitment to the idea of cigarette smoking. Your job consists of producing, advertising, and selling cigarettes to millions of people. If it's true that cigarette smoking causes cancer, then, in a sense, you are partially responsible for the illness and death of a great many people. This would produce a great deal of dissonance: Your cognition "I am a decent, kind human being" would be dissonant with your cognition "I am contributing to the early death of a great many people." In order to reduce this dissonance, you must refute the evidence that suggests a causal link between cigarettes and cancer. Moreover, in order to further convince yourself that you are a good, moral person, you might go so far as to demonstrate how much you disbelieve the evidence by smoking a great deal yourself. If your need is great enough, you might even succeed in convincing yourself that cigarettes are good for people. Thus, in order to convince yourself that you are wise, good, and right, you take action that is stupid and detrimental to your health. This analysis is so fantastic that it's almost beyond belief—*almost*. The following is a verbatim account of the first part of a news item released in November, 1971, by the *Washington Post* News Service.

Jack Landry pulls what must be his 30th Marlboro of the day out of one of the two packs on his desk, lights a match to it and tells how he doesn't believe all those reports about smoking and cancer and emphysema.

He has just begun to market yet another cigarette for Philip Morris U.S.A. and is brimming with satisfaction over its prospects.

But how does he square with his conscience the spending of $10 million in these United States over the next year to lure people into smoking his new brand?

"It's not a matter of that," says Landry, Philip Morris' vice president for marketing. "Nearly half the adults in this country smoke. It's a basic commodity for them. I'm serving a need.

"There are studies by pretty eminent medical and scientific authorities, one on a theory of stress, on how a heck of a lot of people, if they didn't have cigarette smoking to relieve stress, would be one hell of a lot worse off. And there are plenty of valid studies that indicate that cigarette smoking and all those diseases are not related."

His satisfaction, says Landry, comes from being very good at his job in a very competitive business, and he will point out that Philip Morris and its big-selling Marlboro has just passed American Tobacco as the No. 2 cigarette seller in America (R. J. Reynolds is still No. 1).

Why a new cigarette now?

Because it is there to be sold, says Landry.

And therein lies the inspiration of the marketing of a new American cigarette, which Landry predicts confidently will have a 1 percent share of the American market within 12 months. That 1 percent will equal about five billion cigarettes and a healthy profit for Philip Morris U.S.A.[4]

Do you think that any amount of rational evidence or argument could induce Mr. Landry to believe that cigarette smoking causes cancer? At the close of the preceding chapter, we discussed the fact that information campaigns are relatively ineffective when they attempt to change deep-seated attitudes. We can now see precisely why information campaigns are of limited effectiveness. If people are committed to an attitude, the information that the communicator presents arouses dissonance; frequently, the best way to reduce the dissonance is to reject or to distort the evidence. The deeper a person's commitment to an attitude, the greater his tendency to reject dissonant evidence.

The reader may or may not be convinced by the case of Mr. Landry. It is always possible that Landry believed that cigarettes were good for people even before he began to peddle them. Obviously, if this were true, his excitement about the benefits of cigarette smoking could hardly be attributed to dissonance. Much more convincing would be a demonstration of a clear case of attitudinal distortion in a unique event. Such a demonstration was provided several years ago by (of all things) a football game in the Ivy League. It was an important game between Princeton and Dartmouth. It was billed as a grudge match, and this soon became evident on the field: the game earned the reputation of being one of the roughest and dirtiest in the history of either school. On the Princeton team was an All-American named Dick Kazmaier; as the game progressed, it became increasingly clear that the Dartmouth players were out to get him. Whenever he carried the ball, he was gang-tackled, piled on, and mauled. He was finally forced to leave the game with a broken nose. Meanwhile, the Princeton team was not exactly inactive: soon after Kazmaier's injury, a Dartmouth player was carried off the field with a broken leg. Several fistfights broke out on the field in the course of the game, and many injuries were suffered by both sides.

Sometime after the game, a couple of psychologists—Albert Hastorf of Dartmouth and Hadley Cantril of Princeton[5]—visited both campuses with their 16-mm movie projector and showed films of the game to the students on each campus. The students were instructed to be completely objective and, while watching the film, to take notes of each infraction of the rules, how it started, and who was responsible. As you might imagine, there was a huge difference in the way this game was viewed by the students at each university. There was a strong tendency for the students to see their own fellow students as victims of illegal aggression, rather than as perpetrators of illegal aggression. Moreover, this was no minor distortion: it was found that Princeton students saw fully twice as many violations on the part of the Dartmouth players as the Dartmouth students saw. Again, people are not passive receptacles for the deposition of information. The manner in which they view and interpret information depends upon how deeply they are committed to a particular belief or course of action. Individuals will distort the objective world in order to reduce dissonance. The manner in which they will distort and the intensity of their distortion are highly predictable.

Lenny Bruce, a perceptive comedian and social commentator (who almost certainly never read about cognitive dissonance theory) had the following insight into the 1960 presidential election campaign:

> I would be with a bunch of Kennedy fans watching the debate and their comment would be, "He's really slaughtering Nixon." Then we would all go to another apartment, and the Nixon fans would say, "how do you like the shellacking he gave Kennedy?" And then I realized that each group loved their candidate so that a guy would have to be this blatant—he would have to look into the camera and say: "I am a thief, a crook, do you hear me, I am the worst choice you could ever

make for the Presidency!" And even then his following would say, "Now there's an honest man for you. It takes a big guy to admit that. There's the kind of guy we need for President."[6]

People don't like to see or hear things that conflict with their deeply held beliefs or wishes. An ancient response to such bad news was to kill the messenger—literally. A modern-day figurative version of "killing the messenger" is to blame the media for the presentation of material that produces the pain of dissonance. For example, in the summer of 1973, Richard Nixon's deep involvement in the illegal events known as "the Watergate affair" was coming into sharp focus; talk of impeachment was beginning to be heard among members of Congress. When the news magazines reported these events, readers who were committed to Richard Nixon found it difficult to take without lashing out—sometimes violently:

> Sir:
> You infamous bastards will live to regret your continued scurrilous attacks upon the person and integrity of the President of the United States. I hope to live long enough to see that NEWSWEEK (together with The Washington Post, Time and The New York Times) is reduced to ashes and rubble by an incensed public.
> In the event of any civil disorder, which will certainly develop if any formal action is taken to remove President Nixon, I will be in the forefront, lending a hand to destroy all who would be responsible for that dreadful event. And, NEWSWEEK, you will be at the top of the list. Revolution and civil war may bring down our country, but in that atmosphere we can cleanse our nation of you vermin with swift, drumhead justice—on the spot! I further enlighten you to the fact that our armed forces, our police and all related agencies will be with us to bring you down.[7]

Dissonance Reduction and Rational Behavior

I have referred to dissonance-reducing behavior as "irrational." By this I mean that it is often maladaptive, in that it can prevent people from learning important facts or from finding real solutions to their problems. On the other hand, it does serve a purpose: Dissonance-reducing behavior is ego-defensive behavior; by reducing dissonance, we maintain a positive image of ourselves—an image that depicts us as good, or smart, or worthwhile. Again, although this ego-defensive behavior can be considered useful, it can have disastrous consequences. In the laboratory, the irrationality of dissonance-reducing behavior has been amply demonstrated in a number of experiments. A particularly interesting example is provided in a study by Edward Jones and Rika Kohler.[8] These investigators selected individuals who were deeply committed to a position on the issue of racial segregation—some of the subjects were in favor of segregation, and others were opposed to it. These individuals were then allowed to read a series of arguments on both sides of the issue. Some of these arguments were extremely sensible and plausible, and others were so implausible that they bordered on the ridiculous. Jones and Kohler were interested in determining which of the arguments the people would remember best. If people were purely rational, we would expect them to remember the plausible arguments best and the implausible arguments least: why in the world would a person want to keep implausible arguments in his head? Accordingly, the rational man would rehearse and remember all the arguments that made sense and would slough off all ridiculous arguments. What does the theory of cognitive dissonance predict? It is comforting to have all the wise men on your side and all the fools on the other side: When a person reads or hears a silly argument in favor of his own position, it arouses some dissonance, because it raises some doubts about the wisdom of his position or the intelligence of the people who agree with him. Likewise, every time he hears a plausible argument on the other side of the issue, it also arouses some dissonance, because it suggests the possibility that the other side may be right. Because these arguments arouse dissonance, he will try not to think about them—that is, he might not learn them very well, or he might simply forget about them. This is exactly what Jones and Kohler found. Their subjects did not remember in a rational-functional manner. They tended to remember the plausible arguments that were in agreement with their own position, and the *implausible* arguments that were in agreement with the opposing position.

Those of us who have worked with the theory of cognitive dissonance do not deny that man is capable of rational behavior. The theory merely suggests that a good deal of our behavior is not rational—although, from inside, it may seem very sensible indeed. If you ask the hypnotized young man why he wore a raincoat on a sunny day, he'll give you an answer that he feels is sensible; if you ask the vice-president of Philip Morris why he smokes, he'll give you a reason that makes sense to him—he'll tell you how good it is for everyone's health; if you ask Jones and Kohler's subjects why they remembered a particular set of arguments rather than others, they'll insist that the arguments they remembered were a fair and representative sample of those that they read. It is important to note that the world is not divided into rational people on the one side and dissonance-reducers on the other. Although it is undoubtedly true that people are not all the same—and, accordingly, that some people are able to tolerate dissonance better than others—basically, we are all capable of rational behavior and we are all capable of dissonance-reducing behavior, depending upon the circumstances. Occasionally, the same person can manifest both behaviors in rapid succession.

The rationality and irrationality of human behavior will be illustrated over and over again during the next several pages, as we list and discuss some of the wide ramifications of man's need for self-justification. These ramifications run virtually the entire gamut of human behavior, but for the sake of conserving time and space, we will sample only a few of these. Let us begin with the decision-making process—a process that shows man at his most rational and his most irrational in quick succession.

Dissonance as a Consequence of Making a Decision

Suppose you are about to make a decision—about the purchase of a new car, for example. This involves a significant amount of money, so it is, by definition, an important decision. Your family is growing, so you've decided on a station wagon. But what kind? Should it be a VW Microbus, a compact foreign model, or a large, expensive one from General Motors? There are various advantages and disadvantages to each: The Microbus gets good mileage, is roomy, and is "in," but you've heard that it's not very safe. The large GM car is safe, has plenty of room and power, but it's expensive to buy and operate. The more compact car is not as roomy, but you've heard that it has an excellent repair record. My guess is that, *before* you make the decision, you will seek as much information as you can. Chances are you will read *Consumer Reports* to find out what this expert, unbiased source has to say. Perhaps you'll confer with some friends who own the various cars under consideration. You'll probably visit the automobile dealers to test-drive the cars to see how each one feels. All of this predecision behavior is perfectly rational. Let us assume you make a decision—you buy a VW Microbus. What happens next? Your behavior will begin to change: No longer will you seek objective information about all makes of cars. Chances are you may begin to spend more time talking to VW owners. You will begin to talk about the number of miles to the gallon as though it were the most important thing in the world. My guess is that you will not be prone to spend much time thinking about the fact that the wind can make driving a Microbus in windy mountain passes particularly hazardous: your failure to attend to this shortcoming could conceivably cost you your life.

How does this sort of situation come about? Following a decision—especially a difficult one, or one that involves a significant commitment in time, effort, or money—people almost always experience dissonance. This is so because the chosen alternative is seldom entirely positive and the rejected alternatives are seldom entirely negative. In this example, your cognition that you bought a Microbus is dissonant with your cognition about any deficiencies that the car may have. Similarly, all the positive aspects of the other cars that you considered buying but did not buy are dissonant with your cognition that you did not buy one of them. A good way to reduce such dissonance is to seek out exclusively positive information about the car you chose and avoid negative information about it. One source of safe information is advertisements: it is a safe bet that an ad will not run down its own product. Accordingly, one might predict that a person who has recently purchased a new car will begin to read advertisements selectively—he will read more ads about his own car *after the purchase* than people who have *not* recently purchased the same model; moreover, owners of new cars will tend to steer clear of ads for other makes of cars. This is exactly what was found by Danuta Ehrlich and her colleagues[9] in a well-known survey of advertising readership. In short, Ehrlich's data suggest that, *after* decisions, people try to gain reassurance that their decisions were wise by seeking information that is certain to be reassuring.

People do not always need help from Madison Avenue to gain reassurance; they can do a pretty good job of reassuring themselves. An experiment by Jack Brehm[10] demonstrates how this can come about: Posing as a marketing researcher, Brehm showed each of several women eight different appliances (a toaster, an electric coffee maker, a sandwich grill, and the like) and asked that she rate them in terms of how attractive each appliance was to her. As a reward, each woman was told that she could have one of the appliances as a gift—and she was given a choice between two of the products she had rated as being attractive. After she chose one, it was wrapped up and given to her. Several minutes later, she was asked to rate the products again. It was found that after receiving the appliance of her choice, each woman rated the attractiveness of that appliance somewhat higher, and decreased the rating of the appliance that she had a chance to own but decided against. Again, making a decision produces dissonance: cognitions about any negative aspects of the preferred object are dissonant with having chosen it, and cognitions about the positive aspects of the unchosen object are dissonant with *not* having chosen it. To reduce dissonance, people cognitively spread apart the alternatives. That is, *after the decision*, they emphasized the positive attributes of the appliance they decided to own while de-emphasizing its negative attributes; for the appliance they decided *not* to own, they emphasized its negative attributes and de-emphasized its positive attributes. This basic phenomenon has been extended and further clarified by a number of different investigators.[11]

Some Historical Examples of the Consequences of Decisions. It is impossible to overstate the potential importance of this phenomenon. When I mentioned that ignoring danger in order to reduce dissonance could conceivably lead to a person's death, I meant that literally. Suppose a madman has taken over your country and has decided to eradicate all members of your religious group. But you don't know that for sure. What you *do* know is that your country is being occupied, that the leader of the occupation forces does not like your religious group very much, and that, occasionally, members of your religious group are forced to move from their homes and are kept in detention camps. What do you do? You could try to flee from your country; you could try to pass as a member of a different religious group; or you could sit tight and hope for the best. Each of these options is extremely dangerous: It is very difficult to escape or to pass and go undetected; and if you are caught trying to flee or pass, the penalty is immediate execution. On the other hand, deciding to sit tight could be a disastrous decision if it turns out that your religious group *is* being systematically annihilated. Let us suppose that you decide to sit tight. That is an important decision—and, naturally, it produces a great deal of dissonance. In order to reduce dissonance, you convince yourself that you made a wise decision—that is, you convince yourself that, although people of your religious sect are made to move and are being treated unfairly, they are *not* being killed unless they break the law.

Suppose that, months later, a respected man from your town tells you that he has witnessed all the men, women, and children who had recently been deported from the town being butchered mercilessly. I would predict that you would try to dismiss this information as untrue—that you would attempt to convince yourself that the reporter was lying or hallucinating. Accordingly—although, if you had listened to the man who tried to warn you, you might have been able to escape—you end up being slaughtered.

Fantastic? Impossible? How could anyone not take the "respected man" seriously? The events described above are an accurate account of exactly what happened, in 1944, to the Jews in Sighet, a small town in Hungary.[12]

The processes of cognitive distortion and selective exposure to information may have been an important factor in the escalation of the war in Vietnam. In a thought-provoking analysis of the Pentagon Papers, Ralph White suggested that dissonance blinded our leaders to information that was incompatible with the decisions they had already made. As White put it, "There was a tendency, when actions were out of line with ideas, for decision-makers to align their ideas with their actions." To take just one of many examples, the decision to continue to escalate the bombing of North Vietnam was made at the price of ignoring crucial evidence from the CIA and other sources that made it clear that bombing would not break the will of the North

Vietnamese people, but, quite the contrary, would only strengthen their resolve.

> It is instructive, for instance, to compare McNamara's highly factual evidence-oriented summary of the case against bombing in 1966 (pages 555–563 of the Pentagon Papers) with the Joint Chief's memorandum that disputed his conclusion and called the bombing one of our two trump cards, while it apparently ignored all of the facts that showed the opposite. Yet it was the Joint Chiefs who prevailed.[13]

White surmises that the reason that they prevailed was that their advice was consonant with decisions that had already been made and with certain key assumptions that proved to be erroneous.[14]

Escalation is a process that continues to feed on itself. Once a small commitment is made, it sets the stage for ever increasing commitments. The flavor of this kind of cognitive escalation is nicely captured in an analysis of the Pentagon Papers by the news magazine *Time*:

> Yet the bureaucracy, the Pentagon Papers indicate, always demanded new options; each option was to apply more force. Each tightening of the screw created a position that must be defended; once committed, the military pressure must be maintained.[15]

The escalation process has been investigated under controlled experimental conditions. Suppose you would like to enlist someone's aid in a massive undertaking, but you know that the job you have in mind for him is so difficult, and will require so much time or effort, that the person will surely decline. What should you do? One possibility is to get him involved in a much smaller aspect of the job—one that is so easy that he wouldn't dream of turning it down. This action serves to commit him to "the cause." Once he is thus committed, the likelihood of his complying with the larger request increases. This was demonstrated by Jonathan Freedman and Scott Fraser.[16] These experimenters attempted to induce each of several homeowners to put up a huge, ugly sign in his front yard that read "Drive Carefully." Because this sign would have uglified his property, the typical homeowner refused to do it: only 17 percent complied. However, each subject in a different group of homeowners was first "softened up" by an experimenter who "put his foot in the door" by getting him to sign a petition favoring safe driving. Because the signing of a petition is an easy thing, virtually all of them complied. A few weeks later, a different experimenter went to each homeowner with a huge, ugly sign reading "Drive Carefully." More than 55 percent of these homeowners allowed the sign to be put up on their property. Thus, when a person commits himself in a small way, it increases the probability that he will commit himself further in that direction.

The Importance of Irrevocability. One of the key determinants of whether or not a person engages in distortion and reevaluation after a decision is the irrevocability of the decision. This needs some explaining: Occasionally, we make tentative decisions. For example, if you had indicated that you might buy a $100,000 house near San Francisco, but the decision was not finalized, chances are you would not expend any effort trying to convince yourself of the wisdom of the decision; but once you had put your money down and you knew that you couldn't get it back, you would probably start minimizing the importance of the dampness in the basement, the cracks in the foundation, or the fact that it happened to be built on the San Andreas fault. Some evidence for the importance of irrevocability comes from a clever study of the cognitive gyrations of gamblers at a race track. Robert Knox and James Inkster[17] simply intercepted people who were on their way to place $2 bets. They had already decided on their horses and were about to place their bets when the investigators asked them how certain they were that their horses would win. Because they were on their way to the $2 window, their decisions were not irrevocable. The investigators collared other bettors just as they were leaving the $2 window, *after* having placed their bets, and asked them how certain they were that their horses would win. Typically, an individual who had just placed his bet gave his horse a better chance of winning than did one who was about to place his bet. In short, when the decision is irrevocable, more dissonance gets reduced; people are more certain they are right *after* there is nothing they can do about it.

The Decision to Behave Immorally. How can we corrupt an honest person? Conversely, how can we get a person to be *more* honest? One way is to capitalize on the dissonance that results from making a difficult decision. Suppose you are a college student enrolled in a biology course. Your grade will hinge on the final exam that you are now taking. The key question on the exam involves some material that you know fairly well—but, because of anxiety, you draw a blank. You are sitting there in a nervous sweat. You look up and, lo and behold, you happen to be sitting behind a woman who is the smartest person in the class (who also happens, fortunately, to be the person with the most legible handwriting in the class). You glance down and you notice that she is just completing her answer to the crucial question. You know that you could easily read her answer if you chose to. What do you do? Your conscience tells you that it's wrong to cheat—and yet, if you don't cheat, you are certain to get a poor grade. You wrestle with your conscience. Regardless of whether you decide to cheat or not to cheat, you are doomed to experience dissonance. If you cheat, your cognition "I am a decent moral person" is dissonant with your cognition "I have just committed an immoral act." If you decide to resist temptation, your cognition "I want to get a good grade" is dissonant with your cognition "I could have acted in such a way that would have insured that I got a good grade, but I chose not to."

Suppose that, after a difficult struggle, you decide to cheat. How do you reduce dissonance? Before you read on, think about it for a moment. One way to reduce dissonance is to minimize the negative aspects of the action you have chosen (and to maximize the positive aspects)—much the same way the women did after choosing an appliance in Jack Brehm's experiment. In this instance, an efficacious path of dissonance reduction would entail a change in your attitude about cheating. In short, you will adopt a more lenient attitude. Your reasoning might go something like this: "Cheating isn't so bad, under some circumstances. As long as nobody gets hurt, it's really not very immoral—anybody would do it—therefore, it's part of human nature . . . so how could it be bad? If anyone gets caught cheating, he should not be severely punished, but should be treated with understanding."

Suppose that, after a difficult struggle, you decide *not* to cheat. How would you reduce dissonance? Once again, you could change your attitude about the morality of the act—but in the opposite direction. That is, in order to justify the fact that you gave up a good grade, you must convince yourself that cheating is a heinous sin, that it's one of the lowest things a person can do, and that cheaters should be found out and severely punished.

The interesting and important thing to remember, here, is that the initial attitudes of the people hypothetically described above could have been virtually identical. It could be that their decisions were a hair's breadth apart—that one came within an ace of resisting, but decided to cheat, while the other came within an ace of cheating, but decided to resist. Once the decisions have been made, however, their attitudes toward cheating will diverge sharply as a consequence of their decisions.

These speculations were put to the test by Judson Mills[18] in an experiment with sixth-graders. Mills first measured their attitudes toward cheating. He then had them participate in a competitive exam with prizes being offered to the winners. The situation was arranged so that it was almost impossible to win without cheating, and so that it was easy for the children to cheat, thinking it would go undetected. As one might expect, some of the students cheated and others did not. The next day, the sixth-graders were again allowed to indicate how they felt about cheating. In general, those children who had cheated became more lenient toward cheating, and those who resisted the temptation to cheat adopted a harsher attitude toward cheating.

The data from Mills' experiment are provocative indeed. One thing they suggest is that the most zealous opponents of a given position are not those who have always been distant from that position. For example, one might hazard a guess that the people who are most angry at the apparent sexual promiscuity associated with the hippie subculture may *not* be those who have never been tempted to be sexually promiscuous themselves. Indeed, Mills' data suggest the possibility that the people who have the strongest need to crack down hard on this sort of behavior are those who have been sorely tempted, who came dangerously close to giving in to this temptation, but who finally resisted. People who *almost* decide to live in glass houses are frequently the ones who are most prone to throw stones.

Early in this chapter, I discussed the fact that the desire for self-justification is an important reason why people who are strongly committed to an attitude on an issue tend to resist any direct attempts to change that attitude. In effect, such people are invulnerable to the propaganda or education in question. We can now see that the same mechanism that enables a person to cling to an attitude can induce him to *change* an attitude. It depends on which course of action will serve most to reduce dissonance under the circumstances. A person who understands the theory can set up the proper conditions to induce attitude change in other people by making them vulnerable to certain kinds of beliefs. For example, if a modern Machiavelli were advising a contemporary ruler, he might suggest the following strategies based upon the theory and data on the consequences of decisions:

1. If you want someone to form more positive attitudes toward an object, get him to commit himself to own that object.
2. If you want someone to soften his moral attitude toward some misdeed, tempt him so that he performs that deed; conversely, if you want someone to harden his moral attitudes toward a misdeed, tempt him—but not enough to induce him to commit the deed.

The Psychology of Inadequate Justification

Attitude change as a means of reducing dissonance is not, of course, limited to post-decision situations. This can occur in countless other situations, including every time a person says something he doesn't believe or does something stupid or immoral. The effects can be extremely powerful. Let us look at some of them.

In a complex society, we occasionally find ourselves saying or doing things that we don't completely believe. For example, Sam Businessman enters the office and sees his secretary wearing a perfectly atrocious outfit with pink stripes and orange polka dots. "How do you like my new dress?" she asks timidly. "Very pretty," he answers. Theoretically, Sam's cognition "I am a truthful person" is dissonant with his cognition "I said that dress was very pretty, although I believe it to be a disaster." Whatever dissonance may be aroused by this inconsistency can be easily and quickly reduced by Sam's cognition that it's important not to hurt people: "I lied so as not to hurt her; why should I tell her that it's an ugly dress? It serves no useful purpose." This is an effective way of reducing dissonance, because it completely justifies the action Sam took. In effect, the justification is situation-determined. We will call this *external justification*.

But what happens if there is not ample external justification in the situation itself? For example, imagine that Sam Businessman, who is a politically conservative person, finds himself at a cocktail party with many people whom he doesn't know very well. The conversation turns to politics. The people are talking with horror about the fact that the United States seems to be drastically escalating its friendly overtures toward the People's Republic of China. Sam's belief is a complicated one; he has mixed feelings about it, but generally he is opposed to our forming an alliance with the Chinese Communists because he feels that they are evil and we should not compromise with evil. Partly because Sam's companions are sounding so pious, and partly as a lark, he gradually finds himself taking a much more liberal–radical position than the one he really holds. As a matter of fact, Sam even goes so far as to assert that Mao Tse-tung is an extraordinarily gifted leader and that the Chinese people are better off under communism than they've been in hundreds of years. Somebody counters Sam's argument by talking about the millions of people that Mao supposedly murdered in order to achieve a unified government. In the heat of the situation, Sam replies that those figures are grossly exaggerated. Quite a performance for a man who does, in fact, believe that Mao killed millions of innocent people during his rise to power.

When Sam awakes the next morning and thinks back on the evening's events, he gasps in horror. "Oh, my God, what have I done?" he says. He is intensely uncomfortable. Another way of putting it is that he is experiencing a great deal of dissonance. His cognition "I misled a bunch of people; I told them a lot of things about Red China that I don't really believe" is dissonant with his cognition "I am a reasonable, decent, and truthful person." What does he do to reduce dissonance? He searches around for *external justifications*. First, it occurs to Sam that he might have been drunk, and therefore not responsible for what he said. But he remembers that he only had one or two martinis—no external justification there. Because Sam cannot find sufficient external justification for his behavior, it is necessary for him to attempt to justify his behavior internally—by changing his attitude in the direction of his statements. That is, if Sam can succeed in convincing himself that his statements were not so very far from the truth, then he will have reduced dissonance—that is, his behavior of the preceding night will no longer be absurd in his own view. I do not mean to imply that Sam would suddenly become an avowed Maoist. What I do mean is that he might begin to feel a little less harshly about the Chinese Communists than he had felt before he made those statements. Most events of this world are built in such a way that they are neither completely black nor completely white; there are many gray areas. Thus, Sam might begin to take a different look at some of the events that have taken place in China during the past fifty years. He might start by looking into some of Mao's writings and being disposed toward seeing wisdom there that he hadn't seen before. He might also begin to be more receptive to information that indicates the extent of the corruption and brutality of Chiang Kai-shek's government. To repeat: if an individual makes a statement of belief that is difficult to justify *externally*, he will attempt to justify it *internally* by making his attitudes more consistent with the statement.

We have mentioned a couple of forms of external justification. One is the idea that it's all right to tell a harmless lie in order to avoid hurting a person's feelings—as in the case of Sam and his secretary's unattractive dress. Another is when a person is drunk and, therefore, not responsible for his own actions. Still another form of external justification is reward. Put yourself in Sam's shoes for a moment, and suppose that you and I both were at that cocktail party: As the conversation turned to Red China, I pull you aside and say, "Hey, I would like you to come out strongly in favor of Mao Tse-tung and Chinese communism." What's more, suppose I handed you $5000 for doing it. After counting the money, you gasp, put the $5000 in your pocket, return to the discussion, and defend Mao Tse-tung to the hilt. The next morning when you wake up in bed, would you experience any dissonance? I don't think so. Your cognition "I said some things about Mao Tse-tung and Chinese communism that I don't believe" is dissonant with the cognition "I am a truthful and decent person." But, at the same time, you have adequate external justification for having made that statement: "I said those favorable things about Chinese communism in order to earn $5000—and it's worth it." In effect, you have 5000 cognitions that are consonant with having made that statement. You don't have to soften your attitude toward Mao in order to justify that statement—you know why you made the statement: you made it *not* because you think it's true, but in order to get the $5000. You're left with the knowledge that you sold your soul for $5000—and that it was worth it.

Saying is believing; that is, dissonance theory predicts that we begin to believe our own lies—but only if there is not an abundance of external justification for making the statements that run counter to our original attitude. We can now begin to elaborate on our earlier discussion of conformity. Recall that in Chapter 2 we found that, in order to get overt compliance, the greater the reward, the greater the probability that a person will comply. But now we can go one step further: in order to produce *an actual change* in attitudes, the greater the reward, the *less* likely it is that any attitude change will occur. If all I want you to do is to recite a speech favoring Mao Tse-tung, George Wallace, Barry Goldwater, Fidel Castro, or anyone, the most efficient thing for me to do would be to give you the largest possible reward. This would increase the probability that you will comply by making that speech. But suppose I have a more ambitious goal: suppose I want to effect a lasting change in your attitudes and beliefs. In that case, just the reverse is true. The smaller the external reward that I give you to induce you to recite the speech, the more likely it is that you will be forced to seek additional justification, in the form of convincing yourself that the things you said were actually true. This would result in an actual change of attitude, rather than mere compliance. The importance of this technique cannot be overstated. If a person changes his attitude because he makes a public statement for minimal external justification, that attitude change will be relatively permanent; the person is not changing his attitudes because of the reward (compliance) or because an attractive person influenced him (identification). He's changing his attitudes because he has succeeded in *convincing himself* that his previous attitudes were incorrect. This is a very powerful form of attitude change.

Thus far, we have been dealing with highly speculative material. These speculations have been investigated scientifically in several experiments. Among these is a classic study by Leon Festinger and J. Merrill Carlsmith.[19] Festinger and Carlsmith asked college students to perform a very boring and repetitive series of tasks—packing spools, turning screws, and so on. The experimenter then induced them to lie about the task; specifically, he employed them to tell a co-ed (who was waiting to participate in the experiment) that the task she would be performing was interesting and enjoyable. Some of the students were offered twenty dollars for telling the lie, others were offered only one dollar for telling the lie. After the experiment was over, an interviewer asked the "lie-tellers" how they had enjoyed the tasks that they had performed earlier in the experiment. The results were clearcut: Those students who had previously been paid twenty dollars for lying—that is, for saying that the spool-packing had been enjoyable—actually rated it as being dull. This is not surprising—it *was* dull. But what about the students who had been paid only one dollar for telling their fellow student that the task was enjoyable? They did, indeed, rate the task as an enjoyable one. In other words, people who received an abundance of external justification for lying told the lie but didn't believe it, whereas those who told the lie in the absence of a great deal of external justification did, indeed, move in the direction of believing that what they said was true.

Research support for the "saying is believing" phenomenon has extended beyond relatively unimportant attitudes like the dullness of a monotonous task. Attitude change has been shown on such important issues as police brutality and the legalization of marijuana. In one experiment, for example, Arthur R. Cohen[20] induced Yale students to engage in a particularly difficult form of counterattitudinal behavior. Cohen conducted his experiment immediately after a student riot in which the New Haven police had behaved in a rather brutal manner toward the students. The students (who strongly believed that the police had behaved badly) were asked to write an essay in support of the actions taken by the police. Students were urged to write the strongest, most forceful defense of the police actions they could muster. Before writing the essay, students were paid for their efforts. There were four conditions: some students were paid ten dollars; others, five dollars, still others, one dollar; and a fourth group, the paltry sum of fifty cents. After each student wrote his essay, he was asked to indicate his own private attitudes about the police actions. The results are perfectly linear: the smaller the reward, the greater the attitude change. Thus, people who wrote in support of the

New Haven police for the meager sum of fifty cents developed a more favorable attitude toward the actions of police than did the people who wrote the essay for one dollar; the people who wrote the essay for one dollar developed a more favorable attitude toward the actions of the police than did the people who wrote the essay for ten dollars; and so on. The less the external justification in terms of money, the greater the attitude change.[21]

What Is Inadequate Justification? Throughout this section, we have been referring to "inadequate" external justification and "an abundance" of external justification. These terms require some additional clarification. In the Festinger–Carlsmith experiment, all of the subjects did, in fact, agree to tell the lie—including all of those paid only one dollar. In a sense then, one dollar was *adequate*—adequate to induce the subjects to tell the lie; but, as it turns out, it wasn't sufficient to keep them from feeling foolish. In order to reduce their feelings of foolishness, they had to reduce the dissonance that resulted from telling a lie for so paltry a sum. This entailed additional bolstering in the form of convincing themselves that it wasn't completely a lie, and that the task wasn't quite as dull as it seemed at first—as a matter of fact, when looked at in a certain way, it was actually quite interesting.

It would be fruitful to compare these results with Judson Mills' data on the effects of cheating among sixth-graders.[22] Recall that, in Mills' experiment, the decision about whether or not to cheat was almost certainly a difficult one for most of the children. This is why they experienced dissonance regardless of whether they cheated or resisted temptation. One could speculate about what would happen if the rewards to be gained by cheating were very large. For one thing, it would be more tempting to cheat—therefore, more people would actually cheat. But, more important, if the gains for cheating were astronomical, those who cheated would undergo very little attitude change. Much like the college students who lied in Festinger and Carlsmith's twenty-dollar condition, those who cheated for a great reward would have less need to reduce dissonance. In fact, Mills did include this refinement in his experiment, and his results are consistent with this reasoning: Those who cheated in order to obtain a small reward tended to soften their attitudes about cheating more than those who cheated in order to obtain a large reward. Moreover, those who resisted temptation in the face of a large reward tended to *harden* their attitudes about cheating to a greater extent than those who resisted in the face of a small reward—just as one might expect.

Dissonance and the Self-concept. The analysis of the dissonance phenomenon presented in this section requires a departure from Festinger's original theory. In the experiment by Festinger and Carlsmith, for example, the original statement of dissonance went like this: the cognition "I believe the task is dull" is dissonant with the cognition "I said the task was interesting." A few years ago, I reformulated the theory in a way that focuses more attention on the individual's conception of himself.[23] Basically, this reformulation suggests that dissonance is most powerful in situations in which the self-concept is threatened. Thus, for me, the important aspect of dissonance in the situation described above is not that the cognition "I said 'X' " is dissonant with the cognition "I believe 'not X'." Rather, the crucial fact is that I have misled people: the cognition "I have said something I don't believe and it could have bad consequences for people" is dissonant with my self-concept; that is, it is dissonant with my cognition that "I am a decent, reasonable, truthful person."

This formulation is based upon the assumption that most individuals like to think of themselves as decent people who wouldn't ordinarily mislead someone unless there was good reason for it—especially if, in misleading that person, the consequences for him could be disastrous. For example, consider Sam, who believes that marijuana is dangerous and should definitely not be legalized. Suppose he is induced to make a speech advocating the use of marijuana. Suppose further that he makes the statement to an audience consisting of individuals whom he knows to be irrevocably committed to a position opposing the use of marijuana (for example, members of a vice squad, the Daughters of the American Revolution, or prohibitionists). In this case, there are no dangerous consequences for the audience, because they are unlikely to be changed by Sam's communication. That is, the communicator is in little danger of doing anyone any real harm. According to our view of dissonance theory, Sam would not change his attitude, because he is not doing anyone any harm. Similarly, if Sam were asked to make the same statement to a group of individuals whom he knows to be irrevocably committed to the use of marijuana, there would be no possibility of a negative behavioral change in the audience. Again, he stands little chance of doing harm, because the members of his audience already believe what he is telling them. On the other hand, if Sam were induced to make the identical speech to a group of individuals who have no prior information about marijuana, we expect that he would experience much more dissonance than in the other situations. His cognition that he is a good and decent person is dissonant with his cognition that he has said something he doesn't believe; moreover, his statement is likely to have serious *belief* or *behavioral consequences* for his audience. To reduce dissonance, he should convince himself that the position he advocated is correct. This would allow him to believe that he has not harmed anyone. Moreover, in this situation, the smaller the incentive he receives for advocating the position, the greater the attitude change. I recently tested and confirmed this hypothesis in collaboration with Elizabeth Nel and Robert Helmreich.[24] We found an enormous change in attitudes toward marijuana when subjects were offered a small reward for making a video tape recording of a speech favoring the use of marijuana—but only when they were led to believe that the tape would be shown to an audience that was *uncommitted on the issue*. On the other hand, when subjects were told that the tape would be played to people who were irrevocably committed on the subject of marijuana (one way or another), there was relatively little attitude change on the part of the speaker. Thus, lying produces a greater attitude change in the liar when he is undercompensated for lying, especially when the lie is apt to cause another person some harm: the greater the potential harm, the greater the dissonance; the greater the dissonance, the greater the attitude change.*

Inadequate Rewards as Applied to Education. A great deal of research has shown that the insufficient-reward phenomenon applies to

---

*It should be mentioned that, in this as well as in the other experiments discussed here, each subject was completely debriefed as soon as he had finished his role in the experiment. Every attempt was made to avoid causing a permanent change in the attitudes of the subjects. It is always important to debrief subjects after an experiment; this is especially true when the experiment induces a change in an important attitude.

all forms of behavior—not simply the making of counter-attitudinal statements. For example, it has been shown that, if a person actually *performs* a rather dull task for very little external justification, he rates the task as more enjoyable than if he had a great deal of external justification for performing it.[25] This does not mean that people would rather receive low pay than high pay for doing a job. People prefer to receive high pay—and they often work harder for high pay. But if they are offered low pay for doing a job, and still they agree to do it, there is dissonance between the dullness of the task and the low pay. To reduce the dissonance, they attribute good qualities to the job and, hence, come more to enjoy the mechanics of the job with a low salary than with a high salary. This phenomenon may have far-reaching consequences. For example, let's look at the elementary-school classroom. If you want Johnny to recite a foreign-language vocabulary, then you should reward him; gold stars, praise, high grades, presents, and the like are good external justifications. Will Johnny recite the foreign words, just for the fun of it, long after the rewards are no longer forthcoming? In other words, will the high rewards make him enjoy the task? I doubt it. But if the external rewards are not too high, Johnny will add his own justification for performing the foreign language drill; he may even make a game of it. In short, he is more likely to continue to memorize the foreign vocabulary long after school is out and the rewards have been withdrawn.

For certain rote tasks, we, as educators, probably do not care whether Johnny enjoys them or not, as long as he masters them. On the other hand, if Johnny can learn to enjoy them, he will perform them outside of the educational situation. Consequently, with such increased practice, he may come to gain greater mastery over the procedure—and he may retain it indefinitely. Thus, at least under some conditions, it may be a mistake to dole out extensive rewards as an educational device. If a student is provided with just barely enough incentive to perform the task, we may succeed in allowing him to maximize his enjoyment of the task. This may serve to increase his long-range retention and performance. I am not suggesting that inadequate rewards are the only way that people can be taught to enjoy material that lacks inherent attractiveness. What I *am* saying is that piling on excessive external justification inhibits one of the processes that can help set the stage for increased enjoyment.

Several recent experiments by Edward Deci make this point very nicely.[26] Indeed, Deci carries our analysis one step further by demonstrating that offering rewards to individuals for performing a pleasant activity actually decreases the intrinsic attractiveness of that activity. In one experiment, for example, college students worked separately on an interesting puzzle for an hour. The next day, the students in the experimental condition were paid one dollar for each piece of the puzzle they completed. The students in the control group worked on the puzzle as before, without pay. During a third session, neither group was paid. The question is: how much liking did each group have for the puzzles? Deci measured this during the third session by noting whether or not each student worked on the puzzle during a free break when they could do whatever they pleased. The results show a strong tendency for the *unrewarded* group to spend more free time on the task than the rewarded group. The rewarded group did work harder on the task during the rewarded session, but their interest waned in the final session. The unrewarded group showed an increase in interest during the third session.

In a similar vein, Mark Lepper and David Greene found the same kind of relationship with preschool children.[27] Half of the children were induced to work on a set of plastic jigsaw puzzles by the promise of a more rewarding activity later. Others were not promised the more rewarding activity. After playing with the puzzles, *all* of the subjects were allowed to engage in the "more rewarding activity" (but recall that only half of the subjects were led to believe that this was a reward for having worked on the puzzles). A few weeks later, the kids were turned loose on the puzzles. Those who had worked on the puzzles in order to earn the chance to engage in the more rewarding activity spent less of their free time playing with the puzzles. In short, by offering a reward for playing, we succeeded in turning play into work.

Insufficient Punishment. Thus far, we have been discussing what happens when a person's *rewards* for saying something are meager. The same process works for punishment. In our everyday lives, we are continually faced with situations wherein those who are charged with the duty of maintaining law and order are threatening to punish us if we do not comply with the demands of society. As adults, we know that, if we exceed the speed limit and get caught, we will end up paying a substantial fine. If it happens too often, we will lose our license. So we learn to obey the speed limit when there are patrol cars in the vicinity. Youngsters in school know that, if they cheat on an exam and get caught, they could be humiliated by the teacher and severely punished. So they learn not to cheat while the teacher is in the room watching them. But does harsh punishment teach them that it's wrong to cheat? I don't think so. I think that it teaches them to try to avoid getting caught. In short, the use of threats of harsh punishment as a means of getting someone to refrain from doing something that he enjoys doing necessitates constant harassment and vigilance. It would be much more efficient and would require much less noxious restraint if, somehow, people could enjoy doing those things that contribute to their own health and welfare—and to the health and welfare of others. If children would enjoy *not* beating up smaller kids or enjoy *not* cheating or *not* stealing from others, then society could relax its vigilance and curtail its punitiveness. It is extremely difficult to persuade people (especially young children) that it's not enjoyable to beat up smaller people. But it is conceivable that, under certain conditions, they will *persuade themselves* that such behavior is unenjoyable.

Let's take a closer look. Picture the scene: You are the parent of a five-year-old child who enjoys beating up on his three-year-old brother. You've tried to reason with him, but to no avail. So, in order to protect the welfare of the younger child, and (it is hoped) in order to make a "nicer" person out of the older brother, you begin to punish the five-year-old for his aggressiveness. Each parent has at his disposal a number of punishments that range from the extremely mild (a stern look) to the extremely severe (a hard spanking, forcing the child to stand in a corner for two hours, and depriving him of TV privileges for a month). The more severe the threat, the greater the likelihood that the youngster will mend his ways *while you are watching him*. But he may very well hit his brother again as soon as you turn your back.

Suppose instead, that you threaten him with a very mild punishment. In either case (under threat of severe punishment or of mild punishment), the child experiences dissonance. He is aware that he is not beating up his little brother—and also aware that he would very much *like* to beat him up. When the child has the urge to hit his brother and doesn't, he asks himself in effect, "How come I'm not beating up my little brother?" Under severe threat, he has a ready answer in the form of sufficient external justification: "I'm not beating him up because, if I do, that giant over there (my father) is going to spank me, stand me in the corner, and keep me from watching television for a month." The severe threat has provided the child ample external justification for not hitting his brother while he's being watched.

The child in the mild-threat situation experiences dissonance, too. But when he asks himself, "How come I'm not beating up my little brother?" he doesn't have a good answer, because the threat is so mild that it does not provide a superabundance of justification. The child is *not* doing something that he wants to do—and while he does have *some* justification for not doing it, he lacks complete justification. In this situation, he continues to experience dissonance. He is unable simply to reduce the dissonance by blaming his inaction on a severe threat. The child must find a way to justify the fact that he is not aggressing against his little brother. The best way is to try to convince himself that he really doesn't like to beat his brother up, that he didn't want to do it in the first place, that beating up little kids is not fun. The less severe the threat, the less the external justification; the less the external justification, the greater the need for internal justification. Allowing people the opportunity to construct their own internal justification can be a long step toward helping them develop a permanent set of values.

To test this idea, I performed an experiment at the Harvard University nursery school in collaboration with J. Merrill Carlsmith.[28] For ethical reasons, we did not try to change basic values like aggression—parents, understandably, might not approve of our changing important values. Instead, we chose a trivial aspect of behavior—toy preference.

We first asked five-year-old children to rate the attractiveness of several toys; then we chose one toy that a child considered to be quite attractive, and we told him he couldn't play with it. We threatened half of the children with mild punishment for transgression—"I would be a little angry"; we threatened the other half with more severe punishment—"I would be very angry; I would have to take all of the toys and go home and never come back again; I would think you were just a baby." After that, we left the room and allowed the children to play with the other toys—and to resist the temptation of playing with the forbidden ones. All of the children resisted the temptation—none played with the forbidden toy.

On returning to the room, we remeasured the attractiveness of all of the toys. Our results were both striking and exciting. Those children who underwent a mild threat now found the toy less attractive than before. In short, lacking adequate external justification for refraining from playing with the toy, they succeeded in convincing themselves that they hadn't played with it because they didn't really like it. On the other hand, the toy did not become less attractive for those who were severely threatened. These children continued to rate the forbidden toy as highly desirable—indeed, some even found it more desirable than they had before the threat. The children in the severe-threat condition had good external reasons for not playing with the toy—they therefore had no need to find additional reasons —and, consequently, they continued to like the toy.

Jonathan Freedman[29] extended our findings and dramatically illustrated the permanence of the phenomenon. He used as his "crucial toy" an extremely attractive battery-powered robot that scurries around hurling objects at a child's enemies. The other toys were sickly by comparison. Naturally, all of the children preferred the robot. He then asked them not to play with that toy, threatening some children with mild punishment and others with severe punishment. He then left the school and never returned. Several weeks later, a young lady came to the school to administer some paper-and-pencil tests to the children. The children were unaware of the fact that she was working for Freedman or that her presence was in any way related to the toys or the threats that had occurred earlier. But it just so happened that she was administering her test in the same room that Freedman had used for his experiment—the room where the same toys were casually scattered about. After she administered the test to each child, she asked him to hang around while she scored it—and suggested, offhandedly, that he might want to amuse himself with those toys that someone had left in the room.

Freedman's results are highly consistent with our own. The overwhelming majority of the children who had been mildly threatened weeks earlier refused to play with the robot; they played with the other toys instead. On the other hand, the great majority of the children who had been severely threatened did, in fact, play with the robot. In sum, a severe threat was not effective in inhibiting subsequent behavior—but the effect of one *mild* threat inhibited behavior as much as nine weeks later. Again, the power of this phenomenon rests on the fact that the child did not come to devalue this behavior (playing with the toy) because some adult told him it was undesirable; he *convinced himself* that it was undesirable.

My guess is that this process may well apply beyond mere toy preference to more basic and important areas, such as the control of aggression. Partial support for this guess can be derived from some correlational studies performed in the area of child development that indicate that parents who use severe punishment to stop a child's aggression tend to have children who, while not very aggressive at home, display a great deal of aggression at school and at play away from home.[30] This is what we would expect from the compliance model discussed in Chapter 2.

The Justification of Effort

Dissonance theory leads to the prediction that, if a person works hard to attain a goal, that goal will be more attractive to him than to someone who achieves the same goal with little or no effort. An illustration might be useful: Suppose you are a college student who decides to join a fraternity. In order to be admitted, you must pass an initiation; let us assume that it is a rather severe one that involves a great deal of effort, pain, or embarrassment. After successfully completing the ordeal, you are admitted to the fraternity. When you move into the fraternity house, you find that your new roommate has some peculiar habits: for example, he plays his radio loudly after midnight, borrows money without returning it, and occasionally leaves his dirty laundry on your bed. In short, an objective person might regard him as an inconsiderate slob. But you are not an objective person any longer: your cognition that you went through hell and high water to get into the fraternity is dissonant with any cognitions about your life in the fraternity that are negative, unpleasant, or undesirable. In order to reduce dissonance, you will try to see your roommate in the most favorable light possible. Again, there are reality constraints—no matter how much pain and effort you went through, there is no way that an inconsiderate slob can be made to look much like Prince Charming—but, with a little ingenuity, you can convince yourself that he isn't so bad. What some people might call sloppy, for example, you might consider casual. Thus, his playing the radio loudly at night and his leaving his dirty laundry around only serves to demonstrate what an easy-going fellow he is—and because he's so nice and casual about material things, it's certainly understandable that he would forget about the money he owes you.

A Prince Charming he isn't, but he's certainly tolerable. Contrast this with what your attitude would have been had you made no investment of effort: Suppose you had moved into a dormitory and encountered the same roommate. Because there was no investment of effort, there is no dissonance; because there is no dissonance, there is no need for you to see your roommate in a good light. My guess is that you would quickly write him off as an inconsiderate slob and try to make arrangements to move to a different location.

These speculations were tested in an experiment that I performed several years ago in collaboration with my friend Judson Mills.[31] In this study, college women volunteered to join a group that would be meeting regularly to discuss various aspects of the psychology of sex. The women were told that, if they wanted to join, they would first have to go through a screening test designed to insure that all people admitted to the group could discuss sex freely and openly. This instruction served to set the stage for the initiation procedure. One-third of the women were assigned to a severe initiation procedure, which required them to recite aloud (in the presence of the male experimenter) a list of obscene words and a few rather lurid sexual passages from contemporary novels. (It should be mentioned that the experiment was performed in the late fifties, when this kind of procedure was far more embarrassing for most women than it would be today.) One-third of the students underwent a mild procedure, in which they recited a list of words that were sexual but not obscene. The final one-third of the subjects were admitted to the group with out undergoing an initiation. Each subject was then allowed to listen in on a discussion being conducted by the members of the group she had just joined. Although the women were led to believe that the discussion was a "live," ongoing one, what they actually heard was a prerecorded tape. This was done so that each of the women, regard-less of what kind of initiation she went through, would be hearing exactly the same discussion. The taped discussion was arranged so that it was as dull and as turgid as possible. After it was over, each subject was asked to rate the discussion in terms of how much she liked it, how interesting it was, how intelligent the participants were, and so forth.

The results supported the predictions: Those subjects who under-went little or no effort to get into the group did not enjoy the discussion very much. They were able to see it as it was—a dull and boring waste of time. Those subjects who went through a severe initiation, however, succeeded in convincing themselves that the same discussion was rather interesting and worthwhile.

The same pattern of results has been shown by other investigators using different kinds of unpleasant initiations. For example, Harold Gerard and Grover Mathewson[32] conducted an experiment similar in concept to the Aronson–Mills study, except for the fact that subjects in the severe-initiation condition were given painful electric shocks instead of a list of obscene words to read aloud. The results paralleled those of Aronson and Mills: subjects who underwent a series of severe electric shocks in order to become members of a group liked that group better than subjects who underwent a series of mild electric shocks.

It should be clear that we are *not* asserting that people enjoy painful experiences—they do not —nor are we asserting that people enjoy things because they are associated with painful experiences. What we *are* stating is that, if a person goes through a painful experience *in order to attain* some goal or object, that goal or object becomes more attractive. Thus, if on your way to a discussion group you got hit on the head by a brick, you would not like that group any better; but, if you volunteered to get hit on the head by a brick *in order to join* the discussion group, you would definitely like it better.

It should be noted that, in most dissonant situations, there is more than one way to reduce dissonance. In the initiation experiment, for example, we found that people who go through a great deal of effort to get into a dull group convince themselves that the group is more interesting. Is this the only way that they could have reduced dissonance? No. They could have convinced themselves that their effort wasn't so great. Indeed, they might have used both strategies simultaneously. This presents an interesting practical problem: To the extent that all of a subject's energies are not aimed in one direction, the potency of any one particular effect is diminished. Thus, suppose you are a basketball coach and you want your team to have a great deal of team spirit, cohesiveness, and camaraderie. You might put each player through a rugged initiation in order to join the team. Naturally, you would want all of the dissonance produced by the initiation to be reduced by each player's deciding that he likes his teammates more. If a player chooses, instead, to convince himself that, "Ah, wasn't such a tough initiation," he reduces dissonance without increasing his esteem for his teammates. As a coach, you might succeed in channelling the dissonance-reducing energy in the direction of intragroup cohesiveness by making the initiation so severe that a person would be unable to consider it a lark. You might bolster this "channelling" by verbally emphasizing how severe the initiation is, in order to make it even more difficult for a player to think of it as easy.

The Justification of Cruelty

Over and over again we have made the point that we have a need to convince ourselves that we are decent, reasonable people. We have seen how this can cause us to change our attitudes on issues that are important to us. We have seen, for example, that if a person makes a counterattitudinal speech favoring the use and legalization of marijuana for little external justification, and he learns that the video tape of that speech will be shown to a group of persuasible youngsters, he tends to convince himself that marijuana isn't so bad—as a means of making himself feel less like an evil person. In this section, we will discuss a variation on this theme: Suppose you performed an action that caused a great deal of harm to an innocent person. Let us suppose further that the harm was real and unambiguous. Your cognition "I am a decent, fair, and reasonable person" would be dissonant with your cognition "I have hurt another person." If the harm is clear, then you cannot reduce the dissonance by changing your opinion on the issue, thus convincing yourself that you've done no harm, as the people in the marijuana experiment did. In this situation, an effective way to reduce dissonance would be to maximize the culpability of the victim of your action—to convince yourself that the victim deserved what he got, either because he did something to bring it on himself or because he was a bad, evil, dirty, reprehensible person.

This mechanism might even operate if you did not directly cause the harm that befell the victim, if you only disliked him (prior to his victimization) and were hoping that harm would befall him. For example, after four students at Kent State University were shot and killed by members of the Ohio National Guard, several rumors quickly spread to the effect that: (1) both of the slain women were pregnant (and therefore, by implication, were oversexed and wanton); (2) the bodies of all four students were crawling with lice; and (3) the victims were so ridden with syphilis that they would have been dead in two weeks anyway.[33]

These rumors were totally untrue. It *was* true that the slain students were all clean, decent, bright kids. Indeed, two of them were not even involved in the demonstration that resulted in the tragedy, but were peacefully walking across campus when they were gunned down. Why were the townspeople so eager to believe and spread these rumors? It is impossible to know for sure, but my guess is that it was for reasons similar to the reasons that rumors were spread among the people in India studied by Prasad and Sinha (see pp. 87–88)—that is, because the rumors were comforting. Picture the situation: Kent is a conservative town. Many of the townspeople were infuriated at the radical behavior of some of the students. Some probably were hoping that the students would get their comeuppance; but death was, perhaps, more than they deserved. In such circumstances, any information that put the victims in a bad light helped to reduce dissonance by implying that it was, in fact, a good thing that they died. In addition, this eagerness to believe that the victims were sinful and deserved their fate was expressed in ways that were more direct: several members of the Ohio National Guard maintained stoutly that the victims deserved to die; and a Kent high-school teacher, whom James Michener interviewed, even went so far as to state that, "Anyone who appears on the streets of a city like Kent with long hair, dirty clothes or barefooted deserves to be shot." She went on to say that this dictum applied even to her own children.[34]

It is tempting simply to write such people off as crazy—but we should not make such judgments lightly. Although it's certainly true that all people are not as extreme as the high-school teacher, it is also true that just about everyone can be influenced in this direction. To illustrate this point, let us take a look at the behavior of Nikita Khrushchev, just before he became Premier of the Soviet Union: In his memoirs, Khrushchev described himself as a tough and skeptical person who certainly doesn't believe everything he's told. He cited several examples of his own skepticism and reluctance to believe scandalous stories about people, and compared himself favorably, in this regard, with Stalin. But let's look at Khrushchev's credulity when it suited his own needs. Soon after Stalin's death, Beria was on the verge of assuming leadership, but Khrushchev convinced the other members of the Presidium that Beria was a dangerous man. Beria was then arrested, imprisoned, and eventually executed. Dissonance theory would lead to the prediction that, because of his central role in Beria's downfall, Khrushchev might be willing to believe negative things about him—no matter how absurd. But let's allow Khrushchev to tell it in his own words:

> After it was all over [Beria's arrest], Malenkov took me aside and said, "Listen to what my chief bodyguard has to say." The man came over to me and said, "I have only just heard that Beria has been arrested. I want to inform you that he raped my stepdaughter, a seventh-grader. A year or so ago her grandmother died and my wife had to go to the hospital, leaving the girl at home alone. One evening she went out to buy some bread near the building where Beria lives. There she came across an old man who watched her intently. She was frightened. Someone came and took her to Beria's home. Beria had her sit down with him for supper. She drank something, fell asleep, and he raped

her." . . . Later, we were given a list of more than a hundred girls and women who had been raped by Beria. He had used the same routine on all of them. He gave them some dinner and offered them wine with a sleeping potion in it.[35]

It seems fantastic that anyone would believe that Beria actually perpetrated this deed on more than one hundred women. And yet, Khrushchev apparently believed it—perhaps because he had a strong need to believe it.

These examples seem to fit an analysis based on dissonance theory, but they do not offer definitive proof. For example, it might be the case that the National Guardsmen at Kent State believed that the students deserved to die even *before* they fired on them, or that Khrushchev would have been prone to believe those fantastic stories about Beria even before he had caused Beria's demise. It might even be true that Khrushchev *didn't* believe those stories, but merely pretended that he believed them in order to discredit Beria.

In order to be more certain that this process really exists, it is essential for the social psychologist to remove himself from the helter-skelter of the real world (temporarily) and test his predictions in the more controlled world of the experimental laboratory. Ideally, if we want to measure attitude change as a result of dissonant cognitions, it is important to know what the attitudes were *before* the dissonance-arousing event occurred. Such a situation was produced in an experiment performed by Keith Davis and Edward Jones.[36] They persuaded students to volunteer to help with an experiment: each student's participation consisted of watching another student being interviewed and then, on the basis of this observation, telling that other student that he believed him to be a shallow, untrustworthy, and dull person. The major finding in this experiment was that subjects who volunteered for this assignment succeeded in *convincing themselves* that they didn't like the victim of their cruelty. In short, *after* saying things that were certain to hurt the other student, they convinced themselves that he deserved it—that is, they found him less attractive than they did *before* they hurt him. A similar result stems from an experiment by David Glass.[37] In this study, individuals who considered themselves to be good and decent people, when induced to deliver a series of electric shocks to other people, derogated their victims as a result of having caused them this pain. It is interesting to note that this result is clearest among people with high self-esteem. If I consider myself to be a scoundrel, then causing another person to suffer does not introduce as much dissonance; therefore, I have less of a need to convince myself that he deserved his fate. Consider the irony: it is precisely because I think I am such a nice person that, if I do something that causes you pain, I must convince myself that you are a rat. In other words, because nice guys like me don't go around hurting innocent people, you must have deserved every nasty thing I did to you.

There are circumstances that limit the generality of this phenomenon. One of those was mentioned above: namely, people with low self-esteem have less need to derogate their victims. Another factor that limits the derogation phenomenon is the capacity of the victim to retaliate. If the victim is able and willing to retaliate at some future time, then a harm-doer feels that equity will be restored, and he thus has no need to justify his action by derogating his victim. In an ingenious experiment by Ellen Berscheid and her associates,[38] college students volunteered for an experiment in which each of them delivered a painful electric shock to a fellow student; as expected, each subject derogated his victim as a result of having delivered the shock. But half of the students were told that there would be a turnabout —that is, that the other students would be given the opportunity to shock *them*. Those who were led to believe that their victims would be able to retaliate did *not* derogate them. In short, because the victims were able to retaliate, dissonance was reduced. The harm-doers had no need to belittle their victims in order to convince themselves that the victims deserved it.

These results suggest that, during a war, soldiers might have a greater need to derogate civilian victims (because they can't retaliate) than military victims. During the court-martial of Lt. William Calley for his role in the slaughter of innocent civilians at My Lai, his psychiatrist reported that the Lieutenant came to regard the Vietnamese people as less than human. Perhaps the research reported in this section helps to shed some light on this phenomenon. Social psychologists have learned that people do not perform acts of cruelty and come out unscathed. I do not know for sure how Lt. Calley (and thousands of others) came to regard the Vietnamese as subhuman, but it seems reasonable to assume that, when we are engaged in a war in which, through our actions, a great number of innocent people are being killed, we might try to derogate the victims in order to justify our complicity in the outcome. We might poke fun at them, refer to them as "gooks," dehumanize them; but, once we have succeeded in doing that, watch out —because it becomes easier to hurt and kill "subhumans" than to hurt and kill fellow human beings. Thus, reducing dissonance in this way has terrible future consequences—it increases the likelihood that the atrocities we are willing to commit will become greater and greater. We will elaborate on this theme in the next chapter. For now, I would like to enlarge on a point I made in Chapter 1: In the final analysis, each person is accountable for his own actions. Not everyone behaved as Lt. Calley behaved. At the same time, it should be noted that Lt. Calley was not alone in his behavior; he stands as a striking example of a rather common phenomenon. With this in mind, it is important to acknowledge the fact that certain situational factors can exert a very powerful impact upon human actions. Accordingly, before we write off such behavior as merely bizarre, or merely crazy, or merely villainous, it would be wise to examine the situation that sets up the mechanism for this kind of behavior. We can then begin to understand the terrible price we are paying for allowing certain conditions to exist. Perhaps, eventually, we can do something to avoid these conditions. Dissonance theory helps to shed some light on this mechanism.

Of course, this kind of situation is not limited to wars. A great number of violent acts can be perpetrated on innocent victims that can lead to justifications, which, in turn, can produce more violence. Imagine that you live in a society that is unfair to minority groups like blacks and Chicanos. Just to take a wild example, let us pretend that, for several decades, the white majority was not allowing the blacks and Chicanos to attend first-rate public schools, but instead were providing them with a second-rate and stultifying education. As a consequence of this "benign neglect," the average black child and the average Chicano child are less well educated and less motivated than the average white child at the same grade level. They demonstrate this by generally doing poorly on achievement tests. Such a situation provides a golden opportunity for civic leaders to justify their discriminatory behavior and, hence, to reduce dissonance. "You see," they might say, "colored people are stupid (because they perform poorly on the achievement test); see how clever we were when we decided against wasting our resources by trying to provide them with a high-quality education. These people are unteachable." This is what sociologists refer to as a *self-fulfilling prophecy*. It provides a perfect justification for cruelty and neglect. So, too, is the attribution of moral inferiority to blacks and Chicanos. We imprison these people in overcrowded ghettos; and we set up a situation in which the color of a person's skin almost inevitably unleashes forces that prevent him from participating in the opportunities for growth and success that exist for white Americans. Through the magic of television, he sees people succeeding and living in the luxury of middle-class respectability. He becomes painfully aware of the opportunities, comforts, and luxuries that are unavailable to him. If his frustration leads him to violence or if his despair leads him to drugs, it is fairly easy for his white brother to sit back complacently, shake his head knowingly, and attribute this behavior to some kind of moral inferiority. As Edward Jones and Richard Nisbett[39] point out, when some misfortune befalls *us*, we tend to attribute the cause to something in the environment; but when we see the same misfortune befalling *another person*, we tend to attribute the cause to something inherent in his personality.

The Psychology of Inevitability

George Bernard Shaw was hard hit by his father's alcoholism, but he tried to make light of it. He once wrote: "If you cannot get rid of the family skeleton, you may as well make it dance."[40] In a sense, dissonance theory describes the ways that people have of making their skeletons dance—of trying to live with unpleasant outcomes. This is particularly true when a situation arises that is both negative and inevitable. Here, people attempt to make the best of things by cognitively minimizing the unpleasantness of the situation. In one experiment, Jack Brehm[41] got children to volunteer to eat a vegetable that they had previously said they disliked a lot. After they had eaten the vegetable, the experimenter indicated to half of the kids that they could expect to eat much more of that vegetable in the future; the remaining kids were not so informed. The kids who were led to believe that it was inevitable that they would be eating the vegetable in the future succeeded in convincing themselves that that particular vegetable was not so very bad. In short, the cognition "I dislike that vegetable" is dissonant with the cognition "I will be eating that vegetable in the future." In order to reduce the dissonance, the children came to believe that the vegetable was really not as noxious as they had previously thought. John Darley and Ellen Berscheid[42] showed that the same phenomenon works with people as well as with vegetables. In their experiment, college women volunteered to participate in a series of meetings in which each co-ed would be discussing her sexual behavior and sexual standards with another co-ed whom she didn't know. Before beginning these discussion sessions, each woman was given two folders. Each of the folders contained a personality description of a young woman who had supposedly volunteered for the same experience; the descriptions contained a mixture of pleasant and unpleasant characteristics. Half of the subjects were led to believe that they were going to interact with the young woman described in folder *A*, and the remaining subjects were led to believe that they were going to interact with the one described in folder *B*. Before actually meeting these co-eds, the subjects were asked to evaluate each of them on the basis of the personality descriptions that they had read. Those subjects who felt that it was inevitable that they were going to be sharing their intimate secrets with the young woman described in folder *A* found her much more appealing as a person than the one described in folder *B*, whereas those who believed that they were going to have to interact with the young woman described in folder *B* found *her* much more appealing. Just as with vegetables, inevitability makes the heart grow fonder. The knowledge that one is inevitably going to be spending time with another person increases the positive aspects of that person—or, at least, decreases his negative aspects. In short, people tend to make the best of something that they know is bound to occur.

The Importance of Self-esteem

Throughout this chapter, we have seen how a person's commitment to a particular course of action can freeze or change his attitudes, distort his perception, and determine the kind of information he seeks out. In addition, we have seen that a person can become committed to a situation in a number of different ways—by making a decision, by working hard in order to attain a goal, by believing that something is inevitable, by engaging in any action that has serious consequences (such as hurting someone), and so on. As we have mentioned before, the deepest form of commitment takes place in those situations in which a person's self-esteem is at stake. Thus, if I perform a cruel or a stupid action, this threatens my self-esteem, because it turns my mind to the possibility that I am a cruel or stupid person. In the hundreds of experiments that were inspired by the theory of cognitive dissonance, the clearest results were obtained in those situations in which a person's self-esteem was involved. Moreover, as one might expect, we have seen that those individuals with the highest self-esteem experience the most dissonance when they behave in a stupid or cruel manner.

What happens when a person has low self-esteem? Theoretically, if he were to commit a stupid or an immoral action, he would not experience much dissonance. His cognition "I have done an immoral thing" is *consonant* with his cognition "I am a schlunk." In short, a person who believes himself to be a schlunk expects to do schlunky things. Another way of putting it is that a person who has low self-esteem will not find it terribly difficult to commit an immoral action—because committing an immoral action is not dissonant with his self-concept. On the other hand, if a person has high self-esteem, he is more likely to resist the temptation to commit an immoral action, because to behave immorally would produce a great deal of dissonance.

I tested this proposition in collaboration with David Mettee.[43] We predicted that individuals who had a low opinion of themselves would be more likely to cheat (if given the opportunity) than individuals who had a high opinion of themselves. It should be made clear that we were not making the simple prediction that people who believe themselves to be dishonest will cheat more than people who believe themselves to be honest. Our prediction was a little more daring; it was based on the assumption that, if a normal person receives a temporary blow to his self-esteem (for example, if he is jilted by his girl friend or flunks an exam) and thus feels low and worthless, he is more likely to cheat at cards, kick his dog, wear mismatched pajamas, or do any number of things consistent with his having a low opinion of himself. As a function of feeling that they are low people, individuals will commit low acts.

In our experiment, we modified students' self-esteem (temporarily) by giving them false information about their personalities. After taking a personality test, one-third of the students were given positive feedback; specifically, they were told that the test indicated that they were mature, interesting, deep, and so forth. Another one-third of the students were given negative feedback; they were told that the test indicated that they were relatively immature, uninteresting, rather shallow, and the like. The remaining one-third of the students were not given any information about the results of the test.

Immediately afterwards, the students were scheduled to participate in an experiment, conducted by a different psychologist, that had no apparent relation to the personality inventory. As a part of this second experiment, the subjects participated in a game of cards against some of their fellow students. This was a gambling game in which the students were allowed to bet money and were told that they could keep whatever money they won. In the course of the game, the subjects were presented with a few opportunities to cheat in a situation where it seemed impossible that they could be detected. The situation was arranged so that, if a student decided *not* to cheat, he would certainly lose, whereas, if he decided to cheat, he would be certain to win a sizable sum of money.

The results clearly showed that those students who had previously received information designed to lower their self-esteem cheated to a far greater extent than those who had received the high self-esteem information. The control group—those that received no information—fell exactly in between. These findings suggest that it would be well worth the effort of parents and teachers to alert themselves to what could be the far-reaching consequences of their own behavior as it affects the self-esteem of their children and students. Specifically, if it is true that low self-esteem is an important antecedent of criminal or cruel behavior, then we might want to do everything possible to help individuals learn to respect and love themselves.

Physiological and Motivational Effects of Dissonance

How far can the effects of dissonance extend? In the past several years, researchers have shown that it can go beyond attitudes; it can modify the way we experience basic physiological drives. Under certain well-specified conditions, dissonance reduction can lead hungry people to experience less hunger, thirsty people to experience less thirst, and people undergoing intensive electric shock to experience less pain. Here's how it works: If a person is induced to *commit himself* to a situation in which he will be deprived of food or water for a long time, or in which he will experience electric shock, and has *low external justification* for doing this, he will experience dissonance. His cognitions concerning his hunger pangs, his parched throat, or the pain of electrical shock are each dissonant with his cognition that he volunteered to go through these experiences and is not getting very much in return. In order to reduce this dissonance, he convinces himself that the hunger isn't so intense, or that the thirst isn't so bad, or the pain isn't so great. This should not be astonishing. Although hunger, thirst, and pain all have physiological bases, it is a well-documented fact that they have a strong psychological component. For example: through suggestion, mediation, hypnosis, placebo pills, the bedside manner of a skillful physician, or some combination of these, perceived pain can be reduced. Experimental social psychologists have shown that, under conditions of high dissonance arousal, ordinary people, without any special skills in hypnosis or meditation, can accomplish the same ends for themselves.

Thus, Philip Zimbardo and his collegues[44] have subjected many people to intense electric shocks: half of these people were in a high-dissonance condition—that is, they were induced to *commit themselves* to volunteer for the experience and were given very little external justification—and the other half were in a low-dissonance condition—that is, they had no choice in the matter and had a great deal of external justification. The results showed that those people in the high-dissonance condition tended to report that they experienced less pain than people in the low-dissonance condition. Moreover, this phenomenon extended beyond their subjective reports: there is some evidence to indicate that the physiological response to pain (as measured by the galvanic skin response) was somewhat less intense in the high-dissonance condition. In addition, the pain of subjects in the high-dissonance condition interfered *less* with the tasks they were performing. Thus, not only was their pain *reported* as less intense, but it also affected their behavior less intensely.

Similar results have been shown for hunger and thirst. Jack

Brehm[45] reported a series of experiments in which people were deprived of either food or water for long periods of time. In addition to experiencing hunger or thirst, these individuals were experiencing either high or low dissonance for much the same reasons that Zimbardo's subjects were experiencing high or low dissonance. Specifically, some of the subjects had low external justification for undergoing the hunger or thirst, while others had high external justification. For the dissonant subjects, the best available way to reduce the dissonance was to minimize the experience of hunger or thirst. In separate experiments on hunger and thirst, Brehm reported that the subjects in the high-dissonance condition said they were less hungry (or thirsty) than low-dissonance subjects who were deprived of food (or water) for the same length of time. Again, this was no mere verbal report—after the experiment, when all of the subjects were allowed to eat (or drink) freely, the high dissonance subjects actually consumed less food (or water) than the low-dissonance subjects.

A Critical Look at Cognitive Dissonance as a Theory

I'd like to invite the reader backstage again. Recall that, in the preceding chapter (page 74–76), we went backstage to look at how scientists worked to make sense out of conflicting data about how the size of a discrepancy affects opinion change. This time we will go behind the scenes to look at the evolution and development of a theory. In science, theories are almost never static. A theory is proposed in order to make sense out of an occurrence—or even out of a number of apparently unrelated occurrences. By providing us with a new way of looking at the world, a theory can generate new hypotheses, new research, and new facts. Theories are neither right nor wrong. Rather, theories are judged according to how useful they are; they are more or less useful depending upon how well they account for the existing facts and how fruitful they are at generating new information. But no theory provides us with a perfect accounting of the way the world is. Thus, theories are frequently challenged and criticized. These challenges inevitably result in the reformulation of an existing theory or in the invention of an entirely new theory that seems to provide a better fit. When theories are reformulated, they are done so either to increase or decrease their scope. For example, if a theory is too vague or imprecise, an attempt may be made to simplify it, to limit its domain, or to restructure its language in order to increase our certainty about the nature of the prediction being made.

With this in mind, let us examine the theory of cognitive dissonance. As we have seen, dissonance theory has proved to be a useful way of looking at human interaction. In the two decades since its inception, it has inspired more research and has generated more discoveries about social behavior than any other theory in psychology. But there are some serious conceptual problems with the theory as originally stated. Perhaps the major difficulty stems from the fact that the original statement was conceptually vague. Look at the original theoretical statement on page 88. What is a cognition? In what way are cognitions opposite? The vagueness stems from the fact that the scope of the theory was not limited to situations that are inconsistent on logical grounds alone. Rather, the inconsistencies that produce dissonance are *psychological* inconsistencies. Indeed, this makes the theory exciting and increases its scope. Unfortunately, it also renders the theory less than perfectly precise. It would be relatively easy to make a precise statement about the domain of the theory if its predictions were limited to instances of logical inconsistency because there are strict rules for determining whether conclusions do or do not follow from premises on the basis of formal logic. For example, take the famous syllogism:

> All men are mortal.
> Socrates is a man.
> Therefore, Socrates is mortal.

If someone believed that Socrates was not mortal, while accepting the first two premises, this would be a clear case of dissonance.

By contrast, let us take the typical dissonance situation:

> I believe that smoking cigarettes causes cancer.
> I smoke cigarettes.

The cognition "I smoke cigarettes" is not inconsistent with the cognition "cigarette smoking causes cancer" *on formal logical grounds.*

It is inconsistent on psychological grounds; that is, the implications of the two statements are dissonant because we know that most people do not want to die. But it is sometimes difficult to be certain what will be psychologically inconsistent for any one person. For example, suppose you have great admiration for Franklin Delano Roosevelt; then you learn that, throughout his marriage, he was carrying on a clandestine love affair. Will that cause dissonance? It is difficult to know. If you place a high value on marital fidelity *and* you also believe that great men should not violate this sanction, then you will experience some dissonance. To reduce it you will either change your attitudes about Roosevelt or soften your attitudes about marital infidelity. Because a large number of people probably do not hold both of these values simultaneously, however, they will not experience dissonance. Moreover, even if a person *does* hold these two values simultaneously, the cognitions may not be particularly salient —so how do we know whether or not they cause dissonance? This leads us to a major point: Even when the cognitions are undeniably salient the degree of dissonance is certain to be small compared to what it would be if *you* had violated your own values—as was true, for example, in Judson Mills' experiment with the youngsters who cheated on their tests.

In recent years, a great deal of the initial vagueness of the conceptual statement has been reduced by several theorists.[46] For example, as discussed earlier in this chapter, my own research[47] has led me to the conclusion that dissonance effects may be limited to situations in which a person's behavior violates his self-concept. This can happen in one of two ways: (1) if he consciously and knowingly does something stupid; (2) if he does something that hurts another person—even if he does it unknowingly. An example of a stupid action might be going through a severe initiation to get into a group that could easily turn out to be very uninteresting or perhaps volunteering to write a counterattitudinal essay for very little reward. A hurtful, guilt-producing action might be misleading a person by convincing him or her to do something you think might be harmful, saying cruel things to a person who has done you no harm, administering an electric shock to an innocent victim, and so on.

But these changes in the conceptualization of dissonance theory did not come all by themselves. They came gradually—partly as a result of outside criticism. For example, twenty years ago I believed that dissonance could exist between any two cognitions, and that the predicted results would inevitably follow. Mostly, the results *did* follow because, without our realizing it, we were designing our experiments in a manner such that a violation of the self-concept was almost always involved. That is, in our experiments, people were either knowingly committing themselves to stupid activities (like writing a counterattitudinal essay) or doing something immoral (like cheating or deceiving another person). Because we didn't realize at the time that these factors were involved, we were occasionally surprised when what seemed like a clear prediction did not turn out. For example, Milton Rosenberg[48] once performed an experiment similar to Arthur Cohen's experiment (reported on pp. 108–109) in which subjects were paid either a large reward or small reward for writing an essay against their own beliefs. His results came out quite differently from Cohen's. This produced a great deal of confusion. Then, Darwyn Linder and his colleagues[49] noticed what seemed to be a minor difference between the two experiments. The subjects in Cohen's experiment knowingly committed themselves to write an essay favoring the rather brutal actions of the New Haven police during a student demonstration, but they were informed at the outset that they didn't have to do it if they didn't want to. Unlike the participants in Cohen's experiment, Rosenberg's subjects were not given a clear idea of what they were going to do before they agreed to do it. That is, while they were supposedly waiting to participate in one experiment, they were induced to commit themselves to help out another researcher. It wasn't until *after* they had been committed to the task that they realized that they were going to have to write an essay that went against their own beliefs. It was too late to pull out. In this situation, it was easy for the subjects to remove their self-concept from the situation by saying, in effect, "How was I supposed to know?"*

---

*Recall the two ways in which dissonance can be aroused through a violation of the self-concept: (1) knowingly doing something stupid, or (2) doing something that hurts another person. In the first situation, if it's easy to say "How was I supposed to know?" there will be little or no dissonance. In the second situation, the fact that someone gets hurt makes it impossible to avoid dissonance simply by saying, "How was I supposed to know?".

Intrigued by this difference, Linder and his associates then performed an experiment in which they systematically varied the subjects' freedom of choice. They found clear evidence: When the subjects knew what they were letting themselves in for in advance, there was a dissonance effect—those who wrote a counterattitudinal essay for a small reward changed their beliefs in the direction of their essay to a greater extent than those who did it for a large reward. When the subjects did not have this freedom of choice but committed themselves to an unknown task, the results were just the opposite. Thus, Linder's experiment helped to clarify the limitations of dissonance effects and helped to indicate and firm up the direction of the evolution of the theory.

Although the revision of dissonance theory in terms of the self-concept has helped clarify the theory and has led to more precise predictions, the theory is still, of course, not acceptable to everyone. To some, the theory is still somewhat cumbersome. Daryl Bem,[50] for example, was not happy with the theory because it relied too much on the assumption of internal events that are difficult to measure. Bem made an earnest attempt to explain some of the phenomena discovered by dissonance theory in terms that were more concrete and more readily observable. In short, his idea was to move away from a conceptual reliance on such internal states as "cognitions" and "psychological discomfort," and to replace such concepts with the more precise "stimulus–response" language of behaviorism. Bem concentrated his efforts on the area of counterattitudinal advocacy. Let's look at the situation through Bem's eyes.

Suppose you see a woman walk into a cafeteria, survey all of the desserts being offered, pick up a wedge of rhubarb pie, and begin to eat it. What would you conclude? Simple: "She must like rhubarb pie. Given the fact that she has freedom of choice and a great many options, why else would she have chosen rhubarb pie?" So far, so good. Now, suppose *you* walk into a cafeteria, select a wedge of rhubarb pie, and eat it. What would you conclude from your own actions? Simple: "I must like rhubarb pie—why else would I be eating it?" Bem applied this reasoning to an area that the reader is very familiar with by now. Suppose you observe somebody writing an essay favoring the fierce actions of the New Haven police during a student demonstration, and you know he's being paid only fifty cents to do it. Wouldn't you conclude that he must really believe that the actions of the New Haven police were right and reasonable? Why else would he say so? Surely not for the fifty cents. Suppose you find *yourself* writing an essay favoring the fierce actions of the New Haven police for a payment of fifty cents?

In short, Bem's notion is that many of the dissonance effects are nothing more than reasonable inferences that people make about their attitudes based upon their perceptions of their own behavior. To test his notion, Bem has designed a method that is as simple as his theory. He merely describes an experimental procedure to his subjects—for example, he has described Cohen's experiment on attitudes about the behavior of the New Haven police outlined above. He then asks his subjects to guess the real attitude of each of the subjects in the experiment he has just described —for example, how much did each of Cohen's essay writers *really* favor the actions of the New Haven police? Bem's results parallel those of the original experiment: his subjects guessed that the people who wrote essays for fifty cents favoring the actions of the New Haven police must have believed what they said to a greater extent than those who wrote similar essays for five dollars.

Bem's reasoning is elegant in its simplicity; his analysis is certainly more sparse than the more traditional analyses of these data in terms of such hypothetical constructs as psychological discomfort, self concept, and so on. In science, we strive for simplicity and parsimony; if two theories accurately account for a body of data, the simpler one is preferable. But does Bem's conceptualization account for these data as accurately as dissonance theory? At this writing, it's difficult to be certain. It would appear that Bem's research ignores one vital fact: that the actor in a situation has more information than the observer. That is, when I write an essay favoring the brutal behavior of the New Haven police, chances are I *know* what my beliefs were before I wrote it; when you observe me writing an essay favoring the actions of the New Haven police, you *don't know* what my beliefs were beforehand. Both Russell Jones and his colleagues and Jane Piliavin and her colleagues[51] have demonstrated that, when the observers know the prior beliefs of the actor in such a situation, their statements no longer parallel those of the subjects in the original experiment; that is, Bem's results are not replicated. Does this mean that Bem's analysis is inaccurate? Not necessarily. It is always possible that, in a dissonance situation, even the *actor* does not know what his own prior beliefs are—that is, it is conceivable that, prior to writing an essay favoring the actions of the New Haven police, Cohen's subjects may not have had a clear notion of how they felt about it.

Still, it's difficult for me to believe that discomfort does not accompany dissonance. Many investigators who have performed experiments testing hypotheses derived from dissonance theory are convinced that a person experiencing dissonance shows signs of being uncomfortable. Phenomenologically, when a person is placed in a dissonance-producing situation, his behavior does not seem appropriate to the cool, calculated, objective, almost mechanical, unemotional deduction game that Bem believes such situations to be. But such unsystematic perceptions by researchers can hardly be considered to be convincing data. Is there any independent evidence that people experiencing dissonance are in a state of discomfort? Some. Recently, Michael Pallak and Thane Pittman[52] performed an experiment that lends support to the notion that psychological discomfort exists during a state of dissonance. Before we describe their experiment, I should first mention a finding from the psychology of learning: Suppose you are performing a task that has several possible responses that compete for your attention (as opposed to a task in which there is one clear response). If you are in a state of high drive (that is, if you are very hungry, very thirsty, very sexy, or whatever), you will perform more poorly than if you are in a low-drive state. On the other hand, if the task is a clear and simple one, being in a high-drive state seems to energize a person without causing interference; hence, you will be more successful at such a task if you are in a high-drive state. Pallak and Pittman simply put some subjects in a highly dissonant situation and others in a situation that produced very little dissonance. The low-dissonance subjects performed better than the high-dissonance subjects in a complex task (one with many competing responses), whereas the high-dissonance subjects performed better than the lows in a simple task (one with few competing responses). Thus, dissonance arousal seems to act like hunger or thirst. Although these data are not conclusive, they do indicate that something is going on inside the subjects during dissonance arousal that may be akin to psychological discomfort. Accordingly, in my judgment, although Bem's explanation of dissonance phenomena is simple and straightforward, the analysis in terms of "discomfort produced by a violation of the self-concept" strikes me as being a richer and more accurate reflection of the phenomena.

Man Cannot Live by Consonance Alone

Near the beginning of this chapter, I made the point that people are capable of rational, adaptive behavior as well as dissonance-reducing behavior. Let's return to that issue. If a person spends all of his time protecting his ego, he will never grow. In order to grow, we must learn from our mistakes. But if a person is intent on reducing dissonance, he will not admit to his mistakes. Instead, he will sweep his mistakes under the rug, or, worse still, he will turn them into virtues. The autobiographical memoirs of former presidents are full of the kind of self-serving, self-justifying statements that can best be summarized as "if I had it all to do over again, I would not change a thing."[53]

On the other hand, people do frequently grow—people do frequently profit from their mistakes. How? Under what conditions? Ideally, it would be useful for a person to be able to bring himself to say, in effect, "O.K., I blew it. What can I learn from the experience so that I will not end up in this position again?" This can come about in several ways:

1. Through an understanding of our own defensiveness and dissonance-reducing tendencies.
2. Through the realization that performing stupid or immoral actions does not necessarily mean that we are irrevocably stupid or immoral people.
3. Through the development of enough ego strength to tolerate errors in ourselves.
4. Through increasing our ability to recognize the utility of admitting error.

Of course, it is far easier to list these procedures than it is to accomplish them. How does a person get in touch with his own defensiveness and dissonance-reducing tendencies? How can we come to realize that bright, moral people like ourselves can occasionally perform a stupid or immoral action? It is not enough to know it superficially; in order to utilize this knowledge, a person may need to experience it and practice it. A situation that encourages this kind of practice will be discussed in Chapter 8.

5

Human Aggression

Several years ago, I was watching Walter Cronkite on television. In the course of his newscast, he reported an incident in which American planes dropped napalm on a village of South Vietnam believed to be a Viet Cong stronghold. My oldest son, who was about ten at the time, asked brightly, "Hey, Dad, what's napalm?" "Oh," I answered casually, "as I understand it, it's a chemical that both sticks and burns, so that if it gets on a person's skin, he can't remove it, and it burns him pretty badly." And I continued to watch the news. A few minutes later, I happened to glance across at my son and saw tears streaming down his face. Looking at my son, I became dismayed and upset as I

My thinking about the psychology of aggression has been influenced and enriched by a great many casual conversations with Dr. Leonard Berkowitz of the University of Wisconsin, while we were colleagues at the Center for Advanced Study in the Behavioral Sciences. I am pleased to acknowledge my indebtedness to him.

began to think about what had happened to me. Had I become so brutalized that I could answer such a question so matter-of-factly—as if my son had asked me how a baseball is made or how a leaf functions? Had I gotten so accustomed to human brutality?

We're living in an era of unspeakable horror—of infants being bayoneted before the eyes of their parents in Bangladesh; of American soldiers shooting children at point-blank range at My Lai. Of course, events of this kind are not peculiar to the present decade. A friend once showed me a very thin book—only ten or (fifteen pages long—that purported to be a capsule history of the world. It was a chronological listing of the important events in recorded history. Can you guess how it read? Of course—one war after another, interrupted every now and then by a few other events, such as the birth of Jesus and the invention of the printing press. What kind of species is man if the most important events in his brief history are situations in which people kill each other en masse?

Man is an aggressive animal. With the exception of certain rodents, no other vertebrate so consistently and wantonly kills members of his own species. We have defined social psychology as social influence—that is, one person's (or group's) influence on another. The most extreme form of aggression (physical destruction) can be considered to be the ultimate degree of social influence. Is aggression part of the nature of man? Can it be modified? What are the social and situational factors that increase and decrease aggression?

Aggression Defined

It is difficult to present a clear definition of "aggression" because, in the popular vernacular, the term is used in so many different ways. Clearly, the Boston Strangler, who made a hobby of strangling women in their apartments, was performing acts of aggression. But a football player making a driving tackle is also considered aggressive. A tennis player who charges the net is called aggressive. So, too, is a successful insurance salesman who is "a real go-getter." The child who staunchly defends his own possessions against the encroachment of others, and the child who goes out of his way to clobber his brother, are both considered aggressive. On a more subtle level, if a neglected wife sulks in the corner during a party, this may be an act of "passive aggression." Also, a child who wets his bed, a jilted boy friend who threatens suicide, or a student who doggedly attempts to master a difficult mathematical problem could conceivably be labeled as illustrations of an aggressive tendency in human beings. And what of the violence exerted by the state in its attempt to maintain law and order—and the less direct forms of aggression through which people of one race or religion humiliate and degrade people of different races or religions? If all of these behaviors are to be called by the blanket term "aggression," the situation is indeed confused. As a way of increasing our understanding of aggression, we must cut through this morass and separate the "assertive" aspects of the popular definition from the destructive aspects. That is, a distinction can be made between behavior that harms others and behavior that does not harm others. The outcome is important. Thus, according to this distinction, the go-getting salesman or the student doggedly sticking to his mathematical problem would not be considered aggressive, but the behavior of the Boston Strangler, the clobbering child, the suicidal boy friend, and even the sulking, neglected wife would all be considered aggressive.

But this distinction is not altogether satisfactory because, by concentrating on outcome alone, it ignores the intention of the person perpetrating the act, and this is the crucial aspect of the definition of aggression. I would define an act of aggression as a behavior aimed at causing harm or pain. Thus, by this definition, the football player is *not* considered to be performing an act of aggression if his aim is simply to bring down his man as efficiently as possible —but he *is* behaving aggressively if his aim is to cause pain or injury to his man, whether or not he succeeds in doing so. To illustrate, suppose a three-year-old child slaps at his father in anger. The slap may be totally ineffectual—it may even cause his father to laugh. But it is, nonetheless, an aggressive act. Similarly, the same child may, in total innocence, thrust a sharp elbow into his father's eye, causing severe pain and colorful contusions. This would not be defined as an act of aggression, because its painful consequences were unintended.

It might be useful to make one additional distinction within the category of intentional aggression, namely, a distinction between aggression that is an end in itself and aggression that is instrumental in achieving some goal. Thus, a football player might intentionally inflict an injury on the opposing quarterback in order to put him out of the game and thus increase his own team's probability of winning. This would be instrumental aggression. On the other hand, he might perform this action on the last play of the last game of the season to "pay back" the quarterback for some real or imagined insult or humiliation; here, the aggressive act would be an end in itself. Similarly, dropping a bomb on a ball-bearing factory in Munich during World War II can be considered an act of instrumental aggression, while shooting down some defenseless women and children can be considered an act of aggression as an end in itself. The "button man" who, working for the Mafia, guns down a designated victim is probably behaving instrumentally; thrill killers like Leopold and Loeb probably weren't.

Is Aggressiveness Instinctive?

Psychologists, physiologists, ethologists, and philosophers are in disagreement over whether aggressiveness is an innate, instinctive phenomenon or whether such behavior has to be learned. This is not a new controversy: it has been raging for centuries. For example, Jean-Jacques Rousseau's concept of the noble savage[1] (first published in 1762) suggested that man, in his natural state, is a benign, happy, and good creature, and that a restrictive society forces aggressiveness and depravity upon him. Others have taken the view that man in his natural state is a brute, and that only by enforcing the law and order of society can we curb or sublimate his natural instincts toward aggression. Sigmund Freud[2] is a good example of a proponent of this general position. Freud suggested that man is born with a death instinct, *thanatos*: when turned inward, thanatos manifests itself in self-punishment, which, in the extreme case, becomes suicide; when turned outward, this instinct manifests itself in hostility, destructiveness, and murder. "It is at work in every living being and is striving to bring it to ruin and to reduce life to its original condition of inanimate matter."[3] Freud believed that this aggressive energy must come out somehow, lest it continue to build up and produce illness. This notion can be described as a "hydraulic" theory—that is, the analogy is one of water pressure building up in a container: unless aggression is allowed to drain off, it will produce some sort of an explosion. According to Freud, society performs an essential function in regulating this instinct and in helping people to sublimate it—that is, in helping people to turn the destructive energy into acceptable, or even useful, behavior.

Taking the notion of man's natural aggressiveness one step further, there are some scholars who feel that man in his natural state is not only a killer, but that his wanton destructiveness is unique among animals; consequently, these scholars suggest that to call man's behavior brutal is to libel nonhuman species. This point of view has been expressed eloquently by Anthony Storr:

> We generally describe the most repulsive examples of man's cruelty as brutal or bestial, implying by these adjectives that such behaviour is characteristic of less highly developed animals than ourselves. In truth, however, the extremes of 'brutal' behaviour are confined to man; and there is no parallel in nature to our savage treatment of each other. The sombre fact is that we are the cruellest and most ruthless species that has ever walked the earth; and that although we may recoil in horror when we read in newspaper or history book of the atrocities committed by man upon man, we know in our hearts that each one of us harbours within himself those same savage impulses which lead to murder, to torture, and to war.[4]

There is a lack of definitive or even clear evidence on the subject of whether or not aggression is instinctive in man. I suppose that is why the controversy still rages. Much of the evidence, such as it is, stems from observation of, and experimentation with, species other than man. In one such study, for example, Zing Yang Kuo[5] attempted to explode the myth that cats will instinctively stalk and kill rats. His experiment was a very simple one. He raised a kitten in the same cage with a rat. Not only did the cat refrain from attacking the rat, but the two became close companions. Moreover, the cat refused either to chase or to kill other rats. It should be noted, however, that this experiment does not prove that aggressive behavior is not instinctive; it merely demonstrates that aggressive behavior can be inhibited by early experience. Thus, in an experiment reported by Irenäus Eibl-Eibesfeldt,[6] it was shown that rats raised in isolation (that is, without any experience in fighting other rats) will attack a fellow rat when one is introduced into the cage; moreover, the isolated rat uses the same pattern of threat and attack that experienced rats use. Thus, although aggressive behavior can be modified by experience (as shown by Kuo's experiment), Eibl-Eibesfeldt showed that aggression apparently does not need to be learned. On the other hand, one should not conclude from this study that aggressiveness is necessarily instinctive, for as John Paul Scott[7] has pointed out, in order to draw this conclusion, there must be physiological evidence of a spontaneous stimulation for fighting that arises from within the body alone. The stimulus in the above experiment came from the outside—that is, the sight of the new rat stimulated the isolated rat to fight. Scott concluded from his survey of the evidence that there is no inborn need for fighting: if an organism can arrange its life in such a way that there is no outside stimulation to fight, then he will not experience any physiological or mental damage as a result of not expressing aggression. This view contradicts Freud's contention and, in effect, asserts that there is no instinct of aggression.

The argument goes back and forth. Scott's conclusion has been called into question by the distinguished ethologist Konrad Lorenz.[8] Lorenz observed the behavior of certain cichlids, which are highly aggressive tropical fish. Male cichlids will attack other males of the same species apparently as an aspect of territorial behavior—that is, to defend their territory. In its natural environment, the male cichlid does not attack female cichlids, nor does he attack males of a different species—he only attacks males of his own species. What happens if all other male cichlids are removed from an aquarium, leaving only one male alone with no appropriate sparring partner? According to the hydraulic theory of instinct, the need to aggress will build up to the point where the cichlid will attack a fish that doesn't usually serve as an appropriate stimulus for attack; and that is exactly what happens. In the absence of his fellow male cichlids, he attacks males of other species—males that he had previously ignored. Moreover, if *all* males are removed, the male cichlid will eventually attack and kill females.

And the controversy continues. Leonard Berkowitz,[9] one of our nation's leading experts on human aggression, believes that humans are essentially different from nonhumans in that learning plays a more important role in their aggressive behavior. In humans, aggressiveness is a function of a complex interplay between innate propensities and learned responses. Thus, although it is true that many animals from insects to apes will attack an animal who invades his territory, it is a gross oversimplification to imply, as some popular writers have, that man is likewise programmed to protect his territory and behave aggressively in response to specific stimuli. There is much evidence to support Berkowitz's contention that man's innate patterns of behavior are infinitely modifiable and flexible. Indeed, there is even a good deal of evidence for such flexibility among nonhumans. For example, by electrically stimulating a certain area of a monkey's brain, one can evoke an aggressive response in the monkey. This area can be considered to be the neural center of aggression; but that does not mean that, when this area is stimulated, the monkey will always attack. If a monkey is in the presence of other monkeys who are less dominant than he in their social hierarchy, he will indeed attack them when the appropriate area of his brain is stimulated; but if the same area is stimulated while he is in the presence of monkeys who are *more* dominant than he, he will *not* attack; rather, he will tend to flee the scene. Thus, the same physiological stimulation can produce widely different responses, depending upon learning. This appears to be true in spades for humans. Our conclusion from reviewing these data is that, although aggressiveness may have an instinctive component in man, the important point for the social psychologist is that it *is* modifiable by situational factors. How can it be modified? How much can it be modified? Should it be modified? Before getting to these questions, we must first understand what the situational factors are and how they operate.

Frustration

Aggression can be caused by any unpleasant or aversive situation, such as pain, boredom, and the like. Of these aversive situations, the major instigator of aggression is *frustration*. If an individual is thwarted on his way to a goal, the resulting frustration will increase the probability of an aggressive response. This does not mean that frustration *always* leads to aggression or that frustration is the only cause of aggression. There are other factors that will determine whether or not a frustrated individual will aggress—and there are other causes of aggression.

A clear picture of the relation between frustration and aggression emerges from a well-known experiment by Roger Barker, Tamara Dembo, and Kurt Lewin.[10] These psychologists frustrated young children by showing them a roomful of very attractive toys, which they were then not allowed to play with. The children stood outside a wire screen looking at the toys, hoping to play with them—even expecting to play with them—but were unable to reach them. After a painfully long wait, the children were finally allowed to play with the toys. In this experiment, a separate group of children were allowed to play with the toys directly without first being frustrated. This second group of children played joyfully with the toys. But the frustrated group, when finally given access to the toys, were extremely destructive: they tended to smash the toys, throw them against the wall, step on them, and so forth. Thus, frustration can lead to aggression.

It is important to distinguish between frustration and deprivation. Children who simply don't have toys do not necessarily aggress. Rather, the research with children indicates that it was those children who have every reason to expect to play with the toys who experienced frustration when this expectancy was thwarted; this thwarting was what caused the children to behave destructively. In accord with this distinction, the psychiatrist Jerome Frank has pointed out that the two most serious riots by blacks in recent years did *not* take place in the geographical areas of greatest poverty; rather, they took place in Watts and Detroit, where things aren't nearly as bad for blacks as they are in some other sections of the country. The point is, things *are* bad, relative to what "Whitey" has. Revolutions usually are not started by people whose faces are in the mud. They are most frequently started by people who have recently lifted their faces out of the mud, looked around, and noticed that other people are doing better than they are, and that the system is treating them unfairly. Thus, frustration is not simply the result of deprivation; it is the result of *relative deprivation*. Suppose I choose not to be educated and you choose to be educated; if you have a better job than I do, I will not experience frustration when I think about that. But if we've both been educated, and you have a white collar job and I (because I'm black, or a Chicano, or a woman) am handed a broom, I *will* feel frustrated; or, if you find it easy to get an education, but an education is denied me, I will also feel frustrated. This frustration will be exacerbated every time I turn on the TV and see all those beautiful houses that white people live in, and all those lovely appliances for sale to other people, and all of that gracious living and leisure that I cannot share in. When you consider all of the economic and social frustrations faced by minority groups in this affluent society, it is surprising that there are so *few* riots. As long as there is hope that is unsatisfied, there will be aggression. Aggression can be reduced by eliminating hope—or by satisfying it.

A hopeless people is an apathetic people. The South African blacks and the Haitians will not revolt as long as they are prevented from hoping for anything better. The saving grace of the United States is that—theoretically, at least—this is a land of promise. We teach our children to hope, to expect, and to work to improve their lives. But unless this hope stands a reasonable chance of being ful-filled, some turmoil will be inevitable.

Social Learning and Aggression

Although frustration and pain can be considered the major causes of aggression, there are many factors that can intervene, either to induce aggressive behavior in a person who is suffering very little pain or frustration, or, conversely, to inhibit an aggressive response in a person who is frustrated. These factors are the result of social learning. We have already seen how social learning can inhibit an aggressive response: recall that, when we stimulate the area of a monkey's brain that characteristically produces aggressive behavior, the monkey will not aggress if he is in the presence of a monkey whom *he has learned* to fear. Another qualification based upon social learning is the intention attributed to an agent of pain or frustration. One aspect of behavior that seems to distinguish man from other animals is man's ability to take the intentions of others into consid-eration. Consider the following situations: (1) a considerate person accidentally steps on your toe; or (2) a thoughtless person that you know doesn't care about you steps on your toe. Let us assume that the amount of pressure and pain is exactly the same in both cases. My guess is that the latter situation would evoke an aggressive response, but the former would produce little or no aggression. Thus, I am suggesting that frustration and pain do not inexorably produce aggression. The response can be modified—and one of the primary things that can modify aggression is the intention attributed to the frustrator. This phenomenon was demonstrated in an experiment by Shabaz Mallick and Boyd McCandless,[11] in which they frustrated third-grade school children by having another child's clumsiness prevent them from achieving a goal that would have resulted in a cash prize. Some of these children were subsequently provided with a reasonable and "unspiteful" explanation for the behavior of the child who fouled them up. Specifically, they were told that he had been "sleepy and upset." The children in this condition directed much less aggression against the "thwarting" child than did children who were not given this explanation.

On the other side of the coin, certain stimuli can evoke aggressive behavior on the part of individuals who do not appear to be frustrated. In a classic series of experiments, Albert Bandura, and his associates[12] demonstrated that simply seeing another person behave aggressively can increase the aggressive behavior of young children. The basic procedure in these studies was to have an adult knock around a plastic, air-filled "Bobo" doll (the kind that bounces back after it's been knocked down). Sometimes, the adult would accompany his physical aggression with verbal abuse against the doll. The kids were then allowed to play with the doll. In these experiments, not only did the children imitate the aggressive models, they also engaged in other forms of aggressive behavior after having witnessed the aggressive behavior of the adult. In short, the children copied the behavior of an adult; seeing someone else behave aggressively served as an impetus for them to behave aggressively. It is important to note, however, the children did not confine their behavior to mere imitation, but invented new and creative forms of aggression. This indicates that the effect of a model generalizes—it is not simply a matter of the children doing exactly what adults are doing—which means that children can be stimulated to commit a range of aggressive actions. Bandura and

his co-workers have also demonstrated that the outcome was important: if the aggressive model was rewarded for his aggressive behavior, the children who witnessed it were subsequently more aggressive
than those who witnessed the model being punished for aggressing.

Carrying this one step further, Leonard Berkowitz and his
associates[13] have shown that, if an individual is frustrated or angered,
the mere presence of an object associated with aggression will increase his aggressiveness. In one experiment, college students were
made angry: some of them were made angry in a room in which a gun
was left casually lying around, and others, in a room in which a
neutral object (a badminton racket) was substituted for the gun. The
subjects were then given the opportunity to administer some electric
shocks to a fellow college student. Those individuals who had been
made angry in the presence of the aggressive stimulus (the gun)
administered more electric shocks than did those who were made
angry in the presence of the badminton racket. In other words,
certain cues that are associated with aggression will increase a person's tendency to aggress. As Berkowitz puts it, "An angry person
can pull the trigger of his gun if he wants to commit violence; but the
trigger [that is, the sight of the gun] can also pull the finger or
otherwise elicit aggressive reactions from him, if he is ready to
aggress and does not have strong inhibitions against such behavior."[14]

Is Aggression Necessary?

Survival of the Fittest. Some scholars have suggested that certain
kinds of aggression are useful and, perhaps, even essential. Konrad
Lorenz,[15] for example, has argued that aggression is "an essential part
of the life-preserving organization of instincts." Basing his argument
on his observation of nonhumans, he sees aggressiveness as being of
prime evolutionary importance, allowing the young animals to have
the strongest and wisest mothers and fathers and enabling the group
to be led by the best possible leaders. From their study of Old World
monkeys, the anthropologist Sherwood Washburn and the psychiatrist David Hamburg[16] concur. They find that aggression within the
same group of monkeys plays an important role in feeding, repro-

duction, and in determining dominance patterns. The strongest and most aggressive male in a colony will assume a dominant position through an initial display of aggressiveness. This serves to reduce subsequent serious fighting within the colony (the other males know who's boss). Furthermore, because the dominant male dominates reproduction, the colony increases its chances of survival as the strong male passes on his vigor to subsequent generations.

A similar pattern is reported among elephant seals by Burney LeBoeuf.[17] Each year before mating season, pairs of males square off against each other and engage in ferocious blood battles for dominance. The strongest, most aggressive, and shrewdest male is not only number one on the dominance hierarchy among his fellows, but he becomes the number one lovemaker in the group. For example, in one observation, the number one or "alpha" male in a particular rookery of 185 females and 120 males was responsible for half of the observed copulations. In smaller rookeries of 40 or fewer females, the alpha male is typically responsible for 100 percent of the copulations that take place.

With these data in mind, many observers urge caution in attempting to control aggression in man, suggesting that, as in lower animals, aggression is necessary for survival. This reasoning is based, in part, on the assumption that the same mechanism that drives one man to kill his neighbor drives another to "conquer" outer space, "sink his teeth" into a difficult mathematical equation, "attack" a logical problem, or "master" the universe.

But this is probably not true. Overt aggression is no longer necessary for human survival. Moreover, to equate creative activity and high achievement with hostility and aggression is to confuse the issue. It is possible to achieve mastery of a problem or a skill without hurting another person even without attempting to conquer. It is possible to reduce violence without reducing man's curiosity or his desire to solve problems. This is a difficult distinction for us to grasp, because the western mind—and perhaps the American mind in particular—has been trained to equate success with victory, to equate doing well with beating someone. M. F. Ashley Montagu[18] feels that an oversimplification and misinterpretation of Darwin's theory has provided the average man with the mistaken idea that conflict is necessarily the law of life. Ashley Montagu states that it was convenient, during the industrial revolution, for the top dogs, who were exploiting the workers, to justify their exploitation by talking about life being a struggle for survival, and about it's being natural for the fittest (and only the fittest) to survive. The danger, here, is that this kind of reasoning becomes a self-fulfilling prophecy and can cause us to ignore or play down the survival value of nonaggressive and noncompetitive behavior for man and other animals. For example, Peter Kropotkin[19] concluded in 1902 that cooperative behavior and mutual aid have great survival value for many forms of life. There is ample evidence to support this conclusion. The cooperative behavior of certain social insects, such as termites, ants, and bees, is well known. Perhaps not so well known is a form of behavior in the chimpanzee that can only be described as "altruistic." It goes something like this: Two chimpanzees are in adjoining cages. One chimp has food and the other doesn't. The foodless chimpanzee begins to beg. Reluctantly, the "wealthy" chimp hands over some of his food. In a sense, the very reluctance with which he does so makes the gift all the more significant. It indicates that he likes the food and would dearly enjoy keeping it for himself. Accordingly, it suggests that the urge to share may have deep roots, indeed.[20] But Kropotkin's work has not been given much attention—indeed, it has been largely ignored, perhaps because it did not fit in with the temper of the times or with the needs of those who were profiting from the industrial revolution.

Let us look at our own society. As a culture, we Americans seem to thrive on competition; we reward winners and turn away from losers. For two centuries, our educational system has been based upon competitiveness and the laws of survival. With very few exceptions, we do not teach our kids to love learning—we teach them to strive for high grades. When sportswriter Grantland Rice said that what's important is not whether you win or lose, but how you play the game, he was not *describing* the dominant theme in American life, he was *prescribing* a cure for our over-concern with winning. From the Little League ball player who bursts into tears after his team loses, to the college students in the football stadium chanting "We're number one!"; from Lyndon Johnson, whose judgment was almost certainly distorted by his oft-stated desire not to be the first American President to lose a war, to the third-grader who despises his classmate for a

superior performance on an arithmetic test; we manifest a stagger-
ing cultural obsession with victory. Vince Lombardi, a very successful professional football coach, may have summed it all up with the
simple statement "Winning isn't everything, it's the *only* thing."
What is frightening about the acceptance of this philosophy is that it
implies that the goal of victory justifies whatever means we use to
win, even if it's only a football game—which, after all, was first
conceived as a recreational activity. An interesting and appalling
footnote to Lombardi's statement involves the manner in which the
residents of Green Bay, Wisconsin, treated his successor, Dan
Devine when, as coach of the Green Bay Packers in 1974, he had the
misfortune to lead that team to a losing season. As a result, he was the
target of physical threats, his family was insulted, his dog was shot in
front of his house, people made obscene phone calls in the middle of
the night, and false rumors spread that his daughters were the town
sluts and that his wife was an alcoholic.[21]

It is certainly true that, in the early history of man's evolution, a
great deal of aggressive behavior was adaptive. But as we look about
and see a world full of strife, of international and interracial hatred
and distrust, of senseless slaughter and political assassination, we feel
justified in questioning the survival value of this behavior. The biol-
ogist Loren Eisley paid tribute to our ancient ancestors, but warned
against imitating them, when he wrote: "The need is now for a
gentler, a more tolerant people than those who won for us against the
ice, the tiger, and the bear."[22]

Catharsis. There is another sense in which it sometimes has been
argued that aggressiveness serves a useful and perhaps a necessary
function. I refer here to the psychoanalytic position. Specifically, as
mentioned earlier, Freud believed that, unless people are allowed to
express themselves aggressively, the aggressive energy would be
dammed up and would eventually explode, either in the form of
extreme violence or in mental illness. Is there any evidence to support
this contention? The evidence, such as it is, suggests that *conflict about
aggression* can lead to a state of high emotional tension in humans.
This has led some investigators to the faulty conclusion that the
inhibition of an aggressive response in humans produces either serious

symptoms or intensely aggressive behavior. But there is no direct evidence for this conclusion.

"But, still," one might ask, "is the expression of aggression beneficial?" There are at least three ways in which aggressive energy can be discharged: (1) by expending it in the form of physical activity, such as games, running, jumping, punching a bag, and so on; (2) by engaging in a nondestructive form of fantasy aggression—like dreaming about hitting someone, or writing a violent story; and (3) by engaging in direct aggression—lashing out at someone, hurting him, getting him into trouble, saying nasty things about him, and the like.

Let us take the first one—engaging in socially acceptable aggressive behavior. There is widespread belief that this procedure works, and it is amply promoted by psychoanalytically oriented therapists. For example, the distinguished psychiatrist William Menninger has asserted that "competitive games provide an unusually satisfactory outlet for the instinctive aggressive drive."[23] It would seem reasonable to ask if there is any evidence that competitive games reduce aggressiveness. In his careful analysis of the existing data, Berkowitz[24] could find no simple, unequivocal findings to support the contention that intense physical activity reduces aggressiveness. Similarly, in an exhaustive study of college athletes, Warren Johnson[25] found no consistent evidence to support the notion of catharsis. He concluded that, not only is it absurd to argue that wars have been won on the playing fields of Eton, it is even more absurd to hope that we can prevent them there. This is not to say that people do not get pleasure out of these games. They do. But engaging in these games does not decrease aggressiveness.

Let us look at the second form of aggression—fantasy. There is some evidence that engaging in a fantasy of aggression can make people feel better, and can even result in a temporary reduction in aggressiveness. In an interesting experiment by Seymour Feshbach,[26] students were insulted by their instructor; then, half of the students were given the opportunity to write imaginative stories about aggression, while the other half were not given this opportunity. There was also a control group of students who were not insulted. Feshbach's results showed that, immediately afterward, the people who had been given the opportunity to write stories about aggression were slightly less aggressive than were those who were not given this opportunity. It should be pointed out that both of these groups of insulted students were considerably more aggressive than a group of students who were not insulted at all. Thus, the utility of fantasy aggression was limited: it did not reduce a great deal of aggressive energy. It is also important to emphasize that, in fantasy aggression, no one actually gets hurt.

Let us now turn our attention to direct aggression: Does an overt act of aggression reduce the need for further aggression? It is tempting to think so. Most of us, when frustrated or angry have experienced something akin to a relief of tension when we've expressed that anger by yelling, cursing, or shouting epithets at someone. But does such behavior reduce aggressiveness? Under almost all conditions, the answer to this question is no. Indeed, the main thrust of the research on this issue indicates that an overt act of aggression against another person serves to *increase* the aggressor's negative feelings toward the target of the aggression and therefore *increases* the probability of future aggression against that person.

Why? As we have seen in the preceding chapter, when a person does harm to another person, it sets some cognitive processes in motion that are aimed at justifying that act of cruelty. Specifically, when a person hurts another person, he experiences cognitive dissonance. The cognition "I have hurt Sam" is dissonant with the cognition "I am a decent, reasonable, good person." A good way for me to reduce dissonance is to somehow convince myself that hurting Sam was not an indecent, unreasonable, bad thing to do. I can accomplish this by blinding myself to Sam's virtues and by emphasizing his faults; by convincing myself that Sam is an awful person who deserved to be hurt. This would especially hold if the target is an *innocent* victim of my aggression. Thus, in experiments by David Glass and by Keith E. Davis and Edward E. Jones[27] (discussed in the preceding chapter), the subject inflicted either psychological or physical pain on an innocent person who had done the subject no prior harm. The subjects then proceeded to derogate the victim, convincing themselves that he was not a very nice person and therefore that he deserved what he got. This reduces dissonance, all right,

and it also sets the stage for further aggression—once you've derogated a person, it makes it easier for you to hurt him in the future.

But what happens if the victim isn't so innocent? What happens if
he or she has done something to make you angry and, therefore, does
indeed deserve retaliation. Here the situation becomes more complex
and therefore more interesting. One of several experiments performed to test this issue was a brilliantly conceived doctoral dissertation by Michael Kahn.[28] In Kahn's experiment, a technician, taking
some physiological measurements from college students, made some
derogatory remarks about these students. In one experimental condition, the subjects were allowed to vent their hostility by expressing their feelings about the technician to his employer—an action
that looked as though it would get the technician into serious trouble,
perhaps even cost him his job. In another condition, they were not
provided with the opportunity to express any aggression against the
person who had aroused their anger. What would psychoanalytic
theory predict would occur? That's easy: the inhibited group would
experience tension, a good deal of anger, and hostile feelings toward
the technician, while the group that expressed their feelings would
feel relieved, relaxed, and not as hostile toward the technician. In
short, according to psychoanalytic theory, expressing hostility would
serve as a *catharsis*—that is, it would purge the insulted subjects of
their hostile feelings. Being a good Freudian, Kahn expected these
results. He was surprised and (to his credit) excited to find evidence
to the contrary. Specifically, those who were allowed to express their
aggression subsequently felt greater dislike and hostility for the
technician than did those who were inhibited from expressing their
aggression. In other words, expressing aggression did not inhibit the
tendency to aggress, it tended to increase it—even when the target
was not simply an innocent victim.

What Kahn's experiment illustrates is that, when a person is
made angry, he frequently engages in over-kill. In this case, costing
the technician his job is a serious over-kill compared to the harm that
the technician perpetrated. The over-kill produces dissonance in
much the same way that hurting an innocent person produces dissonance. That is, there is a discrepancy between what the person did
to you and the force of your retaliation. That discrepancy must be

justified—and just as in the "innocent victim" experiments, the justification takes the form of derogating the object of your wrath *after* you've hurt him.

But what happens if you can arrange it so that retaliation is not allowed to run roughshod? That is, what if the degree of retaliation is reasonably controlled in a way such that it is not wildly more intense than the action that precipitated it? In such a circumstance, I would predict that there would be little or no dissonance. "Sam has insulted me; I've paid him back; we're even. I have no need to retaliate further." This is what was found in an experiment by Anthony Doob and Larraine Wood.[29] As in Kahn's experiment, Doob and Wood arranged things so that their subjects were humiliated and annoyed by an accomplice. In one condition, they were given the opportunity to retaliate by administering a series of electric shocks to their tormentor. In this situation, once the score was evened, they had no further need to punish their tormentor. But those subjects who had not been given the opportunity to retaliate *did* choose to punish their tormentor subsequently. Thus, we have seen that retaliation can reduce the need for further aggression if something akin to equity has been restored. It is important to note that most situations in the real world are not as neat as the Doob and Wood situation where retaliation can be made functionally similar to the original act. In my opinion, the real world is usually closer to the situation in Michael Kahn's experiment: retaliation typically outstrips the original act by a great deal. For example, whatever the students at Kent State University might have been doing to the members of the Ohio National Guard (shouting obscenities, teasing, taunting), it hardly merited their being shot and killed. Moreover, most victims of massive aggression are totally innocent. In all of these situations, the opposite of catharsis takes place. Thus, once I have shot some dissenting students at Kent State, I will convince myself that they *really* deserved it, and I will hate dissenting students even more than I did before I shot them; once I have slaughtered some women and children at My Lai, I will be even more convinced that Orientals aren't really human than I was before I slaughtered them; once I have denied black people a decent education, I will become even more convinced that they are stupid and couldn't have profited from a good education to begin with. In most situations, violence does *not* reduce the tendency toward violence: violence breeds more violence.

It should be clear to the reader that there is an important difference between being angry and expressing that anger in a violent and destructive manner. To experience anger in appropriate circumstances is normal and harmless. Indeed, there is very little one can do to avoid anger. It is certainly possible to express that anger in a nonviolent manner, for example, by a forceful and simple statement: "I am very angry at you because of what you did." Indeed, such a statement in and of itself is a vehicle for self-assertion and probably serves to relieve tension and to make the angered person feel better. At the same time, because the target does not get hurt, such a response does not set in motion those cognitive processes that would lead the angered person to justify his or her behavior by putting down the target person. More will be said on this issue in Chapter 8.

Catharsis and Public Policy. What does all of this tell us about public policy? In spite of the evidence against the catharsis hypothesis, it still seems to be widely believed by most average people—including those people who make important decisions that affect all of us. Thus, it is frequently argued that playing football[30] or watching people getting murdered on the TV screen[31] serves a valuable function in draining off aggressive energy. As we have seen, neither seems to be true. Recall that Albert Bandura and his associates found consistent evidence to support the notion that children use adult aggressors as models for their own behavior. They beat the hell out of a "Bobo" doll after watching an adult hit the doll. This phenomenon is not limited to preschool children: several investigators have shown that seeing films of a vicious fight increased the aggressive behavior of a wide range of subjects, including juvenile delinquents, normal female adults, hospital attendants, and high-school boys.[32] Indeed, after surveying the evidence in their report to the Surgeon General, psychologists Robert Liebert and Robert Baron state that, of eighteen studies on this issue, sixteen support the notion that watching violence increases subsequent aggression among the observers.

The evidence suggests that violence on TV is potentially dangerous, in that it serves as a model for behavior—especially for children. And what do we see on TV? In the fall of 1969, George Gerbner and his associates conducted an exhaustive survey of television programming during prime time and on Saturday mornings. He found that violence prevailed in eight out of every ten plays. Moreover, the rate of violent episodes was eight per program hour. Cartoons—which are the favorite viewing matter of most young children—contain the most violence. Of the ninety-five cartoon plays analyzed in this study, only *one* did not contain violence.

Spokesmen for the major TV networks have attempted to shrug off the Bandura experiments because they do not involve aggression against people. After all, who cares about what a kid does to a "Bobo" doll? Recent experimental evidence demonstrates, however, that the effects of watching violence are *not* limited to walloping a "Bobo" doll: it induces kids to wallop each other as well. In one study, Liebert and Baron[33] exposed a group of subjects to a TV production of "The Untouchables," an extremely violent cops-and-robbers type of program. In a control condition, a similar group of children were exposed to a TV production of a highly action-oriented sporting event for the same length of time. The children were then allowed to play in another room with a group of other children. Those who had watched the violent TV program showed far more aggression against the other children than those who had watched the sporting event.

Finally, back in the real world, several studies show that those children who watch more aggressive programs on TV show more evidence of turning to aggressiveness as a solution to their problems.[34] It should be noted that these correlational studies are not conclusive by themselves—that is, they do not prove that watching violence on TV causes kids to choose aggressive solutions. It may be that kids who happen to like aggression (for some other reason) watch a lot of TV aggression and *also* choose aggressive ways to solve their problems. This is precisely why the evidence from controlled experiments is so important: in the Liebert and Baron study, we *know* that it was watching "The Untouchables," *and nothing else*, that produced the aggressive behavior in the kids—because a similar group of kids that watched a sports event behaved less aggressively than those who watched "The Untouchables."

In sum, there is fairly clear evidence that watching violent behavior on TV will increase the aggressive behavior of children. But children *do* tend to find such fair entertaining. Accordingly, because this kind of programming is probably a good way to sell "Barbie" and "Ken" dolls, the networks will not curtail it—unless there is a public outcry. In the face of mounting evidence from psychological laboratories that links viewing of aggressive behavior with performing aggressive behavior, the amount of violence on NBC *increased* between 1968 and 1969. Moreover, in 1975 it was estimated that, by age 15, the average child will have witnessed more than 15,000 killings on TV.

The effect of media violence or violent behavior may not be limited to young children. The following news story was distributed by the Associated Press on November 23, 1971:

> Witnesses say a gunman armed with two rifles and dressed in Army fatigues yelled and laughed hysterically as he moved through a paint brush factory on a fatal shooting spree. Five workers died. Three other persons, including the alleged assailant and a policeman, were wounded. [The alleged assailant] . . . fired about a dozen shots. They killed two men. . . . Still firing, the gunman returned to a storage room where police later found two other bodies. Another man shot in the shipping department died en route to a hospital. . . . Police, unable to arrive at a motive for the rampage, were exploring possible parallels to a recent "Hawaii Five-O" television segment involving a multiple slaying. . . . Many characteristics, including the assailant's garb, method of operation and a bag of candy found in his pocket, resembled the television program. . . . Receipts found for one rifle and ammunition were dated shortly after the broadcast.

And this was not an isolated incident. In 1975, a national magazine reported the following occurrences:

> In San Francisco, three teen-age girls lured two younger girls down a lonely path and sexually molested them. In Chicago, two boys attempted to extort $500 from a firm by means of a bomb threat. In Boston, a youthful gang set a woman on fire with gasoline. In all three cases police officials concluded that the crimes had been directly inspired by shows the adolescents had recently watched on prime-time television.[35]

It would appear that Oscar Wilde was correct when he said that life imitates art. But surely, those individuals who produce, package, and distribute violence on TV and in films are aware of these data. What are they doing about it? Very little. Most of these individuals simply view themselves as hard-working people who are merely responding to the needs and tastes of the public. For example, Samuel Arkoff, board chairman of American International Pictures (one of our leading manufacturers of violent films), said: "Maybe the need to view violence will someday be reduced to watching pro football."[36] Unfortunately, the data indicate that this need is being increased, not satiated, by people like Mr. Arkoff. How responsible are these people? "The effects on society?" asks Joe Wizan, another producer of violent films. "I don't give it a thought. Psychiatrists don't have the answers, so why should I?"[37]

Aggression to Attract Public Attention. There is still another function that violent aggression might serve. In a complex and apathetic society like ours, it might be the most dramatic way for an oppressed minority to attract the attention of the silent majority. No one can deny that the effects of the Watts and Detroit riots served to alert a large number of decent but apathetic people to the plight of black people in America, and no one can doubt that the bloodshed at the state prison at Attica, New York, has led to increased attempts at prison reform. Are such outcomes worth the dreadful price in human lives? I cannot answer that question. But, as a social psychologist, what I can say (again and again) is that violence almost never ends simply with a rectification of the conditions that brought it about. Violence breeds violence—not only in the simple sense of the victim striking back against his enemy, but also in the infinitely more complex and more insidious sense of the attacker seeking to justify his violence by exaggerating the evil that exists in his enemy and thereby increasing the probability that he will attack him again (and again, and again . . .). There never was a war to end all wars—quite the contrary: bellicose behavior strengthens bellicose attitudes, which increase the probability of bellicose behavior. We must search for alternative solutions. A milder form of instrumental aggression might serve to redress social ills without producing an irreconcilable cycle of conflict. The strike, the boycott, the nonviolent sit-in have all been used effectively in this decade to awaken this nation to real griev- ances. Accordingly, I would echo Loren Eisley's call for a gentler people and for a people more tolerant of differences between one another—but not a people tolerant of injustice: a people who will love and trust one another, but who will yell, scream, strike, boy- cott, march, sit-in (and even vote) to eliminate injustice and cruelty. Again, as we have seen in countless experiments, violence cannot be turned on and off like a faucet. Research has shown over and over again that the only solution is to find ways of reducing violence *as we continue to reduce the injustice that produces the frustrations that fre- quently erupt in violent aggression.*

Toward the Reduction of Violence

If we assume, then, that the reduction of man's propensity toward aggressiveness is a worthwhile goal, how should we proceed? It is tempting to search for simple solutions. No less an expert than the president of the American Psychological Association has suggested, in his presidential address, that we develop an anticruelty drug to be fed to people (especially national leaders) as a way of reduc- ing violence on a universal scale.[38] The quest for such a solution is understandable and even somewhat touching; but it is extremely unlikely that a drug could be developed that would reduce cruelty without completely tranquilizing the motivational systems of its users. Chemicals cannot make the fine distinction that psychological processes can. Thus, we can conceive of a gentle, peace-loving man like Albert Einstein, who is simultaneously a fountainhead of creative energy, courage, and resourcefulness. Such men are produced by a subtle combination of physiological and psychological forces, of in- herited capacities and learned values. It is difficult to conceive of a chemical that could perform as subtly. Moreover, chemical control of human behavior has the quality of an Orwellian nightmare. Whom would we trust to use such methods?

There probably are no simple and foolproof solutions. But let's speculate about some complex and less foolproof possibilities based upon what we've learned so far.

Pure Reason. I am certain that we could construct a logical, reasonable set of arguments depicting the dangers of aggression and the misery produced (not only in victims, but in aggressors) by aggressive acts. I'm even fairly certain that we could convince most people that the arguments were sound; clearly, most people would agree that war is hell and that violence in the streets is undesirable. But such arguments probably would not significantly curtail aggressive behavior, no matter how sound, no matter how convincing. The individual—even if he is convinced that aggression, in general, is undesirable—will behave aggressively, unless he firmly believes that aggressiveness is undesirable for him. As Aristotle observed more than 2000 years ago, many people cannot be persuaded by rational argument alone—especially when the issue concerns their own personal behavior: "For argument based on knowledge implies instruction, and there are people whom one cannot instruct."[39] Moreover, because the problem of the control of aggression is one that first occurs in early childhood—that is, at a time when the individual is too young to be reasoned with—logical arguments are of little value. It is for these reasons that social psychologists have searched for alternative techniques of persuasion. Many of these have been developed with young children in mind, but are adaptable to adults as well.

Punishment. To the average citizen, an obvious way of reducing aggression is to punish it. If one man robs, hits, or kills another, the simple solution is to put him in prison or, in extreme cases, to kill him. If a child aggresses against his parents, siblings, or peers, we can spank him, scream at him, remove his privileges, or make him feel guilty. The assumption here is that this punishment "will teach him a lesson," that he will "think twice" before he performs that activity again, and that the more severe the punishment, the better. But it is not that simple. Severe punishment has been shown to be effective temporarily, but, unless used with extreme caution, it can have the opposite effect in the long run. Observations of parents and children in the real world have demonstrated time and again that parents who use severe punishment tend to produce children who are extremely aggressive.[40] This aggressiveness usually takes place outside the home, where the child is distant from the punishing agent. But these naturalistic studies are inconclusive. They don't necessarily prove that punishment for aggression, in and of itself, produces aggressive children. Parents who resort to harsh punishment probably do a lot of other things as well—that is, they are probably harsh and aggressive people. Accordingly, it may be that their children are simply copying the general aggressive behavior of their parents. Indeed, it has been shown that, if children are physically punished by an adult who had previously treated them in a warm and nurturant manner, they tend to comply with the adult's wishes when the adult is absent from the scene. On the other hand, children who are physically punished by an impersonal, cold adult are far less likely to comply with the adult's wishes once the adult has left the room. Thus, there is some reason to believe that punishment can be useful if it is applied judiciously in the context of a warm relationship.

One other factor of great significance to the efficacy of punishment is its severity or restrictiveness. A severe or restrictive punishment can be extremely frustrating; because frustration is one of the primary causes of aggression, it would seem wise to avoid using frustrating tactics when trying to curb aggression. This point was demonstrated very nicely in a study by Robert Hamblin and his colleagues.[41] In this study, hyperaggressive boys were punished by their teacher by having privileges taken away from them. Specifically, the boys had earned some tokens that were exchangeable for a wide variety of fun things; but each time a boy aggressed, he was deprived of some of the tokens. During and after the application of this technique, the frequency of aggressive actions among these boys practically doubled. It is reasonable to assume that this was the result of an increase in frustration.

Severe punishment frequently results in compliance, but it rarely produces internalization. In order to establish long term nonaggressive behavior patterns, it is important to induce a child to internalize a set of values that denigrates aggressiveness. In experiments discussed more fully in Chapter 4, both Merrill Carlsmith and I and Jonathan Freedman[42] demonstrated that, with young children, threats of mild punishments are far more effective than threats of severe punishments. Although these investigations dealt with toy preference in children, I would speculate that threats of mild punishment would curb aggression in the same way. Suppose a mother threatens to punish her child in order to induce him to refrain, momentarily, from aggressing against his little brother. If she is successful, the child will experience dissonance. The cognition "I like to wallop my little brother" is dissonant with the cognition "I am refraining from walloping my little brother." If he were severely threatened, he would have an abundantly good reason for refraining: he would be able to reduce dissonance by saying, "The reason that I'm not hitting my brother is that I'd get the daylights beaten out of me if I did—but I sure would like to." However, suppose his mother threatens to use a punishment that is mild rather than severe—a punishment just barely strong enough to get the child to stop his aggression. In this instance, when he asks himself why he's not hitting his infinitely hittable little brother at the moment, he can't use the threat as a way of reducing dissonance—that is, he can't easily convince himself that he would be walloped if he hit the kid, simply because it's not true—yet he must justify the fact that he's not hitting his brother. In other words, his external justification (in terms of the severity of the threat) is minimal; therefore, he must add his own justification in order to justify his restraint. He might, for example, convince himself that he no longer enjoys hitting his little brother. This would not only explain, justify, and make sensible his momentary peaceful behavior, but, more important, *it would decrease the probability of his hitting his little brother in the future.* In short, a counteraggressive value would have been internalized: he would have convinced *himself* that, for *him*, hitting someone is not a good or fun thing to do.

Although this process has been shown to work in several highly controlled laboratory experiments, it has one major practical drawback: before it can be applied, it is essential for the parent to know, for each child, exactly what sort of threat to use. It is important that it not be too severe, or else the child will have no need to seek additional justification for his lack of aggression. On the other hand, it must be severe enough for him to refrain from aggressing momentarily. This is crucial because if a parent administers a threat or a punishment that is not quite severe enough to get the child to desist momentarily, the entire process will backfire: the child will consciously decide not to stop his aggression, *even though* he knows that he will be punished for it. This child experiences dissonance, too: the cognition "I am aggressing" is dissonant with the congnition "I will be punished for it." How does the child reduce dissonance? He does so by convincing himself that it's worth it—that it's so enjoyable to hit his little brother that he's willing even to be punished for it. This reasoning serves to increase the long-term attractiveness of aggressive behavior. Thus, although threats of mild punishment can be an effective means of helping a child to become less aggressive, the technique cannot be used lightly or thoughtlessly. Careful consideration must be given to the precise level of intensity of the threat to be administered. This, of course, will vary somewhat from child to child. For some children, a stony stare from father may be too severe; for others, a hard spanking may not be severe enough. Again, the proper level can be found—but not easily. The important point is that a threat that is not severe enough to bring about a momentary change in behavior will actually increase the attractiveness of the unwanted behavior.

Punishment of Aggressive Models. A variation on the theme of punishment involves punishing someone else. Specifically, it has been argued that it might be possible to reduce aggression by presenting the child with the sight of an aggressive model who comes to a bad end. The implicit theory here is that the individual who is exposed to this sight will, in effect, be vicariously punished for his own aggression and, accordingly, will become less aggressive. It is probable that, in our nation's past, public hangings and floggings were arranged by people who held this theory. Does it work? Gross data from the real world does not support the theory. For example, according to the President's Commission on Law Enforcement,[43] the existence and use of the death penalty does not decrease the homicide rate. Moreover, on the level of casual data, the mass media frequently depict aggressive people as highly attractive (Bonnie and Clyde, for example, or Butch Cassidy and the Sundance Kid), even though they are eventually punished. This tends to induce individuals to identify with these violent characters.

The evidence from controlled experiments presents a more precise picture. Typically, in these experiments, children watch a film of an aggressive person who, subsequently, is either rewarded or punished for his aggressiveness. Later, the children are given an opportunity to be aggressive under circumstances similar to the ones shown in the film. The consistent finding is that the children who watched the film in which the aggressive person was punished display significantly less aggressive behavior than the children who watched the film of the person being rewarded.[44] As mentioned previously, there is also some evidence to indicate that the kids who watched the aggressive film character being punished displayed less aggressive behavior than did children who watched an aggressive film character who was neither rewarded nor punished. On the other hand—and this is most crucial to our discussion—seeing a model being punished for aggression did not decrease the general level of aggression below that of a group of children who were never exposed to an aggressive model. In other words, the major thrust of the research seems to indicate that seeing an aggressor rewarded will increase aggressive behavior in a child, and that seeing him punished will *not* increase the child's aggressive behavior (but it's not clear that seeing an aggressor punished will *decrease* his aggressive behavior). It might be just as effective not to expose the child to aggressive models at all. The implications of this research for the portrayal of violence in the mass media have already been discussed.

Rewarding Alternative Behavior Patterns. Another possibility that has been investigated is to ignore a child when he behaves aggressively and to reward him for nonaggressive behavior. This strategy is based, in part, upon the assumption that young children (and perhaps adults as well) frequently behave aggressively as a way of attracting attention. For them, being punished is preferable to being ignored. Paradoxically, then, punishing aggressive behavior may actually be interpreted as a reward—"Hey, look, gang! Mommy pays attention to me every time I slug my little brother. I think I'll do it again." This idea was tested in an experiment conducted at a nursery school by Paul Brown and Rogers Elliot.[45] The nursery-school teachers were instructed to ignore all aggressive behavior on the part of the kids. At the same time, the teachers were asked to be very attentive to the children, and especially to give them a lot of attention when they were doing things incompatible with aggression—such as playing in a friendly manner, sharing toys, and cooperating with others. After a few weeks, there was a noticeable decline in aggressive behavior. In a more elaborate experiment, Joel Davitz[46] demonstrated that frustration need not necessarily result in aggression—rather, it *can* lead to constructive behavior, if such behavior has been made attractive and appealing by prior training. In this study, children were allowed to play in groups of four. Some of these groups were rewarded for constructive behavior, while others were rewarded for aggressive or competitive behavior. Then the kids were deliberately frustrated. This was accomplished by building up the expectation that they would be shown a series of entertaining movies and be allowed to have fun. Indeed, the experimenters went so far as to begin to show a movie and to hand out candy bars to be eaten later. But then the frustration was administered: the experimenter abruptly terminated the movie at the point of highest interest and took the candy bars away. The children were then allowed to play freely. Those children who had been trained for constructive behavior displayed far more constructive activity and far less aggressive activity than those in the other group.

This research is encouraging indeed. It is unlikely that parents can ever succeed in building an environment for their children that is totally free of frustrations. Even were this possible, it would not be desirable, because the world outside is full of frustrating situations, and a child who is sheltered from frustration will experience greater pain and turmoil when he is finally exposed to frustrating events. But it *is* possible to train children to respond to frustrating events in ways that are constructive and satisfying, rather than in ways that are violent and destructive.

The Presence of Nonaggressive Models. An important curb to aggressive behavior is the clear indication that such behavior is inappropriate. And the most effective indicator is *social*—that is, the presence of other people in the same circumstances who are restrained and relatively unaggressive. For example, in a study by Robert Baron and Richard Kepner,[47] subjects were insulted by an individual and then observed that individual receiving electric shocks at the hands of a third person. The third person either delivered intense electric shocks or very mild electric shocks. There was also a control group in which subjects did not observe a model administering shocks. Subjects were then given the opportunity to shock their tormentor. Those who had witnessed a person delivering intense shocks delivered more intense shocks than those in the control condition; those who had witnessed a person delivering a mild shock delivered milder shocks than those in the control condition. Does this paradigm seem familiar? The reader can readily see that the expression of aggressive behavior, like the expression of *any* behavior, can be viewed as an act of conformity. Specifically, in an ambiguous situation, people look to other people for a definition of what is appropriate. Recall that in Chapter 2 we described the conditions under which you might belch at the dinner table of a Turkish dignitary. Here we are suggesting that, if you and your friends are frustrated or made angry and, all around you, people in your group are throwing snowballs at your tormentors, it will increase the probability that you will throw snowballs; if they are merely talking forcefully, it will increase the probability that you will talk forcefully; and, alas, if the people in your group are swinging clubs at the heads of their tormentors, it will increase the probability that you yourself will pick up a club and start swinging.

Building Empathy Toward Others. Seymour Feshbach notes that most people find it difficult to inflict pain purposely on another human being, unless they can find some way of dehumanizing their victim. "Thus the policeman becomes a 'pig,' and the student a 'hippie.' The Asiatic becomes a 'Gook,' 'yellow people are treacherous,' and besides, 'we all know that life is cheap in the orient.' "[48] As I have noted time and again in this book, the kind of rationalization that Feshbach points out not only makes it possible for us to aggress against another person, but it also guarantees that we will continue to aggress against him. Recall the example of the schoolteacher living in Kent, Ohio, who, after the killing of four Kent State students by Ohio National Guardsmen, told author James Michener[49] that anyone who walks on the street barefoot deserves to die. This kind of statement is understandable only if we assume that it was made by someone who had succeeded in dehumanizing the victims of this tragedy. We can deplore the process of dehumanization, but, at the same time, an understanding of the process can help us to reverse it. Specifically, if it is true that most individuals must dehumanize their victims in order to commit an extreme act of aggression, then, by building empathy among people, aggressive acts will become more difficult to commit. Indeed, Norma and Seymour Feshbach[50] have demonstrated a negative correlation between empathy and aggressiveness in children: the more empathy a person has, the less he resorts to aggressive actions.

Exactly how empathy among people can be fostered is a complex problem. We are not quite ready to discuss it, at this point; but in Chapters 7 and 8, we will suggest how it might be nurtured. First, however, we must take a closer look at the other side of the coin: dehumanization; the kind of dehumanization that occurs in prejudice; the kind of dehumanization that not only hurts the victim, but hurts the oppressor as well. Read the first paragraph of the next chapter and you'll see what I mean.

6

Prejudice

A white policeman yelled, "Hey, boy! Come here!" Somewhat bothered, I retorted: "I'm no boy!" He then rushed at me, inflamed, and stood towering over me, snorting, "What d'ja say, boy?" Quickly he frisked me and demanded, "What's your name, boy?" Frightened, I replied, "Dr. Poussaint. I'm a physician." He angrily chuckled and hissed, "What's your first name, boy?" When I hesitated he assumed a threatening stance and clenched his fists. As my heart palpitated, I muttered in profound humiliation, "Alvin."

He continued his psychological brutality, bellowing, "Alvin, the next time I call you, you come right away, you hear? You hear?" I hesitated. "You hear me, boy?"[1]

Hollywood would have had the hero lash out at his oppressor and emerge victorious. But in the real world, Dr. Poussaint simply slunk away, humiliated—or, in his own words, "psychologically castrated." The feeling of helplessness and powerlessness that is the harvest of the oppressed almost inevitably leads to a diminution of self-esteem that begins even in early childhood. Many years ago, Kenneth and Mamie Clark[2] demonstrated that black children, some of whom were only three years old, were already convinced that being black was not a good thing—they rejected black dolls, feeling that white dolls were prettier and generally superior. This experiment suggests that educational facilities that are "separate but equal" are never equal because they imply to the minority child that he is being segregated because there is something wrong with him. Indeed, this experiment played a major role in the Supreme Court decision (*Brown* v. *Board of Education*) that declared segregated schools to be unconstitutional.

This diminution of self-esteem is not limited to blacks: it affects other oppressed groups as well. In a study similar to the Clark and Clark experiment, Philip Goldberg[3] demonstrated that women have been taught to consider themselves the intellectual inferiors of men. In his experiment, Goldberg asked a number of female college students to read several scholarly articles, and to evaluate them in terms of their competence, style, and so on. For some students, specific articles were signed by male authors (for example, John T. McKay); for others, the same articles were signed by female authors (for example, Joan T. McKay). The female students rated the articles much higher if they were "written" by a male author than if they were "written" by a female author. In other words, these women had "learned their place"—they regarded output of other females as necessarily inferior to that of males, just as the black youngsters learned to regard black dolls as inferior to white dolls. This is the legacy of a prejudiced society.

Stereotypes and Attributions

Social scientists have defined "prejudice" in a variety of ways. Technically, there are positive and negative prejudices; I can be prejudiced against modern artists or prejudiced in favor of modern artists. This means that, before I am introduced to Sam Smear (who I've been told is a modern artist), I will be inclined to like or dislike him—and I will be inclined to expect to see certain characteristics in him. Thus, if I associate the concept "modern artist" with effeminate behavior, I would be filled with shock and disbelief if Sam Smear were to swagger through the door looking for all the world like the middle linebacker for the Green Bay Packers. If I associate the concept "modern artist" with a radical-liberal political view, I would be astonished if Sam Smear were wearing a William Buckley political button.

In this chapter, we will not be discussing situations that concern prejudice "in favor of" people; accordingly the working definition of prejudice that we will employ will be limited to negative attitudes. We will define prejudice as a hostile or negative attitude toward a distinguishable group based on generalizations derived from faulty or incomplete information. For example, when we say that an individual is prejudiced against blacks, we mean that he is oriented toward behaving with hostility against blacks; he feels that, with perhaps one or two exceptions, all blacks are pretty much the same; the characteristics he assigns to blacks are either totally inaccurate or, at best, based upon a germ of truth that he zealously applies to the group as a whole.

The generalization of characteristics or motives to a group of people is called "stereotyping." To stereotype is to assign identical characteristics to any person in a group, regardless of the actual variation among members of that group. Thus, to believe that blacks are full of a natural sense of rhythm, or that Jews are materialistic, is to assume that virtually all blacks are rhythmic, or that virtually all Jews go around gathering possessions. Stereotyping is not necessarily an intentional act of abusiveness, however: it is frequently merely a way of simplifying our view of the world, and we all do it to some extent. Most of us have a specific picture in our mind when we hear the words "Irish priest" or "New York cab driver" or "Italian barber." To the extent that the stereotype is based on experience and is at all accurate, it is an adaptive, short-hand way of dealing with the world. On the other hand, if it blinds us to individual differences within a class of people, it is maladaptive and potentially dangerous. Moreover, most stereotypes are not based upon valid experience, but are based on hearsay or images concocted by the mass media, or are generated within our heads as ways of justifying our own prejudices and cruelty.

Like the self-fulfilling prophecy discussed earlier in this book, it is helpful to think of blacks or Chicanos as stupid, if it justifies our depriving them of an education, and it is helpful to think of women as being biologically predisposed toward domestic drudgery, if we want to keep them tied to the vacuum cleaner. In such cases, stereotyping is, indeed, abusive. It should be plain, moreover, that stereotyping can be painful to the target, even if the stereotype would seem to be neutral or positive. For example, it is not necessarily negative to attribute "ambitiousness" to Jews or "a natural sense of rhythm" to blacks; but it is abusive, if only because it robs the individual Jew or black person of his right to be treated as an individual with his own individual traits, be they positive or negative.

A special case of stereotyping is attribution. When an event occurs, there is a tendency among individuals to try to attribute a cause to that event. Specifically, if a person performs an action, observers will make inferences about what caused that behavior. Such causal inferences are called *attributions*. For example, if the tight end on your favorite football team drops an easy pass, there are many possible explanations: perhaps the sun got in his eyes; maybe he was up late the night before drinking with his friends; perhaps he was distracted by worry over the ill health of his child; maybe he dropped it on purpose because he bet on the other team; maybe he "heard footsteps"; or, perhaps he just happens to be an untalented player. Note that each of the above attributions about the cause of the tight end's bobble has a very different set of ramifications. You'd feel differently about the person if he were worried about his child's illness than if he had bet on the other team.

This need to find a cause for another person's behavior is part of a human tendency to go beyond the information given. It is often functional. For example, suppose you have just moved into a strange town where you have no friends and you are feeling very lonely. There is a knock on the door and it is Joe, a neighbor who shakes your hand and welcomes you to the neighborhood. You invite him in. He stays for about twenty minutes, during which time you and he have an interesting conversation. You feel really good about the possibility of having discovered a new friend. As he gets up to leave, he says, "Oh by the way, if you ever need some insurance, I happen to be in the business and I'd be happy to discuss it with you," and he leaves his card. Is he your friend who happens to be selling insurance or is he an insurance salesman who is pretending to be your friend in order to sell you insurance? It is important to know, because you must decide whether or not to pursue a relationship with him. To repeat, in making attributions, the individual must go beyond the information given. We do not *know* the reason why the tight end dropped the pass. We are guessing. Thus, the attributor's causal interpretations may be accurate or erroneous, functional or dysfunctional.

In recent years, the phenomenon of attribution has been explored in a systematic manner by a number of investigators,[4] and their major findings have been loosely organized into a theory. Attribution theory deals with the rules that most people use in attempting to infer the causes of the behavior they observe. The theory also deals with the different kinds of situations that produce different kinds of attributions. There is a stock joke (that predates attribution theory) about a Protestant and a Catholic who happen to notice a priest entering a brothel. The Protestant clucks his tongue and smiles smugly as he reflects on the hypocrisy of the Catholic Church. The Catholic beams proudly as he reflects on the fact that, when a member of *his* church is dying, even in a brothel, he is entitled to the Holy Sacrament, and a priest will enter the brothel to administer it. What the joke illustrates, of course, is that people make attributions that are consistent with their beliefs or prejudices. If Mr. Bigot sees a well-dressed, white, Anglo-Saxon Protestant sitting on a park bench sunning himself at three o'clock on a Wednesday afternoon, he thinks nothing of it. If he sees a well-dressed black man doing the same thing, he is liable to leap to the conclusion that the person is unemployed—and he becomes infuriated, because he assumes that his hard-earned taxes are paying that shiftless good-for-nothing enough in welfare subsidies to keep him in good clothes. If Mr. Bigot passes Mr. Anglo's house and notices that a trash can is overturned and some garbage is strewn about, he is apt to conclude that a stray dog has been searching for food. If he passes Mr. Garcia's house and notices the same thing, he is inclined to become annoyed, and to assert that "those people live like pigs." Not only does prejudice influence his attributions and conclusions, his erroneous conclusions justify and intensify his negative feelings. Thus, the entire attribution process can spiral. Prejudice causes particular kinds of negative attributions or stereotypes that can, in turn, intensify the prejudice.

The attribution process has been demonstrated most clearly in recent research on sex roles. For example, let's look at a well-controlled experiment by Shirley Feldman-Summers and Sara Kiesler.[5] When confronted with the phenomenon of a highly successful female physician, male undergraduates perceived her as being less competent and having had an easier path toward success than a successful male physician. Female undergraduates saw things a little differently. They did not see either the male physician or the female physician as being less competent, but they saw the male as having had an easier time of it. Both males and females attributed higher motivation to the female physician. It should be noted that attributing a high degree of motivation to a woman can be one way of implying that she has less actual skill than her male counterpart. This possibility comes into focus when we examine a similar study by Kay Deaux and Tim Emswiller[6] in which they showed that, if the sex role stereotype is strong enough, even members of the stereotyped group tend to buy it. Specifically, male and female students were confronted with a highly successful performance by a fellow student on a complex perceptual task, and were asked to account for it. When it was a male who had succeeded, both male and female students attributed his success to his ability; when it was a female who succeeded, both male and female students attributed her success to *luck*. Interestingly enough, this tendency that women have to downplay the ability factor in a woman's success begins early in life and *even applies to self-attributions*. In a recent study, John Nicholls[7] found that, while fourth-grade boys attributed their own successful outcome on a difficult intellectual task to their ability, girls tended to derogate their own successful performance. Moreover, he also found that, while boys had learned to protect their egos by attributing their own failures to bad luck, girls took more of the blame for failures on themselves. Putting all of this research together, it appears that the stereotype of the incompetent woman is so strong in our society that a highly successful woman is seen by others, *and by herself*, either as a rare person with an extraordinary high degree of motivation or as simply lucky. More will be said on the issue of the female sex role in a moment.

In his classic book *The Nature of Prejudice*, the late Gordon Allport reported the following dialogue:

> *Mr. X:* The trouble with the Jews is that they only take care of their own group.
>
> *Mr. Y:* But the record of the Community Chest campaign shows that they gave more generously, in proportion to their numbers, to the general charities of the community, than do non-Jews.
>
> *Mr. X:* That shows they are always trying to buy favor and intrude into Christian affairs. They think of nothing but money; that is why there are so many Jewish bankers.
>
> *Mr. Y:* But a recent study shows that the percentage of Jews in the banking business is negligible, far smaller than the percentage of non-Jews.
>
> *Mr. X:* That's just it; they don't go in for respectable business; they are only in the movie business or run night clubs.[8]

This dialogue illustrates the insidious nature of prejudice far better than a mountain of definitions. In effect, the prejudiced Mr. X is saying "Don't trouble me with facts, my mind is made up." He makes no attempt to dispute the data as presented by Mr. Y. He either proceeds to distort the facts in order to make them support his hatred of Jews, or he bounces off them, undaunted, to a new area of attack. A deeply prejudiced person is virtually immune to information. It is reasonably safe to assume that all of us are prejudiced—whether it is against an ethnic, national, or racial group, against specific geographical areas as places to live, or against certain kinds of food. Let's take food as an example: In this culture, we tend not to eat insects. Suppose someone (like Mr. Y) were to tell you that caterpillars, grasshoppers, or ants were a great source of protein and, when carefully prepared, were extremely tasty. Would that convince you to eat them? Probably not. Like Mr. X, you'd probably find some other reason for your prejudice, such as the fact that insects are ugly. After all, in this culture, we eat only aesthetically beautiful creatures—like lobsters!

Gordon Allport wrote his book in 1954; the dialogue between

Mr. X and Mr. Y might seem somewhat dated to a reader in the 1970s. Do people really think that way? Is there anyone so simple-minded as to believe the old inaccurate stereotypes about Jewish bankers? I'm afraid so. In 1974, the most powerful military officer in the United States, General George S. Brown, Chairman of the Joint Chiefs of Staff, in a public speech referring to "Jewish influence in Congress," said, ". . . it is so strong you wouldn't believe, now. . . . They own, you know, the banks in this country, the newspapers. Just look at where the Jewish money is."⁹ Not all prejudiced think-ing is as obvious as that of Allport's Mr. X or as blatantly misinformed as General Brown's statement about Jewish bankers. Many indi-viduals who regard themselves as fair-minded, decent people are capable of a more subtle form of prejudice. For the relatively secure member of the dominant majority, it is sometimes difficult to em-pathize with the plight of the victim of prejudice. He may *sympathize*, and wish that it weren't so; occasionally, however, a little hint of self-righteousness may creep into his attitude, a slight tendency to lay part of the blame on the victim. This may take the form of the "well-deserved reputation." It goes something like this: "If the Jews have been victimized throughout their history, they must have been doing *something* wrong." Or "If those people don't *want* to get into trouble, why don't they just . . . " (stay out of the headlines; keep their mouths shut; don't go where they're not wanted; or whatever). Such a suggestion constitutes a demand that the outgroup conform to standards that are more stringent than those that are set for the majority.

Ironically, this tendency to blame the victim for his victimization is motivated by a desire to see the world as a just place. As Melvin Lerner and his colleagues have shown,¹⁰ people tend to assign re-sponsibility for any inequitable outcome that is otherwise difficult to account for. For example, if two people work equally hard on the same task, and, by a flip of a coin, one receives a sizable reward and the other receives nothing, observers show a strong tendency to rate the unlucky person as having worked less hard. Apparently, people find it scary to think about living in a world where hard workers can get no pay—therefore, they decide that the unpaid worker must not have worked very hard, even though they saw that the reward was determined by a mere flip of a coin. By the same token, if six million

Jews get butchered for no apparent reason, it is somehow comforting to believe that they must have done something to deserve it.*

Confessions of a Male Chauvinist

About 50 years ago, Karl Pearson, a distinguished British scientist and mathematician concluded his study on ethnic differences by stating: "Taken on the average and regarding both sexes, this alien Jewish population is somewhat inferior physically and mentally to the native (British) population."[11] On the basis of his findings, Pearson argued against allowing the immigration of East European Jews into Great Britain. Most liberal-minded scientists are now sophisticated enough to demand more valid data than those collected by Pearson. For example, we are sophisticated enough to know that standard IQ tests are prejudiced instruments that unintentionally discriminate in favor of white, middle-class suburbanites by stating their examples in terms and phrases that are more familiar to children reared in the suburbs than to children reared in the ghetto or on the farm. Thus, before we conclude that it was stupidity that caused a black person, a Chicano, or the resident of a rural community to do poorly on an IQ test, we demand to know whether or not the IQ test was culture-free. But we are not sophisticated enough to escape completely from certain kinds of prejudice. Let me state a personal example. In the first edition of this book, while discussing individual differences in persuasibility, I made the point that women seem more persuasible than men. This statement was based upon a well-known experiment by Irving Janis and Peter Field. A close inspection of this experiment, however, suggests that it was weighted unintentionally against women in much the same way that IQ tests are weighted against rural and ghetto residents. The topics of the persuasive arguments included civil defense, cancer research, von Hindenberg, and so on—topics that the culture trains men and boys to take a greater interest in than

---

*The astute reader may have noticed that this is a milder form of our tendency to derogate a person that *we* have victimized. In Chapter 4, we saw that, if X hurts Y, he tends to derogate Y, turn him into a non-person, and hurt him again. Now we see that, if X notices that Y has gotten the short end of the stick, he somehow feels that Y must have done something to deserve it.

women and girls. Thus, the results may simply indicate that people are more persuasible on topics that they don't care about or don't know about. If someone were to perform a similar experiment using topics that women were brought up to value, the chances are that men would end up looking more persuasible than women. Of course, the mere fact that women are raised not to be interested in certain "male only" topics is in and of itself a tragic consequence of sex discrimination.

Five years ago, when I was writing the first edition of this book, I was unaware of the possible artifact in the experiment by Janis and Field until it was called to my attention (gently but firmly) by a friend who happens to be both a woman and a social psychologist. The lesson to be gained from this example is a clear one: When we are reared in a prejudiced society, we often accept those prejudices uncritically. It is easy to believe that women are gullible because that is the stereotype that is held by the society. Thus, we tend not to look at supporting scientific data critically and, without realizing it, we use the data as scientific support for our own prejudice.

Carrying this one step further, Daryl and Sandra Bem[12] suggest that the prejudice against women that exists in our society is an example of a *nonconscious ideology*—that is, a set of beliefs that we accept implicitly but of which we are unaware because we cannot even conceive of alternative conceptions of the world. In this culture, for example, we are socialized in such a way that it is difficult for us to imagine a woman going out to work as a physicist or a crane operator while her husband stays home vacuuming the floor and taking care of the kids. If we were to hear of such a situation, we would leap to the conclusion that something was wrong with the husband. Why? Because such an arrangement is not held to be a real option in our society. Much as a fish is unaware that his environment is wet, we don't even notice the existence of this ideology because it is so totally prevalent.

Recall the example in Chapter 1 in which little Mary received a Suzie Homemaker set ("complete with her own little oven") for her birthday: By the time she was nine, she was conditioned to know that her place was in the kitchen. This was done so thoroughly that her father was convinced that "housewifery" was genetic in origin. This is no mere fantasy. Studies by Ruth Hartley[13] indicate that, by age *five*, children have already developed clearly defined notions of what constitutes appropriate behavior for women and men. This non-conscious ideology can have vast consequences for society. For example, Jean Lipman-Blumen[14] reports that the vast majority of women who, in early childhood, acquired a traditional view of their sex role (that is, "a woman's place is in the home") opt not to seek advanced education; on the other hand, those women who had acquired a more egalitarian view of sex roles show a much stronger tendency to aspire to advanced education.

The example of my own nonconscious chauvanism is instructive. To me, it indicates that current trends in the direction of the raising of women's consciousness are not only benefitting women, but they are benefitting men as well. To use Lipman-Blumen's example, my guess is that the next 10 years will show an increase in the extent to which women seek advanced education as their view of their sex role begins to change. In addition, to the extent that my friends are able to help me see my own blind spots, they help me to become a better scientist and a less biased person.

Let us broaden this example. In recent years, our society has become increasingly aware of the discrimination and stereotyping that occurs as a result of differential sex roles. The notion of sex roles, or roles appropriate to sex identity, is quite useful in understanding the pressures that society places on both men and women. The most striking feature differentiating male and female sex roles is the great diversity of acceptable role behaviors available to men and the lack of such choice and diversity for women. Traditionally, femininity has consistently been correlated with high anxiety, low self-esteem, and low social acceptance.[15] The female role has been centered around the home, children, and marriage, with limited access to higher status or to more differentiated jobs.

The sex-role socialization process has led us to regard the roles of females and males as characteristically rigid and limiting. Sex-role researchers and feminists alike find that such traditional labeling is antithetical to a rich and full growth process. Sandra Bem advocates that people reduce this sex-role stereotyping by becoming more "androgynous": "That is, they should be encouraged to be both instrumental and expressive, both assertive and yielding, both masculine and feminine—depending upon the situational appropriateness of these various behaviors."[16]

Women, like the members of many minorities, are rewarded for actions that support the notion that they are inferior, passive, dependent, and neurotic. Consequently, the self-fulfilling prophecy is in effect: if a woman were to attempt to view herself as different from the socially accepted norm, she would inevitably experience some discomfort by dint of the fact that her behavior would be discrepant from the self-concept that she had been developing since childhood. For example, as mentioned earlier, if a crane operator and a housewife were to change roles, it is clear that much dissonance would be aroused, especially when interacting with their peers. In this manner, a socially conditioned stereotype tends to be perpetuated. If a woman attempts to deviate from her rigid sex role by being assertive or by seeking an unconventional job, she is risking the loss of friendships and is encouraging even more prejudiced feelings in others. If individuals need to compare themselves to similar others, stepping out of an accepted role is less likely to occur, particularly if most women and minority members are insecure and have low self-esteem. Indeed, only the very secure might venture into unconventional roles.

Causes of Prejudice

It should be clear that prejudice is pervasive and that each of us pays a huge price for it. Now let's look at what causes prejudice. As we have seen, one determinant of prejudice in a person is a need for self-justification. In the last two chapters, for example, we have shown that, if we have done something cruel to a person or a group of people, we derogate that person or group in order to justify our cruelty. If we can convince ourselves that a group is unworthy, subhuman, stupid, or immoral, it helps *us* to keep from feeling immoral if we enslave them, deprive them of a decent education, or murder them. We can then continue to go to church and to feel like good Christians, because it isn't a fellow human that we've hurt. Indeed, if we're skillful enough, we can even convince ourselves that the barbaric slaying of old men, women, and children is a Christian virtue—as the crusaders did when, on their way to the holy land, they butchered European Jews in the name of the Prince of Peace. Again, as we have seen, this act of self-justification serves to intensify subsequent brutality.

Of course, there are other human needs in addition to self-justification. For example, there are status and power needs. Thus, an individual who is low on the socioeconomic hierarchy may need the presence of a downtrodden minority group in order to be able to feel superior to somebody. Several studies have shown that a good predictor of a person's degree of prejudice is whether or not his social status is low or declining. Regardless of whether it is prejudice against blacks[17] or against Jews,[18] if a person's social status is low or declining, he is apt to be more prejudiced than someone whose social status is high or rising. It has been found that people who are at or near the bottom in terms of education, income, and occupation are not only highest in their dislike of blacks, but they are also the ones most likely to resort to violence in order to prevent the desegregation of the schools.[19]

These findings raise some interesting questions. Are people of low socioeconomic and educational status more prejudiced because (1) they need someone to feel superior to, (2) they most keenly feel competition for jobs from minority group members, (3) they are more frustrated than most people and, therefore, more aggressive, or (4) their lack of education increases the probability of their taking a simplistic, stereotypic view of the world? It is difficult to disentangle these variables, but it appears to be true that each of these phenomena contributes to prejudice. Indeed, it should be clear that there is no single cause of prejudice. Prejudice is determined by a great many factors. Let's take a look at the major determinants of prejudice.

In this chapter, we will discuss four basic causes of prejudice: (1) economic and political competition or conflict, (2) displaced aggression, (3) personality needs, and (4) conformity to existing social norms. These four causes are not mutually exclusive—indeed, they may all operate at once—but it would be helpful to determine how important each cause is, because any action we are apt to recommend in an attempt to reduce prejudice will depend on what we believe to be the major cause of prejudice. Thus, for example, if I believe that bigotry is deeply ingrained in the human personality, I might throw my hands up in despair and conclude that, in the absence of deep psychotherapy, the majority of prejudiced people will always be prejudiced. This would lead me to scoff at attempts to reduce prejudice by reducing competitiveness or by attempting to counteract the pressures of conformity.

Economic and Political Competition. Prejudice can be considered to be the result of economic and political forces. According to this view, given that resources are limited, the dominant group might attempt to exploit or derogate a minority group in order to gain some material advantage. Prejudiced attitudes tend to increase when times are tense and there is a conflict over mutually exclusive goals. This is true whether the goals are economic, political, or ideological. Thus, prejudice has existed between Anglo and Mexican-American migrant workers as a function of a limited number of jobs, between Arabs and Israelis over disputed territory, and between Northerners and Southerners over the abolition of slavery. The economic advantages of discrimination are all too clear when one looks at the success certain craft unions have had, over the years, in denying membership to women and members of ethnic minorities, thus keeping them out of the relatively high-paying occupations they control. For example, in a recent study, it was found that only 2.7 percent of union-controlled apprenticeships were filled by blacks as of 1966—an increase of only 1 percent over the previous ten years. Moreover, in the mid-sixties, the U.S. Department of Labor surveyed four major cities in search of minority-group members serving as apprentices among union plumbers, steamfitters, sheetmetal workers, stone masons, lathers, painters, glaziers, and operating engineers. In the four cities, they failed to find a single black person thus employed. Clearly, prejudice pays off for some people.[20]

It has also been shown that discrimination, prejudice, and negative stereotyping increase sharply as competition for scarce jobs increases. Thus, in one of his classic early studies of prejudice in a small industrial town, John Dollard documented the fact that, although there was initially no discernible prejudice against Germans in the town, it came about as jobs became scarce:

Local whites largely drawn from the surrounding farms manifested considerable direct aggression toward the newcomers. Scornful and derogatory opinions were expressed about these Germans, and the native whites had a satisfying sense of superiority toward them. . . . The chief element in the permission to be aggressive against the Germans was rivalry for jobs and status in the local woodenware plants. The native whites felt definitely crowded for their jobs by the entering German groups and in case of bad times had a chance to blame the Germans who by their presence provided more competitors for the scarcer jobs. There seemed to be no traditional pattern of prejudice against Germans unless the skeletal suspicion of all out-groupers (always present) be invoked in this place.[21]

Similarly, Americans harbored little or no negative feeling toward the Chinese immigrants who were working on the construction of the transcontinental railroad during the middle of the nineteenth century. At that time, jobs were plentiful and the Chinese were performing an arduous job for very little pay. They were generally regarded as sober, industrious, and law-abiding. After the completion of the railroad, however, jobs became more scarce; moreover, when the Civil War ended, there was an influx of former soldiers into this already tight job market. This was immediately followed by a dramatic increase in negative attitudes toward the Chinese: the stereotype changed to "criminal," "conniving," "crafty," and "stupid." A recent poll conducted by the National Opinion Research Center indicates that this tendency is still with us. In 1971, most anti-black prejudice was found in groups that were just one rung above the blacks socioeconomically. Moreover, this tendency is most pronounced in situations in which the two groups were in close competition for jobs.[22]

These data appear to indicate that competition and conflict breed prejudice. At the same time, there is some ambiguity in interpreting the data, because, in some instances, the variables of competition are intertwined with such other variables as educational level and family background. In order to determine whether competition causes prejudice in and of itself, an experiment is needed. But how can we proceed? Well, if conflict and competition lead to prejudice, it should be possible to produce prejudice in the laboratory. This can be done by the simple device of (1) randomly assigning people of differing backgrounds to one of two groups, (2) making those groups distinguishable in some arbitrary way, (3) putting those groups into a situation in which they are in competition with each other, and (4) looking for evidence of prejudice. Such an experiment was conducted by Muzafer Sherif and his colleagues[23] in the natural environment of a Boy Scout camp. The subjects were normal, well-adjusted, twelve-year-old boys who were randomly assigned to one of two groups, the *Red Devils* and the *Bulldogs*. Within each group, the kids were taught to cooperate. This was done largely through arranging activities that made each group highly intradependent. For example, within each group, individuals cooperated in building a diving board for the swimming facility, preparing group meals, building a rope bridge, and so on.

After a strong feeling of cohesiveness developed within each group, the stage was set for the conflict. The researchers arranged this by setting up a series of competitive activities in which the two groups were pitted against each other in such games as football, baseball, and tug-of-war. In order to increase the tension, prizes were awarded to the winning team. This resulted in some hostility and ill will during the games. In addition, the investigators devised rather diabolical devices for putting the groups into situations specifically designed to promote conflict. In one such situation, a camp party was arranged. The investigators set it up so that the *Red Devils* were allowed to arrive a good deal earlier than the *Bulldogs*. In addition, the refreshments consisted of two vastly different kinds of food: about half of the food was fresh, appealing, and appetizing; the other half was squashed, ugly, and unappetizing. Perhaps because of the general competitiveness that already existed, the early arrivers confiscated most of the appealing refreshments, leaving only the less interesting, less appetizing, squashed, and damaged food for their adversaries. When the *Bulldogs* finally arrived and saw how they had been taken advantage of, they were understandably annoyed—so annoyed that they began to call the exploitive group rather uncomplimentary names. Because the *Red Devils* believed that they deserved what they got (first come, first served), they resented this treatment and re-sponded in kind. Name-calling escalated into food-throwing and, within a very short time, a full-scale riot was in progress.

Following this incident, competitive games were eliminated and a great deal of social contact was initiated. Once hostility had been aroused, however, simply eliminating the competition did not eliminate the hostility. Indeed, hostility continued to escalate, even when the two groups were engaged in such benign activities as sitting around watching movies. Eventually, the investigators succeeded in reducing the hostility. Exactly how this was accomplished will be discussed later in this chapter.

The "Scapegoat" Theory of Prejudice. In the preceding chapter, we made the point that aggression is caused, in part, by frustration and such other unpleasant or aversive situations as pain or boredom. In that chapter, we saw that there is a strong tendency for a frustrated individual to lash out at the cause of his frustration. Frequently, however, the cause of a person's frustration is either too big or too vague for direct retaliation. For example, if a six-year-old child is humiliated by his teacher, how can he fight back? The teacher has too much power. But this frustration may increase the probability of his aggressing against a less powerful bystander—even if the bystander had nothing to do with his pain. By the same token, if there is mass unemployment, who is the frustrated, unemployed worker going to strike out against—the economic system? The system is much too big and much too vague. It would be more convenient if he could find something or someone less vague and more concrete to blame for his unemployment. The President? He's concrete, all right, but also much too powerful to strike at with impunity.

The ancient Hebrews had a custom that is noteworthy in this context. During the days of atonement, a priest placed his hands on the head of a goat while reciting the sins of the people. This symbolically transferred the sin and evil from the people to the goat. The goat was then allowed to escape into the wilderness, thus clearing the community of sin. The animal was called a scapegoat. In modern times the term "scapegoat" has been used to describe a relatively powerless innocent who is made to take the blame for something that is not his fault. Unfortunately, he is not allowed to escape into the wilderness, but is usually subjected to cruelty or even death. Thus, if an individual is unemployed, or if inflation has depleted his savings, he can't very easily beat up on the economic system, but he can find a scapegoat. In Nazi Germany, it was the Jews; in the rural South, it was black people. Several years ago, Carl Hovland and Robert Sears[24] found that, in the period between 1882 and 1930, they could predict the number of lynchings in the South in a given year from a knowledge of the price of cotton during that year. As the price of cotton dropped, the number of lynchings increased. In short, as people experienced an economic depression, they probably experienced a great many frustrations. These frustrations apparently resulted in an increase in lynchings and other crimes of violence.

It is difficult to be certain whether these lynchings were motivated by the psychological aspects of frustration or whether they were partly due to the kind of economic competition that we discussed earlier. As for the persecution of the Jews in Nazi Germany, the zeal with which the Nazis carried out their attempt to erase all members of the Jewish ethnic group (regardless of economic status) strongly suggests that the phenomenon was not exclusively economic or political, but was (at least in part) psychological.[25] Solider evidence comes from a well-controlled experiment by Neal Miller and Richard Bugelski.[26] Individuals were asked to state their feelings about various minority groups. Some of the subjects were then frustrated by being deprived of an opportunity to attend a film, and were given an arduous and difficult series of tests instead. They were then asked to restate their feelings about the minority groups. These subjects showed some evidence of increased prejudicial responses following the frustrating experience. A control group that did not go through the frustrating experience did not undergo any change in prejudice.

Additional research has helped to pin down the phenomenon even more precisely. In one experiment, Donald Weatherley[27] subjected college students to a great deal of frustration. Some of these students were highly anti-Semitic; others were not. The subjects were then asked to write stories based upon pictures that they were shown. For some of the subjects, the characters in these pictures were assigned Jewish names; for the others, they were not. There were two major findings: (1) after being frustrated, anti-Semitic subjects wrote stories that directed more aggression toward the Jewish characters than did people who were not anti-Semitic; and (2) there was no difference between the anti-Semitic students and the others when the characters they were writing about were not identified as Jewish. In short, frustration leads to a specific aggression—aggression against someone you hate.

The general picture of scapegoating that emerges is that individuals tend to displace aggression onto groups that are visible, that are relatively powerless, and that are disliked to begin with. Moreover, the form the aggressiveness takes depends on what is allowed or approved by the ingroup in question: lynchings and pogroms are not frequent occurrences, unless they are deemed appropriate by the dominant culture or subculture.

The Prejudiced Personality. As we have seen, the displacement of aggression onto scapegoats may be a human tendency, but it is not true that all people do it to a like degree. We have already identified socioeconomic status as a cause of prejudice. Also, we have seen that people who dislike Jews are more apt to displace aggression onto them than are people who do not dislike Jews. We can now carry this one step further: There is some evidence to support the notion of individual differences in a general tendency to hate. In other words, there are people who are predisposed toward being prejudiced, not solely because of immediate external influences, but because of the kind of people that they are. Theodor Adorno and his associates[28] refer to these individuals as "authoritarian personalities." Basically, the authoritarian personality has the following characteristics: he tends to be rigid in his beliefs; he tends to possess "conventional" values; he is intolerant of weakness (in himself as well as in others); he tends to be highly punitive; he is suspicious; and he is respectful of authority to an unusual degree. The instrument developed to determine authoritarianism (called the F scale) measures the extent to which each person agrees or disagrees with such items as these:

1. Sex crimes such as rape and attacks on children deserve more than mere imprisonment; such criminals ought to publicly whipped, or worse.
2. Most people don't realize how much our lives are controlled by plots hatched in secret places.
3. Obedience and respect for authority are the most important virtues children should learn.

A high degree of agreement with such items indicates authoritarianism. The major finding is that people who are high on authoritarianism do not simply dislike Jews or dislike blacks, but, rather, they show a consistently high degree of prejudice against *all* minority groups.

Through an intensive clinical interview of people high and low on the *F* scale, Adorno and his colleagues have traced the development of this cluster of attitudes and values to early childhood experiences in families that are characterized by harsh and threatening parental discipline. Moreover, people high on the *F* scale tend to have parents who use love and its withdrawal as their major way of producing obedience. In general, the authoritarian personality, as a child, tends to be very insecure and highly dependent on his parents; he fears his parents and feels unconscious hostility against them. This combination sets the stage for the emergence of an adult with a high degree of anger, which, because of fear and insecurity, takes the form of displaced aggression against powerless groups, while the individual maintains an outward respect for authority.

Although research on the authoritarian personality has added to our understanding of the possible dynamics of prejudice, it should be noted that the bulk of the data are correlational: that is, we know only that two variables are related—we cannot be certain what causes what. Consider, for example, the correlation between a person's score on the *F* scale and the specific socialization practices he was subjected to as a child. Although it's true that adults who are authoritarian and highly prejudiced had parents who tended to be harsh and to use "conditional love" as a socialization technique, it is not necessarily true that this is what *caused* them to develop into prejudiced people. It turns out that the parents of these people tend, themselves, to be highly prejudiced against minority groups. Accordingly, it may be that the development of prejudice in some people may be due to conformity through the process of *identification*, as described in Chapter 2. That is, it may be true that a child consciously picks up his beliefs about minorities from his parents because he identifies with them. This is quite different from, and much simpler than, the explanation offered by Adorno and his colleagues, which is based on the child's unconscious hostility and repressed fear of his parents.

This is not to imply that, for some people, prejudice is not deeply rooted in unconscious childhood conflicts. Rather, it is to suggest that many people may have learned a wide array of prejudices on Mommy's or Daddy's knee. Moreover, some people may conform to prejudices that are limited and highly specific, depending upon the norms that exist in their subculture. Let's take a closer look at the phenomenon of prejudice as an act of conformity.

Prejudice through Conformity. It is frequently observed that there is more prejudice against blacks in the South than in the North. This often manifests itself in stronger attitudes against racial integration. For example, in 1942, only 4 percent of all Southerners were in favor of the desegregation of transportation facilities, while 56 percent of all Northerners were in favor of it.[29] Why? Was it because of economic competition? Probably not; there is more prejudice against blacks in those southern communities in which economic competition is low than in those northern communities in which economic competition is great. Are there relatively more authoritarian personalities in the South than in the North? No. Thomas Pettigrew[30] administered the *F* scale widely in the North and in the South, and found that the scores are about equal for Northerners and Southerners. In addition, although there is more prejudice against blacks in the South, there is *less* prejudice against Jews in the South than there is in the nation as a whole; the prejudiced personality should be prejudiced against everybody—the Southerner isn't.

How, then, do we account for the animosity toward blacks that exists in the South? It could be due to historical causes: the blacks were slaves, the Civil War was fought over the issue of slavery, and so on. This could have created the climate for greater prejudice. But what sustains this climate? One possible clue comes from the observation of some rather strange patterns of racial segregation in the South. One example, that of a group of coal miners in a small mining town in West Virginia, should suffice: the black miners and the white miners developed a pattern of living that consisted of total and complete integration while they were under the ground, and total and complete segregation while they were above the ground. How can we account for this inconsistency? If you truly hate someone, you want to keep away from him—why associate with him below the ground and not above the ground?

Pettigrew has suggested that the explanation for these phenomena is *conformity*. In this case, people are simply conforming to the norms that exist in their society (above the ground!). The historical events of the South set the stage for greater prejudice against blacks, but it is conformity that keeps it going. Indeed, Pettigrew believes that, although economic competition, frustration, and personality needs account for some prejudice, the greatest proportion of prejudiced behavior is a function of slavish conformity to social norms.

How can we be certain that conformity is responsible? One way is to determine the relation between a person's prejudice and his general pattern of conformity. For example, a study of interracial tension in South Africa[31] showed that those individuals who were most likely to conform to a great variety of social norms also showed a higher degree of prejudice against blacks. In other words, if conformists are more prejudiced, it suggests that prejudice may be just another thing to conform to. Another way to determine the role of conformity is to see what happens to a person's prejudice when he moves to a different area of the country. If conformity is a factor in prejudice, we would expect individuals to show dramatic increases in their prejudice when they move into areas in which the norm is more prejudicial, and to show dramatic decreases when they are affected by a less prejudicial norm. And that is what happens. In one study, Jeanne Watson[32] found that people who had recently moved to New York City and had come into direct contact with anti-Semitic people became more anti-Semitic themselves. In another study, Pettigrew found that, as Southerners entered the army and came into contact with a less discriminatory set of social norms, they became less prejudiced against blacks.

The pressure to conform can be relatively overt, as in the Asch experiment. On the other hand, conformity to a prejudicial norm might simply be due to the unavailability of accurate evidence and a preponderance of misleading information. This can lead people to adopt negative attitudes on the basis of hearsay. Examples of this kind of stereotyping behavior abound in the literature. For example, consider Christopher Marlowe's *The Jew of Malta* or William Shakespeare's *The Merchant of Venice*. Both of these works depict the Jew as a conniving, money-hungry, bloodthirsty, cringing coward. We might be tempted to conclude that Marlowe and Shakespeare had had some unfortunate experiences with unsavory Jews, which resulted in these bitter and unflattering portraits—except for one thing: the Jews had been expelled from England some 300 years before these works were written. Thus, it would seem that the only thing with which Marlowe and Shakespeare came into contact was a lingering stereotype. Unfortunately, their works not only reflected the stereotype, but undoubtedly contributed to it as well.

Bigoted attitudes can also be fostered intentionally by a bigoted society. For example, one investigator[33] interviewed white South Africans in an attempt to find reasons for their negative attitudes toward blacks. What he found was that the typical white South African was convinced that the great majority of crimes were committed by blacks. This was erroneous. How did such a misconception develop? The individuals reported that they saw a great many black convicts working in public places—they never saw any white convicts. Doesn't this prove that blacks are convicted of more crimes than whites? No. In this case, it was merely a reflection of the fact that the rules forbade white convicts from working in public places! In short, a society can *create* prejudiced beliefs by law or by custom. In our own society, until very recently, newspapers tended to identify the race of a criminal or suspect if he was nonwhite, but never bothered to mention the wrong-doer's race if he happened to be white. This has undoubtedly contributed to a distorted picture of the amount of crime committed by nonwhites. Again, until very recently, it was rare to see a black face on television in a nonstereotypic role or in a commercial. This created the illusion that blacks are inconsequential members of our society—people who don't use aspirin or shaving cream, who don't have real problems or real emotions. Moreover, if the participation of blacks is limited to stereotypic roles like the characters in "Amos 'n Andy" or the song-and-dance man on a variety show, this strengthens the stereotype that blacks are stupid, shiftless, lazy, and have a natural sense of rhythm. In the past several years, black athletes have been appearing on TV screens with greater frequency; I would guess that whites from rural northern towns who do not have much direct contact with blacks would be surprised to learn that there actually are blacks who are unable to run the 100-yard dash in less than 10 seconds!

Of course, the same problem affects the portrayal of women. When the media portray women through news reports, in documentaries, or in situation comedies, they are not, in general, seen as authority figures, intellectuals, or adventurous people. Instead, they are frequently viewed as simple-minded individuals who get turned on by such boring issues as which laundry detergent or toilet paper to buy. We tend to believe or accept things that we see with great frequency—unless there are powerful reasons against doing so. Moreover, it is very difficult for us to account for what is not represented. Thus, if we never see women in powerful roles, it is easy to conclude that they are incapable of using power effectively.

Stateways Can Change Folkways

In 1954, the United States Supreme Court declared that separate but equal schools were, by definition, unequal. In the words of Chief Justice Earl Warren, when black children are separated from white children on the basis of race alone, it "generates a feeling of inferiority as to their status in the community that may affect their hearts and minds in a way unlikely ever to be undone." Without our quite realizing it, this decision launched our nation into one of the most exciting, large-scale social experiments ever conducted.

In the aftermath of this historic decision, many people were opposed to integrating the schools on "humanitarian" grounds. They predicted a holocaust if the races were forced to mingle in schools. They argued that you cannot legislate morality—meaning that, although you can force people to attend the same school, you cannot force people to like and respect each other. This echoed the sentiments of the distinguished sociologist, William Graham Sumner, who, years earlier had stated that "stateways don't change folkways." They urged that desegregation be delayed until attitudes could be changed.

Social psychologists at that time, of course, believed that the way to change behavior is to change attitudes. Thus, if you can get bigoted adults to become less prejudiced against blacks, then they will not hesitate to allow their children to attend school with blacks. Although they should have known better, many social scientists were relatively confident that they could change bigoted attitudes by launching information campaigns. They took a "16-millimeter" approach to the reduction of prejudice: if prejudiced people believe that blacks are shiftless and lazy, then all you have to do is show them a *movie*—a movie depicting blacks as industrious, decent people. The idea is that you can combat misinformation with information. If Shakespeare believes that Jews are conniving bloodsuckers because he has been exposed to misinformation about Jews, tell him the truth, and his prejudice will fade away. If a white South African believes that blacks commit most of the crimes, show him the white convicts, and he'll change his beliefs. Unfortunately, it is not quite that simple. Whether prejudice is largely a function of economic conflict, conformity to social norms, or deeply rooted personality needs, it is not easily changed by an information campaign. Over the years, most people become deeply committed to their prejudicial behavior. To develop a liberal attitude to blacks when all of your friends and associates are still prejudiced is no easy task. A mere movie cannot undo a way of thinking and a way of behaving that has persisted over the years.

As the reader of this book has learned, where important issues are involved, information campaigns fail, because people are inclined not to sit still and take in information that is dissonant with their beliefs. Paul Lazarsfeld,[34] for example, described a series of radio broadcasts presented in the early forties that were designed to reduce ethnic prejudice by presenting information about various ethnic groups in a warm and sympathetic manner. One program was devoted to a description of Polish-Americans, another was devoted to Italian-Americans, and so forth. Who was listening? The major part of the audience for the program about Polish-Americans consisted of Polish-Americans. And guess who made up the major part of the audience for the program on Italian-Americans? Right. Moreover, as we've seen, if people are compelled to listen to information that is uncongenial, they will reject it, distort it, or ignore it—in much the same way that Mr. X maintained his negative attitude against Jews despite Mr. Y's information campaign, and in much the same way that the Dartmouth and Princeton students distorted the film of the football game they watched. For most people, prejudice is too deeply rooted in their own belief systems, is too consistent with their day-to-day behavior, and receives too much support and encouragement from the people around them to be reduced by a book, a film, or a radio broadcast.

The Effects of Equal-Status Contact. Although changes in attitude will affect changes in behavior, as we have seen, it is often difficult to change attitudes through education. What social psychologists have long known, but have only recently begun to understand, is that *changes in behavior can affect changes in attitudes.* On the simplest level, it has been argued that, if blacks and whites could be brought into direct contact, prejudiced individuals would come into contact with the reality of their own experience, not simply a stereotype; eventually, this would lead to greater understanding. The contact must take place in a situation in which blacks and whites have equal status, of course; many whites have always had a great deal of contact with blacks, but typically in situations in which the blacks played such menial roles as slaves, porters, dishwashers, shoe-shine boys, washroom attendants, and domestics. This kind of contact serves only to increase stereotyping by whites, and thus adds fuel to their prejudice against blacks. It also serves to increase the resentment and anger of blacks. Until recently, equal-status contact has been rare, both because of educational and occupational inequities in our society and because of residential segregation. The 1954 Supreme Court decision was the beginning of a gradual change in the frequency of equal status contact.

Occasionally, even before 1954, isolated instances of equal-status integration had taken place. The effects tended to support the notion that behavior change will produce attitude change. In a typical study, Morton Deutsch and Mary Ellen Collins[35] examined the attitudes of whites toward blacks in public housing projects. Specifically, in one housing project, black and white families were assigned to buildings in a segregated manner—that is, they were assigned to separate buildings in the same project. In another project, the assignment was integrated—black and white families were assigned to the same building. Residents in the integrated project reported a greater positive change in their attitudes towards blacks subsequent to their moving into the project than did residents of the segregated project. From these findings, it would appear that stateways *can* change folkways, that you *can* legislate morality—not directly, of course, but through the medium of equal-status contact. It seems clear that if diverse racial groups can be brought together under conditions of equal status, they stand a chance of getting to know each other better. This can increase understanding and decrease tension, *all other things being equal.**

The Vicarious Effects of Desegregation. It wasn't until much later that social psychologists began to entertain the notion that desegregation can affect the values of people who do not even have the opportunity to have direct contact with minority groups. This can occur through the mechanisms that we have referred to in Chapter 4 as the *psychology of inevitability.* Specifically, if I know that you and I will inevitably be in close contact, and I don't like you, I will experience dissonance. In order to reduce dissonance, I will try to convince myself that you are not as bad as I had previously thought. I will set about looking for your positive characteristics, and will try to ignore, or minimize the importance of, your negative characteristics. Accordingly, the mere fact that I know that I must at some point be in *close contact* with you will force me to change my prejudiced attitudes about you, *all other things being equal.* Laboratory experiments have confirmed this prediction: For example, children who believed that they must inevitably eat a previously disliked vegetable began to convince themselves that the vegetable wasn't so bad.[36] Similarly, college women who knew they were going to have to work intimately with a woman who had several positive and negative qualities developed a great fondness for that woman before they even met her; this did not occur when they were *not* let to anticipate working with her in the future.[37]

Admittedly, it's a far cry from a bowl of vegetables to relations between blacks and whites. Few social psychologists are so naive as to believe that racial intolerance, which is deep-seated, can be eliminated by people reducing their dissonance through coming to terms with what they believe to be inevitable events. I would suggest that, under ideal conditions, such events *can* produce a *diminution* of hostile feelings in *most* individuals. I will discuss what I mean by "ideal condi-

---

*It should be noted that the study alluded to in this paragraph took place in public housing projects rather than in private residential areas. This is a crucial factor that will be discussed in a moment.

tions" in a moment; but first, let us put a little more meat on those theoretical bones. How might the process of dissonance reduction take place?

Turn the clock back to the late 1950s. Imagine a 45-year-old white male whose 16-year-old daughter attends a segregated school in the Deep South. Let us assume that he has a negative attitude toward blacks, based in part on his belief that blacks are shiftless and lazy and that all black males are oversexed and potential rapists. Suddenly, the edict is handed down by the Justice Department: the following autumn, his fair-haired, nubile daughter must go to an integrated school. All of the state and local officials, while perhaps not liking the idea, clearly convey the fact that there's nothing that can be done to prevent it—it's the law of the land and it must be obeyed. The father might, of course, refuse to allow his child to obtain an education, or he could send her to an expensive private school. But such measures are either terribly drastic or terribly costly. So he decides that he must send her to an integrated school. His cognition that his fair-haired young daughter must inevitably attend the same school with blacks is dissonant with his cognition that blacks are shiftless rapists. What does he do? My guess is that he will begin to re-examine his beliefs about blacks. Are they *really* all that shiftless? Do they *really* go around raping people? He may take another look—this time, with a strong inclination to look for the good qualities in blacks rather than to concoct and exaggerate bad, unacceptable qualities. I would guess that, by the time September rolls around, his attitude toward blacks would have shifted in a positive direction. Again, this analysis is vastly oversimplified. But look at the advantages this process has over an information campaign: A mechanism has been triggered that *motivates* the individual to alter his negative stereotype of blacks.

This analysis strongly suggests that a particular kind of public policy would be most potentially beneficial to society—a policy that is the exact opposite of what has been generally recommended. As mentioned previously, following the 1954 Supreme Court decision, there was a general feeling that integration must proceed slowly. Most public officials and many social scientists believed that, in order to achieve harmonious racial relations, integration should be delayed until people could be re-educated to become less prejudiced. In short, the general belief in 1954 was that the behavior (integration) must *follow* a cognitive change. My analysis suggests that the best way to produce eventual interracial harmony would be to launch into behavioral change. Moreover, *and most important,* the sooner the individuals are made to realize that integration is inevitable, the sooner their prejudiced attitudes will begin to change. On the other hand, this process can be (and has been) sabotaged by public officials through fostering the belief that integration can be circumvented or delayed. This serves to create the illusion that the event is not inevitable. In such circumstances, there will be no attitude change; the result will be an increase in turmoil and disharmony. Let's go back to our previous example: if the father of the fair-haired daughter is led (by the statements and tactics of a governor, a mayor, a school-board chairman, or a local sheriff) to believe that there's a way out of integration, it is clear that he will feel no need to re-examine his negative beliefs about blacks. The result is apt to be violent opposition to integration.

Consistent with this reasoning is the fact that, as desegregation has spread, favorable attitudes toward desegregation have increased: in 1942, only 30 percent of the whites in this country favored desegregated schools; by 1956, the figure rose to 49 percent; finally, in 1970, as it became increasingly clear that school desegregation was inevitable, fully 75 percent of the white population was in favor of it. The change in the South (taken by itself) is even more dramatic: in 1942, only 2 percent of the whites in the South favored integrated schools; in 1956, while most southerners still believed that the ruling could be circumvented, only 14 percent favored desegregation; but by 1970, as desegregation continued, just under 50 percent favored it. Of course, such statistical data does not constitute absolute proof that the reason people are changing their attitudes toward school desegregation is that they are coming to terms with what is inevitable—but the data are highly suggestive.

In a careful analysis of the process and effects of school desegregation, Thomas Pettigrew raised the question of why violence occurred during the desegregation of some communities, such as Little Rock and Clinton, and not in others, such as Norfolk and Winston-Salem. His conclusion, which lends further support to our reasoning, was that "violence has generally resulted in localities where at least some of the authorities give prior hints that they would gladly return to segregation if disturbances occurred; peaceful integration has generally followed firm and forceful leadership."[38] In other words, if people were not given the opportunity to reduce dissonance, there was violence. As early as 1953, Kenneth B. Clark[39] noticed the same phenomenon during the desegregation in some of the border states. He discovered that immediate desegregation was far more effective than gradual desegregation. Moreover, violence occurred in those places where ambiguous or inconsistent policies were employed or where community leaders tended to vacillate. The same kind of thing happened when military units began to desegregate during World War II: trouble was greatest where policies were ambiguous.[40]

But All Other Things Are Not Always Equal. In the preceding section, I presented an oversimplified view of a very complex phenomenon. I did this intentionally as a way of indicating how things can proceed theoretically under ideal conditions. But conditions are seldom ideal. There are almost always some complicating circumstances. Let us now look at some of the complications, and then proceed to discuss how these complications might be eliminated or reduced.

When I discussed the fact that prejudice was reduced in an integrated housing project, I made special note of the fact that it was a *public* housing project. Some complications are introduced if it involves privately owned houses: Primarily, there is a strong belief among whites that, when blacks move into a neighborhood, real-estate values decrease. This belief introduces economic conflict and competition, which mitigate against the reduction of prejudiced attitudes. Indeed, systematic investigations of integrated *private* housing shows an increase in prejudiced attitudes among the white residents.[41]

Moreover, as I mentioned, the experiments on the psychology of inevitability were done in the laboratory where the dislikes involved were almost certainly not as intense or as deep-seated as racial prejudice. Although it is encouraging to note that these findings were paralleled by the data from desegregation in the real world, it would be naive and misleading to conclude that the way to desegregation will always be smooth as long as individuals are given the opportunity to come to terms with inevitability. Frequently, trouble begins once desegregation starts. This is due, in part, to the fact that the contact between black and white children (especially if it is begun in high school) is usually not equal-status contact. Picture the scene: A 16-year-old black from a poor family, after being subjected to a second-rate education, is suddenly dropped into a learning situation in a predominately white middle-class school taught by white middle-class teachers, where he finds he must compete with middle-class whites who have been reared to hold middle-class values. In effect, he is thrust into a highly competitive situation for which he is unprepared, a situation in which the rules are not his rules and the payoffs are made for abilities that he has not yet developed. He is competing in a situation that, psychologically, is far removed from his home turf. Ironically enough, these factors tend to produce a diminution of his self-esteem—the very factor that led to the Supreme Court decision in the first place.[42]

Thus, a newly desegregated high school is typically a tense place. It is natural for black students to attempt to raise their self-esteem. One way of raising self-esteem is to stick together, lash out at whites, assert their individuality, reject white values and white leadership, and so on.[43]

Let me sum up the discussion thus far: (1) Equal-status contact under the ideal conditions of no economic conflict can and does produce increased understanding and a diminution of prejudice.[44] (2) The psychology of inevitability can and does set up pressures to reduce prejudiced attitudes, and can set the stage for smooth, non-violent school desegregation, *under ideal conditions*. (3) Where economic conflict is present (as in integrated neighborhoods of private domiciles) there is often an increase in prejudiced attitudes. (4) Where school desegregation results in a competitive situation involving serious inequities for blacks, there is often an increase in hostility of blacks toward whites that is at least partially due to an attempt to regain some lost self-esteem.

Interdependence—A Possible Solution. School desegregation can open the door to increased understanding among students but, by itself, it is not the ultimate solution. The issue is not simply getting kids of various races and ethnic backgrounds into the same school—it's what happens after they get there that is crucial. As we have seen, if the atmosphere is a highly competitive one, whatever tensions exist initially might actually be increased as a result of contact. The tension that is frequently the initial result of school desegregation reminds me somewhat of the behavior of the children in the experiment by Muzafer Sherif and his colleagues.[45] Recall that hostility was produced between two groups by placing them in situations of conflict and competition. Once the hostility was established, it could no longer be reduced simply by removing the conflicts and the competition. As a matter of fact, once distrust was firmly established, bringing the groups together in equal-status, noncompetitive situations served to *increase* the hostility and distrust. For example, the children in these groups had trouble with each other even when they were simply sitting near each other watching a movie.

How did Sherif eventually succeed in reducing the hostility? By placing these groups of children in situations in which they were mutually interdependent—situations in which they had to cooperate with each other in order to accomplish their goal. For example, the investigators set up an emergency situation by damaging the water-supply system. The only way that the system could be repaired was if the children cooperated immediately. On another occasion, the camp truck broke down while the kids were on a camping trip. In order to get the truck going again, it was necessary to pull it up a rather steep hill. This could only be accomplished if all of the kids pulled together—regardless of whether they were *Bulldogs* or *Red Devils*. Eventually, there was a diminution of hostile feelings and negative stereotyping. The boys made friends across groups, they began to get along better, and they began to cooperate spontaneously.

The key factor seems to be *mutual interdependence*—a situation wherein the individuals need one another and are needed by one another in order to accomplish their goal. Several researchers have demonstrated the benefits of cooperation in well-controlled laboratory experiments. Morton Deutsch, for example, has shown that problem-solving groups are both friendlier and more attentive when a cooperative atmosphere is introduced than when a competitive atmosphere prevails.

Unfortunately, cooperation and interdependence are not characteristic of the process that exists in most school classrooms, even at the elementary level. We have already alluded to the competitive nature of the process; let us take a closer look at it. First, let's define "process." Whenever people interact, two things exist simultaneously. One of these is the content and the other is the process. By content, we simply mean the substance of their encounter; by process, we mean the dynamics of the encounter. In a classroom, for example, the content could be arithmetic, geography, social studies, or music; the process is the manner in which these lessons are taught. I would argue that it is through the process that the pupils learn a great deal about the world they live in. Indeed, I would even go so far as to say that, in many respects, the process is a more important source of learning than the content itself. In our observations of elementary-school classrooms, the most typical situation we saw was this: The teacher stands in front of the class, asks a question, and waits for one of the children to answer it. Most frequently, six to ten children strain in their seats and wave their hands to attract the teacher's attention. They seem eager to be called upon. Several other students sit quietly with their eyes averted, as if trying to make themselves invisible. When the teacher calls on one of the students (indeed, she or he can only call on one), there are looks of disappointment, dismay, and unhappiness on the faces of those students who were eagerly raising their hands but were not called on. If the student who is called upon comes up with the right answer, the teacher smiles, nods approvingly, and goes on to the next question. This is a great reward for the student who happens to be called on. At the same time that the fortunate student is coming up with the right answer and being smiled upon by the teacher, an audible groan can be heard coming from the children who were striving to be called upon but were ignored. It is obvious that they are disappointed because they missed an opportunity to show the teacher how smart and quick they are.

Through this process, the students learn several things. First, they learn that there is one and only one expert in the classroom: the teacher. They also learn that there is one and only one correct answer to any question that the teacher asks: namely, the answer that the teacher has in mind. The students' task is to figure out which answer the teacher expects. The students also learn that the payoff comes from pleasing the teacher by actively displaying how quick, smart, neat, clean, and well-behaved they are. If they do this successfully, they will gain the respect and love of this powerful person. This powerful person will then be kind to them and will tell their parents what wonderful children they are. There is no payoff for them in consulting with their peers. Indeed, their peers are their enemies—to be beaten. To collaborate with them may mean punishment—especially if this collaboration occurs during a test.

The game is very competitive and the stakes are very high—because, in an elementary-school classroom, the kids are competing for the respect and approval of one of the two or three most important people in their world (important for most students, anyway). If you are a student who knows the correct answer and the teacher calls on one of the other kids, it is likely that you will sit there hoping and praying that the kid will come up with the wrong answer so that you will have a chance to show the teacher how smart you are. Those who fail when called upon, or those who do not even raise their hands and compete, have a tendency to resent the kids who succeed. Frequently, the "losers" become envious and jealous of the successful students; perhaps they try to tease them or put them down by referring to them as "teacher's pets." They might even use physical aggression against them in the school yard. The successful students, for their part, often hold the unsuccessful students in contempt; they consider them to be dumb and uninteresting. The upshot of this process—which takes place, to a greater or lesser extent, in most classrooms—is that friendliness and understanding is not promoted among *any* of the children in the same classroom. Quite the reverse. The process tends to create enmity, even among kids of the same racial group. When ethnic or racial unfamiliarity is added, or when tension brought about by forced busing flavors the stew of an already unhappy process, the situation can become extremely difficult and unpleasant.

Although competitiveness in the classroom is typical, it is not inevitable. In my own research, I found that many classroom teachers were eager to try more cooperative techniques. Accordingly, my colleagues and I developed a simple method wherein children were put into interdependent learning groups; we systematically compared their performance, happiness, and liking for one another with that of children in more traditional, competitive classroom situations.[46] We called our method the jigsaw technique because it works very much like a jigsaw puzzle. An example will clarify this: In our initial experiment, we entered a fifth-grade classroom in which the kids were studying biographies of great Americans. The upcoming lesson happened to be a biography of Joseph Pulitzer. First, we constructed a biography of Joseph Pulitzer that consisted of six paragraphs. Paragraph one was about Joseph Pulitzer's ancestors and how they came to this country; paragraph two was about Joseph Pulitzer as a little boy and how he grew up; paragraph three was about Joseph Pulitzer as a young man, his education, and his early employment; paragraph four was about Joseph Pulitzer as a middle-aged man and about how he founded his newspaper; and so forth. Each major aspect of Joseph Pulitzer's life was contained in a separate paragraph. We mimeographed our biography of Joseph Pulitzer and cut each copy of the biography into six one-paragraph sections and gave every child in each of the six-person learning groups one paragraph about Joseph Pulitzer's life. Thus, each learning group had within it the entire biography of Joseph Pulitzer, but each individual child had no more than one-sixth of the story. Just like a jigsaw puzzle: each child had one piece of the puzzle, and each child was dependent on all of the other children in the group for the completion of the big picture. In order to learn about Joseph Pulitzer, each child had to master a paragraph and teach it to the others. Each student took his paragraph and went off by himself where he could learn it. In learning the paragraph, the child was free to consult with his counterpart in one of the other learning groups. That is, if Johnnie had been dealt Joseph Pulitzer as a young man, he might have consulted with Millie, who was in a different learning group and had also been dealt Pulitzer as a young man. They could use each other to rehearse and to clarify for themselves what were the important aspects of that phase of Joseph Pulitzer's life. A short time later, the kids came back into session with their six-person groups. They were informed that they had a certain amount of time to communicate that knowledge to each other. They were also informed that, at the end of that time (or soon thereafter), they were going to be tested on their knowledge.

When thrown on their own resources, the children eventually learned to teach each other and to listen to each other. The children came to learn that none of them could do well without the aid of each person in the group—and that each member had a unique and essential contribution to make. Suppose you and I are children in the same group. You've been dealt Joseph Pulitzer as a young man; I've been dealt Pulitzer as an old man. The only way I can learn about Joseph Pulitzer as a young man is to pay close attention to what you are saying. You are a very important resource for me. The teacher is no longer the sole resource—she isn't even an important resource; indeed, she isn't even in the group. Instead, every kid in the circle becomes important to me. I do well if I pay attention to other kids; I do poorly if I don't. I no longer get rewarded for trying to please the teacher at your expense. It's a whole new ball game.

But cooperative behavior doesn't happen all at once. Typically, it requires several days for the children to use this technique effectively. It is very difficult to break old habits. These young kids in our experimental group had grown accustomed to competing during all of their previous years in school. Typically, for the first few days, kids tried to compete—even though competitiveness was now dysfunctional. Let me illustrate with an actual example that was quite typical of the way the children stumbled toward the learning of the cooperative process: In one of our groups there was a male Chicano whom we will call Carlos. Carlos was not very articulate in English (it was his second language). He had learned over the years how to keep quiet in class because frequently, when he had spoken up in the past, he was ridiculed. In this instance, he had a great deal of trouble communicating his paragraph to the other kids; he was very uncomfortable about it. He liked the traditional way better. This is not surprising when you look at it because, in the system we introduced, Carlos was forced to speak, whereas always before he could de-individuate himself and keep a low profile in the classroom. But the situation was even more complex than that—it might even be said that the teacher and Carlos had entered into a conspiracy, that they were in collusion. Carlos was perfectly willing to be quiet. In the past, the teacher called on him occasionally; typically, he would stumble, stammer, and fall into an embarrassed silence. The other kids would make fun of him. The teacher had learned not to call on him anymore. This decision probably came from the purest of intentions—the teacher simply did not want to humiliate him. But, by ignoring him, she had written him off. The implication was that he was not worth bothering with—at least the other kids in the classroom got that message. They believed that there was one good reason why the teacher wasn't calling on Carlos—that he was stupid. Indeed, it is likely that even Carlos began to draw this conclusion. This is part of the dynamic of how desegregation, when coupled with a competitive process, can produce unequal-status contact and can result in even greater enmity between ethnic groups and a loss of self-esteem for members of disadvantaged ethnic minorities.[47]

Let us go back to our six-person group. Carlos, who had to report on Joseph Pulitzer's young manhood, was having a very hard time. He stammered, hesitated, and fidgeted. The other kids in that circle were not very helpful. They had grown accustomed to a competitive process and they responded out of this old, over-learned habit. They knew what to do when a kid stumbles—especially a kid whom they believed to be stupid: they ridiculed him, put him down, and teased him. During our experiment, it was Mary who was observed to say: "Aw, you don't know it, you're dumb, you're stupid. You don't know what you're doing." In our initial experiment, the groups were being loosely monitored by a research assistant who was floating from group to group. When this incident occurred, our assistant made one intervention. The intervention went something like this: "OK, you can do that if you want to. It might be fun for you, but it's *not* going to help you learn about Joseph Pulitzer's young manhood. The exam will take place in about an hour." Notice how the reinforcement contingencies have shifted. No more does the child gain much from putting Carlos down—in fact, she now stands to lose a great deal. After a few days and several similar experiences, it began to dawn on these kids that the *only* way they could learn about Joseph Pulitzer's young manhood was by paying attention to what Carlos had to say. And what gradually happened was that they began to develop into pretty good interviewers. Instead of ignoring or ridiculing Carlos when he was having a little trouble communicating what he knew, they began asking probing questions—the kinds of questions that made it easier for Carlos to communicate what was in his head. Carlos began to respond to this treatment by becoming more relaxed; with increased relaxation came an improvement in his ability to communicate. After a couple of weeks, the other children concluded that Carlos wasn't nearly as dumb as they thought he was. They began to see things in him that they never saw before. They began to like him. Carlos began to enjoy school more and began to see the Anglo kids in his group not as tormentors but as helpful and responsive people.

We have now replicated the experiment in scores of classrooms. The results are clearcut and consistent. Children in the interdependent, "jigsaw" classrooms grew to like each other better, developed a greater liking for school, and developed greater self-esteem than children in traditional classrooms. The increase in liking among kids in the jigsaw classrooms crossed ethnic and racial boundaries. Moreover, subsequent research[48] indicates that, while the exam performance of white kids is about the same, the exam performance of members of ethnic minorities is higher in the jigsaw classrooms than in the traditional classrooms. Finally, teachers enjoyed using our technique: most of the teachers who agreed to use the jigsaw method as part of our experiment continued to use it *after* the experiment was over—and, at this writing (some three years later), most are still using the technique with continued success and satisfaction.

Although interdependence—especially through the jigsaw technique—is clearly a promising strategy, it should be clear that it works best with young children before prejudiced attitudes have an opportunity to become deeply ingrained. Prejudice is a complex phenomenon. No one solution is *the* solution. As we have seen, many aspects of our society are changing simultaneously—more equitable exposure of ethnic minorities via the mass media, greater educational opportunities, and so on. It is a slow process, and equity is still a long distance away. And yet, prejudice is on the wane, and this is encouraging. Recall that, at one time, it was argued that desegregation would be impossible; it was once believed that a good deal of prejudice is generally the result of a deeply rooted personality disorder that must be cured before desegregation can proceed. The evidence indicates that, for the vast majority of individuals, this has not been true. The first wedge in the diminution of prejudice is desegregation. In the words of Thomas Pettigrew, one of our most tireless investigators in this area,

> Some cynics have argued that successful racial desegregation in the South will require an importation of tens of thousands of psychotherapists and therapy for millions of bigoted southerners. Fortunately for desegregation, psychotherapists, and southerners, this will not be necessary; a thorough repatterning of southern interracial behavior will be sufficient therapy in itself.[49]

Although Pettigrew may have been overly optimistic, it seems as though we are beginning to learn how prejudice can be reduced.

In the next two chapters, we will broaden the base of our discussion on prejudice and prejudice reduction. In Chapter 7, we will look at the positive or negative feelings that a person can have for another, and investigate why some individuals like each other and some dislike each other. In Chapter 8, we will look at a technique aimed at increasing interpersonal understanding through honest face-to-face communication.

7

Attraction: Why People Like Each Other

Early in this book I described several situations, in the laboratory and in the real world, in which people turned their backs on the needs of their fellow human beings. I mentioned incidents in which people watched someone being killed without attempting to help; in which people walked casually by, around, and over a woman with a broken leg lying on a Fifth Avenue sidewalk; in which people, hearing a woman in the next room apparently fall off a step ladder and injure herself, did not so much as ask if she needed assistance. I also described a situation in which people went a step further by apparently causing a person to suffer severe pain: a large number of individuals, in blind obedience to the commands of an authority figure, continued to administer severe electric shocks to another human being even after the person screamed in pain, pounded on the door, begged to be released, and then fell into an ominous silence. Finally, we saw how people, through fear, hate, and prejudice, can deprive one another of their civil rights, rob one another of their freedom, and even destroy one another.

With all of these events in mind, I asked if there is any way to diminish aggression and to encourage people to take responsibility for the welfare of their fellow human beings. In this chapter, I will ask this question in a more formal manner: what do we know about the factors that cause one person to like another?

The question is almost certainly an ancient one. The first amateur social psychologist, who must have lived in a cave, undoubtedly wondered what he could do to make the fellow in a nearby cave like him more or dislike him less—or, at least, to make him refrain from clubbing him on the head. Perhaps he bared his teeth as a means of showing his neighbor that he was tough and might bite a chunk out of the latter's leg, if the neighbor behaved aggressively. As luck would have it, this simple gesture worked, and the baring of teeth, now called a smile, gradually evolved into a social convention—a way of getting people not to hurt us and perhaps even to like us. Charles Darwin presents an interesting discussion of this phenomenon in a little book called *The Expression of Emotions in Man and Animals*.[1]

After several thousand years, people are still speculating about the antecedents of attraction—how to behave so that the guy at the next desk, in the next house, or in the next country likes us more, or at least refrains from putting us down or trying to destroy us. What do we know about the causes of attraction? When I ask my friends why they like some of their acquaintances better than others, I get a wide variety of responses. The most typical responses are that people like most (1) those whose beliefs and interests are similar to their own; (2) those who have some skills, abilities, or competencies; (3) those with some pleasant or "admirable" qualities, such as loyalty, reasonableness, honesty, and kindness; and (4) those who like them in return.

These reasons make good sense. They are also consistent with the advice given by Dale Carnegie in a book with the chillingly manipulative title *How to Win Friends and Influence People*.[2] Manipulative title notwithstanding, this interpersonal recipe book seems to have been exactly what people were looking for: it proved to be one of the best sellers of all time. That's not surprising. Americans seem to be deeply concerned with being liked and making a good impression. A series of polls conducted among high-school students during the 1940s and 1950s[3] indicated that their most important concern was the way others reacted to them—and their overwhelming desire was for people to like them more. Such concerns may be greatest during adolescence when the peer group assumes enormous importance, but the desire to be liked is certainly not limited to American adolescents. The search for simple formulae for how to please other people seems universal: Dale Carnegie's book was translated into thirty-five different languages and was avidly read around the globe. Carnegie's advice is deceptively simple: if you want someone to like you, be pleasant, pretend that you like him, feign an interest in things that he's interested in, "dole out praise lavishly," and be agreeable.

Is it true? Are these tactics effective? To a limited extent they *are* effective. There are data from well-controlled laboratory experiments that indicate that we like people with pleasant characteristics more than those with unpleasant characteristics[4]; we like people who agree with us more than people who disagree with us; we like people who like us more than people who dislike us; we like people who cooperate with us more than people who compete with us; we like people who praise us more than people who criticize us; and so on. These aspects of interpersonal attraction can be gathered under one sweeping generalization: we like people whose behavior provides us with maximum reward at minimum cost.[5]

It should be readily apparent that a general reward theory of attraction covers a great deal of ground. For example, it would allow us to explain the fact that we like people who are pretty more than people who are homely, because pretty people bring us "aesthetic" rewards.[6] At the same time, it would allow us to predict that we will like people with opinions similar[7] to ours because, when we run into such people, they reward us by providing us with consensual validation for our beliefs—that is, by helping us to believe that our opinions are "correct." Moreover, as we learned in the preceding chapter, one way that prejudice and hostility can be reduced is by changing the environment in such a way that individuals cooperate with each other rather than compete. Another way of stating this relation is that cooperation leads to attraction. Thus, whether the environment is a summer camp, as in Muzafer Sherif's experiments,[8] or a classroom situation, as in the experiments by Aronson and his colleagues,[9] there is an increase in mutual attraction if people spend some time cooperating with each other. Cooperative behavior is clearly rewarding by definition—a person who cooperates with us is giving us aid, listening to our ideas, making suggestions, and sharing our load.

A general reward–cost theory can explain a great deal of human attraction, but not all of it—the world is not that simple. For example, a reward–cost theory of attraction would lead us to suspect that, all other things being equal, we would like people who live in close proximity to us, because we can get the same reward at less cost by traveling a short distance than we can by traveling a great distance. Indeed, it does tend to be true that people do seem to have more friends who live close by than friends who live far away; but this does not necessarily mean that it is their physical proximity that makes them attractive: their physical proximity may simply make it easier to get to know them, and once we get to know them, we tend to like them. Moreover, as we pointed out earlier in this book, individuals also like things or people for which or for whom they have suffered. For example, recall the experiment I did in collaboration with Judson Mills[10] in which we found that people who went through an unpleasant initiation in order to become members of a group liked that group better than did those who became members by paying a smaller price in terms of time and effort. Where is the reward? The reduction of suffering? The reduction of dissonance? How does the reward become attached to the group? It is not clear.

Moreover, simply knowing that something is rewarding does not necessarily help us to predict or understand a person's behavior. For example, recall that, in Chapters 2, 3, and 4, we analyzed why a person conforms and why he changes his attitudes, and we discussed several reasons: out of a desire to win praise, to be liked, to avoid ridicule; out of a desire to identify with someone whom he respects or admires; out of a desire to be right; or out of a desire to justify his own behavior. In some way, all of these behaviors make sense, or feel good, or both, and therefore can be considered rewards. But simply to label them as rewards tends to obscure the fact that there are important differences in kind among them. Although both the desire to be right and the desire to avoid ridicule, when gratified, produce a state of satisfaction, it is frequently the case that the behaviors a person must employ to gratify these needs are opposite in kind. For example, in judging the size of a line, a person might conform to group pressure out of a desire to avoid ridicule, but he might deviate from the unanimous opinion of the other group members out of a desire to be right. Little understanding is gained by covering both behaviors with the blanket phrase "reward." For the social psychologist, a far more important task is to attempt to determine the conditions under which one or the other course of action will be taken. This point will become clearer as we begin to discuss some of the research on interpersonal attraction.

The Effects of Praise and Favors

Recall that Dale Carnegie advised us to "dole out praise lavishly." That makes sense: surely, we can "win friends" by praising our teachers' ideas or our employees' efforts. But does it *always* work? Let's take a closer look. Common sense suggests that there are situations in which criticism might be more useful than praise. For example, suppose you are a brand-new college instructor lecturing to a class full of graduate students and presenting a theory that you are developing. In the rear of the classroom are two students. One of these people is nodding and smiling and looks as though he is in rapture. At the close of your presentation, he comes up and tells you that you are a genius and that your ideas are the most brilliant he's ever heard. It feels good to hear that, of course. But the other person shakes her head and scowls occasionally during your presentation, and afterward, she comes up and tells you that there are several aspects of your theory that don't make sense. Moreover, she points these out in some detail and with a note of disdain in her voice. That evening, while ruminating on what was said, you realize that the remarks made by the second person, although somewhat extreme and not completely accurate, did contain some worthwhile points and forced you to rethink a few of your assumptions. This eventually leads you to a significant modification of your theory. Which of these two people will you like better? I don't know. Although praise is clearly rewarding, disagreement that leads to improvement may carry its own rewards. Because I am, at this point, unable to predict, in advance, which of these behaviors is more rewarding, it is impossible to be sure which of the two students you will like better.

Let us take a different example, one that involves the attribution of ulterior motives to the praiser. Suppose that Sam is a draftsman, and that he produces an excellent set of blueprints. His boss says, "Nice work, Sam." That phrase will almost certainly function as a reward, and Sam's liking for his boss will probably increase. But suppose Sam is having an off day and produces a sloppy set of blueprints—and knows it. The boss comes along and emits the exact same phrase in exactly the same tone of voice. Will that phrase function as a reward in this situation? I am not sure. Sam *may* interpret the statement as his boss's attempt to be encouraging and nice, even in the face of a poor performance; and, because of the boss's display of considerateness, Sam may come to like him even more than he would have had he, in fact, done a good job. On the other hand, Sam may attribute all kinds of ulterior motives to his boss: he may leap to the conclusion that his boss is being sarcastic, manipulative, dishonest, nondiscriminating, patronizing, or stupid—any one of which could reduce Sam's liking for him. A general reward–cost theory loses a good deal of its value if our definition of what constitutes a reward is not clear. As situations become complex, we find that such general notions decrease in value, because a slight change in the social context in which the reward is provided can change a "reward" into a punishment.

Research in this area indicates that, although people like to be praised and tend to like the praiser,[11] they also dislike being manipulated. If the praise is too lavish, if it seems unwarranted, or (most important) if the praiser is in a position to benefit from ingratiating himself, then he is not liked very much. Edward E. Jones and his students[12] have carried out a great deal of research on this problem. In a typical experiment, an accomplice watched a young woman being interviewed, and then proceeded to evaluate her. The evaluations were prearranged so that some women heard a positive evaluation, some heard a negative evaluation, and some heard a neutral evaluation. In one experimental condition, the evaluator was supplied with an ulterior motive: in this condition, the subjects were informed in advance that the evaluator was a graduate student who needed subjects for her own experiment, and would be asking her (the subject) to volunteer. The results showed that subjects liked those evaluators who praised them better than those who provided them with a negative evaluation—but there was a sharp drop in how much they liked the praiser with the ulterior motive. As Jones puts it, "flattery will get you *somewhere*."

By the same token, we like people who do us favors. Favors can be considered rewards, and we do tend to like people who provide us with this kind of reward. For example, in a classic study by Helen Hall Jennings,[13] it was shown that, among girls in a reformatory, the most popular were those who performed the most services for others —specifically, those who initiated new and interesting activities and helped other girls become a part of these activities. Our liking for people who do us favors extends even to situations in which these favors are not intentional. This was demonstrated by Albert and Bernice Lott[14] in an experiment on young children. The researchers organized children into groups of three for the purpose of playing a game that consisted of choosing various pathways on a board. Those who were lucky enough to choose the safe pathways won the game; making the wrong choice led to disaster. The children were, in effect, walking single file in an imaginary mine field, whose mines remained active even after they were exploded. If the child at the front of the line chose the wrong path, he was "blown up" (out of the game), and the child next in line would, of course, choose a different path. Leaders who happened to choose correctly led the others to a successful completion of the game. The results indicated that those children who were rewarded (by arriving safely at the goal) showed a greater liking for their teammates (who, of course, had been instrumental in helping them achieve the reward) than did those children who did not reach the final goal. In short, we like people who contribute to our victory more than those who do not—even if they had no intention of doing us a favor.

But, as with those who praise us, we do not always like people who do favors for us; specifically, we do not like people whose favors seem as though they may have some strings attached to them. Such strings constitute a threat to the freedom of the receiver. People do not like to receive gifts, if a gift is expected in return; moreover, people do not like to receive favors from individuals who are in a position to benefit from that favor. Let's take an example: If you were a teacher, you might enjoy receiving gifts from your students. On the other hand, you might be made pretty uncomfortable if a borderline student presented you with an expensive gift just before you were about to grade his or her term paper. Strong support for this reasoning comes from an experiment by Jack Brehm and Ann Cole.[15] In this experiment, college students were asked to participate in a study (which the experimenter characterized as important) in which they would be giving their first impressions of another person. As each subject was waiting for the experiment to begin, the "other person" (actually a stooge) asked permission to leave the room for a few moments. In one condition, he simply returned after a while and resumed his seat. In the other condition, he returned carrying two cokes—one for himself and one for the subject. Subsequently, each subject was asked to help the stooge perform a dull task. Interestingly enough, those students who had *not* been given the coke by the stooge were more likely to help him than those who *had* been given the coke.

The upshot of this research is that favors and praise are not universal rewards. For a starving rat or a starving person, a bowl of dry cereal is a reward—it is a reward during the day or during the night, in winter or in summer, if offered by a male or by a female, and so on. Similarly, for a drowning man, a rescue launch is a reward under all circumstances. That is, such rewards are "transsituational." But praise, favors, and the like are not transsituational: whether or not they function as rewards depends upon minor situational variations, some of which can be extremely subtle. Indeed, as we have seen, praise and favors can even function to make the praiser or the favor-doer less attractive than he would have been had he kept his mouth shut or kept his hands in his pockets. Thus, Dale Carnegie's advice is not always sound. If you want someone to like you, doing him a favor as a technique of ingratiation is indeed risky.

Getting someone to do *you* a favor is a more certain way of using favors to increase your attractiveness. Recall that, in Chapter 4, I described a phenomenon that we called "the justification of cruelty." Briefly, I pointed out that, if a person causes harm to another, he will attempt to justify his behavior by derogating the victim. We are now prepared to take a look at the other side of that coin: if we do someone a favor, we must justify this action by convincing ourselves that the recipient of this favor is an attractive, likable, deserving sort of fellow. In effect, we will say to ourselves, "Why in the world did I go to all of this effort (or spend all of this money, or whatever) for Sam? Because Sam's a hell of a nice guy, that's why!"

This notion is far from novel; it seems to be a part of folk wisdom. Moreover, the technique was used with great success by no less a scientist than Benjamin Franklin in 1736. Franklin, disturbed by the political opposition and apparent animosity of a member of the Pennsylvania State legislature, set out to win him over.

> . . . I did not . . . aim at gaining his favour by paying any servile respect to him but, after some time, took this other method. Having heard that he had in his library a certain very scarce and curious book I wrote a note to him expressing my desire of perusing that book and requesting he would do me the favour of lending it to me for a few days. He sent it immediately and I return'd it in about a week with another note expressing strongly my sense of the favour. When we next met in the House he spoke to me (which he had never done before), and with great civility; and he ever after manifested a readiness to serve me on all occasions, so that we became great friends and our friendship continued to his death. This is another instance of the truth of an old maxim I had learned, which says, "He that has once done you a kindness will be more ready to do you another than he whom you yourself have obliged."[16]

While Benjamin Franklin was clearly pleased with the success of his maneuver, it is not entirely clear whether his success was due to this technique or to any one of many charming aspects of his personality. Franklin's notion was put to a more elaborate, well-controlled experimental test by Jon Jecker and David Landy.[17] In this experiment, students participated in a concept-formation task that enabled them to win a rather substantial sum of money. After the experiment was over, one-third of the subjects were approached by the experimenter, who explained that he was using his own funds for the experiment and was running short—which would mean that he might be forced to stop the experiment. He asked, "As a special favor to me, would you mind returning the money you won?" Another one-third of the subjects were approached, *not* by the experimenter, but by the departmental secretary, who asked them if they would return the money as a special favor to the psychology department's research fund, which was running low. The remaining one-third of the subjects were not asked to return their winnings as a special favor to anyone. Finally, the subjects were asked to fill out a questionnaire in which they got a chance to rate the experimenter. Those subjects who had been cajoled into doing a special favor for the experimenter found him most attractive—they had convinced themselves that he was a decent, deserving fellow.

Similar results were obtained in an experiment by Melvin Lerner and Carolyn Simmons,[18] in which groups of subjects were allowed to observe a student who appeared to be receiving a series of electric shocks as part of an experiment in learning. After watching for a while, some groups of subjects were allowed to vote (by private ballot) on whether or not the "victim" should continue to receive electric shocks. Other groups of subjects were not allowed to vote on this procedure. All subjects who were allowed to vote did, indeed, vote for the termination of the shocks; but some groups of voting subjects were successful in effecting a termination of the shocks, while others were not. It turned out that the subjects who were successful at stopping the shocks rated the victim as significantly more attractive than did those who were not allowed to vote, or those whose vote was ineffective. Thus, doing a favor for someone will increase your liking for that person, but only if the effort that you expend results in a successful outcome.

Personal Attributes

As I have already mentioned, there are several personal characteristics that play an important role in determining the extent to which a person will be liked.[19] Thus, people tend to like others who are sincere, competent, intelligent, energetic, and so on. Most of these studies were done in the manner of a public opinion poll—that is, people were simply asked to describe the attributes of people they like and those of people they dislike. In studies of this sort, it is difficult to establish the direction of causality: Do we like people who have pleasant attributes, or do we tend to convince ourselves that our friends tend to have these pleasant attributes? Chances are that causality flows in both directions. In order to be sure that people with certain positive personal attributes are liked better than others, it is necessary to examine this relation under more controlled conditions than exists in the opinion poll. In this section, we will examine closely two of the most important personal attributes: competence and physical attractiveness.

Competence. It would seem obvious that, all other things being equal, the more competent a person is, the more we will like him or her. This is probably because people have a need to be right; we stand a better chance of being right if we surround ourselves with highly able, highly competent people. But, as we continue to learn in this chapter, factors that determine interpersonal attraction are often complex; they cannot always be spelled out in simple terms. As for competence, there is a great deal of apparently paradoxical evidence in the research literature that demonstrates that, in problem-solving groups, the participants who are considered to be the most competent and the best idea men tend *not* to be the ones who are best liked.[20] How can we explain this apparent paradox? One possibility is that, although we like to be around competent people, a person who has a great deal of ability may make us uncomfortable. He may seem unapproachable, distant, superhuman. If this were true, we might like him more were he to show some evidence of fallibility. For example, if a person were a brilliant mathematician as well as a great basketball player and a fastidious dresser, I might like him better if, every once in a while, he misadded a column of numbers, blew an easy layup, or appeared in public with a gravy stain on his tie.

Several years ago, I was speculating about this phenomenon when I chanced upon some startling data from a Gallup poll: when John Kennedy was President, his personal popularity actually increased immediately after his abortive attempt to invade Cuba at the Bay of Pigs in 1961. This was startling, in view of the fact that this attempted invasion was such a phenomenal blunder that it was immediately dubbed (and is still commonly known as) "the Bay of Pigs fiasco." What can we make of it? This was a situation in which a national leader committed one of history's truly great blunders (up until that time, that is) and, miraculously, people came to like him more for it. Why? One possibility is that John Kennedy may have been "too perfect."

In 1961, John Kennedy stood very high in personal popularity.

He was a character of almost storybook proportions. Indeed, his regime was referred to as "Camelot." Kennedy was young, handsome, bright, witty, charming, and athletic; he was a voracious reader, a master political strategist, a war hero, and an uncomplaining endurer of physical pain; he had a beautiful wife (who spoke several foreign languages), two cute kids (one boy and one girl), and a talented, close-knit family. Some evidence of fallibility (like being responsible for a major blunder) could have served to make him more human in the public eye and, hence, more likable.

Alas, this is only one of several possible explanations, and (as the reader knows all too well by now) the real world is no place to test such a hypothesis. In the real world, there are too many things happening simultaneously, any one of which could have increased Kennedy's popularity. For example, after the fiasco occurred, President Kennedy did not try to make excuses or to pass the buck; rather, he manfully accepted full responsibility for the blunder. This selfless action could have done much to make him more attractive in the eyes of the populace. In order to test the proposition that evidence of fallibility in a highly competent person may make him better liked, an experiment was needed. One of the great advantages of an experiment is that it eliminates or controls extraneous variables (such as the selfless assumption of responsibility) and allows us, therefore, to assess more accurately the effect of one variable on another.

I performed such an experiment in collaboration with Ben Willerman and Joanne Floyd.[21] Each subject listened to a simple tape recording featuring one of four stimulus persons: (1) a nearly perfect person; (2) a nearly perfect person who commits a clumsy blunder; (3) a mediocre person; and (4) a mediocre person who commits a clumsy blunder. In preparation, each subject was told that he would be listening to a person who was a candidate for the "College Quiz Bowl," and that he would be asked to rate the candidate by the kind of impression he made, by how likable he seemed, and so forth. Each tape consisted of an interview between the candidate (stimulus person) and an interviewer, and contained a set of extremely difficult questions posed by the interviewer; the questions were of the kind that are generally asked on the "College Quiz Bowl." On one tape, the stimulus person showed a high degree of competence—indeed, he seemed to be virtually perfect, answering 92 percent of the questions correctly—and, in the body of the interview, when asked about his activities in high school, he modestly admitted that he had been an honor student, the editor of the yearbook, and a member of the track team. On another tape, the stimulus person (actually the same actor using the same tone of voice) was presented as a person of average ability: he answered only 30 percent of the questions correctly and, during the interview, he admitted that he had received average grades in high school, had been a proofreader on the yearbook staff, and that he had tried out for the track team but had failed to make it. On the other two recordings (one of the "superior" person and one of the "average" person), the stimulus person committed an embarrassing blunder: near the end of the interview, he clumsily spilled a cup of coffee all over himself. This "pratfall" was created by making a tape recording that included sounds of commotion and clatter, the scraping of a chair, and the anguished voice of the stimulus person saying, "Oh my goodness, I've spilled coffee all over my new suit." To achieve maximum control, this tape was reproduced, and one copy was spliced onto a copy of the tape of the superior person, while the other copy was spliced onto a copy of the tape of the average person. This gave us four experimental conditions: (1) a person of superior ability who blundered, and (2) one who did not; and (3) a person of average ability who blundered, and (4) one who did not.

The superior person who committed a blunder was rated most attractive; the average person who committed the same blunder was rated least attractive. The perfect person (no blunder) was second in attractiveness, and the mediocre person (no blunder) finished third. Clearly, there was nothing inherently attractive about the simple act of spilling a cup of coffee: although it did serve to add an endearing dimension to the perfect person, making him more attractive, the same action served to make the mediocre person appear that much more mediocre and, hence, less attractive. This experiment presents stronger evidence to support our contention that, although a high degree of competence does make a person attractive, some evidence of fallibility increases his attractiveness still further. This finding has been dubbed "the pratfall effect."

More complex experiments have since produced some interesting refinements of this general finding. Basically, the pratfall effect holds most clearly when, within the head of the observer, there is some implicit threat of competition with the stimulus person. Thus, an experiment by Kay Deaux[22] demonstrates that the pratfall effect applies most strongly to males. She found that, although most males in her study preferred the highly competent man who committed a blunder, women showed a tendency to prefer the highly competent nonblunderer, regardless of whether the stimulus person was male or female. Similarly, my colleagues and I found that males with a moderate degree of self-esteem are most likely to prefer the highly competent person who commits a blunder, while males with low self-esteem (who apparently feel little competitiveness with the stimulus person) prefer the highly competent person who *doesn't* blunder.[23]

It should be emphasized that no sizable proportion of people—regardless of their own level of self-esteem—preferred the mediocre person. I want to take special pains to make this point because of a rather striking political event that occurred in the early 1970s, when Richard Nixon was at the height of his popularity. On the advice of his Attorney General, Nixon tried, in vain, to appoint to the Supreme Court two extraordinarily mediocre lower-court judges. In defending these nominees, Senator Roman Hruska argued (seriously, I'm afraid) that, while it was true that these men were mediocre, the mediocre citizens of this country needed someone on the Supreme Court to represent them too! Again, it should be clear that our data do not support this argument.

Physical Attractiveness. Ask a teacher or an employer whether a man's handsomeness or a woman's beauty has any effect in determining his or her advancement, salary, or grade, and most will laugh and indicate that the question is absurd; but ask him whether he's aware of the physical attractiveness of his students or employees and (if he's honest) he'll probably admit that he is. Chances are that their physical attractiveness will affect his judgment of them, whether he realizes it or not. Indeed, the image of the dumb but beautiful secretary who can't type is a familiar sexist "cartoon" in our society. Is the cartoon accurate? Yes. And it's not limited to stereotypically sexist situations—it cuts both ways. Several experiments have underscored what many of us have long suspected: if you want people to like you and treat you well, it pays to be beautiful. We like beautiful and handsome people better than homely people, and we attribute all kinds of good characteristics to them.

In one study by Elaine Walster and her associates,[24] students at the University of Minnesota were randomly matched by computer for blind dates. They had previously been given a battery of personality tests. Which of their many characteristics determined whether or not they liked each other? Was it their masculinity, feminity, dominance, submission, dependence, independence, intelligence, or attitude similarity? It was none of these things. The one determinant of whether or not a couple liked each other and actually repeated their date was their physical attractiveness. If a handsome man was paired with a beautiful woman, they were most likely to desire to see each other again.

In another study, Karen Dion and her colleagues[25] showed college students photographs of three other college-age people; one was physically attractive, one was average, and the third was unattractive. The subjects were asked to rate each of the people depicted on these photographs on twenty-seven different personality traits, and were asked to rate their future happiness. The physically attractive people were assigned by far the most desirable traits and the greatest prognosis for happiness. This was true whether it was men rating men, men rating women, women rating men, or women rating women.

This is not simply a conceit held by college students. Karen Dion and Ellen Berscheid[26] found that, even as early as nursery school, children are responsive to the physical attractiveness of their peers. In their study, Dion and Berscheid first had several independent judges (graduate students) rate the physical attractiveness of nursery-school students. Then they determined who liked whom among the children themselves. The clearest results were obtained for the males: the physically attractive boys were liked better than the physically unattractive boys. Moreover, unattractive boys were considered to be more aggressive than their attractive counterparts; and, when the children were asked to name the classmates that "scared them," they tended to nominate the unattractive children. Of course, it may be that the homely boys *were* more aggressive and *did* behave in a more scary manner. The researchers did not observe the actual behavior of the children in the nursery school. At the same time, there is independent evidence that people do tend to attribute less blame to physically attractive kids, regardless of the facts. This datum emerges from another study by Karen Dion.[27] Women were asked to examine reports of rather severe classroom disturbances, apparently written by a teacher. Attached to each report was a photo of the child who was said to have initiated the disturbance. In some instances, the photo was that of an attractive boy or girl; in others, the photo was that of an unattractive boy or girl. The women tended to place more blame on the unattractive children, and to leap to the conclusion that this was part of their everyday behavior. When the child was pictured as physically attractive, however, adults tended to excuse their disruptive behavior. As one woman put it, " . . . she plays well with everyone, but like anyone else, a bad day can occur. Her cruelty . . . need not be taken too seriously." When a physically unattractive girl was pictured as the culprit in exactly the same situation described in exactly the same way, a typical respondent said: "I think the child would be quite bratty and would probably be a problem to teachers. She would probably try to pick a fight with other children her own age. . . . All in all, she would be a real problem."

In a different vein, Harold Sigall and I[28] demonstrated that good-looking women have more impact on men than homely women—for better or for worse. In this experiment, a woman was made to appear either physically attractive or unattractive. This was accomplished by taking a naturally beautiful woman and, in the unattractive condition, providing her with loose, ill-fitting clothing, fitting her with a frizzy blond wig that did not quite match her skin coloring, and making her complexion look oily and unwholesome. Then, posing as a graduate student in clinical psychology, she interviewed several college males. At the close of the interview, she gave each subject her own personal, clinical evaluation of him. Half of the subjects received evaluations that were highly favorable, and the other half evaluations that were very unfavorable. We found that, when she was homely, the men didn't seem to care much whether they received a good evaluation or a poor evaluation from her: in both situations, they liked her a fair amount. When she was beautiful, however they liked her a great deal when she gave them a favorable evaluation, but, when she gave them an unfavorable evaluation, they disliked her more than in any of the other conditions. Interestingly enough, although the men who were evaluated negatively by the attractive woman said that they didn't like her, they did express a great desire to return in order to interact with her in a future experiment. These data seem to indicate that the negative evaluations from the beautiful woman were so important to the subjects that they wanted the opportunity to return so as to induce her to change her evaluations of them.

Finally, in an interesting study, Harold Sigall and Nancy Ostrove[29] showed that people tend to favor a beautiful woman unless they suspect her of misusing her beauty. Both male and female college students were allowed to read an account of a criminal case in which the defendent was clearly guilty of a crime. Each subject then "sentenced" the defendent to a prison term that he or she considered appropriate. The results showed that when the crime was unrelated to attractiveness (burglary), the sentences were much more lenient when the defendent was physically attractive. When the crime was related to her attractiveness (a swindle in which the defendent induced a middle-aged bachelor to invest some money in a nonexistent corporation), the sentences were much harsher for the physically attractive defendent. These results parallel those of Sigall and Aronson (described above) inasmuch as they both indicate that a woman's physical attractiveness can have a powerful impact on the way she is treated—for better or worse—depending upon exactly how that attractiveness is used.

Taking all of this research into consideration, it appears to be true that physical beauty is more than skin-deep. We are more affected by physically attractive people than by physically unattractive people, and, unless we are specifically abused by them, we tend to like them better. Moreover, in situations involving trouble and turmoil, beautiful people tend to be given the benefit of the doubt—they receive more favorable treatment than homely people. This begins at a very young age. The disconcerting aspect of these data is that there is a strong possibility that such preferential treatment contains the seeds of a self-fulfilling prophecy: we know that, if people are treated poorly (or well), it affects the way they come to think of themselves. Thus, homely children may come to think of themselves as "bad" or unlovable, if they are continually treated that way. Ultimately, they may begin to behave in a way that is consistent with this self-concept, a way that is consistent with how they were treated to begin with.

Please note that, thus far, our discussion of beauty has been limited to "visual" beauty. But there are other kinds of beauty. It turns out that our visual perception exercises a terribly conservative influence on our feelings and behavior. We are wedded to our eyes—especially as a means of determining physical attractiveness. And, as we have seen, once we have categorized a person as pretty or homely, we tend to attribute other qualities to that person—for example, pretty people are likely to strike us as being more warm, sexy, exciting, and delightful than homely people. In the next chapter, I will be discussing sensitivity-training groups. Some of these groups allow people to engage in nonvisual sensory experiences. For example, one such experience enables people to "turn off their eyes" and become acquainted with each other solely through the sense of touch. After participating in one of these exercises, group members typically report a dramatic diminution of their prior stereotypes. Basically, individuals find that there is little "homeliness" in a nonvisual situation. Moreover, participants are frequently astonished to learn that, for example, the incredibly warm, gentle, and sensitive person that they had been having a nonvisual encounter with is, "in reality," the funny-looking guy with the pimples. I doubt that, after even one such nonvisual encounter with him, a person could ever relate to him again as merely a funny-looking guy with pimples. To the extent that such experiences can enable people to become aware of the nonvisual aspects of beauty, some of the unfairness due to the inequitable distribution of physical beauty that we have discussed may be reduced.

Similarity and Attraction

Sam goes to a cocktail party and is introduced to Marty. While they chat for only a few moments, it turns out that they agree completely on several issues, including the inequity of the income-tax structure, the status of Douglas MacArthur in world history, and the superiority of Beefeater gin. Upon returning home, Sam announces to his wife that he likes Marty a great deal and that he considers him to be a wonderful and intelligent person. Literally dozens of tightly controlled experiments by Donn Byrne and his associates[30] have shown over and over again that, if all you know about a person are his opinions on several issues, the more similar his opinions are to yours, the more you like him.

Why is agreement important? There are at least two possibilities: (1) The person who shares our opinion on an issue provides us with a kind of social validation for our beliefs—that is, he provides us with the feeling that we are right. This is rewarding; hence, we like those who agree with us. If a person disagrees with us, this suggests the possibility that we may be wrong. This is punishing; hence, we don't like people who disagree with us. (2) It is likely that we make certain negative inferences about the character of a person who disagrees with us on a substantive issue, not simply because his disagreement indicates that we may be wrong, but, rather, because we suspect that his opinion on that issue indicates that he is the kind of person we have found in the past to be unpleasant, immoral, or stupid. For example, suppose you believe that the penalties for using drugs are too severe. You then meet a man who tells you that he believes that drug users should be put away for several years. I then come along, ask you if you liked that man, and you say "No." Am I to conclude that (1) you didn't like him because hearing him state his belief suggested to you that your belief might be wrong, or (2) you didn't like him because, in your experience, people who favor harsh punishments for drug users tend to be unpleasant, immoral, inhuman, bigoted, harsh, cruel, conventional, punitive, and stupid?

Both of these factors undoubtedly play a role. There is some evidence to suggest that the second factor may be of less importance. This stems from Harold Sigall's brilliant investigation of the psychological effects of conversion.[31] Sigall showed that, if people are highly involved with an issue, they prefer a "disagreer" to an "agreer," if they can succeed in converting him to their way of thinking. In short, Sigall demonstrated that people like converts better than loyal members of the flock. Apparently, the competence that a person feels when he induces someone to convert overcomes any tendency that he might have to actively dislike the other person for being the sort who would hold an "awful" opinion to begin with.

Liking Leads to Liking

There is still another reason why we tend to like people who hold opinions that are similar to ours. It may be that, all other things being equal, if we learn that a person's opinion is similar to our own, we might be prone to believe that he will really like us, if and when he gets to know us. This can be very important because, as it turns out, the single most powerful determinant of whether one person will like another is whether the other likes that person.

Several investigators have demonstrated that being liked indeed does make the heart grow fonder.[32] Furthermore, it has been shown that the greater a person's insecurity and self-doubt, the fonder he will grow of the person who likes him. In a study by Elaine Walster,[33] university co-eds, while waiting to participate in an experiment, were approached by a rather smooth, good-looking, well-dressed young man who was, in fact, an accomplice in the employ of the experimenter. The smooth young man struck up a conversation with the subject, indicated that he liked her, and proceeded to make a date. At this point, the experimenter entered and led the young woman into a different room for the experiment itself. The young woman was told that the purpose of the study was to compare the results of various personality tests that she (the subject) had previously taken. In the course of this procedure, the young woman was allowed to read an evaluation of her own personality. Half of the girls read descriptions of themselves that were highly positive, designed expressly to raise their self-esteem temporarily. The other girls read descriptions that were quite negative; these were designed to lower their self-esteem temporarily and, thus, to increase their feelings of insecurity. Finally, as part of the experiment, the girls were asked to rate how much they liked a wide variety of people—a teacher, a friend, ". . . and since we have one space left, why don't you also rate that fellow whom you were waiting with?" Those women who received unfavorable information about themselves (from the personality test) showed far more liking for their male admirer than did those who received favorable information about themselves. In short, we like to be liked—and the more insecure we feel, the more we appreciate being liked and, consequently, the more we like someone who likes us.

One of the implications of this experiment is that people who are secure about themselves are less "needy"—that is, they are less likely to accept overtures from just any person who comes along. Just as a starving person will accept almost any kind of food and a well-fed person can be more selective, so too will an insecure person accept almost anyone who expresses interest, while a secure person will be more selective. Moreover, a person who feels insecure may even seek out a less attractive person because he or she may feel that this lowers the possibility of being rejected. This implication was tested in an interesting experiment by Sara Kiesler and Roberta Baral[34] who led male college students to believe that they'd either done very well or very poorly in a test of intellectual achievement. They then took a break and the experimenter joined the student for a cup of coffee. As they entered the coffee shop, the experimenter "recognized" a female student seated alone at a table, joined her and introduced the male subject to her. Of course, the female student was a confederate, intentionally planted there. Half of the time, the confederate was made up to look attractive; the other half of the time, she was "uglified." The investigators observed the degree of romantic interest displayed by the male subjects: did they ask to see her again, did they offer to pay for her coffee, did they ask for her phone number, did they try to get her to stay longer, and so on. Interestingly enough, those who were induced to feel secure about themselves (had been led to believe that they had performed well on the test) showed more romantic interest toward the "attractive" woman; those who were induced to feel insecure, showed more romantic interest toward the "unattractive woman."

The Relation Between Similarity and Being Liked. We have already seen that the factors that determine whether or not a person will be liked are not as simple as Dale Carnegie would have us believe. Let's push this further by taking a look at the two variables that we have recently discussed: similarity and being liked. Because we like people who hold opinions that are similar to ours, and because we like people who like us, shouldn't it follow that we will like a person a great deal if we learn that he is *both* similar *and* that he likes us? No. The evidence suggests that these two factors are not additive. Edward Jones, Linda Bell, and I[35] performed an experiment that demonstrated that, although it's nice to be liked by someone who shares our opinions and values, it's apparently far more exciting to be liked by someone who doesn't. Each of the college women in this experiment had a brief conversation with another woman in which she discovered either that they were in agreement or in disagreement on a number of issues. After the conversation, the subject was allowed to eavesdrop on a conversation that the other woman (actually a stooge) was having with a third person. During this conversation, the other woman discussed her feelings about the subject: in one condition, she indicated that she liked her; in another condition, she indicated that she disliked her. How did this affect the subject's feelings about the stooge? The subjects tended to have the greatest liking for people with *dissimilar* attitudes who *liked* them. Thus, although we generally like people who have attitudes similar to our own, if we encounter someone who likes us in spite of the fact that our opinions differ, we are inclined to infer that there must be something special and unique about us that he finds attractive. In short, people tend to suspect that, where opinions differ, "He likes me for myself—not for my opinions." Because this realization is especially gratifying, we tend to like that person most.

And Opposites Do Attract—Sometimes.   The old adage seems to be right: birds of a feather do tend to flock together—that is, people who share opinions that are similar tend to like each other. As we have just learned, however, it's far more complicated than that: if someone likes us, we like him better if he is *different* from us. These data are consistent with some of the findings of investigators who have studied relationships that are more enduring than those that can be produced in the sociopsychological laboratory. Robert Winch,[36] for example, who has done exhaustive studies of the personality characteristics of several engaged and married couples, finds that, under certain conditions, opposites attract—that is, people tend to choose people who have needs and characteristics that complement (rather than coincide with) their own needs and characteristics.

The reader will note that I used the term "under some conditions," because it turns out that there are contradictory data in this research area: some investigators find that married couples tend to have complementary need systems; others find that married couples tend to have similar need systems. My guess is that whether birds of a feather flock together or whether opposites attract depends on which personality characteristics are under consideration. Imagine a person who values neatness and tidiness: such a person would be disinclined to marry someone who was casual to the point of slovenliness. Similarly, the slob would not be too happy with an overly neat person. It would seem reasonable to assume that neat birds would flock with other neat birds and slobs would flock with slobs. By the same token, a person who was extroverted might not get along too well with an introverted person whose idea of a good time was to sit home watching TV. On the other hand, if we look at a different set of characteristics—say, nurturance and dependency—then a different picture emerges: a person who is very nurturant might be miserable if he found himself in a relationship with a highly independent person. By the same token, what could be better for a dependent individual than to live out his life with his head on the bosom of someone who really enjoyed being nurturant? The same holds true for masculinity–femininity, assertiveness–passivity, and dominance–submissiveness. And, in a somewhat more facetious vein, what union could be happier than that of a sadist with a masochist?

In long-term relationships, sociological factors also combine with need-complementarity to play a sizable role in determining the extent to which two people will be attracted to each other and stay together. Society sets forth certain "role norms" for married couples: for example, society expects husbands to be relatively dominant and wives to be relatively submissive. If the complimentarity of the needs of a couple coincide with the role norms set forth by society, it increases the chances of marital happiness. It should also be noted that, although the notion of need-complimentarity and the notion of opinion similarity frequently lead to opposite predictions about attraction, this is not necessarily true. People with certain complementary personality needs can be in complete agreement in their opinions about a given issue. To use an example just mentioned, it seems likely that a dominant male and a submissive female will share the same opinions concerning sex roles in marriage—that a man should be dominant and a woman submissive. It should be obvious to the reader that these role norms are continually in flux; my own guess (and hope) is that the nineteenth-century role norm of the submissive wife is currently in the process of being changed.

The Gain and Loss of Esteem

We have seen that our being liked by a person increases the likelihood that we will like him. Let us take a closer look at this relation: Imagine that, at a cocktail party, you meet a young man for the first time and have an animated conversation with him. After a while, you excuse yourself to refill your glass. You return and find him with his back turned to you, deep in conversation with another person—and he's talking about you. So, naturally, you pause to listen. Clearly, the things he says about you will have an impact upon how you feel about him. It is obvious that he has no ulterior motives; indeed, he doesn't even know that you are eavesdropping. Thus, if he tells his partner that he was impressed by you, that he liked you, that he found you bright, witty, charming, gracious, honest, and exciting, my guess is that this would have a positive effect on your liking for him. On the other hand, if he indicates that he was unimpressed, that he disliked you, that he found you to be dull, boring, dishonest, stupid, and vulgar, my guess is that this would have a negative effect on your liking for him.

So far so good. But I'm sure that's not very interesting to you; you've always known that. Everyone and his grandmother knows that the more good things we hear about outselves, the better we like the speaker (unless he's trying to con us), and the more bad things we hear about ourselves, the more we dislike the person who says them. Everybody knows it—but it happens to be untrue. Imagine this: You have attended seven consecutive cocktail parties and, miracle of miracles, the same general event has occurred each time: you chat with a man for several minutes, you leave, and when you come back, you overhear him talking about you. It's the same man each time. His responses might remain constant throughout his seven encounters with you, or they might vary. There are four possibilities that are particularly interesting to me: (1) you overhear the person saying exclusively positive things about you on all seven occasions; (2) you overhear him saying exclusively negative things about you on all seven occasions; (3) his first couple of evaluations are exclusively negative, but they gradually become increasingly positive until they equal his statements in the exclusively positive situation, and then level off; and (4) his first couple of evaluations are exclusively positive, but they gradually become more negative until they equal his statements in the exclusively negative situation, and then level off. Which situation would render him most attractive to you? Which situation would render him least attractive to you?

According to a simple reward–cost idea of liking, you should like him most in the first situation, in which he says exclusively positive things, and you should like him least (or dislike him most) in the second situation, in which he says exclusively negative things. This seems obvious. Because positive statements are rewarding, the more the better; because negative statements are punishing, the more the worse.

A few years ago, I developed a gain–loss theory of interpersonal attraction that makes a rather different prediction.[37] My idea is a very simple one. It suggests that increases in positive, rewarding behavior from another person have more impact on an individual than constant, invariant reward from that person. Thus, if we take being liked as a reward, a person whose liking for us increases over time will be liked better than one who has always liked us. This would be true even if the *number* of rewards were greater from the latter person. Similarly, losses in rewarding behavior have more impact than constant punitive behavior from another person. Thus, a person whose esteem for us decreases over time will be disliked more than someone who has always disliked us—even if the number of punishments were greater from the latter person. To return to the cocktail party for a moment, I would predict that you would like the individual most in the *gain* situation (where he begins by disliking you and gradually increases his liking) and that you would like him least in the *loss* condition (where he begins by liking you and gradually decreases his liking for you).

In order to test my theory, I needed an experimental analogue of the cocktail-party situation—but, for reasons of control, I felt that it would be essential to collapse the several events into a single long session. In such an experiment, it is important that the subject be absolutely certain that his evaluator is totally unaware that he (the evaluator) is being overheard: this eliminates the possibility of the subject's suspecting that the evaluator is intentionally flattering him when he says positive things. This situation presents a difficult challenge for the experimentalist. The central problem in devising a way to perform the experiment was one of credibility: How do we provide a believable situation in which, in a relatively brief period of time, the subject (1) interacts with a preprogrammed confederate, (2) eavesdrops while the preprogrammed confederate evaluates him to a third party, (3) engages in another conversation with the confederate, (4) eavesdrops again, (5) converses again, (6) eavesdrops again—and so on, through several pairs of trials. To provide any kind of a cover story would indeed be difficult; to provide a sensible cover story that would prevent subjects from becoming suspicious would seem impossible. But, in collaboration with Darwyn Linder, I did devise such a situation.[38] The devices we used to solve these problems are intricate, and they provide a unique opportunity to look behind the scenes of an unusually fascinating sociopsychological procedure. Accordingly, I would like to describe this experiment in some detail, in the hope that it will provide the reader with an understanding of some of the difficulties and excitements involved in conducting experiments in social psychology.

When the subject arrived for the experiment, the experimenter greeted her and led her to an observation room that was connected to the main experimental room by a one-way window and an audio-amplification system. The experimenter told the subject that two girls were scheduled for this hour: one would be the subject and the other would help perform the experiment—and that because she had arrived first, she would be the helper. The experimenter asked her to wait while he left the room to see if the other girl had arrived yet. A few minutes later, through the one-way window, the subject was able to see the experimenter enter the experimental room with another female student (the paid confederate). The experimenter told the confederate to be seated for a moment and that he would return shortly to explain the experiment to her. He then reentered the observation room and began the instructions to the real subject (who believed herself to be the confederate). The experimenter told her that she was going to assist him in performing a verbal conditioning experiment on the other student; that is, he was going to reward the other student for certain words she used in conversation. He told the subject that these rewards would increase the frequency with which the other girl would use these words. He went on to say that his particular interest was "not simply in increasing the output of those words that I reward; that's already been done. In this experiment, we want to see if the use of rewarded words generalizes to a new situation from the person giving the reward when the other girl is talking to a different person who does not reward those specific words." Specifically, the experimenter explained that he would try to condition the other girl to increase her output of plural nouns by subtly rewarding her with an "mmm hmmm" every time she said a plural noun. "The important question is: will she continue to use an abundance of plural nouns when she talks to you, even though you will not be rewarding her?" The subject was then told that her tasks were: (1) to listen in and record the number of plural nouns used by the other girl while the latter was talking to the experimenter, and (2) to engage the other girl in a series of conversations (in which the use of plural nouns would not be rewarded) so that the experimenter could listen and determine whether generalization occurred. The experimenter told the subject that they would alternate in talking to the girl (first the subject, then the experimenter, then the subject) until each had spent seven sessions with her.

The experimenter made it clear to the subject that the other girl must not know the purpose of the experiment, lest the results be contaminated. He explained that, in order to accomplish this, some deception must be used. The experimenter said that, as much as he regretted the use of deception, it would be necessary for him to tell the girl that the experiment was about interpersonal attraction. ("Don't laugh, some psychologists are actually interested in that stuff.") He said that the other girl would be told that she was to carry on a series of seven short conversations with the subject and that, between each of these conversations, both she and the subject would be interviewed—the other girl by the experimenter and the subject by an assistant in another room—to find our what impressions they had formed. The experimenter told the subject that this "cover story" would enable the experimenter and the subject to perform their experiment on verbal behavior, because it provided the other girl with a credible explanation for the procedure they would follow.

The major variable was introduced during the seven meetings that the experimenter had with the confederate. During their meetings, the subject was in the observation room, listening to the conversation and dutifully counting the number of plural nouns used by the confederate. Because she had been led to believe that the confederate thought that the experiment involved impressions of people, it was quite natural for the experimenter to ask the confederate to express her feelings about the subject. Thus, the subject heard herself being evaluated by a fellow student on seven successive occasions.

Note how, by using a cover story that *contains* a cover story involving "interpersonal attraction," we were able to accomplish our aim without arousing suspicion—only four of eighty-four subjects were suspicious of this procedure.

There were four major experimental conditions: (1) positive—the successive evaluations of the subject made by the confederate were all highly positive; (2) negative—the successive evaluations were all very negative; (3) gain—the first few evaluations were negative, but they gradually became more positive, reaching an asymptote at a level equal to the level of the positive evaluations in the positive condition; and (4) loss—the first few evaluations were positive, but they gradually became negative, leveling off at a point equal to the negative evaluations in the negative condition.

The results confirmed our predictions: the subjects in the gain condition liked the confederate significantly better than the subjects in the positive condition. By the same token, the subjects in the loss condition had a tendency to dislike the confederate more than the subjects in the negative condition. It should be stressed that a general reward—cost theory would lead us to a simple algebraic summation of rewards and punishments and, accordingly, would have led to somewhat different predictions. The results are in line with our general theoretical position: a gain has more impact on liking than a set of events that are all positive, and a loss tends to have more impact on liking than a set of events that are all negative. Spinoza may have had something like this in mind when, nearly 300 years ago, he observed:

> Hatred which is completely vanquished by love passes into love, and love is thereupon greater than if hatred had not preceded it. For he who begins to love a thing which he was wont to hate or regard with pain, from the very fact of loving, feels pleasure. To this pleasure involved in love is added the pleasure arising from aid given to the endeavor to remove the pain involved in hatred accompanied by the idea of the former object of hatred as cause.[39]

It should be emphasized that there are two important conditions necessary for the gain–loss effect to be operative. First, it is not just any sequence of positive or negative statements, but an integrated sequence that implies a change of heart. In other words, if you indicate that you think I'm stupid and insincere, and later you indi-cate that you think I'm generous and athletic, this does not constitute a gain according to my definition—or Spinoza's. On the other hand, if you indicate that I'm stupid or insincere and subsequently indicate that you've changed your mind—that you now believe me to be smart and sincere—this is a true gain because it involves a reversal, a replacement of a negative attitude with its opposite. David Mettee and his colleagues[40] performed an experiment that demonstrated this distinction. A gain effect occurred only when a change in heart was made explicit. Second, the change in attitude must be gradual. The reason for this should be clear: An abrupt about-face is viewed by the stimulus person with confusion and suspicion—especially if it occurs on the basis of very little evidence. If Mary thinks that Sam is stupid after three encounters, but brilliant after the fourth encounter, such a dramatic shift is bound to arouse suspicion on Sam's part. A gradual change, on the other hand, makes sense; it does not produce suspicion and hence produces an intensification of the person's liking for his or her evaluator.[41]

The Care and Feeding of Friendship

One of the implications of gain–loss theory is that, in the words of the well-known ballad, "You always hurt the one you love." That is, once we have grown certain of the rewarding behavior of a person, that person may become less potent as a source of reward than a stranger. We have demonstrated that a gain in liking is a more potent reward than the absolute level of the liking; accordingly, it is likely that a close friend (or a mother, a brother, or a mate) is behaving near ceiling level and, therefore, cannot provide us with a gain. To put it another way, because we have learned to expect love, favors, and praise from a friend, such behavior is not likely to represent a gain in his esteem for us. By the same token, the good friend has great potential as a punisher. The closer the friend and the greater his past history of invariant esteem and reward, the more devastating is the withdrawal of his esteem. In effect, then, he has power to hurt the one he loves—but very little power to reward him.

An example may help to clarify this point. After fifteen years of marriage, a doting husband and his wife are getting dressed to attend a formal dinner party. He compliments her on her appearance— "Gee, honey, you look great." She hears his words, but they may not fill her with delight. She already knows that her husband thinks she's attractive; she will not turn cartwheels at hearing about it for the thousandth time. On the other hand, if the doting husband (who in the past was always full of compliments) were to tell his wife that he had decided that she was losing her looks and that he found her quite unattractive, this would cause her a great deal of pain, because it represents a distinct loss of esteem.

Is she doomed to experience either boredom or pain? No, because there are other people in the world. Mr. and Mrs. Doting arrive at the party and a total stranger engages Mrs. Doting in conversation. After a while, he says, with great sincerity, that he finds her very attractive. My guess is that she would not find this at all boring. It represents a distinct gain for her, it makes her feel good, and it increases the attractiveness of the stranger.

This reasoning is consistent with previous experimental findings. O. J. Harvey[42] found a tendency for subjects to react more positively to strangers than to friends, when each were designated as the sources of relatively positive evaluations of the subjects. Moreover, subjects tended to react more negatively to friends than to strangers, when each were designated as the sources of negative evaluations of the subjects. Similarly, several experiments have shown that strangers have more impact on the behavior of young children than either parents or other familiar adults.[43] It is reasonable to assume that children are accustomed to receiving approval from parents and other adults with whom they are familiar. Therefore, additional approval from them does not represent much of a gain. However, approval from a stranger *is* a gain and, according to gain–loss theory, should result in a greater improvement in performance.

These results and speculations suggest a rather bleak picture of the human condition—we seem to be forever seeking favor in the eyes of strangers while, at the same time, we are being hurt by friends and other familiar people. Before we jump to this conclusion, however, let us take a few steps backward and look at the impact that gain or loss of esteem has on the behavior of individuals—quite aside from its effect on the perceived attractiveness of the evaluator. One study is highly pertinent in this respect: Joanne Floyd[44] divided a group of young children into pairs, so that each child was either with a close friend or with a stranger. One child in each pair was then allowed to play a game in which he earned several trinkets. He was then instructed to share these with his partner. The perceived stinginess of the sharer was manipulated by the experimenter: some subjects were led to believe that the friend (or stranger) was treating them generously, and others were led to believe that the friend (or stranger) was treating them in a stingy manner. Each subject was then allowed to earn several trinkets of his own, and was instructed to share them with his partner. As expected, the subjects showed the most generosity in the gain and the loss conditions—that is, they gave most trinkets to generous strangers and stingy friends. In short, they were relatively stingy to stingy strangers (and why not? the strangers behaved as they might have been expected to behave), and to generous friends ("Ho-hum, my friend likes me—so what else is new?"). But when it looked as though they might be gaining a friend (the generous stranger), they reacted with generosity; likewise, when it looked as though they might be *losing* one (the stingy friend), they also responded with generosity. Although it appears to be true that "you always hurt the one you love," the hurt person appears to be inspired to react kindly—rather than "in kind"—in an attempt to re-establish the positive intensity of the relationship. This suggests the comforting possibility that individuals are inclined to behave in a way that will preserve stability in their relations with others.

Let us return to Mr. and Mrs. Doting for a moment: Although Mr. Doting has great power to hurt his wife (by telling her that he thinks she's losing her looks), Mrs. Doting is apt to be very responsive to such criticism, and will likely strive to regain his interest—either by making herself more attractive or by broadening her intellectual or emotional repertoire. Of course, the burden of pleasing one's partner should not fall completely on the woman—although, in our culture, traditionally and stereotypically it has. A relationship becomes truly creative and continues to grow when both partners strive to grow and change in creative ways—and, in all of this, "authenticity" assumes great importance. Carrying this speculation a step further, I would suggest that, the more honest and authentic a relationship, the less the possibility of reaching the kind of dull and deadening plateau on which the Dotings appear to be stuck. What I am suggesting is that an analysis that suggests that close friends and marriage partners are the ones that are least likely to provide us with gains in esteem is most characteristic of relationships in which people are not open or honest with each other. In a closed relationship, people tend to suppress their minor annoyances and to keep their negative feelings to themselves. This results in a fragile plateau that appears positive but that can be devastated by a sudden shift in sentiment. But in an open, honest, "authentic" relationship, one in which people are better able to share their true feelings and impressions (even their negative ones), no such plateau is reached. Rather, there is a continuous zigzagging of sentiment around a point of relatively high esteem. In a relationship of this sort, the partners are reasonably close to the gain condition of the gain–loss experiment. In this light, Dale Carnegie's advice can be seen to be inadequate. If two people are genuinely fond of each other, they will have a more satisfying and exciting relationship over a longer period of time if they are able to express whatever negative feelings they may have than if they are completely "nice" to each other at all times.

Indeed, it is my guess that no formula will be successful over the long haul. That is, an attempt to utilize our knowledge of the antecedents of interpersonal attraction inauthentically *in order* to induce a positive response from another person will not be very successful. In the long run, authenticity is essential for the maintenance and growth of the attraction between people. In the next chapter, I will discuss the advantages of authenticity in human relations in greater detail.

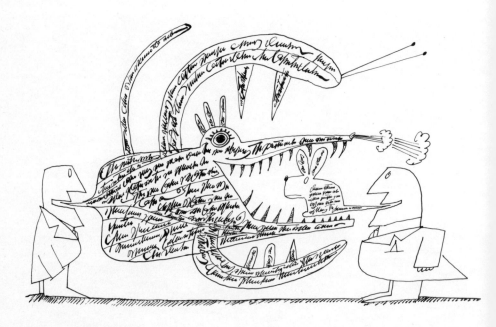

8

Communication in Sensitivity-Training Groups

In Chapter 2, we came upon a scene in which a group of people were sitting around in a circle passing judgments on the size of a line. This was the setting of Solomon Asch's classic experiment on conformity. As you recall, the behavior of most of the people in that circle was inauthentic—that is, they were making statements that were quite different from their real perceptions. They had an agenda in mind, and it was hidden from one of the individuals in the group: their agenda was to attempt to influence or manipulate that person's behavior. What I would like to describe for you in this chapter is quite a

A great deal of my thinking about sensitivity-training groups has been influenced by Michael Kahn, a highly innovative T-group theorist and trainer. Indeed, much of what is original in this chapter can be safely attributed to him. I am also indebted to David Bradford; many ideas contained in this chapter emerged during a series of endless conversations and arguments we had while we were in the process of collaborating on a forthcoming book on sensitivity training.

different kind of group. In this group, from ten to twenty people are sitting around in a circle. Unlike the group in the line-judging experiment, this group has no specific task agenda. Typically, the members have no intention of solving any specific problem. The intent of the group is not to manipulate anyone. Quite the contrary —the intent is to be authentic and to talk straight. The group I am describing is usually referred to as an encounter group, sensitivity-training group, or human-relations training group (T-group for short). The various terms are often used interchangeably but, in fact, they do connote differences in orientation and technique.

Broadly speaking, the term "T-group" refers to the more conservative, more traditional group, in which the primary emphasis is on verbal behavior and the group discussions are almost exclusively confined to the here and now. It is associated with East Coast centers, principally the National Training Laboratories in Bethel, Maine. The term "encounter group" is most often associated with the more radical wing of the human-potential movement; the activities of such groups often include a heavy dose of such nonverbal procedures as touching, body movement, dance, massage, and so on. Although they tend to be associated with such West Coast centers as Esalen Institute, encounter groups may be found throughout the United States. In recent years, many of the more traditional T-groups have incorporated some of these nonverbal procedures, but they still remain relatively conservative. I will use the term "T-group" throughout this chapter; the groups that I will be describing are more toward the traditional end of the spectrum, althought they may make use of some of the more recent innovations usually associated with the term "encounter group."

Although these groups have been in existence since just after World War II, they have burgeoned and proliferated dramatically in the past ten years. They are held in all sections of the country and their members include individuals from all walks of life. There have been specialized groups consisting solely of college students, high-school teachers, corporation presidents, police officers, hippies, members of the State Department, or delinquents; there have been groups for married couples, unmarried couples, and families; there have been confrontation groups, with hippies and cops in one, blacks and whites in another, and managers and their employees in another. But most groups have been heterogeneous—the same group might contain a lawyer, a laborer, a nun, a divorcee, a happily married woman, a banker, a student. T-groups have become a phenomenon of the sixties and seventies—they have received wide (and often sensational) publicity; they have been treated with an uncritical, cultish, almost religious zeal by some of their proponents; and they have been castigated by the right wing as an instrument of the devil, as a subversive form of brainwashing that is eating away at the fabric and soul of the nation. In my judgment, sensitivity-training groups are neither the panacea nor the menace that they frequently are made out to be. When properly used, they can be enormously useful as a means of increasing a person's self-awareness and enriching human relations. When abused, they can be a waste of time—or, in extreme cases, they might even provide people with some very painful experiences whose effects can persist long beyond the termination of the group.

The primary focus in this chapter will be on the sensitivity-training group as an instrument of communication. Although there are all kinds of groups, I will discuss only the traditional T-groups. I will attempt to describe them from within and from without, to discuss what happens in a group, what gets learned, and what the inherent problems and dangers are.

What Is a T-group?

In this section I will attempt to provide a general statement of what a T-group is and what it isn't. Subsequently, I will elaborate on this general overview. Let us begin by describing what a T-group isn't. Typically, it is not a therapy group—that is, it is not designed to cure mental illness; indeed, people with serious emotional problems are discouraged from attending. It is not a seminar—that is, it is not a group in which members communicate facts and abstract concepts about the world. It is not a group in which the leader is a traditional teacher, who tries to impart knowledge by lecturing to the members as though they were an audience. Neither is it a committee that performs tasks or solves problems that have originated outside the group itself.

A T-group experience is educational—but educational in a way that is different from what we are accustomed to. It is different both in the *content* of the material that is learned and in the *process* by which the learning takes place.

The Content: What Gets Learned. Generally, a person in a T-group learns things about himself and his relations with other people. It can be said that, in a college psychology course, I learn how people behave; in a T-group, I learn how *I* behave. But I learn much more than that: I also learn how others see me, how my behavior affects them, and how I am affected by other people.

Historically, T-groups began as a means of teaching people "interpersonal skills." For example, a business executive, a minister, a labor leader, or a school teacher might come to learn things about being a skillful leader—how to get the best out of people, how to give orders without infuriating the recipient, or how to negotiate a contract without coming to blows. While these skills are still being learned in T-groups, the emphasis has begun to shift in recent years toward more personal goals, such as learning to understand one's own feelings and those of other people. Thus, many people are motivated to participate in a T-group because they believe that there may be something missing in their lives. A person may feel alienated from other people; he may feel that life is going by too quickly; he may feel that he wants something more out of life than waking up in the morning, eating breakfast, going to work, coming home, watching television, and going to sleep. In short, many people are searching for greater understanding and greater enrichment of their lives through these groups. This does not mean that a person has to be in the middle of an existential crisis in order to join a group; many people join because they have specific confusions and are searching for specific answers: "Why do I have trouble getting along with my children (or my employees, or women)?" "Why do other people make friends easily, while I tend to be alone?" "Why do I have difficulty in opening up to people?" "What is there about people that makes them so untrustworthy?" "How can I handle my anger?" "Am I really the bitch that my ex-husband says I am?" "What do I do that turns people off?" "Why is it that, when I meet a guy, all he wants to do is take me to bed?"

In addition to allowing a person the opportunity to achieve highly personal and individual goals, most groups attempt to provide an atmosphere wherein the participants can attempt to achieve a number of general goals:

1. To develop a spirit of inquiry, a willingness to examine one's own behavior and to experiment with one's role in the world.
2. To develop an awareness of more things about more people.
3. To develop greater authenticity in interpersonal relations; to feel freer to be oneself and not feel compelled to play a role.
4. To develop the ability to act in a collaborative and mutually dependent manner with peers, superiors, and subordinates, rather than in an authoritative or submissive manner.
5. To develop the ability to resolve conflicts and disputes through problem solving, rather than through coercion or manipulation.

The Process: How Things Are Learned. The single most important distinguishing characteristic of a T-group is the method by which people learn. Again, a T-group is not a seminar or a lecture course. Although a great deal of learning *does* occur, it's not the kind of learning that can be easily transmitted verbally in a traditional teacher–student relationship. It is learning through doing, learning through experience. In a T-group, people learn by trying things out, by getting in touch with their feelings and by expressing those feelings to other people, either verbally or nonverbally. "Trying things out" not only helps the individual understand his own feelings, it also allows him the opportunity of benefitting from learning about how his behavior affects other people. If I want to know whether or not people find me to be a cold, aloof, unemotional person, I simply *behave*—and then others in the group will tell me how my behavior makes them feel.

An implicit assumption underlying these groups is that very little can be gained if someone tells us how we are *supposed* to feel, how we are *supposed* to behave, or what we are *supposed* to do with our lives. A parallel assumption is that a great deal can be gained if we understand *what* we're feeling, if we understand the kinds of interpersonal events that trigger various kinds of feelings, if we understand how our behavior is read and understood by other people, and if we understand the wide variety of options available to us. The role of the

T-group leader is not to present us with answers, but simply to help establish an atmosphere of trust and of intensive inquiry in which we are willing to look closely at our own behavior and the behavior of others.

It is in this sense that a T-group is not a therapy group. The leader does not attempt to interpret our motives or probe into our experiences outside of the group; in addition, he tends to discourage other group members from doing this. Instead, he simply encourages us to behave and to react to the behavior of others.

The Cultural Island. As we race through life, we are frequently distracted. Thoughts about the work we must do compete for our attention with the person we are supposedly listening to now; thoughts about the person we must see during the *next* hour distract us from the work we are trying to do now; as we stand at the cocktail party, balancing a drink in one hand and holding a cigarette in the other, "listening" to the pompous fellow in the flashy suit, we glance over his shoulder to see who else is at the party, and we begin to wonder why we didn't go to that other party instead. This kind of distraction is minimized in a T-group, because there is literally no alternative to paying attention. Here, we are in a room—on a "cultural island"—with several other people for two weeks (or ten days, or a weekend) with nothing to do, no agenda to work, and no one directing us toward any specific action. We are meeting for twelve to sixteen hours a day—there's nothing else happening. Initially, this can be somewhat frightening as we realize how difficult it is to interact with people in the absence of conversational crutches (the weather, have you seen any good films lately, and so on). Then, as we learn to pay attention to others, to listen, to look, we begin to pick up nuances of speech and behavior that we didn't think we were capable of noticing. We also begin to listen to ourselves more, to pay attention to those rumblings in our gut and to try to make sense out of them in the context of what is going on in the room, *outside* of our gut.

Okay, but what happens? How do people get started? What is there to talk about? Typically, the group begins with the leader (trainer) outlining the "housekeeping" schedule: when meals will be served, how long each session will last before it breaks, and so on. He may or may not proceed to outline his philosophy of groups and the limits of his own participation. He may or may not discuss the "contract"—what the participants do *not* have to do. In any case, he soon falls into silence. Minutes pass. They seem like hours. The group members may look at each other or out the window. Typically, the participants will look at the trainer for guidance or direction. None is forthcoming. After several minutes, someone might express his discomfort. This may or may not be responded to. Eventually, in a typical group, someone will express some annoyance at the leader: "I'm getting sick of this. This is a waste of time. How come you're not doing your job? What the hell are we paying you for? Why don't you tell us what we're supposed to do?" There may be a ripple of applause in the background. But someone else might jump in and ask the first person why he's so bothered by a lack of direction—does he need someone to tell him what to do? And the T-group is off and running.

Learning from Each Other

How does learning occur? How can we learn from people who are not experts? We learn through communicating. But we all know how to communicate—or do we? Occasionally, in our everyday lives, when we think we are communicating something to a person, that person is hearing something entirely different. Suppose, for example, that Fred has warm feelings for Jack but, out of shyness or out of a fear of being rejected, he finds it difficult to express these feelings directly. He may choose to communicate those warm feelings by engaging in a teasing, sarcastic kind of banter. Jack may not understand this as warmth, however; indeed, the sarcasm might hurt him. Furthermore, in our culture, it is difficult to communicate hurt feelings, because it indicates weakness and vulnerability. So Jack keeps quiet. Thus, Fred, oblivious to the fact that his behavior is disturbing to Jack, continues to express his warmth via sarcastic jocularity—continuing to hurt the person he likes—until succeeds in driving him away. Not only does Fred lose out on what could have been a warm relationship, but, also, to the extent that this is his common *modus operandi*, Fred has failed to learn from this experience, and may continue to alienate the very people toward whom he feels most warmly.

It may be useful to view the interaction between two people as a chain of events, as illustrated in the following figure.

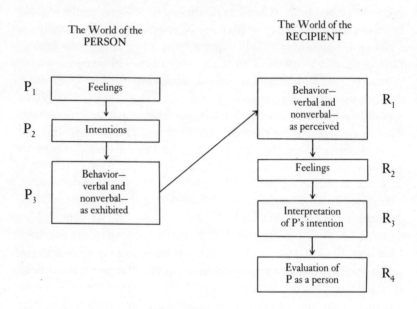

The Person (*P*) has some feelings about the Recipient (*R*). He intends to communicate a particular feeling. This manifests itself in some kind of behavior—some words, a gesture, a smile, a look, or whatever. The Recipient perceives this behavior in his own way, based upon his own needs, feelings, past history, opinions about *P*, and so on. This perception of *P*'s behavior evokes a feeling in *R* (warmth, anger, annoyance, love, fear, or whatever). This feeling is quickly translated into an interpretation of what *P*'s intentions were, which, in turn, flows into an evaluation of what kind of a person *P* is.

There are possibilities for error along any point in the links of this chain. Thus, to return to our example, Fred (*P*) has some warm, loving feelings (P_1) toward Jack. He intends to communicate these (P_2)—but he does it in an oblique, noncommittal, self-protective way:

he teases Jack, makes fun of his clothes, is jocular and sarcastic (P_3). Jack perceives this sarcasm and teasing (R_1); it causes him pain (R_2); and he decides that Fred was trying to put him down (R_3). He concludes, therefore, that Fred is a cruel, aggressive, unfriendly person (R_4).

Error can occur in a different part of the chain. Imagine a totally new situation in which Fred is completely direct and honest, but Jack is suspicious. Suppose that Fred expresses his warmth directly—by putting his arm around Jack's shoulder, by telling Jack how much he likes him, and so on. But in this case, such behavior may be too fast for Jack. Accordingly, Jack may feel uncomfortable, and, instead of simply admitting his discomfort, he may interpret Fred's behavior as manipulative in its intent: he may evaluate Fred as an insincere, political, manipulative person.

The process described above may be familiar to readers of this book: it has been discussed in Chapter 6 under the term *attribution*. If we see a person behaving in a particular way, we have a strong tendency to attribute some motive or personality disposition to him on the basis of his behavior. If this process can be explored and examined, there is a great deal of potential learning in the encounter for both Fred and Jack. Is Fred too scared to display his warm feelings openly? Is Jack too suspicious to accept genuine warmth without villifying Fred? These are important questions whose answers can produce a lot of insight, *but the opportunity for gaining this insight rarely occurs in the real world*. This learning can occur only if Fred and Jack share their feelings with each other. The T-group provides an atmosphere in which these feelings can be expressed and worked through. The group accomplishes this by encouraging the participants to stay with their feelings and to avoid "short-circuiting" the process by skipping from Fred's behavior (P_3) all the way to Jack's attribution (R_3), and, ultimately, to Jack's evaluation of Fred (R_4), without exploring the preceding and intervening events.

Openness and the Need for Privacy

Basically, then, a T-group is a setting in which people are provided with the opportunity to "talk straight" to each other—and to "listen straight." The emphasis is on the *here and now*, rather than on past history. Thus, a participant is *not* encouraged, for example, to explain to everyone the kind of person she is, nor is she encouraged to reveal her childhood experiences, her job anxieties, or the intricacies of her sex life. She *may* talk about these things if she chooses, but she usually learns more if she simply allows events to happen, reacts to the events openly as she experiences them, and allows others to respond to her as she *is* rather than as she describes herself to be. "Openness" is the key aspect of behavior in a T-group. Many critics of T-groups have reacted against the emphasis on openness, because they believe that it violates the dignity of the individual and his need for privacy. But, in this context, openness does not mean detailed self-revelation; it simply means straight talk between two or more people. In a competently conducted T-group, a norm is established that provides each member with the right to as much physical and emotional privacy as he desires. Participants are encouraged to resist any pressure to make them reveal things that they would rather hold private. But if a member does wish to express something in a group, he is helped to learn how to express it directly, rather than obliquely. For example, if Bill is angry at Ralph, it is his right to keep that anger to himself, if he so chooses. But if he chooses to express his anger, it is much more useful (for Bill, for Ralph, and for everyone else concerned) if he expresses it directly by telling Ralph about his feelings than it is if he expresses it by any one of a number of indirect means—such as making snide remarks or sarcastic statements, grunting whenever Ralph talks, making fun of Ralph covertly, or lifting his eyes toward the ceiling, so that everyone can feel his contempt for Ralph. If Bill makes a snide remark, someone in the group will almost invariably ask him if he has any feelings about Ralph that he wants to share with the group. He is not forced to share his feelings—but he's discouraged from talking in riddles and encouraged to translate the muddy language of sarcasm into straight talk.

　　This is not to deny that, in some groups, a great deal of coercion is used to make people reveal things that they might prefer not to reveal. Sigmund Koch, a vocal and erudite critic of the human-potential movement, provides a graphic description of some of the more lurid and extreme examples of coercive groups. But he goes beyond that and asserts that *all* T-groups constitute a threat to human dignity and "a challenge to any conception of the person that would make life worth living."[1] Koch has sounded a warning siren that is well worth heeding. Personally, I would prefer not to participate in a group that invaded my privacy and pressured me to make self-revealing statements against my better judgment; but I believe that Koch's condemnation of all T-groups on these grounds is based upon a misunderstanding of the term "openness" and an overgeneralization of his limited exposure to the goings on in "far-out" groups. At the same time, I would agree with Koch to the extent of advising people to steer clear of encounter groups, unless they are competently conducted and unless they practice the value that no one has to do anything that he doesn't want to do. More will be said about this near the end of the chapter.

Characteristics of Effective Feedback

The Importance of Immediacy. As I mentioned previously, members of T-groups are encouraged to express their feelings directly and openly. When the participants abide by this norm, each is able to receive immediate feedback on how people interpret what he says and does. In this way, a participant is able to gain insight into the impact that his actions and statements have on other people. Once he gains this insight, he is free to do whatever he wants with it: that is, people are not advised to perform only those actions that no one finds objectionable; rather, they are allowed to see the consequences of their behavior and to decide whether the price they are paying is worth it. They are also given the opportunity of finding out that there may be more options open to them than they may have realized. To illustrate, suppose I perform an action that angers my wife. If she doesn't express this anger, I may never become aware of the fact that the action I've performed makes her angry. On the other hand, suppose she gives me immediate feedback; suppose she tells me how these actions on my part make her feel angry. Then, I have at least two options: I can continue to behave in that way, or I can stop behaving in that way—the choice is mine. The behavior may be so important that I don't want to give it up. Conversely, my wife's feelings may be so important that I choose to give up the behavior. In the absence of any knowledge of how my behavior makes her feel, I don't have a choice. Moreover, knowing exactly how she feels about a particular set of actions may allow me to explore a *different* set of actions that may satisfy my needs as well as her needs.

The value of feedback is not limited to the recipient. Frequently, in providing feedback, people discover something about themselves and their own needs. If a woman feels, for example, that it's "wrong" to experience anger, she may block out her awareness of this feeling. When the expression of such feelings is legitimized, she has a chance to bring them out in the open, look at them, and to become aware that her expression of anger has not caused the world to come to an end. Moreover, the direct expression of a feeling keeps the encounter on the up-an-up and, thus, helps to prevent the escalation of negative feelings. For example, if my wife has learned to express her anger directly, it keeps our discussion on the issue at hand. If she suppresses the anger, but it leaks out in other ways—at different times and in different situations—I do not know where her hostility is coming from.

For example, suppose we are at a party and I begin to tell a "hilarious" story. When I am midway through my story, my wife says, "Oh, come on, now—I'm sure no one is interested in that tired old joke you keep telling," and she abruptly changes the subject. I am stunned, because I have no idea that her need to put me down is a result of some anger that she felt toward me for something I had done two weeks earlier, some anger that she was unwilling or unable to express at the time. Indeed, she herself may not know what caused her to interrupt my "hilarious" story. My response to the put-down might be to become self-righteous about being abused for no apparent reason. This makes me angry, and the escalation is on.

Feelings versus Evaluations. People often need some coaching in how to provide feedback. We often do it in a way that angers or upsets the recipient, thereby causing more problems than we solve. Indeed, one of the aspects of T-groups that sometimes frightens and confuses people who have never been in a properly conducted group is that their prior experiences with providing and receiving feedback have not always been pleasant. This is one of the reasons why it is so difficult to communicate what happens in a T-group to people who have never experienced one. Specifically, when we describe this aspect of a T-group, we are describing behavior of a sort that all of us have had experience with—much of it unpleasant. And yet, we're trying to say that such behavior can be productive in a T-group. To say this, however, may make the group seem to be a magical, mystical thing, which it's not. The way this can happen is better illustrated than described in the abstract. I will do this by providing an example of dysfunctional feedback, and of how people can be taught to modify their method of providing feedback (without modifying its quality) in order to maximize communication and understanding. This example is an event that occurred in an actual group session.

In the course of the group meeting, one of the members (Sam) looked squarely at another member (Harry) and said, "Harry, I've been listening to you and watching you for a day and a half, and I think you're a phoney." Now, that's quite an accusation. How can Harry respond? Another way of asking the question is: What are Harry's options? He has several: he can (1) agree with Sam; (2) deny the accusation and say that he's not a phoney; (3) say, "Gee, Sam, I'm sorry that you feel that way"; (4) get angry and call Sam some names; or (5) feel sorry for himself and go into a sulk. Taken by themselves, none of these responses is particularly productive. In the "real world," it is unlikely that Sam would have come out with this statement; if he had come with it, there almost certainly would have been trouble. But doesn't Sam have the right to express this judgment? After all, he's only being open.

This seems to be a dilemma: T-groups encourage openness, but openness can hurt people. The solution to this dilemma is rather simple: It is possible to be open and, at the same time, to express oneself in a manner that causes a minimum of pain. The key rests in the term *"feeling"*: Sam was not expressing a feeling, he was expressing a judgment. As I mentioned previously, openness in a T-group means the open expression of feelings. By "feeling," I mean, specifically, anger or joy, sadness or happiness, annoyance, fear, discomfort, warmth, and the like. In the terms of the figure on page 254, Sam has leapt to R_4, instead of sharing R_1 and R_2.

How was this encounter handled in the T-group? In this situation, the group leader intervened by asking Sam if he had any *feelings* about Harry. In our society, people are not accustomed to expressing feelings. It is not surprising, then, that Sam thought for a moment and then said, "Well, I *feel* that Harry is a phoney." Of course, this not a feeling, as defined above. This is an opinion or a judgment expressed in the terminology of feelings. A judgment is nothing more or less than a feeling that is inadequately understood or inadequately expressed. Accordingly, the leader probed further by asking Sam *what* his feelings were. Sam still insisted that he felt that Harry was a phoney. "And what does that do to you ?" asked the leader. "It annoys the hell out of me," answered Sam. Here, another member of the group intervened and asked for data: "What kinds of things has Harry done that annoyed you, Sam?" Sam, after several minutes of probing by various members of the group, admitted that he got annoyed whenever Harry showed affection to some of the women in the group. On further probing, it turned out that Sam perceived Harry as being very successful with women. What eventually emerged was that Sam owned up to a feeling of jealousy and envy —that Sam wished that he had Harry's smoothness and success with women. Note that Sam had initially masked this feeling of envy; rather, he had discharged his feelings by expressing disdain, by saying that Harry was a phoney. This kind of expression is ego-protecting: because we live in a competitive society, if Sam had admitted to feeling envious, it would have put him "one down" and put Harry "one up." This would have made Sam vulnerable—that is, it would have made him feel weak in relation to Harry. By expressing disdain, however, Sam succeeded in putting *himself* "one up." Although his behavior was successful as an ego-protecting device, it didn't contribute to Sam's understanding of his own feelings and of the kinds of events that caused those feelings; and it certainly didn't contribute to Sam's understanding of Harry or to Harry's understanding of Sam (or, for that matter, to Harry's understanding of himself). In short, Sam was communicating ineffectively. As an ego-defensive measure, his behavior was adaptive; as a form of communication, it was extremely maladaptive. Thus, although it made Sam vulnerable to admit that he envied Harry, it opened the door to communication; eventually, it helped them to understand each other. Moreover, a few other men also admitted that they felt some jealousy about Harry's behavior with women. This was useful information for Harry, in that it enabled him to understand the effects his behavior had on other people.

As we know, Harry has several options: he can continue to behave as he always has, and let other people continue to be jealous and, perhaps, to express their jealousy in terms of hostility; or he can modify his behavior in any one of a number of ways in order to cause other people (and, ultimately, himself) less difficulty. *The decision is his.* Should he decide that his "enviable" behavior is too important to give up, he has still gained enormously from his encounter with Sam in the T-group. Specifically, if a similar situation occurs in the real world, Harry, who now knows the effect his behavior may have on other men, will not be surprised by their responses, will be more understanding, will be less likely to overreact, and so forth.

But who needs a group? Couldn't Sam and Harry have done just as well by themselves? No. They almost certainly would have ended simply by calling each other names, hurting each other's feelings, and making each other angry. But suppose they had the benefit of a trained counselor in human relations—wouldn't that be as good as a group? Probably not. One of the great advantages and excitements about the T-group is that we don't deal with expert opinion (in the traditional sense). Rather, each person is considered an expert on his own feelings. By sharing their feelings, the other members of the group can be enormously helpful to Sam and Harry. Specifically, the other group members contributed to the data Harry was gathering by expressing their own feelings about Harry's behavior.

Indeed, if the other members of the group do not spontaneously express their feelings, the group leader might specifically ask them to do so. Why is this important? Let's take two opposite cases. First, let us assume that Sam was the only person in the room who felt envious. In that case, it would have been relatively safe to conclude that the situation was largely Sam's problem, and he could then work on it. Sam would have gained the understanding that he is inordinately jealous or envious of people who do particular things, as evidenced by the fact that no one else experienced such feelings toward Harry. On the other hand, if it came out (as it did in reality) that several people also felt envious of Harry, it would be clear that the problem was one that Harry himself might want to face up to.

This is another reason why it is important for the group that each member be honest and open in expressing his feelings. If all of the members of the group actually experienced envy of Harry, but (out of kindness, or fear, or shyness) none of them admitted to it, then it would have left Sam with the feeling that he was an extraordinarily envious person. If, on the other hand, very few of the other members felt this envy, but they wanted to support Sam and did so by claiming this feeling of enviousness, then this would have left Harry with the erroneous belief that his behavior was causing a lot of negative feelings in other people. It would also leave Sam with the erroneous belief that his behavior was not extraordinary. Thus, a desire to protect Sam would certainly not be doing him any good—it would be protecting him from an understanding of himself.

Of course, the preceding example was a relatively easy one to deal with. It ended up with Sam feeling admiration and envy for Harry. But what if Sam hates Harry—should he express his hatred? What if Sam believes that Harry is an evil person—should he express that belief? Here again, we can see the difference between a feeling and an evaluation. It would be useful if Sam would express the feelings underlying his judgments and evaluations. Did Harry do something that hurt Sam and made him angry? Is this why Sam hates Harry and thinks he's an evil person? Sam will not get very far by discussing Harry's evilness. *Sam*: "I hate you, Harry; you are evil." *Harry*: "No, I'm not." *Sam*: "Well, that is the way I see it; I'm just giving you feedback like we're supposed to do in here." *Harry*: "That's your problem—besides, you're not so great yourself." By calling Harry names, Sam sets up the situation in a way that invites Harry to defend himself and to counterattack, rather than to listen. But if Sam were to lead with his own feelings ("I am hurt and angry"), it would invite Harry into a discussion about what he (Harry) did to hurt and anger Sam. This is not to say that it is pleasant to hear someone say that he is angry at us or hurt by us—it's not. But it helps us to pay attention and to try to deal with the problem at hand.

Why is it tempting for Sam to call Harry evil, rather than to talk about his own hurt? The reasons for this behavior should be clear by now. Being hurt puts us "one down"—it makes us vulnerable. In this society, we tend to glide through life protecting ourselves; in effect, each of us wears a suit of behavioral armor, so that other people can't hurt us. This results in a lot of inauthentic behavior—that is, we mask our true feelings from other people. This is often accomplished through the process of short-circuiting. Sometimes, we are so successful at it that we mask our feelings from ourselves as well.

In summary, then, feedback expressed in terms of feelings is a lot easier for the recipient to listen to and deal with than feedback in the form of judgments and evaluations. This is true for two major reasons: First, a person's opinions and judgments about another person are purely a matter of conjecture. Thus, Sam's opinions about Harry's being a phoney and about Harry's being an evil person may reflect reality, or they may, just as likely, not: they are merely Sam's theories about Harry. Only Harry knows for sure whether he's being a phoney; Sam is only guessing. But Sam's statement that he is feeling envious or angry is not a guess or a theory—it is an absolute fact. Sam is not guessing about his feelings—he knows them; indeed, he is the only person in the world who knows them for sure. Harry may or may not care about Sam's intellectual theories or pontifical judgments, but, if he is desirous of interacting with Sam, he is probably very interested in knowing about Sam's feelings and what role he (Harry) plays in triggering those feelings.

The second major reason why feedback expressed in terms of feelings is preferable to feedback expressed in terms of judgments is that, when Sam states an opinion or a judgment about Harry, he is saying something about Harry only, but when he states a *feeling* about Harry, he is also talking about himself. Thus, the statement of feeling is a gift: metaphorically, it is Sam opening the door to his home and letting Harry in. When Sam states a judgment about Harry, however, he is storming Harry's barricades and laying something on him. Harry has good reason to resist this, because Sam has no right to be in his home without an invitation. Harry can let him in by telling him what his feelings are; likewise, Sam can let Harry in by telling him what *his* feelings are.[2]

Feelings and Intentions. Frequently, in a T-group (or in the "real world"), one person will say or do something that hurts another. If the recipient (*R*) *does* get to the point of expressing his hurt, the person (*P*) may insist that hurting wasn't his intention. It is important that he expresses this; but, in a T-group, it is important to move beyond this. If *P* says, "Oh, I'm sorry, I didn't mean to hurt you—I really like you," and *R* answers by saying "Oh, that's fine, I feel better about it now," that may smooth things over and make things tolerable. Much of the time, all we're after is interpersonal relations that are tolerable. But sometimes we want more than that—we want to learn something about ourselves and the other person. We accomplish this by moving beyond our tendency to paper over events such as this—by moving toward an exploration of the process. "Why is it that I hurt people when I don't intend to?" or, "Why am I so easily hurt?"

If *P* does not *intend* to hurt *R*, there is often a tendency for him to deny the legitimacy of *R*'s hurt, saying, in effect, "What right do you have to be hurt, now that you know that I didn't intend to hurt you?" Again, this kind of attitude does not increase *P*'s learning. If I spilled a cup of hot tea on my friend's lap, the fact that I did not intend to does not completely remove the hurt. I may want to reach out to my friend and express concern that he's hurt—and then examine my own clumsiness, to try to learn from it, so that the probability of my doing it in the future will be reduced. At the same time, it may be that the tea wasn't all that hot. The group may be useful in helping my friend and me explore the ins and outs of this complex relationship—not to decide who is right and who is wrong, but to help us understand ourselves, each other, and the nature of our relationship. In a T-group, people do not attempt to decide who is right and who is wrong; rather, an attempt is made to determine what can be learned. If a person is misunderstood, it is not enough for him to sulk and say, "Alas, nobody understands me." It can be far more productive if he tries to find out why it is that people don't understand him, and what he can do to increase the probability that he will be understood in the future. In order to accomplish this, each individual must assume some part of the responsibility for what happens to him.

The Role of the Group Leader

The leader* or "trainer" of a T-group is not a therapist or a teacher, and he does not function as one. Typically, he does not offer depth interpretations of the behavior of members of the group, nor does he spend much time in delivering lectures to the participants. He is, first and foremost, a member of the group. That means that his feelings are as much a part of the group process as the feelings of any other member of the group. He does not hold himself aloof from the group, and his feelings are not hidden from the group. Unlike a therapist, he is not in any assymetrical relationship to the group, doing all the listening and none of the disclosing. As a member, it is also appropriate for him to receive feedback from the participants. This can be an extremely important function, for the manner in which he gives and receives feedback serves as a model for the other participants. If he gives feedback openly and without evaluation and receives feedback without being defensive, his group will learn faster.

But, of course, he is also a professional who has had more experience in such matters than the other participants; although he will disclose his own feelings, he does other things as well: He may underscore what is going on so that important events do not slide by. He may occasionally make a "group-level" intervention, describing where the group seems to be headed, in terms of its own dynamics. He will help individuals work through their encounters, helping the participants to discuss their feelings (rather than their judgments), until such time as the group members themselves learn to do this for one another. Again, this learning is facilitated by the way he discusses his own feelings. He also lends support to those group members who are taking risks and making themselves vulnerable, until the partici-

---

*In this section, I am attempting to describe the behavior of a competent T-group trainer. I should acknowledge that there are many variations in style among competent trainers: some intervene much more readily than others, some use structured exercises more frequently than others, and so on. Thus, in a sense, there is no such thing as a "typical" trainer. At the same time, I would imagine that very few trainers would find serious fault with the behavior of the trainer described in this section.

pants learn to support one another. This is an extremely important function of the trainer. It is through his attitude and behavior that a general atmosphere of caring and supportiveness develops. Thus, a well-run T-group is not run in an atmosphere of tugging and shouting (as is frequently implied by the mass media); rather, it is the atmosphere of care and support, encouraged and modeled by the trainer, that makes it possible for the people in the group to try things out and, ultimately, to learn.

This does not mean that the trainer is wishy-washy or bland. He will express a wide range of emotions—including anger, fear, and envy—if he experiences them. The learning of the group members is facilitated in large part by the ability of the trainer to express a wide range of feelings clearly and authentically while, at the same time, helping to create an atmosphere of psychological safety in the group.

Occasionally, the leader must step in to prevent a group member from getting hurt. Thus, if a person is being unfairly criticized or "blindsided," the leader should intervene. When I use the term "blindsided," I am referring to a situation like the one that developed between Sam and Harry: When Sam called Harry a phoney, Harry was left in a very difficult and painful position. He was being nailed, but, because he didn't know what he had done to elicit the attack, he didn't know "where it was coming from." How could Harry defend himself? Recall that the leader intervened by taking the spotlight (momentarily) off of Harry and focusing it on Sam, where it properly belonged. This intervention served to protect Harry from the pain and embarrassment of an unjust attack, without protecting him from learning something of importance from Sam, once Sam was able to rephrase his statement in a more fair and more useful manner.

There are some situations in which it is imperative, in my opinion, for a trainer to intervene (as in the above example). But the trainer should not do all of the work: maximal learning occurs when the group has learned to do its own work. Thus, from the trainer's perspective, in many situations, an act of nonintervention can be more helpful than an act of intervention—no matter how brilliant that act of intervention might be. The purpose of a group is *not* for the trainer to show the participants how brilliant he is. Experience helps a trainer to determine when and how to intervene in a wide variety of situations. It also helps him decide when not to intervene. The more experienced the trainer, the less likely is he to commit a serious blunder. In addition, everything is grist for the mill, in a T-group— even the trainer's blunders. The more experienced the trainer, the more able he will be to help convert a blunder of his own into a learning experience for the group. It is a truism that, because of the very nature of the T-group, anything that happens can be useful, as long as it gets properly processed. The experienced trainer may not be able to avoid error, but he is able to help process that error and, thus, to contribute to the learning of the participants.

The trainer attempts to facilitate the workings of the group, helping the group to unfold in its own way, rather than dominating it or forcing it into a specific mold. By the same token, he attempts to hold the door open to all of the members, inviting them to participate without forcing them to do so. Occasionally, a participant will be hurting badly, because he has something to say but is afraid to take the risk of leaping onto center stage. The experienced trainer often becomes aware of this and may, with a word, a look, a nod, or a gesture, invite him in.

Although not a therapist, the trainer is in a unique and powerful position in the group. This means that he sometimes must use caution, lest he have *too much* impact on the group members. For example, even when he has strong feelings about an event, he will often refrain from jumping in with an expression of those feelings until after others have had the opportunity to express theirs. In addition, because of his role and power, it is likely that some members of the group will be reminded of their relations with other powerful figures in their lives; because of the permissive atmosphere of the group, they may choose the leader as the target of some of their hostile feelings toward others in positions of authority. This is a tricky situation; but, if it is useful, the leader may allow it to happen. Subsequently, he may want to explore with the group, and with the particular member, the extent to which the leader's behavior may have elicited the hostility, and the extent to which the hostility may have been a response to his role. In any event, the leader must learn to come to terms with his own power; for him to ignore it, or to pretend that it isn't there, could be malfunctional for the group.

The Application of T-group Learning to the World Outside

Throughout this chapter we have made a distinction between the T-group and the "real world." This can be misleading. In most respects, the T-group is a real-world situation. The people in these groups do not play games with each other; their interactions are real, their emotions are real, the difficulties they get into with other people are real. There is one major difference between human interactions in the T-group and human interactions elsewhere. In the T-group, the norm is openness; accordingly, the participants are oriented toward making themselves vulnerable and are set *not* to take advantage of one another's vulnerability. This is not true outside the T-group; we cannot expect others to be vulnerable, nor can we be certain that others will not take advantage of our vulnerability.

Let me illustrate: When two or more people are engaged in some sort of relationship, whether it be in a T-group or in the outside world, they usually have some feelings about each other. If these feelings are not understood, they can get in the way of the task at hand. But let us take the situation outside of the T-group: Suppose that you and I are members of a six-member committee to raise funds for underprivileged children. Suppose that you are intelligent, creative, athletic, wealthy, and personable. I'm feeling competitive with you; I want the other committee members to like and admire me more than they like and admire you. Because of those feelings, if you propose an idea for raising funds, I will be prone to find fault with it, to ridicule it, to argue it down, even if it's a good idea—*especially* if it's a good idea.

But suppose I've just come back from a T-group. How does that help me? Would I immediately stand up, cross over to where you are sitting, put my hand on your shoulder and say, "I'm feeling jealous and competitive; but you have great ideas and are a terrific guy—I want to support your ideas"? I doubt it. First of all, I'd be frightened to do that. Because we are not in the relatively protected environment of a T-group, you may not be inclined to interact according to the norm of openness. You might take advantage of the vulnerable position that my confession has left me in, and proceed to put me down.

There is no group of people to rally round us and help us work through our confrontation. There isn't an experienced trainer present to intervene in order to help me salvage the pieces of my shattered ego.

Furthermore, because you have not agreed to be in my T-group, I have no business using my openness as a means of forcing you to play my game with me. If there is one thing that sensitivity training should have taught me, it is to be sensitive to you and your style, so as not to coerce you into being more open than you feel like being. An excellent example of half-baked sensitivity training on the rampage was portrayed in the film *Bob, Carol, Ted and Alice*. In one scene, the heroine, fresh from a weekend encounter and feeling self-righteously open, is about to leave a restaurant when the headwaiter says that he hopes she enjoyed the meal. "Do you really mean that?" she asks.

Well, then, if these specific techniques are not transferable to the outside world, is T-group training of any value? Yes: the important learning is more than mere techniques—and such learning *is* transferable. Specifically, I can apply any insights I may have had about myself in the T-group and any communication skills (talking and listening) that I learned in the T-group. To illustrate, let us go back to the committee meeting: When you propose a good idea, I feel awful. I also feel a compulsion to find fault with your idea. But if, in the T-group, I had learned to confront my feelings of envy and competitiveness, I may stop and think about whether your idea was *really* a bad one, or whether I'm just being competitive again. If I can be aware of my jealousy and my need to compete, perhaps I can curb them and, thereby, become a more productive committee member. Subsequently, if I get to know you better and begin to trust you, I may decide to share with you (in private) my prior feelings of competitiveness. Perhaps I can do it in a way that will serve to invite you into a closer, more honest relationship, without attempting to *force* you into one.

Research on T-groups: Do They Really Work?

Most people who have participated in a competently conducted T-group *know* that something important happens there. They know it because they have experienced important changes in themselves and have seen others change. Moreover, nearly all T-group leaders can show you a great many letters from "satisfied customers." Carl Rogers, one of the better known group leaders, has published a typical response from a participant.

> I am more open, spontaneous. I express myself more freely. I am more sympathetic, empathic and tolerant. I am more confident. I am more religious in my own way. My relations with my family, friends and co-workers are more honest and I express my likes and dislikes and true feelings more openly. I admit ignorance more readily. I am more cheerful. I want to help others more.[3]

Although it is encouraging and gratifying to know that individuals feel better about themselves and their relations with others, these spontaneous testimonials do not, of course, constitute scientific data. The problem is that only a small percentage of the participants send spontaneous letters. What about the others? It is possible that little of importance happened to them.

One step beyond letters, in terms of scientific rigor, are questionnaires. With a questionnaire study, we can get responses from a random sample of participants and not simply from those who choose to write letters. Several studies have been done in which questionnaires were mailed to the individuals after their participation in a T-group. Almost all of these studies show that the vast majority of participants feel that they've benefitted a great deal from their experience. But still, this is not totally satisfying.

What is the baseline for change? In the absence of a control condition, it is impossible to know what really happened. These problems were solved nicely in a recent study by Nancy Adler and Daniel Goleman.[4] These investigators tested the hypothesis that participation in a T-group would be beneficial in helping individuals achieve whatever goals they set for themselves. For example, an individual might want to become less shy and more assertive; would participation in a T-group facilitate this change? The answer appears to be yes. High school students who participated in a T-group made more progress in accomplishing their own goals than those who had not participated in a T-group. While this study is an improvement over many of the earlier studies, it still leaves many questions unanswered. Somehow, the self-report of a participant does not seem very objective. It would be helpful to know several additional things: What were the specific outcomes? If some of those events had been changed, would the same results have occurred? Unless he knows for sure "what causes what," the hard-headed scientist remains somewhat skeptical—and with good reason. After all, the "good" outcome reported by a person may be nothing more than a subtle bit of self-deception. The participants spent a lot of time and effort in that group; if the experience were worthless, they would feel absurd. It is always possible that they convinced themselves that it was an important event, in much the same way that the co-eds did in the initiation experiment that Judson Mills and I conducted (pp. 118–119).

On the other hand, it is not my intention to minimize the importance of a person's awareness of his own feelings and his belief about the accomplishment of his goals. If a person feels better about himself because he has gone through a T-group, this is not to be brushed off simply because one is not clear about the exact antecedents of this change. Indeed, in my opinion, if a single T-group experience results in a person's feeling more sensitive, more understanding, more tolerant, and all those other things reported by the participant in Carl Rogers' group, then that is ample justification for the existence of T-groups. Moreover, if these effects persist for several months (as reported by many participants), then it is hard to argue against its being a real and significant event in the individual's life—regardless of whether we, as scientists, fully understand the phenomenon.

These two sides of the question do not exclude each other. The humanist can continue to revel in the impact that group experiences have on participants, without necessarily denigrating the scientist who is trying to determine whether the effects extend beyond the self-reports of the participants; the scientist can continue to try to find out "if" and "why" in precise ways, without disparaging T-groups simply because the phenomenon is difficult to investigate in as precise a manner as he would like.

Why are T-groups so hard to investigate? Basically, because it's difficult for the scientist to control and manipulate the variables that supposedly produce the outcomes. So many things are happening at once in a T-group that, after it is over, it is impossible to know what factors were crucial in making a person feel good. Ideally, the hard-headed scientist is tempted to plant a couple of stooges in a T-group, have them behave in a well-controlled, predetermined manner, and measure the effects this would have on the other participants. Such a procedure would encompass the controls and the impact that constitute the kind of experiment that has played such a major role in increasing our understanding of the social animal. But this kind of procedure is simply not feasible. The T-group is one of the few sanctuaries of honesty left on this planet. The implicit (and often explicit) assumption of the participants is that people are at least *trying* to be honest. For the experimental social psychologist to bring in his apparatus of deception would be a serious violation of this implicit contract.

What we are left with is some kind of compromise. Most of the research done on T-groups lacks the control and precision of the laboratory experiments that we've been discussing throughout this volume. It remains difficult to be certain about what causes what. At the same time, after surveying the research literature, I am compelled to draw the conclusion, albeit tentatively, that important changes do take place in T-groups, and that these changes are demonstrable beyond the individual's own self-report. In several studies, for example, it has been shown that other people outside of the T-group can see changes in participants that are consistent with the stated goals of the T-group and with the individual's own self-report.[5] Basically, here's how these studies were done. An industrial organization allowed a few of its managers to participate in a T-group. Several weeks later, the back-home colleagues of those individuals were asked if they had noticed any changes in their on-the-job behavior. As a control, the same respondents were also asked to rate any changes in the on-the-job behavior of managers who had *not* been in a T-group. By and large, the data show a tendency for managers who had participated in T-groups to be viewed by their associates as having changed more than managers who had not. Specifically, the T-groupers were seen to be more sensitive; to have more communication skills and more leadership skills; to be more considerate of others, more relaxed, and more insightful; and so on. These data suggest that the effects are not simply a matter of self-deception on the part of the participants; they indicate that real changes occur that can be perceived by other people. These findings are encouraging, but not perfect. It is always possible that some of the raters were aware of which of their colleagues had or had not been to a T-group; if this were true, it could conceivably have influenced their rating. Again, in the natural environment of an industrial organization, it is difficult to eliminate this possibility.[6]

Several experiments using a different strategy have yielded interesting and reliable data. For example, in a well-controlled experiment, Irwin Rubin[7] assessed the effects of a T-group on reducing ethnic prejudice. We have seen that people coming out of a T-group are generally more accepting of themselves and feel more sensitive, more empathic, more tolerant, and so forth. If this general feeling of self-acceptance, sensitivity, and tolerance is more than an empty self-assessment, it should result in a person's being less prejudiced against minority groups. Rubin simply administered a test designed to measure ethnic prejudice to a large group of people. Half of those people then went through a T-group experience. He then remeasured the ethnic prejudice of all of the individuals. Those who had gone through the T-group showed a sharp reduction in ethnic prejudice; those who had not gone through the T-group showed no sizable change.

Two recent experiments have shown conclusively that, after participating in a sensitivity-training group, people become more hypnotizable.[8] Now, it may seem that susceptibility to hypnotism is not a very desirable outcome—but consider what it means: Several researchers have demonstrated that people who are less suspicious and more trusting than others are more easily hypnotized. The fact that participating in a T-group increases the ease with which a person can be hypnotized suggests strongly that T-groups foster a sense of trust in their participants. These are exciting findings for two reasons: (1) generally, it is not easy to help people to learn to trust each other using other techniques; and (2) from a scientific point of view, susceptibility to hypnosis, because it is involuntary in nature, is a very convincing outcome—far more convincing than a person's own self-assessment of his increase in trust.

In another experiment, Marvin Dunnette[9] organized and set up ten separate T-groups. Some of these groups were led by well-trained, highly competent trainers; others were led by trainers having only a little prior experience. In addition, three groups of a different sort were set up: these were run as discussion groups in which the participants talked about current events, played games, solved puzzles, and so on. Before the groups started, and again after several sessions, the members were measured for their empathy with other people in their group—specifically, on how well they could predict the preferences of the members of their own group for various activities, occupations, and the like. The members of the T-groups showed a greater increase in empathy than the members of the other groups. Moreover, within the T-groups themselves, the greatest eventual empathy occurred in those groups having the more competent leaders and showing more member interaction.

This last experiment is of interest not only for its results and for its methodological soundness but, in addition, because it was conducted by an experimenter who was seriously skeptical about T-groups. Just a year earlier, Marvin Dunnette (along with John Campbell) wrote a highly critical review of research on T-groups. After performing his own experiment, Dunnette wrote:

> These results seem to me to be firm evidence that T-groups may be accomplishing what their advocates claim for them. . . . It appears from these meager but provocative results that T-groups may truly be a medium for getting to know others better—that the Quest for Love may properly be sharpened, focused, and guided by the T-group experience.[10]

What Constitutes a Good or a Bad Outcome?

T-groups have been criticized because occasionally, following a group experience, an individual may seek psychological counseling. What does this mean? Is it a good outcome or a bad outcome? It's hard to be certain. It could be that the individual was hurt by the T-group experience. It might also indicate that, as a result of the T-group experience, certain emotional problems *that always were there* came into clear focus, and the individual was able to see for the first time that he was in need of therapy. Alternatively, it might mean that the group provided him with the courage to seek out the therapy that he already knew he needed. Or, it might simply mean that he wanted therapy, and thought he could get it cheaply in a T-group; when this failed, he sought the therapy from a more appropriate source. With this in mind, it is instructive to compare two recent articles on T-groups by psychiatrists. In one, Ralph Cranshaw[11] cited three cases of individuals who needed psychiatric hospitalization following their experiences in sensitivity-training groups. He considered this a tragic outcome, and laid the blame for it on the groups, implying that the sensitivity-training movement was irresponsibly experimenting with human beings. In another article in the same journal, James Cadden and his associates[12] reported on a sensitivity program for incoming medical students. These investigators found that the program had a beneficial effect—it helped some of their students become aware of a need for psychiatric counseling. Moreover, the number of serious psychiatric crises among these students was lower than that for similar groups in previous years. This was attributed to the fact that the T-group enabled the individuals to handle their crises more effectively.

Some Dangers of Group Encounter— Let the Buyer Beware

The dynamics of a T-group are powerful. This means that a group encounter can be an exciting, exhilarating, enriching experience in which a great many emotions are felt and in which a lot of learning takes place. But, as with any powerful situation, there are some dangers. Individuals frequently experience anger and frustration, physical or emotional attraction for another member of the group, and intense joy or sadness. These experiences can produce understanding and growth, if they are discussed and worked through. However, if they are ignored or are mishandled by the group, they can produce upset, pain, humiliation, and loss of dignity, which could persist long after the group encounter has terminated.

Suppose you are a person who is interested in joining a group. Has the preceding paragraph frightened you? Good! Has it scared you out of considering a group experience? I hope not. The occurrence of serious disturbances in groups run by well-trained professional leaders is extremely small. After a thorough study of groups conducted under the auspices of the National Training Laboratories, Charles Seashore stated: "The incidence of serious stress and mental disturbance during sensitivity training is difficult to measure but it is estimated to be less than one percent of participants and in almost all cases occurs in persons with a history of prior disturbances."[13]

The question to be asked is: "How do I maximize the probability of having a good experience and minimize the probability of having a bad one?" Basically, there are two ways: first, make certain you do not join a group unless it is being conducted by a skilled, experienced, competent trainer; and second, make certain that the philosophy and techniques of the group are consistent with your own values. I will address the remainder of this section to those readers who are thinking about joining a group. The rest of you can skip to the next section, "The T-group and Empathy Formation."

The Competency of the Trainer. In recent years, with the burgeoning of interest in group encounter, the demand for groups has exceeded the supply of competent trainers. Into this breech has leapt the well-meaning individual who, fresh from an exciting experience as a participant in a T-group, has decided to "turn on" his friends by setting himself up as a group leader. *Stay Away!* No matter how good his intentions may be, he is almost certainly not equipped to handle a group. The vast majority of "bad trips" we hear and read about have occurred in just such groups. Leading a group is a very subtle business that requires a great deal of training, experience, and sensitivity, as well as a strong sense of responsibility. Don't trust it to amateurs! Moreover, even a psychologist with a Ph.D., though he may be licensed and accredited to do therapy, may not be an appropriate group leader if he has not had the requisite training. There are a few centers in the country that offer training and internships in group leadership to qualified individuals. The most well established is the National Training Laboratory (NTL) in Washington, D.C. There also exists an organization that has been formed for the primary purpose of examining and accrediting trainers—the International Association of Applied Social Science (IAASS). Its procedures for accreditation are extremely rigorous. Accordingly, the only sure-fire way of being certain that your leader is competent and well-trained is to write to IAASS, at 1755 Massachusetts Ave. NW, Washington, DC 20036, for a list of its accredited members.

Types of Groups. In this chapter, we have been describing relatively conservative groups—groups in which there is a maximum of freedom, a minimum of coercion, and few "far-out" procedures. This happens to be the kind of group that I am most comfortable with. But, as we have indicated, there are all kinds of groups. Let's look at a couple of extreme examples: some groups are conducted in the nude. There is a lot of learning that can take place in such a group—for example, people have a chance to overcome excessive modesty, hang-ups about their bodies, and so on. It *can* be a freeing experience. But if *you* don't feel ready for such an experience, you should make certain that you don't wander into this kind of group by accident. There are also groups in which a great deal of screaming, yelling, and physical violence is encouraged. This may have some value for some people; if you're *not* one of these people, however, you shouldn't stumble into such a group. In short, you should do everything you can to inform yourself of the nature of the group before agreeing to participate.

In general, you might want to steer clear of groups that do not allow you to say "no." As Michael Kahn[14] puts it, no one should be forced to do something he doesn't want to do. Indeed, in a recent study of outcomes of encounter groups, Morton Lieberman and his associates[15] found that groups conducted by coercive, forceful leaders have a tendency to produce more casualties than other kinds of groups. I would argue that they probably produce less long-term learning as well. Often a forceful, dynamic, coercive leader can "make things happen," and, by so doing, can produce temporary "highs" in some of the participants. But the ultimate goal of a group is not to get "high" but to learn some things about group dynamics and about oneself that can be important outside of the group situation. And learning is most likely to occur if the individual takes the initiative on his own.

In his analysis of the T-group, Kahn makes the point that coercion can be subtle—it need not be a function of a forceful leader—but can be a norm that develops gradually and undramatically within the group itself. He, therefore, suggests that the word "no" should be actively supported by the leader—in this way, the freedom *not* to comply becomes a norm. This does not mean that it's always good for group members to avoid situations that look frightening or painful—sometimes, important growth is possible in those situations—but the individual himself should be the one to make the decision. He should be encouraged to try if he feels ready—and equally encouraged to decline if he does not. Growth is an exciting (and often painful) experience—but no one person can "grow" another. A person indicates that he's ready to grow when he takes that first step *on his own*, and not because he is being coerced.

The T-group and Empathy Formation

In the chapters devoted to aggression and prejudice, the point was made that it is a lot easier to hurt or kill another person if he has first been dehumanized. When we think of a South Vietnamese peasant as a "gook," we feel less guilty about putting the torch to his house or killing his wife and children. When we think of a police officer as a "pig" or a student as a "long-haired weirdo," it keeps *us* from hurting as we proceed to hurt *him*. One of the aspects of T-groups that is most exciting is the potential to reverse this process. As the research literature indicates, when individuals are in a situation in which they are talking straight and listening to each other, they begin to gain mutual understanding. Understanding does not always lead to attraction: I may understand you and decide that you are not *my kind* of person, but I would have difficulty concluding that you are not a person. Accordingly, I might choose not to be your friend or never to associate with you, but it would be very difficult for me to choose to hurt or to kill you without anticipating a great deal of guilt and emotional pain.

In my experience with groups, I have seen this happen on

countless occasions. I have seen blacks and whites (or members of the Establishment and rebellious youngsters) enter with some sullen suspicion, gradually bring some of their feelings of animosity and distrust out in the open, and occasionally yell at each other in exasperation, frustration, and anger. But, in most cases, they eventually begin to listen to each other and to process their own feelings honestly and openly. Rarely do they end up by flinging themselves into each other's arms; but rarely do they leave without some awareness of the other person *as a person*. At the beginning of this chapter, I said that T-groups were not the panacea that their extreme advocates occasionally make them out to be. I repeat that statement here: T-groups probably cannot save the world all by themselves; but, when properly used, they offer a viable technique for increasing self-awareness and understanding among people.

9

Social Psychology as a Science

The distinguished Soviet psychologist Pavel Semonov once observed that man satisfies his hunger for knowledge in two ways: (1) he observes his environment and tries to organize the unknown in a sensible and meaningful way (this is science); and (2) he reorganizes the known environment in order to create something new (this is art). From my own experience, I would add the observation that, in social psychology, the two are often blended: the experimentalist uses art to enrich his science. In this chapter, I will try to communicate how this happens.

In Chapter 2, I described an incident at Yosemite National Park.

Many of the ideas contained in this chapter first saw the light of day several years ago in an article I wrote for *The Handbook of Social Psychology* in collaboration with J. Merrill Carlsmith. I am pleased to acknowledge Dr. Carlsmith's important contribution to my thinking on this topic.

Briefly, what happened was this: when awakened by sounds of distress, a great many campers rushed to the aid of the person who needed help. Because the behavior of these campers was decidedly different from the behavior of witnesses to the Genovese murder (thirty-eight people watched a woman being stabbed to death without attempting to help in any way), I speculated about what may have caused this difference in behavior in the two situations. But no matter how clever or adroit my speculations might have been, no amount of thinking and cogitation could make us certain that these speculations were correct. The reason for this is that there are literally dozens of differences between the Yosemite campground situation and the Genovese murder case. How can we be certain that the factor that I mentioned constitutes a crucial difference—the difference that made the difference?

We ran into a similar problem in Chapter 7. In that chapter, we mentioned the almost unbelievable fact that, while John Kennedy was president, his personal popularity underwent an increase immediately after he committed a great blunder. That is, after Kennedy's tragic miscalculation known as the Bay of Pigs fiasco, a Gallup poll showed that people liked him better than they had just before that incident. We speculated about what could have caused that shift toward greater popularity, and suggested that it might have been because committing a blunder served to make Kennedy seem more human, thus making people feel closer to him. But, because there were many factors involved in Kennedy's behavior, it is impossible to be certain that my speculation was accurate. In order to get some definitive evidence in support of the proposition that blunders can humanize people who appear perfect, it was necessary to go beyond observation. We had to design an experiment that allowed us to control for extraneous variables and test the effects of a blunder on attraction in a less complex situation.

This is why social psychologists perform experiments. Although some experiments in social psychology are exciting and interesting in form and content, the process of designing and conducting experiments in social psychology is not fun and games. It is time-consuming and laborious work, and it almost always puts the experimenter in an ethical bind. Moreover, in striving for control, the experimenter must often concoct a situation that bears little resemblance to the real-world situation from which he got his original idea. In fact, a frequent criticism is that laboratory experiments are unrealistic and contrived imitations of human interaction that don't reflect the "real world" at all. But is this true?

Perhaps the best way to answer this question is to examine one laboratory experiment closely, considering its advantages and disadvantages, as well as an alternative, more realistic approach that might have been used to study the same issue. An experiment performed by Judson Mills and me[1] suits our purpose. The reader may recall that, in this experiment, we showed that people who expended great effort (by undergoing a severe initiation) to gain membership into a group liked the group more than did people who became members with little or no effort.

Here's how the experiment was performed: Sixty-three college women who initially volunteered to participate in several discussions on the psychology of sex were subjects of the study. Each person was tested individually. At the beginning of the study, the experimenter explained that he was studying the "dynamics of the group-discussion process." He said that the actual topic of the discussion wasn't important to him, but that he had selected "sex" in order to be certain of having plenty of participants, because most people are interested in sex. But he also explained that he had encountered a major drawback because he had chosen sex as the topic: specifically, because of shyness, many people found it difficult to discuss sex in a group setting. Because any impairment of the flow of the discussion could seriously invalidate his results, he needed to know if the subjects felt any hesitancy to enter a discussion about sex. When the subjects heard this, each and every one indicated that she would have no difficulty. These elaborate instructions were used to set the stage for the important event to follow. The reader should note how the experimenter's statements tend to make the following material believable.

Up to this point, the instructions had been the same for each subject. Now it was time to give each of the people in the various experimental conditions a different experience—an experience that the experimenters believed would make a difference. This is called the *independent variable*.

Subjects were randomly assigned in advance to one of three conditions: a condition in which one-third of them would go through a severe initiation, one in which one-third would go through a mild initiation, and one in which one-third would not go through any initiation at all. For the no-initiation condition, subjects were simply told that they could now join the discussion group. For the severe- and mild-initiation conditions, however, the experimenter told each subject that, because he needed to be positive that she could discuss sex openly, he had developed a screening device, a test for embarrassment, which he then asked her to take. This test constituted the initiation. For the severe-initiation condition, the test was highly embarrassing: it required the subject to read aloud, to the male experimenter, a list of twelve obscene words and two detailed descriptions of sexual activity taken from current novels. (This may not seem terribly embarrassing to today's reader, but remember, this was in 1959!) The mild-initiation subjects had only to read aloud a list of words related to sex that were not obscene.

After the initiation, each subject was allowed to eavesdrop on a group discussion being conducted by members of the group that she had just joined. In order to control the content of this material, it was actually a tape recording; but the subjects were led to believe that it was a live discussion. Thus, all subjects—regardless of whether they had gone through a severe initiation, a mild initiation, or no initiation—listened to the same group discussion. The group discussion was about as dull and as boring as possible; it involved a halting, inarticulate analysis of the secondary sex characteristics of lower animals— changes in plumage among birds, intricacies of the mating dance of certain spiders, and the like. The tape contained long pauses, a great deal of hemming and hawing, interruptions, incomplete sentences, and so on, all designed to make it boring.

At the end of the discussion, the experimenter returned with a set of rating scales on which the subject was to rate how interesting and worthwhile the discussion had been. This is called the *dependent variable*, because, quite literally, the response is assumed to be "dependent" upon which of the experimental conditions the subject had been assigned to.

The results supported the hypothesis: Women who went through a mild initiation, or no initiation at all, saw the group discussion as relatively dull. But those who suffered in order to be admitted to the group thought it was really an exciting discussion. Remember, it was *exactly the same discussion* that all the students were rating.

Judson Mills and I spent several hundred hours in designing this experiment, creating a credible situation, writing a script for the tape recording of the group discussion, rehearsing the actors who played the roles of group members, constructing the initiation procedures and the measuring instruments, recruiting volunteers to serve as subjects, pilot-testing the procedure, running the subjects through the experiment, and explaining the true purpose of the experiment to each subject (the reason for the deception, what it all meant, and so forth). What we found out was that people who go through a severe initiation in order to gain entry into a group tend to like that group better than people who go through a mild initiation (or no initiation at all). Surely, there must be a much simpler way! The reader may have noticed a vague resemblance between the procedure used by Mills and me and other initiations, such as those used by primitive tribes and those used by some college fraternities and other exclusive clubs or organizations. Why, then, didn't Judson Mills and I take advantage of the real-life situation, which is not only easier to study but also far more dramatic and realistic? Let's look at the advantages: real-life initiations would be more severe (that is, they would have more impact on the members); we would not have had to go to such lengths to design a group setting that the participants would find convincing; the social interactions would involve real people, rather than mere voices from a tape recording; we would have eliminated the ethical problem created by the use of deception and the use of a difficult and unpleasant experience in the name of science; and finally, it could all have been accomplished in a fraction of the time that the experiment consumed.

Thus, when we take a superficial look at the advantages of a natural situation, it appears that Mills and I would have had a much simpler job if we had studied existing fraternities. Here's how we might have done it: We could have rated each group's initiation for severity, and later interviewed the members to determine how much they liked their group. If the members who had undergone a severe initiation liked their fraternities more than the mild- or no-initiation fraternity members, the hypothesis would be supported. Or would it? Let's take a closer look at why people bother to do experiments.

If we were to ask the man on the street to name the most important characteristic of a laboratory experiment, he would probably say "control." And this *is* a major advantage. Experiments have the advantage of controlling the environment and the variables so that the effects of each variable can be precisely studied. By taking our hypothesis to the laboratory, Mills and I eliminated a lot of the extraneous variation that exists in the real world. The severe initiations were all equal in intensity; but this would have been difficult to match, had we used several "severe-initiation" fraternities. Further, the group discussion was identical for all subjects; in the real world, however, fraternity members would have been rating fraternities that were, in fact, different from each other. Assuming we had been able to find a difference between the "severe-initiation" fraternities and the "mild-initiation" fraternities, how would we have known whether this was a function of the initiation rather than of the differential likableness that already existed in the fraternity members themselves? In the experiment, the *only* difference was the severity of the initiation, so we know that any difference was due to that procedure.

The Importance of Random Assignment

Control *is* a very important aspect of the laboratory experiment, but it's not the major advantage of this procedure. A still more important advantage is that subjects can be randomly assigned to the different experimental conditions. This means that each subject has an equal chance to be in any condition in the study. Indeed, the random assignment of subjects to conditions is the crucial difference between the experimental method and nonexperimental approaches. And the great advantage of the random assignment of people to conditions is this: any variables that haven't been thoroughly controlled are almost certain to be distributed randomly across the various conditions. This means that it is extremely unlikely that such variables would affect our results in a systematic fashion. An example might help to clarify this point: Suppose you are a scientist and you have the hypothesis that marrying beautiful women makes men happy. How do you test this hypothesis? Let us say that you proceed to find a thousand men who are married to beautiful women and a thousand men who are married to ugly women, and you give them all a "happiness" questionnaire. Lo and behold, the men married to beautiful women *are* happier than the men married to ugly women. Does this mean that being married to a beautiful woman makes you happy? No. It may be that happy men are sweeter, more good-humored, and easier to get along with, and that, consequently, beautiful women (who have a competitive advantage over ugly women) seek these men out and marry them. So it may be that being happy *causes* men to marry beautiful women. The problem doesn't end there. It is also possible that there is some third factor that causes *both* happiness *and* being married to a beautiful woman. One such factor could be money: it is conceivable that being rich helps make men happy, and that their being rich is what attracts the beautiful women. So it's possible that neither causal sequence is true—it is possible that happiness does not cause men to marry beautiful wives and that beautiful wives do not cause men to be happy.

And the problem is even *more* complicated. It's more complicated because we usually have no idea what these third factors might be. In the case of the happiness study, it could be wealth; it could also be that handsomeness causes men to be happy and also attracts beautiful women; it could be social grace, athletic ability, power, popularity, using the right toothpaste, being a snappy dresser, or any of a thousand qualities that the poor researcher does not know about and could not possibly account for. But if he performs an experiment, he can randomly assign his subjects to various experimental conditions. Although this procedure does not eliminate differences due to any of these variables (money, social grace, athletic ability, and the like), it neutralizes them by distributing these characteristics *randomly* across various experimental conditions. That is, if subjects are randomly assigned to experimental conditions, there will be approximately as many rich men in one condition as in the others, as many socially adept men in one condition as the others, and as many athletes in one condition as in the others. Thus, if we do find a difference between conditions, it is virtually impossible that this would be due to individual differences in any single characteristic, because *all* of these characteristics had equal (or nearly equal) distribution across all of the conditions.

Admittedly, the particular example of happy men and beautiful wives does not easily lend itself to the confines of the experimental laboratory. But let us fantasize about how we would do it if we could: Ideally, we would take fifty men and randomly assign twenty-five to beautiful wives and twenty-five to ugly wives. A few months later, we could come back and administer the happiness questionnaire. If we find that the men we assigned to the beautiful wives are happier than the men we assigned to the ugly wives, we would know what caused their happiness—*we* did! In short, their happiness couldn't easily be attributed to social grace, or handsomeness, or money, or power—these were randomly distributed among the experimental conditions. It almost certainly must have something to do with their wives' characteristics.

To repeat, this example is somewhat fantastic—even social psychologists must stop short of arranging marriages for scientific purposes. But this does *not* mean that we cannot test important, meaningful, relevant events under controlled laboratory conditions. This book is loaded with such examples. Let's look at one of these examples as a way of clarifying the advantages of the experimental method: In Chapter 5, I reported a correlation between the amount of time a childs spends watching violence on TV and his tendency to choose aggressive solutions to his problems. Does that mean that watching aggression on TV causes kids to become aggressive? Not necessarily. It might. But it might also mean that aggressive kids simply like to watch aggression, and that these kids would be just as aggressive if they watched "Captain Kangaroo" all day long. But then some experimenters came along and proved that watching violence increases violence.[2] How? By randomly assigning some kids to a situation in which they watched an episode of "The Untouchables"—a TV series in which people beat, kill, rape, bite, and slug each other for fifty minutes per episode. As a control, they randomly assigned some other kids to a situation in which they watched an athletic event for the same length of time. The crucial point: each kid stood *an equal chance* of being selected to watch "The Untouchables"; therefore, any differences in character structure among the kids in this experiment were neutralized across the two experimental conditions. Thus, when the investigators found that the kids who watched "The Untouchables" showed more aggressiveness afterward than those who watched the athletic event, it does suggest quite strongly that watching violence can lead to violence.

Let us return to the initiation experiment: If we conducted a survey and found that members of severe-initiation fraternities find each other more attractive than do members of mild-initiation fraternities, then we would have evidence that severity of initiation and liking for other members of a fraternity are *positively correlated*. By "positively correlated" we mean that the more severe the initiation, the more a member will like his group. No matter how highly correlated the two variables are, however, we cannot conclude, from our survey data alone, that severe initiations *cause* liking for the group. All we can conclude from such a survey is that these two factors are associated with each other.

It is possible that the positive correlation between severe initiations and liking for other members of a fraternity exists not because severe initiations *cause* members to like their groups more, but for just the opposite reason. It could be that high attractiveness in a group causes severe initiations. If group members see themselves as highly desirable, they may try to keep the situation that way by maintaining an elite group. Thus, they might require a severe initiation in order to discourage people from joining, unless those people have a high desire to do so. From our survey data alone, we cannot conclude that this explanation is false and that severe initiations really do lead to liking. The data give us no basis for making this choice, because they tell us nothing about cause and effect. Moreover, as we have seen in our previous example, there could be a third variable that causes both severe initiations *and* liking. Who would like to give and receive a severe initiation? Why, people with strong sadomasochistic tendencies, of course. Such people may like each other not because of the initiation but because "birds of a feather" tend to like each other. Although this may sound like an outlandish explanation, it is certainly possible. What is more distressing for the researcher are the countless other possible explanations that he can't even think of. The experimental method, based, as it is, on the technique of random assignment to experimental conditions, eliminates all of these in one fell swoop. The sadomasochists in the experiment have just as much chance of being assigned to the no-initiation condition as to the severe-initiation condition. In the real-world study, alas, most of them would most certainly *assign themselves* to the severe-initiation condition, thus making the results uninterpretable.

The Challenge of Experimentation
in Social Psychology

Control versus Impact. All is not so sunny in the world of experimentation. There are some very real problems connected with doing experiments. I mentioned that control is one of the major advantages of the experiment; yet, it is impossible to exercise complete control over the environment of human subjects. One of the reasons why many psychologists work with rats, rather than people, is that it enables the researcher to control almost everything that happens to his subjects from the time of their birth until the time he completes the experiment—climate, diet, exercise, degree of exposure to playmates, absence of traumatic experiences, and so on. Social psychologists do not keep human subjects in cages in order to control their experiences. Although this makes for a happier world for the subjects, it also makes for a slightly sloppy science.

Control is further limited by the fact that individuals differ from one another in countless subtle ways. We try to make statements about what people do. By this we mean, of course, what most people do most of the time under a given set of conditions. To the extent that unmeasured individual differences are present in our results, our conclusions may not be precise for all people. Differences in attitudes, values, abilities, personality characteristics, and recent past experiences can affect the way people respond in an experiment. Thus, even with our ability to control the experimental situation itself, the same situation may not affect each person in exactly the same way.

Furthermore, when we do succeed in controlling the experimental setting so that it is exactly the same for every person, we run the real risk of making the situation so sterile that the subject is inclined not to take it seriously. The word "sterile" has at least two meanings: (1) germ-free, and (2) ineffective or barren. The experimenter should strive to make it as "germ-free" as possible without making it barren or "unlifelike" for the subject. If a subject doesn't find the events of an experiment interesting and absorbing, the chances are that his reactions will not be spontaneous and that our results, therefore, will have little meaning. Thus, in addition to control, it is just as essential that an experiment have impact upon the subjects. They must take the experiment seriously and become involved in it, lest it not affect their behavior in a meaningful way. The difficulty for social psychologists is that these two crucial factors, impact and control, often work in opposite ways: as one increases, the other tends to decrease. This is the dilemma that faces experimenters: how to maximize impact upon the subjects without sacrificing control over the situation. This requires considerable creativity and ingenuity in the design and construction of experimental situations. This leads us into the problem of realism.

Realism. Early in this chapter, I mentioned that a frequent criticism of laboratory experiments is that they are artificial and contrived imitations of the world, that they aren't "real." What do we mean by "real"? As J. Merrill Carlsmith and I have pointed out,[3] an experiment can be realistic in two separate ways: If an experiment has impact upon a subject, forces him to take the matter seriously, and involves him in the procedures, we can call this *experimental realism.* Quite apart from this is the question of how similar the laboratory experiment is to the events that frequently happen to people in the outside world. This can be termed *mundane realism.* Often, a confusion between experimental realism and mundane realism is responsible for the criticism that experiments are artificial and worthless because they don't reflect the real world.

Perhaps the difference between the two realisms can be illustrated by an example of a study high in experimental realism but low in mundane realism. Recall the experiment by Stanley Milgram[4] discussed in Chapter 2, in which each subject was asked to deliver a series of shocks, of increasing intensity, to another person who was supposedly wired to an electrical apparatus in an adjoining room. Now, honestly—how many times in our everyday life are we asked to deliver electric shocks to people? It's unrealistic—but unrealistic only in the mundane sense. Did the procedure have experimental realism—that is, was the subject wrapped up in it, did he take it seriously, did it have impact on him, was it part of *his* real world at that moment? Or was he merely play-acting, not taking it seriously, going through the motions, ho-humming it? Milgram reports that his subjects experienced a great deal of tension and discomfort. But I'll let Milgram describe, in his own words, what a typical subject looked like:

I observed a mature and initially poised businessman enter the laboratory smiling and confident. Within 20 minutes he was reduced to a twitching, stuttering wreck, who was rapidly approaching a point of nervous collapse. He constantly pulled on his earlobe, and twisted his hands. At one point he pushed his fist into his forehead and muttered: "Oh God, let's stop it." And yet he continued to respond to every word of the experimenter, and obeyed to the end.[5]

This hardly seems like the behavior of a person in an unrealistic situation. The things that were happening to Milgram's subjects were *real*—even though they didn't happen to them in their everyday existence. Accordingly, it would seem safe to conclude that the results of this experiment are a reasonably accurate indication of the way people would react if a similar set of events *did* occur in the real world.

Deception. The importance of experimental realism can hardly be overemphasized. The best way to achieve this essential quality is to design a setting that will be absorbing and interesting to the subjects. At the same time, it is frequently necessary to disguise the true purpose of the study. This puts the sociopsychological experimenter in the position of a film director who's setting the stage for action but not telling the actor what the play is all about. Such settings are called *cover stories*, and are designed to increase experimental realism by producing a situation in which the subject can act naturally, without being inhibited by knowing just which aspect of his behavior is being studied. For example, in the Aronson–Mills initiation study, subjects were told that they were taking a test for embarrassment, in order to screen them for membership in a group that would be discussing the psychology of sex—this was the cover story. In reality, they were being subjected to an initiation to see what effect, if any, this would have on their liking for the group. If the subjects had been aware of the true purpose of the study before their participation, the results would have been totally meaningless. Researchers who have studied this issue have shown that, if a subject knows the true purpose of the experiment, he does *not* behave naturally but either tries to perform in a way that puts him in a good light or tries to "help out" the experimenter by behaving in a way that makes the experiment come out as predicted. Both of these outcomes are disastrous for the experimenter. The experimenter can usually succeed in curbing the subject's desire to be "helpful," but the desire to "look good" is more difficult to curb. Most people do not want to be thought of as weak, abnormal, unattractive, stupid, or crazy. Thus, if given a chance to figure out what the experimenter is looking for, most people will try to make themselves look good or "normal." For example, in an experiment designed specifically to elucidate this phenomenon,[6] when subjects were told that a particular outcome indicated that they possessed a "good" personality trait, they exhibited the behavior necessary to produce that outcome far more often than when they were told that it reflected a negative trait. Although this behavior is understandable, it does interfere with meaningful results. It is for this reason that subjects are deceived about the true nature of the experiment.

To illustrate, let's look again at Solomon Asch's classic experiment on conformity.[7] Recall that, in this study, a student was assigned the task of judging the relative size of a few lines. It was a simple task. But a few other students (who were actually accomplices of the experimenter) purposely stated an incorrect judgment. When faced with this situation, a sizable number of the subjects yielded to the implicit group pressure and stated the incorrect judgment. This was, of course, a highly deceptive experiment. The subjects thought that they were participating in an experiment on perception, but, actually, it was their conformity that was being studied. Was this deception necessary? I think so. Let's play it back without deception: Imagine yourself a subject in an experiment in which the experimenter said, "I am interested in studying whether or not you will conform in the face of group pressure," and then he told you what was going to happen. My guess is that you wouldn't conform. My guess is that almost *no one* would conform—because conformity is considered to be a weak and unattractive behavior. What could the experimenter have concluded from this? That people tend to be nonconformists? Such a conclusion would be erroneous and misleading. Such an experiment would be meaningless.

Recall Milgram's experiments on obedience: He found that 62 percent of the average citizens in his experiment were willing to administer intense shocks to another person in obedience to the experimenter's command. Yet, each year, when I describe the experimental situation to the students in my class and ask them if *they* would obey such a command, only about 1 percent indicate that they would. Does this mean that my students are nicer people than Milgram's subjects? I don't think so. I think it means that people, if given half a chance, will try to look good. Thus, unless Milgram had used deception, he would have come out with results that simply do not reflect the way people behave when they are led to believe that they are in real situations. If we were to give people the opportunity to sit back, relax, and make a guess as to how they would behave if . . . , we would get a picture of how people would like to be, rather than a picture of how people are.

Ethical Problems. Using deception may be the best (and perhaps the *only*) way to get useful information about the way people behave in most complex and important situations, but it *does* present the experimenter with a serious ethical problem. Basically, there are three problems:

> 1. It is simply unethical to tell lies to people. This takes on even greater significance in the post-Watergate era, when it has been revealed that government agencies have bugged citizens illegally, that presidents tell outright lies to the people who elected them, and that all manner of dirty tricks, fake letters, forged documents, and so on, have been used by people directly employed by the president. Can social scientists justify adding to the polution of deception that currently exists?
>
> 2. Such deception frequently leads to an invasion of privacy. When the people serving as subjects do not know what the experimenter is really studying, they are in no position to give their informed consent. For example, in Asch's experiment, it is conceivable that some students might not have agreed to participate, had they known in advance that Asch was interested in examining their tendency toward conformity, rather than their perceptual judgment.
>
> 3. Experimental procedures often entail some unpleasant experiences, such as pain, boredom, anxiety, and the like.

Do the ends justify the means? This is a debatable point. Some argue that, no matter what the goals of this science are and no matter what the accomplishments, it's not worth it if people are deceived or put through some discomfort. Others, on the opposite end of the spectrum, insist that social psychologists are finding things out that may have profound benefits for mankind, and, accordingly, almost any price is worth paying for the results.

My own position is somewhere in between. I believe that the science of social psychology is important, and I also believe that experimental subjects should be protected at all times. This means at least five things:

1. Procedures that cause intense pain or discomfort should be avoided, if at all possible. If the experimenter exercises a great deal of ingenuity and caution, he can usually succeed in testing his hypothesis without using extreme methods. Although a less intense procedure usually produces results that are less clear, experimenters might choose to sacrifice some clarity in the interests of protecting their subjects.

2. Experimenters should be ever alert to alternative procedures to deception. If some other viable procedure can be found, it should be used.

3. Experimenters should provide their subjects with the real option of quitting the experiment if their discomfort becomes too intense.

4. The experimenter should spend considerable time with each subject at the close of the experimental session, carefully explaining the experiment, its true purpose, the reasons for the deception, and so on. He should go out of his way to protect the dignity of the subject, to avoid making him feel stupid or gullible about having "fallen for" the deception. He should make certain that the subject leaves the scene in good spirits—feeling good about himself and about his role in the experiment. This can be accomplished by any earnest experimenter who is willing to take the time and effort to repay the subject (with information and consideration) for the very important role the subject has played in the scientific enterprise.

5. Finally, the experimenter should not undertake an experiment that entails deception or discomfort "just for the hell of it." Before entering the laboratory, the experimenter should be certain that the experiment is sound and important—that he is seeking the answer to an interesting question and that he is seeking it in a careful and well-organized manner.

Most experimenters in social psychology are extremely sensitive to the needs of their subjects. Although some experiments entail procedures that cause a considerable amount of discomfort, the vast majority of these procedures contain a great many safeguards for the protection of subjects. For example, from the point of view of subject discomfort, most readers would agree that Stanley Milgram's experiment on obedience is one of the most difficult studies reported in this book. Yet it is evident that Milgram worked hard after the experiment to turn the overall experience into a useful and exciting one for his subjects. It is also clear that he was successful: Some time after the experiment, 83.7 percent of the participants reported that they were glad to have taken part in the study; 15.1 percent reported neutral feelings; and only 1.3 percent stated that they were sorry they participated. Furthermore, a university psychiatrist interviewed a sample of the subjects and found no injurious effects—rather, the typical response was that their participation was instructive and enriching.

The Postexperimental Session. The postexperimental session, sometimes called debriefing, is an extremely important part of the experiment. Not only is it of great value as a means of undoing some of the discomforts and deceptions that occurred during the experimental session, it also provides the experimenter with an opportunity to instruct the subject so that the experiment can become an educational experience. In addition, it allows the experimenter to determine the extent to which his procedure worked—and to find out from the one person who knows best (the subject) how he might improve the procedure. In short, the prudent experimenter regards his subjects as colleagues—not as objects. For those of you who have never had first-hand experience with a debriefing session, a description of exactly what is involved and how subjects are treated may provide a more complete understanding of the experimental technique.

At first, the experimenter encourages the subject to give his overall reaction to the experiment and to ask any questions he might have. He then tries to determine why the subject responded as he did and whether he interpreted the procedures the way they were intended. If there was any deception involved, was the subject suspicious of the cover story? If the subject was suspicious, the experimenter must decide whether his suspicions were great enough to have affected his behavior. If so, then the subject's responses cannot be included in the data of the experiment. Because the researcher is interested in how subjects spontaneously behave, any responses that are motivated by suspicions cannot be spontaneous, and are most likely invalid. If more than a few subjects must be discarded for reasons of suspiciousness, the entire experiment must be scrapped.

Throughout this first part of the debriefing, the experimenter probes to try to learn as precisely as possible what the subject's reactions were, and whether he was suspicious. The subject is then informed of the deception. It is important that the pace be gradual and the manner gentle, so that the subject isn't suddenly confronted with the information. I can picture Lucy (in the "Peanuts" comic strip) as the world's worst experimenter. How might she break the news to Charlie Brown? "You've been fooled; we've been lying to you and you fell for it—ha! ha!" Clearly, this kind of approach must be avoided.

Every experimenter has his own technique for debriefing. I will discuss my own procedure in some detail: I begin by asking the subject whether the experiment was perfectly clear—if he has any questions about either the purpose or the procedure. I usually ask some open-ended questions—for example, I might simply ask him to tell me frankly how the experiment struck him. Because people do react differently, it does help me to know his feelings. I then begin zeroing in by asking him if any part of the procedure seemed odd, confusing, or disturbing to him. If he does have any suspicions, they will probably be revealed by this procedure, or at least I will see signs that indicate the need for further probing; but, if not, I continue toward greater specificity and ask if he thinks there may be more to the experiment than meets the eye. This is a giveaway. It tells him, in effect, that there *was* more than meets the eye. Many subjects will indicate that they do think so. This does not necessarily mean that they had strong and definite suspicions; it means, rather, that some people know that deception is frequently a part of certain psychology experiments, and that they are vaguely suspicious about the probability of this being one of those. My own questioning may have helped confirm these suspicions. It is important that we recognize the subject's lack of gullibility. It is also important that we communicate that being fooled by the procedure is not a matter of stupidity or gullibility, but that it is a function of the procedure—because if it's a good experiment, *virtually everyone* gets fooled. This is crucial: being "taken in" hurts only if it leads us to conclude that we are extraordinarily stupid or gullible. But this is not true with these experiments. If the experiment is a good one, *everyone* will be "taken in." Accordingly, it is imperative that the experimenter take the time and trouble to make this clear to the subject. This one factor is frequently the crucial determinant of whether the subject goes home feeling good about his participation or feeling like a fool. Any experimenter who doesn't take special care with this part of the experiment has no business in a sociopsychological laboratory.

If the subject voices specific suspicions, I invite him to say how they might have affected his behavior. His answer to this question is crucial. If he does have some clear suspicions (right or wrong), and if these did affect his behavior, I will discard his data. Obviously, this decision is made in ignorance of whether or not his results supported the hypothesis! If he is not on target, I will tell him that it was reasonable for him to be suspicious, that there *is* more to the experiment, and I will then proceed to describe what we're studying and the reasons for using deception. I try to level with the subjects by sharing my own discomfort about using deception. I also try hard to explain why I think the results might be important.

If the subject is feeling uncomfortable, or angry, or disdainful, I want to know it so I can deal with it. But most subjects are polite. To help the subject build up the courage to tell me off (if he feels like it), I try to share my own questions and criticisms about the procedure and its impact, in the hope that this will remove any reluctance he may feel in talking about his skepticisms, his feeling that the whole experiment seemed trivial and meaningless, his annoyance, his discomfort, or the fact that the procedure had more of an impact on him than I had intended. Subjects are usually eager to help me improve the experiment, and frequently have provided me with many valuable suggestions.

To close the session, I ask that subjects try to keep their laboratory experiences secret. If future subjects know the study's purpose in advance, their reactions will be invalid and could lead to our drawing incorrect conclusions about the results. To avoid this waste of time, experimenters need to secure the help of each person participating in the study. I have had good success at maintaining secrecy by emphasizing the great harm that would be done to the scientific community if sophisticated subjects provided me with results that falsely supported my hypothesis.[8]

In this chapter, I have tried to present the advantages of the experimental method, and I have tried to show how complex and challenging it is to design a laboratory experiment in social psychology. In addition, I have tried to share some of the excitement I feel in overcoming difficulties, and tried to explore the ways I attempt to insure the well-being, as well as the learning, of my subjects. Experimental subjects have contributed a great deal to our understanding; we are in their debt. The knowledge, information, and insights described in the first eight chapters of this book are based upon the techniques and procedures discussed in this chapter, as well as upon the cooperation of our experimental subjects. Ultimately, our understanding of the social animal in all of his complexities rests on our ingenuity in developing techniques for studying his behavior that are well-controlled and impactful without violating the essential dignity of those individuals who contribute to our understanding by serving as experimental subjects.

The Morality of Discovering Unpleasant Things

There is one additional ethical consideration—a rather knotty one: the moral responsibility of the scientist for what he discovers. Throughout this book, I have been dealing with some extremely powerful antecedents of persuasion. This was particularly true in Chapter 4, in which I discussed techniques of self-persuasion, and in some of the subsequent chapters, in which I discussed some of the applications of these techniques. Self-persuasion is a very powerful force because, in a very real sense, the "persuadee" never knows what hit him. He comes to believe that a particular thing is true, not because J. Robert Oppenheimer or T. S. Eliot or Joe "The Shoulder" convinced him that it was true—he comes to believe it because he has convinced himself. What's more, he frequently does not know why or how he came to believe it. This renders the phenomena not only powerful, but frightening as well. As long as I know why I came to believe X, I am relatively free to change my mind; but if all I know is that X is true—and that's all there is to it—I am far more likely to cling to that belief, even in the face of disconfirming evidence.

The mechanisms that I described can be used to get people to brush their teeth, to stop bullying smaller people, to reduce pain, or to love their neighbors. Many people might consider these to be good outcomes; but they are manipulative just the same. Moreover, the same mechanisms can also be used to get people to buy particular brands of toothpaste and perhaps to vote for particular political candidates. Isn't it immoral to uncover ways of manipulating people?

As the reader of this volume must know by this time, as a real person living in the real world, I have a great many values—and I've made no effort to conceal them; they stick out all over the place. For example, I would like to eliminate bigotry and cruelty. If I had the power, I would employ the most humane and effective methods at my disposal in order to achieve those ends. I am equally aware that, once the methods are developed, others might use them in an attempt to achieve ends that I might not agree with. This causes me great concern. I am also aware that you may not share my values—therefore, if you believe that these techniques are powerful, *you* should be concerned.

At the same time, I should hasten to point out that the phenomena I have been describing are not new. It was not a social psychologist who got Mr. Landry hooked on Marlboros, and it was not a social psychologist who induced Lt. Calley to wantonly kill Vietnamese civilians. They did what they did on their own. Social psychologists are attempting to understand these phenomena and scores of others that take place in the world every day, phenomena that have been occurring since the time that the first two people on earth began interacting. By understanding these phenomena, the social psychologist may be able to help people to refrain from a particular kind of behavior when the people themselves decide that it is maladaptive.

But the mere fact that a working social psychologist knows that the phenomena he or she is working with are not of his or her own creation does not free us from moral responsibility. Our research often crystallizes these phenomena into highly structured, easily applicable techniques. There is always the possibility that some individuals may develop these techniques and use them for their own ends.

In the hands of a demagogue, these techniques could conceivably turn our society into an Orwellian nightmare. It is not my intention to preach about the responsibilities of social psychologists. What I am most cognizant of are what I believe to be *my own* responsibilities. Briefly, they are to educate the public about how these techniques might be used, to remain vigilant against their abuse, and to continue to do research aimed at furthering our understanding of the social animal, of how he thinks and how he behaves.

Notes

Chapter 1. What Is Social Psychology?

1. James Michener, *Kent State*: *What Happened and Why* (New York: Random House, 1971).

2. Kenneth Clark and Mamie Clark, "Racial Identification and Preference in Negro Children," in *Readings in Social Psychology*, ed. T. M. Newcomb and E. L. Hartley (New York: Holt, 1947), pp. 169–178.

3. Jonathan Harris, *Hiroshima*: *A Study in Science, Politics, and the Ethics of War* (Menlo Park, Calif.: Addison-Wesley, 1970).

4. Michener, *op. cit.*

5. Ellen Berscheid; personal communication.

6. Philip Zimbardo, *The Psychological Power and Pathology of Imprisonment* (a statement prepared for the U.S. House of Representatives Committee on the Judiciary; Subcommittee No. 3: Hearings on Prison Reform, San Francisco, Calif., October 25, 1971), p. 3.

Chapter 2.   Conformity

1. Copyright © 1933, 1961 by James Thurber. From "The Day the Dam Broke," in *My Life and Hard Times* (New York: Harper, 1933), pp. 41, 47. (Originally printed in *The New Yorker*.)

2. Stanley Schachter, "Deviation, Rejection, and Communication," *Journal of Abnormal and Social Psychology*, 46 (1951): 190–207.

3. Albert Speer, *Inside the Third Reich: Memoirs*, tr. Richard Winston and Clara Winston (New York: Macmillan, 1970).

4. *Playboy*, January, 1975, p. 78.

5. Solomon Asch, "Effects of Group Pressure Upon the Modification and Distortion of Judgement," in *Groups, Leadership and Men*, ed. M. H. Guetzkow (Pittsburgh: Carnegie, 1951), pp. 117–190. Solomon Asch, "Studies of Independence and Conformity: A Minority of One Against a Unanimous Majority," *Psychological Monographs*, 70 (1956): No. 9, Whole No. 416.

6. Morton Deutsch and Harold Gerard, "A Study of Normative and Informational Social Influence Upon Individual Judgment," *Journal of Abnormal and Social Psychology*, 51 (1955): 629–636.

7. Jane Mouton, Robert Blake, and Joseph Olmstead, "The Relationship Between Frequency of Yielding and the Disclosure of Personal Identity," *Journal of Personality*, 24 (1956): 339–347.

8. Michael Argyle, "Social Pressure in Public and Private Situations," *Journal of Abnormal and Social Psychology*, 54 (1957): 172–175.

9. Solomon Asch, "Effects of Group Pressure Upon the Modification and Distortion of Judgment," in *Groups, Leadership and Men*, ed. M. H. Guetzkow (Pittsburgh: Carnegie, 1951), pp. 117–190.

10. Bernard Mausner, "The Effect of Prior Reinforcement of the Interaction of Observer Pairs," *Journal of Abnormal and Social Psychology*, 49 (1954): 65–68. Bernard Mausner, "The Effect of One's Partner's Success in a Relevant Task on the Interaction of Observed Pairs," *Journal of Abnormal and Social Psychology*, 49 (1954): 557–560. Solomon Goldberg and Ardie Lubin, "Influence as a Function of Perceived Judgment Error," *Human Relations*, 11 (1958): 275–281.

11. Stanley Milgram, "Nationality and Conformity," *Scientific American*, 205 (5) (1961): 45–51. R. Frager, "Conformity and Anti-

conformity in Japan," *Journal of Personality and Social Psychology*, 15 (1970): 203–210.

12. Frank W. Schneider, "Conforming Behavior of Black and White Children," *Journal of Personality and Social Psychology*, 16 (1970): 466–471.

13. Gordon Allport, The Nature of Prejudice (Cambridge, Mass.: Addison-Wesley, 1954): 13–14.

14. James Dittes and Harold Kelley, "Effects of Different Conditions of Acceptance Upon Conformity to Group Norms," *Journal of Abnormal and Social Psychology*, 53 (1956): 100–107.

15. Leon Festinger, "A Theory of Social Comparison Processes," *Human Relations*, 7 (1954): 117–140.

16. Stanley Schachter and Jerome Singer, "Cognitive, Social, and Physiological Determinants of Emotional State," *Psychological Review*, 69 (1962): 379–399.

17. William James, *Principles of Psychology* (New York: Smith, 1890).

18. Herbert Kelman, "Processes of Opinion Change," *Public Opinion Quarterly*, 25 (1961): 57–78.

19. Charles Kiesler, Mark Zanna, and James De Salvo, "Deviation and Conformity: Opinion Change as a Function of Commitment, Attraction, and Presence of a Deviate," *Journal of Personality and Social Psychology*, 3 (1966): 458–467.

20. Carolin Kuetner, Edward Lichtenstein, and Hayden Mees, "Modification of Smoking Behavior: A Review," *Psychological Bulletin*, 70 (1968): 520–533.

21. Stanley Milgram, "Behavioral Study of Obedience," *Journal of Abnormal and Social Psychology*, 67 (1963): 371–378. Stanley Milgram, "Some Conditions of Obedience and Disobedience to Authority," *Human Relations*, 18 (1965): 57–76.

22. Stanley Milgram, "Some Conditions of Obedience and Disobedience to Authority," *Human Relations*, 18 (1965): 57–76.

23. John Darley and Bibb Latané, "Bystander Intervention in Emergencies: Diffusion of Responsibility," *Journal of Personality and Social Psychology*, 8 (1968): 377–383. Bibb Latané and John Darley, "Group Inhibition of Bystander Intervention in Emergencies," *Journal of Personality and Social Psychology*, 10 (1968): 215–221. Bibb Latané and Judith Rodin, "A Lady in Distress: Inhibiting

Effects of Friends and Strangers on Bystander Intervention," *Journal of Experimental and Social Psychology*, 5 (1969): 189–202.

24. Bibb Latané and Judith Rodin, "A Lady in Distress: Inhibiting Effects of Friends and Strangers on Bystander Intervention," *Journal of Experimental Social Psychology*, 5 (1969): 189–202.

25. Darley and Latané, *op. cit.*

26. Irving Piliavin, Judith Rodin, and Jane Piliavin, "Good Samaritanism: An Underground Phenomenon?" *Journal of Personality and Social Psychology*, 13 (1969): 289–299.

27. Robert A. Baron, "Magnitude of Model's Apparent Pain and Ability to Aid the Model as Determinants of Observer Reaction Time," *Psychonomic Science*, 21 (1970): 196–197.

Chapter 3.   Mass Communication, Propaganda, and Persuasion

1. *Newsweek*, June 2, 1974, p. 79. John J. Occonner, "They Sell All Kinds of Drugs on Television," *The New York Times*, March 10, 1974, p. D15.

2. Philip Mann and Ira Iscoe, "Mass Behavior and Community Organization: Reflections on a Peaceful Demonstration," *American Psychologist*, 26 (1971): 108–113.

3. Joe McGinniss, *The Selling of the President 1968* (New York: Pocket Books, 1970), p. 160.

4. Daryl Bem, *Beliefs, Attitudes, and Human Affairs* (Belmont, Calif.: Brooks/Cole, 1970).

5. Robert Zajonc, "The Attitudinal Effects of Mere Exposure," *Journal of Personality and Social Psychology Monograph Supplement*, 9 (1968): 1–27.

6. Philip Zimbardo and Ebbe Ebbesen, *Influencing Attitudes and Changing Behavior* (Reading, Mass.: Addison-Wesley, 1969).

7. Aristotle, "Rhetoric," tr. W. Rhys Roberts, in *Aristotle, Rhetoric and Poetics* (New York: Modern Library, 1954), p. 25.

8. Carl Hovland and Walter Weiss, "The Influence of Source Credibility on Communication Effectiveness," *Public Opinion Quarterly* 15 (1951): 635–650.

9.   Elliot Aronson and Burton Golden, "The Effect of Relevant and Irrelevant Aspects of Communicator Credibility on Opinion Change," *Journal of Personality*, 30 (1962): 135–146.

10. *The New York Times*, February 17, 1974.

11. Elaine Walster, Elliot Aronson, and Darcy Abrahams, "On Increasing the Persuasiveness of a Low Prestige Communicator," *Journal of Experimental Social Psychology*, 2 (1966): 325–342.

12. Elaine Walster and Leon Festinger, "The Effectivenese of 'Overheard' Persuasive Communications," *Journal of Abnormal and Social Psychology*, 65 (1962): 395–402.

13. Judson Mills and Elliot Aronson, "Opinion Change as a Function of Communicator's Attractiveness and Desire to Influence," *Journal of Personality and Social Psychology*, 1(1965): 173–177.

14. George Hartmann, "A Field Experiment on the Comparative Effectiveness of 'Emotional' and 'Rational' Political Leaflets in Determining Election Results," *Journal of Abnormal and Social Psychology*, 31 (1936): 336–352.

15. Howard Leventhal, "Findings and Theory in the Study of Fear Communications," in *Advances in Experimental Social Psychology*, Vol. 5, ed. L. Berkowitz (New York: Academic Press, 1970), pp. 119–186.

16. Carl Hovland, Arthur Lumsdain, and Frederick Sheffield, *Experiments on Mass Communication* (Princeton: Princeton University Press, 1949).

17. Norman Miller and Donald Campbell, "Recency and Primacy in persuasion as a Function of the Timing of Speeches and Measurements," *Journal of Abnormal and Social Psychology*, 59 (1959): 1–9.

18. Philip Zimbardo, "Involvement and Communication Discrepancy as Determinants of Opinion Conformity," *Journal of Abnormal and Social Psychology*, 60 (1960): 86–94.

19. Carl Hovland, O. J. Harvey, and Muzafer Sherif, "Assimilation and Contrast Effects in Reaction to Communication and Attitude Change," *Journal of Abnormal and Social Psychology*, 55 (1957): 244–252.

20. Elliot Aronson, Judith Turner, and J. Merrill Carlsmith, "Communication Credibility and Communication Discrepancy as De-

terminants of Opinion Change," *Journal of Abnormal and Social Psychology*, 67 (1963): 31–36.

21. Irving L. Janis, Donald Kaye, and Paul Kirschner, "Facilitating Effects of 'Eating-While-Reading' on Responsiveness to Persuasive Communications," *Journal of Personality and Social Psychology*, 1 (1965): 181–186.

22. Jonathan Freedman and David Sears, "Warning, Distraction and Resistance to Influence," *Journal of Personality and Social Psychology*, 1 (1965): 262–266.

23. William McGuire and Dimitri Papageorgis, "The Relative Efficacy of Various Types of Prior Belief—Defense in Producing Immunity Against Persuasion," *Journal of Abnormal and Social Psychology*, 62 (1961): 327–337.

24. Lance Canon, "Self-confidence and Selective Exposure to Information," in *Conflict, Decision and Dissonance*, ed. L. Festinger (Stanford: Stanford University Press, 1964), pp. 83–96.

25. Leon Festinger and Nathan Maccoby, "On Resistance to Persuasive Communications," *Journal of Abnormal and Social Psychology*, 68 (1964): 359–366.

Chapter 4.   Self-Justification

1. Jamuna Prasad, "A Comparative Study of Rumors and Reports in Earthquakes," *British Journal of Psychology*, 41 (1950): 129–144.

2. Durganand Sinha, "Behavior in a Castastrophic Situation: A Psychological Study of Reports and Rumours," *British Journal of Psychology*, 43 (1952): 200–209.

3. Leon Festinger, *A Theory of Cognitive Dissonance* (Stanford: Stanford University Press, 1957).

4. *Austin American*, Nov. 18, 1971, p. 69.

5. Albert Hastorf and Hadley Cantril, "They Saw a Game: A Case Study," *Journal of Abnormal and Social Psychology*, 49 (1954): 129–134.

6. Lenny Bruce, *How to Talk Dirty and Influence People* (Chicago: Playboy Press, and New York: Pocket Books, 1966), pp. 232–233.

7. *Newsweek*, Letter to the Editor, June 18, 1973.

8. Edward Jones and Rika Kohler, "The Effects of Plausibility on the Learning of Controversial Statements," *Journal of Abnormal and Social Psychology*, 57 (1958): 315–320.

9. Danuta Ehrlich, Isaiah Guttman, Peter Schönbach, and Judson Mills, "Postdecision Exposure to Relevant Information," *Journal of Abnormal and Social Psychology*, 54 (1957): 98–102.

10. Jack Brehm, "Postdecision Changes in the Desirability of Alternatives," *Journal of Abnormal and Social Psychology*, 52 (1956): 384–389.

11. Leon Festinger and Nathan Maccoby, "On Resistance to Persuasive Communications," *Journal of Abnormal and Social Psychology*, 68 (1964): 359–366.

12. Elie Wiesel, *Night* (New York: Avon, 1969).

13. Ralph White, "Selective Inattention," *Psychology Today*, November 1971, pp. 47–50, 78–84.

14. For a penetrating analysis of the process involved in a number of disastrous political decisions, see Irving Janis' book, *Victims of Groupthink* (Boston: Houghton Mifflin, 1972).

15. "Pentagon Papers: The Secret War," *Time*, June 28, 1971, p. 12.

16. Jonathan Freedman and Scott Fraser, "Compliance Without Pressure: The Foot-in-the-Door Technique," *Journal of Personality and Social Psychology*, 4 (1966): 195–202.

17. Robert Knox and James Inkster, "Postdecision Dissonance at Post Time," *Journal of Personality and Social Psychology*, 8 (1968): 319–323.

18. Judson Mills, "Changes in Moral Attitudes Following Temptation," *Journal of Personality*, 26 (1958): 517–531.

19. Leon Festinger and J. Merrill Carlsmith, "Cognitive Consequences of Forced Compliance," *Journal of Abnormal and Social Psychology*, 58 (1959): 203–210.

20. Arthur Cohen, "An Experiment on Small Rewards for Discrepant Compliance and Attitude Change," in *Explorations in Cognitive Dissonance*, by J. W. Brehm and A. R. Cohen (New York: Wiley, 1962), pp. 73–78.

21. It should be mentioned, in passing, that the "saying-is-believing" phenomenon has produced some controversial data. The weight of evidence tends to support the analysis presented in this text. For a

more detailed discussion of this issue, read Elliot Aronson, "The Theory of Cognitive Dissonance: A Current Perspective," in *Advances in Experimental Social Psychology*, Vol. 4, ed. L. Berkowitz (New York: Academic Press, 1969), pp. 1–34.

22. Mills, *op. cit.*

23. Elliot Aronson, "Dissonance Theory: Progress and Problems," in *Theories of Cognitive Consistency: A Sourcebook*, ed. R. P. Abelson, E. Aronson, W. J. McGuire, T. M. Newcomb, M. J. Rosenberg, and P. H. Tannenbaum (Chicago: Rand McNally, 1968), pp. 5–27. Elliot Aronson, "The Theory of Cognitive Dissonance: A Current Perspective," in *Advances in Experimental Social Psychology*, Vol. 4, ed. L. Berkowitz (New York: Academic Press, 1969), pp. 1–34.

24. Elizabeth Nel, Robert Helmreich, and Elliot Aronson, "Opinion Change in the Advocate as a Function of the Persuasibility of His Audience: A Clarification of the Meaning of Dissonance," *Journal of Personality and Social Psychology*, 12 (1969): 117–124.

25. Jonathan Freedman, "Attitudinal Effects of Inadequate Justification," *Journal of Personality*, 31 (1963): 371–385.

26. Edward Deci, *Intrinsic Motivation* (New York: Plenum, 1975). Edward Deci, "Effects of Externally Mediated Rewards on Intrinsic Motivation," *Journal of Personality and Social Psychology*, 18 (1971): 105–115.

27. Mark R. Lepper and David Greene, "Turning Play into Work: Effects of Adult Surveillance and Extrinsic Rewards on Children's Intrinsic Motivation," *Journal of Personality and Social Psychology*, 31 (1975): 479–486.

28. Elliot Aronson and J. Merrill Carlsmith, "Effect of the Severity of Threat on the Devaluation of Forbidden Behavior," *Journal of Abnormal and Social Psychology*, 66 (1963): 584–588.

29. Jonathan Freedman, "Long-term Behavioral Effects of Cognitive Dissonance," *Journal of Experimental Social Psychology*, 1 (1965): 145–155.

30. Robert Sears, John Whiting, Vincent Nowlis, and Pauline Sears, "Some Child-rearing Antecedents of Aggression and Dependency in Young Children," *Genetic Psychology Monographs*, 47 (1953): 135–234.

31. Elliot Aronson and Judson Mills, "The Effect of Severity of Initiation on Liking for a Group," *Journal of Abnormal and Social Psychology*, 59 (1959): 177–181.

32. Harold Gerard and Grover Mathewson, "The Effects of Severity of Initiation on Liking for a Group: A Replication," *Journal of Experimental Social Psychology*, 2 (1966): 278–287.

33. James Michener, *Kent State: What Happened and Why* (New York: Random House, 1971).

34. *Ibid.*

35. Nikita Khrushchev, *Krushchev Remembers*, tr. and ed. Strobe Talbott. (Boston: Little, Brown, 1970).

36. Keith Davis and Edward Jones, "Changes in Interpersonal Perception as a Means of Reducing Cognitive Dissonance," *Journal of Abnormal and Social Psychology*, 61 (1960): 402–410.

37. David Glass, "Changes in Liking as a Means of Reducing Cognitive Discrepancies Between Self-esteem and Aggression," *Journal of Personality*, 32 (1964): 531–549.

38. Ellen Berscheid, David Boye, and Elaine Walster, "Retaliation as a Means of Restoring Equity," *Journal of Personality and Social Psychology*, 10 (1968): 370–376.

39. Edward Jones and Richard Nisbett, *The Actor and The Observer: Divergent Perceptions of the Causes of Behavior* (New York: General Learning Press, 1971).

40. George Bernard Shaw; *Selected Prose*, ed. Diarmuid Russel (New York: Dodd, Mead, 1952).

41. Jack Brehm, "Increasing Cognitive Dissonance by a *Fait-Accompli*," *Journal of Abnormal and Social Psychology*, 58 (1959): 379–382.

42. John Darley and Ellen Berscheid, "Increased Liking as a Result of the Anticipation of Personal Contact," *Human Relations*, 20 (1967): 29–40.

43. Elliot Aronson and David Mettee, "Dishonest Behavior as a Function of Different Levels of Self-esteem," *Journal of Personality and Social Psychology*, 9 (1968): 121–127.

44. Philip Zimbardo, *The Cognitive Control of Motivation* (Glenview, Ill.: Scott, Foresman, 1969).

45. Jack Brehm, "Motivational Effects of Cognitive Dissonance," in
     Nebraska Symposium on Motivation, 1962 (Lincoln: University of
     Nebraska Press, 1962), pp. 51–77.

46. Jack W. Brehm and Arthur R. Cohen, *Explorations in Cognitive
     Dissonance* (New York: Wiley, 1962).

47. Elliot Aronson, "The Cognitive and Behavioral Consequences of
     the Confirmation and Disconfirmation of Expectancies," (Harvard
     University, 1960, unpublished manuscript). Elliot Aronson and
     J. M. Carlsmith, "Performance Expectancy as a Determinant of Ac-
     tual Performance," *Journal of Abnormal and Social Psychology*, 65
     (1962): 178–182. Elliot Aronson and David R. Mettee, "Dishonest
     Behavior as a Function of Differential Levels of Induced Self-
     esteem," *Journal of Personality and Social Psychology*, 9 (1968):
     121–127. Elizabeth Nel, R. Helmreich, and Elliot Aronson, "Opin-
     ion Change in the Advocate as a Function of the Persuasibility
     of His Audience: A Clarification of the Meaning of Dissonance,"
     Journal of Personality and Social Psychology, 12 (1969): 117–124.
     Elliot Aronson, Thomas Chase, Robert Helmreich, and Ronald
     Ruhnke, "A Two-Factor Theory of Dissonance Reduction: The
     Effect of Feeling Stupid or Feeling 'Awful' on Opinion change,"
     International Journal for Research and Communication, (Fall, 1975;
     in press).

48. M. J. Rosenberg, "When Dissonance Fails: On Eliminating Eval-
     uation Apprehension from Attitude Measurement," *Journal of
     Personality and Social Psychology*, 1 (1965): 28–42.

49. Darwyn E. Linder, Joel Cooper, and Edward E. Jones, "Decision
     Freedom as a Determinant of the Role of Incentive Magnitude in
     Attitude Change," *Journal of Personality and Social Psychology*, 6
     (1967): 245–54.

50. Daryl J. Bem, "Self-perception: An Alternative Interpretation of
     Cognitive Dissonance Phenomena," *Psychological Review*, 74
     (1967): 183–200.

51. Russell A. Jones, Darwyn E. Linder, Charles A. Kiesler, Mark
     Zanna, and Jack M. Brehm, "Internal States or External Stimuli:
     Observers' Attitude Judgments and the Dissonance Theory—
     Self-persuasion Controversy," *Journal of Experimental Social Psy-
     chology*, 4 (1968): 247–269. Jane A. Piliavin, I. M. Piliavin, E. P.
     Loewenton, C. McCauley, and P. Hammond, "On Observers'

Reproductions of Dissonance Effects: The Right Answers for the Wrong Reasons?", *Journal of Personality and Social Psychology*, 13 (1969): 98–106.

52. Michael S. Pallak and Thane S. Pittman, "General Motivational Effects of Dissonance Arousal," *Journal of Personality and Social Psychology*, 21 (1972): 349–358.

53. Lyndon B. Johnson, *The Vantage Point: Perspectives of the Presidency 1963–69*, (New York: Holt, Rinehart and Winston, 1971).

Chapter 5.   Human Aggression

1. Jean-Jacques Rousseau, *The Social Contract* and *Discourses* (New York: Dutton, 1930).

2. Sigmund Freud, *Beyond the Pleasure Principle* (London: Hogarth Press and Institute of Psycho-Analysis, 1948).

3. Sigmund Freud, "Why War" (letter to Albert Einstein, 1932), in *Collected Papers*, Vol. 5, ed. Ernest Jones (New York: Basic Books, 1959), p. 282.

4. Anthony Storr, *Human Aggression* (New York: Bantam, 1970).

5. Zing Yang Kuo, "Genesis of the Cat's Response to the Rat," in *Instinct* (Princeton: Van Nostrand, 1961), p. 24.

6. Irenäus Eibl-Eibesfeldt, "Aggressive Behavior and Ritualized Fighting in Animals," in *Science and Psychoanalysis*, Vol. VI (*Violence and War*), ed. J. H. Masserman (New York: Grune and Stratton, 1963).

7. John Paul Scott, *Aggression* (Chicago: University of Chicago Press, 1958).

8. Konrad Lorenz, *On Aggression*, tr. Marjorie Wilson (New York: Harcourt, Brace and World, 1966).

9. Leonard Berkowitz, "The Frustration–Aggression Hypothesis Revisited," in *Roots of Aggression: A Re-examination of the Frustration–Aggression Hypothesis*, ed. L. Berkowitz (New York: Atherton, 1968).

10. Roger Barker, Tamara Dembo, and Kurt Lewin, "Frustration and Regression: An Experiment with Young Children," *University of Iowa Studies in Child Welfare*, 18 (1941): 1–314.

11. Shabaz Mallick and Boyd McCandless, "A Study of Catharsis of Aggression," *Journal of Personality and Social Psychology*, 4 (1966): 591–596.

12. Albert Bandura, Dorothea Ross, and Sheila Ross, "Transmission of Aggression Through Imitation of Aggressive Models," *Journal of Abnormal and Social Psychology*, 63 (1961): 575–582. Albert Bandura, Dorothea Ross, and Sheila Ross, "A Comparative Test of the Status Envy, Social Power, and Secondary Reinforcement Theories of Identificatory Learning," *Journal of Abnormal and Social Psychology*, 67 (1963): 527–534. Albert Bandura, Dorothea Ross, and Sheila Ross, "Vicarious Reinforcement and Imitative Learning," *Journal of Abnormal and Social Psychology*, 67 (1963): 601–607

13. Leonard Berkowitz and Anthony LePage, "Weapons as Aggression-eliciting Stimuli," *Journal of Personality and Social Psychology*, 7 (1967): 202–207.

14. Leonard Berkowitz, *Control of Aggression* (unpublished, 1971), p. 68.

15. Konrad Lorenz, *On Aggression*, tr. Marjorie Wilson (New York: Harcourt, Brace and World, 1966).

16. Sherwood Washburn and David Hamburg, "The Implications of Primate Research," in *Primate Behavior: Field Studies of Monkeys and Apes*, ed. I. DeVore (New York: Holt, Rinehart and Winston, 1965), pp. 607–622.

17. Burney LeBoeuf, "Male–Male Competition and Reproductive Success in Elephant Seals," *American Zoologist*, 14 (1974): 163–176.

18. M. F. Ashley Montagu, *On Being Human* (New York: Hawthorne Books, 1950).

19. Peter Kropotkin, *Mutual Aid* (New York: Doubleday, 1902).

20. Henry Nissen, "Social Behavior in Primates," in *Comparative Psychology*, ed. C. P. Stone (3rd ed.; New York: Prentice-Hall, 1951), pp. 423–457.

21. *Time*, October 7, 1974.

22. Loren Eisley, *The Immense Journey* (New York: Random House, 1946), p. 140.

23. William Menninger, "Recreation and Mental Health," *Recreation*, 42 (1948): 340–346.

24. Leonard Berkowitz, *Control of Aggression* (unpublished, 1971).

25. Warren Johnson, "Guilt-free Aggression for the Troubled Jock," *Psychology Today*, October 1970, pp. 70–73.

26. Seymour Feshbach, "The Drive-reducing Function of Fantasy Behavior," *Journal of Abnormal and Social Psychology*, 50 (1955): 3–11.

27. David Glass, "Changes in Liking as a Means of Reducing Cognitive Discrepancies between Self-esteem and Aggression," *Journal of Personality*, 32 (1964): 531–549. Keith E. Davis and Edward E. Jones, "Changes in Interpersonal Perception as a Means of Reducing Cognitive Dissonance," *Journal of Abnormal and Social Psychology*, 61 (1960): 402–410. See also Arnold H. Buss, "Physical Aggression in Relation to Different Frustrations," *Journal of Abnormal and Social Psychology*, 67 (1963): 1–7.

28. Michael Kahn, "The Physiology of Catharsis," *Journal of Personality and Social Psychology*, 3 (1966): 278–298. See also: Leonard Berkowitz, James Green, and Jacqueline Macaulay, "Hostility Catharsis as the Reduction of Emotional Tension," *Psychiatry*, 25 (1962): 23–31; and Richard DeCharms and Edward J. Wilkins, "Some Effects of Verbal Expression of Hostility," *Journal of Abnormal and Social Psychology*, 66 (1963): 462–470.

29. Anthony N. Doob and Larraine Wood, "Catharsis and Aggression: The Effects of Annoyance and Retaliation on Aggressive Behavior," *Journal of Personality and Social Psychology*, 22 (1972): 156–162.

30. Konrad Lorenz, *On Aggression*, tr. Marjorie Wilson (New York: Harcourt, Brace and World, 1966). William Menninger, "Recreation and Mental Health," *Recreation*, 42 (1948): 340–346.

31. Joseph Klapper, *The Effects of Mass Communication* (Glencoe, Ill.: Free Press, 1960).

32. Donald Hartmann, *The Influence of Symbolically Modeled Instrumental Aggressive and Pain Cues on the Disinhibition of Aggressive Behavior* (unpublished doctoral dissertation, Stanford University, 1965). Richard Walters and Edward Thomas, "Enhancement of Punitiveness by Visual and Audiovisual Displays," *Canadian Journal of Psychology*, 16 (1963): 244–255.

33. Robert Liebert and Robert Baron "Some Immediate Effects of Televised Violence on Children's Behavior," *Developmental Psychology*, 6 (1972): 469–475.

34. Monroe Lefkowitz, Leonard Eron, and Leopold Walder, *Television Violence and Child Aggression: A Follow-up Study* (Report to the National Institutes of Mental Health, 1971). J. J. McIntyre and J. J. Teevan, *Television and Deviant Behavior* (Report to the National Institutes of Mental Health, 1971). J. R. Dominick and B. S. Greenberg, *Girls' Attitudes Toward Violence as Related to T.V. Exposure, Family Attitudes, and Social Class* (Report to the National Institutes of Mental Health, 1971).

35. *Newsweek*, March 10, 1975.

36. "The Violence Bag," *Newsweek*, December 13, 1971, p. 110.

37. *Ibid.*

38. Kenneth Clark, "The Pathos of Power: A Psychological Perspective," *American Psychologist*, 26 (1971): 1047–1057.

39. Aristotle, "Rhetoric," in *Aristotle, Rhetoric and Poetics*, tr. W. Rhys Roberts (New York: Modern Library, 1954), p. 22.

40. Robert Sears, Eleanor Maccoby, and Harry Levin, *Patterns of Child Rearing* (Evanston, Ill.: Row, Peterson, 1957). Diana Baumrind, "Effects of Authoritative Parental Control on Child Behavior," *Child Development*, 37 (1966): 887–907. Wesley Becker, "Consequences of Different Kinds of Parental Discipline," in *Review of Child Development Research*, Vol. 1, ed. M. L. Hoffman and L. W. Hoffman (New York: Russell Sage, 1964).

41. Robert Hamblin, David Buckholt, Donald Bushell, Desmond Ellis, and Daniel Ferritor, "Changing the Game from 'Get the Teacher' to 'Learn'," *Trans-Action*, January 1969, pp. 20–31.

42. Elliot Aronson and J. Merrill Carlsmith, "The Effect of the Severity of Threat on the Devaluation of Forbidden Behavior," *Journal of Abnormal and Social Psychology*, 66 (1963): 584–588. Jonathan Freedman, "Long-term Behavioral Effects of Cognitive Dissonance," *Journal of Experimental Social Psychology*, 1 (1965): 145–155.

43. U.S. President's Commission on Law Enforcement and Administration of Justice, *The Challenge of Crime in a Free Society: A Report.* (Washington, DC: U.S. Government Printing Office, 1967).

44. Albert Bandura, Dorothea Ross, and Sheila Ross, "Imitation of Film-mediated Aggressive Models," *Journal of Abnormal and Social Psychology*, 66 (1963): 3–11. Albert Bandura, Dorothea Ross, and Sheila Ross, "Vicarious Reinforcement and Imitative Learning," *Journal of Abnormal and Social Psychology*, 67 (1963): 601–607.

45. Paul Brown and Rogers Elliott, "Control of Aggression in a Nursery School Class," *Journal of Experimental Child Psychology*, 2 (1965): 103–107.

46. Joel Davitz, "The Effects of Previous Training on Postfrustration Behavior," *Journal of Abnormal and Social Psychology*, 47 (1952): 309–315.

47. Robert A. Baron and C. Richard Kepner, "Model's Behavior and Attraction toward the Model as Determinants of Adult Aggressive Behavior," *Journal of Personality and Social Psychology*, 14 (1970): 335–344.

48. Seymour Feshbach, "Dynamics and Morality of Violence and Aggression: Some Psychological Considerations," *American Psychologist*, 26 (1971): 281–292.

49. James Michener, *Kent State: What Happened and Why* (New York: Random House, 1971).

50. Norma Feshbach and Seymour Feshbach, "The Relationship Between Empathy and Aggression in Two Age Groups," *Developmental Psychology*, 1 (1969): 102–107.

Chapter 6. Prejudice

1. Alvin Poussaint, "A Negro Psychiatrist Explains the Negro Psyche," in *Confrontation* (New York: Random House, 1971), pp. 183–184.

2. Kenneth Clark and Mamie Clark, "Racial Identification and Preference in Negro Children," in *Readings in Social Psychology*, ed. T. M. Newcomb and E. L. Hartley (New York: Holt, 1947), pp. 169–178.

3. Philip Goldberg, "Are Women Prejudiced against Women?" *Trans-Action*, April 1968, pp. 28–30.

4. Edward E. Jones and Keith E. Davis, "From Acts to Dispositions: The Attribution Process in Person Perception," in *Advances in Experimental Social Psychology*, ed. L. Berkowitz, Vol. 2 (New York: Academic Press, 1965). Harold H. Kelley, "The Processes of Causal Attribution," *American Psychologist*, 28 (1973): 107–128.

5. Shirley Feldman-Summers and Sara B. Kiesler, "Those Who Are Number Two Try Harder: The Effect of Sex on Attributions of

Causality," *Journal of Personality and Social Psychology*, 30 (1974): 846–855.

6. Kay Deaux and Tim Emswiller, "Explanations of Successful Performance on Sex-linked Tasks: What Is Skill for the Male Is Luck for the Female," *Journal of Personality and Social Psychology*, 29 (1974): 80–85.

7. John G. Nicholls, "Causal Attributions and Other Achievement-Related Cognitions: Effects of Task Outcome, Attainment Value, and Sex," *Journal of Personality and Social Psychology*, 31 (1975): 379–389.

8. Gordon Allport, *The Nature of Prejudice* (Cambridge, Mass.: Addison-Wesley, 1954), pp. 13–14.

9. *Newsweek*, November 25, 1974, p. 39.

10. Melvin Lerner, "Evaluation of Performance as a Function of Performer's Reward and Attractiveness," *Journal of Personality and Social Psychology*, 1 (1965): 355–360.

11. Karl Pearson and M. Moul, "The Problem of Alien Immigration into Great Britain, Illustrated by an Example of Russian and Polish Jewish Children," *Annals of Eugenics*, 1 (1925): 5–127.

12. Daryl Bem and Sandra Bem, "We're All Non-conscious Sexists," *Psychology Today*, November (1970): 22–26, 115–116.

13. Ruth Hartley, "Children's Concepts of Male and Female Roles," *Merrill-Palmer Quarterly*, 6 (1960): 83–91.

14. Jean Lipman-Blumen, "How Ideology Shapes Women's Lives," *Scientific American*, 226 (1) (1972): 34–42.

15. Susan W. Gray, "Masculinity–Femininity in Relation to Anxiety and Social Acceptance," *Child Development*, 28 (1957): 203–214.

16. Sandra L. Bem, "Sex Role Adaptability: One Consequence of Psychological Androgyny," *Journal of Personality and Social Psychology*, 31 (1975): 634–643. Phyllis Chesler, *Women and Madness* (New York: Avon Books, 1972).

17. John Dollard, *Caste and Class in a Southern Town* (New Haven: Yale University Press, 1937).

18. Bruno Bettelheim and Morris Janowitz, *Social Change and Prejudice, Including Dynamics of Prejudice* (New York: Free Press, 1964).

19. Melvin Tumin, Paul Barton, and Bernie Burrus, "Education, Prejudice, and Discrimination: A Study in Readiness for Desegregation," *American Sociological Review*, 23 (1958), 41–49.

20. Mitchel Levitas, *America in Crisis* (New York: Holt, Rinehart and Winston, 1969).

21. John Dollard, "Hostility and Fear in Social Life," *Social Forces*, 17 (1938): 15–26.

22. Andrew Greeley and Paul Sheatsley, "The Acceptance of Desegregation Continues to Advance," *Scientific American*, 225 (6) (1971): 13–19.

23. Muzafer Sherif, O. J. Harvey, B. Jack White, William Hood, and Carolyn Sherif, *Intergroup Conflict and Cooperation: The Robbers Cave Experiment* (Norman, Okla.: University of Oklahoma Institute of Intergroup Relations, 1961).

24. Carl Hovland and Robert Sears, "Minor Studies of Aggression: Correlation of Lynchings with Economic Indices," *Journal of Psychology*, 9 (1940): 301–310.

25. Albert Speer, *Inside the Third Reich: Memoirs*, tr. Richard Winston and Clara Winston (New York: Macmillan, 1970).

26. Neal Miller and Richard Bugelski, "Minor Studies in Aggression: The Influence of Frustrations Imposed by the In-group on Attitudes Expressed toward Out-groups," *Journal of Psychology*, 25 (1948): 437–442.

27. Donald Weatherley, "Anti-Semitism and the Expression of Fantasy Aggression," *Journal of Abnormal and Social Psychology*, 62 (1961): 454–457.

28. Theodor Adorno, Else Frenkel-Brunswik, Daniel Levinson, and R. Nevitt Sanford, *The Authoritarian Personality* (New York: Harper, 1950).

29. Greeley and Sheatsley, *op. cit.*

30. Thomas Pettigrew, "Regional Differences in Anti-Negro Prejudice," *Journal of Abnormal and Social Psychology*, 59 (1959): 28–36.

31. Thomas Pettigrew, "Personality and Sociocultural Factors and Intergroup Attitudes: A Cross-national Comparison," *Journal of Conflict Resolution*, 2 (1958): 29–42.

32. Jeanne Watson, "Some Social and Psychological Situations Related to Change in Attitude," *Human Relations*, 3 (1950): 15–56.

33. Ian MacCrone, *Race Attitudes in South Africa* (London: Oxford University Press, 1937).

34. Paul Lazarsfeld, ed., *Radio and the Printed Page* (New York: Duell, Sloan & Pearce, 1940).

35. Morton Deutsch and Mary Ellen Collins, *Interracial Housing: A Psychological Evaluation of a Social Experiment* (Minneapolis: University of Minnesota Press, 1951). See also Daniel Wilner, Rosabelle Walkley, and Stuart Cook, *Human Relations in Interracial Housing* (Minneapolis: University of Minnesota Press, 1955).

36. Jack Brehm, "Increasing Cognitive Dissonance by a *Fait-Accompli*," *Journal of Abnormal and Social Psychology*, 58 (1959): 379–382.

37. John Darley and Ellen Berscheid, "Increased Liking as a Result of the Anticipation of Personal Contact," *Human Relations*, 20 (1967): 29–40.

38. Thomas Pettigrew, "Social Psychology and Desegregation Research," *American Psychologist*, 16 (1961): 105–112.

39. Kenneth Clark, "Desegregation: An Appraisal of the Evidence," *Journal of Social Issues*, 9 (1953): No. 4.

40. Samuel Stouffer, Edward Suchman, Leland DeVinney, Shirley Star, and Robin Williams, Jr., "The American Soldier: Adjustment During Army Life," in *Studies in Social Psychology in WW II*, Vol. 1 (Princeton: Princeton University Press, 1949).

41. Bernard Kramer, *Residential Contact as a Determinant of Attitudes Toward Negroes* (unpublished doctoral dissertation, Harvard University, 1951). Alvin Winder, "White Attitudes Towards Negro—White Interaction in an Area of Changing Racial Composition," *American Psychologist*, 7 (1952): 330–331.

42. Steven Asher and Vernon Allen, "Racial Preference and Social Comparison Processes," *Journal of Social Issues*, 25 (1969): 157–166. Walter Stephan and J. C. Kennedy, "An Experimental Study of Inter-ethnic Competition in Segregated Schools," *Journal of School Psychology*, 13 (1975): 234–247. Harold Gerard and Norman Miller, *School Desegregation* (New York: Plenum, 1976, in press).

43. Julius Lester, "Beep! Beep! Bang! Umgawa! Black Power!" in *Confrontation: Issues of the 70's*, ed. R. Kytle (New York: Random House, 1971), pp. 162–181.

44. Deutsch and Collins, *op. cit.*

45. Muzafer Sherif and Carolyn Sherif, *An Outline of Social Psychology* (New York: Harper & Bros., 1956). Sherif, Harvey, White, Hood, and Sherif, *op. cit.*

46. Elliot Aronson, with Nancy Blaney, Jev Sikes, Cookie Stephan, and Matthew Snapp, "Busing and Racial Tension: The Jigsaw Route to Learning and Liking," *Psychology Today*, February 1975, pp. 43–50.

47. Walter Stephan, "An Experimental Study of Inter-ethnic Competition in Segregated Schools," *Journal of School Psychology*, 13 (1975): 234–247.

48. David Rosenfield, William Lucker, Jev Sikes, and Elliot Aronson, *The Interdependent Classroom: A Technique for Improving Minority Performance* (manuscript in preparation, 1976).

49. Thomas Pettigrew, "Social Psychology and Desegregation Research," *American Psychologist*, 15 (1961): 61–71.

Chapter 7. Attraction: Why People Like Each Other

1. Charles Darwin, *The Expression of Emotions in Man and Animals* (New York: Appleton, 1910).

2. Dale Carnegie, *How to Win Friends and Influence People* (New York: Simon & Schuster, 1937).

3. H. H. Remmers and D. H. Radler, "Teenage Attitudes," *Scientific American*, 198 (6) (1958): 25–29.

4. Thomas Lemann and Richard Solomon, "Group Characteristics as Revealed in Sociometric Patterns and Personality Ratings," *Sociometry*, 15 (1952): 7–90.

5. George Homans, *Social Behavior: Its Elementary Forms* (New York: Harcourt, Brace and World, 1961).

6. Elaine Walster, Vera Aronson, Darcy Abrahams, and Leon Rottman, "Importance of Physical Attractiveness in Dating Behavior," *Journal of Personality and Social Psychology*, 5 (1966): 508–516.

7. Donn Byrne, "Attitudes and Attraction," in *Advances in Experimental Social Psychology*, Vol. 4, ed. L. Berkowitz (New York: Academic Press, 1969).

8. Muzafer Sherif and Carolyn Sherif, *Groups in Harmony and Tension* (New York: Harper & Bros., 1953). Muzafer Sherif, O. J. Harvey, B. Jack White, William Hood, and Carolyn Sherif, *Intergroup Conflict and Cooperation: The Robbers Cave Experiment* (Norman, Okla.: University of Oklahoma Institute of Intergroup Relations, 1961).

9. Elliot Aronson, with Nancy Blaney, Jev Sikes, Cookie Stephan, and Matthew Snapp, "Busing and Racial Tension: The Jigsaw Route to Learning and Liking," *Psychology Today*, February 1975, pp. 43–50.

10. Elliot Aronson and Judson Mills, "The Effect of Severity of Initiation on Liking for a Group," *Journal of Abnormal and Social Psychology*, 59 (1959): 177–181.

11. Morton Deutsch and Leonard Solomon, "Reactions to Evaluations by Others as Influenced by Self-evaluations," *Sociometry*, 22 (1959): 93–112.

12. Edward Jones, *Ingratiation* (New York: Appleton-Century-Crofts, 1964).

13. Helen Hall Jennings, *Leadership and Isolation* (2nd ed.; New York: Longmans, Green, 1959).

14. Bernice Lott and Albert Lott, "The Formation of Positive Attitudes Toward Group Members," *Journal of Abnormal and Social Psychology*, 61 (1960): 297–300.

15. Jack Brehm and Ann Cole, "Effect of a Favor which Reduces Freedom," *Journal of Personality and Social Psychology*, 3 (1966): 420–426.

16. J. Bigelow, ed., *The Autobiography of Benjamin Franklin* (New York: G. P. Putnam's Sons, 1916), pp. 216–217.

17. Jon Jecker and David Landy, "Liking a Person as a Function of Doing Him a Favor," *Human Relations*, 22 (1969): 371–378.

18. Melvin Lerner and Carolyn Simmons, "Observer's Reaction to the 'Innocent Victim': Compassion or Rejection?" *Journal of Personality and Social Psychology*, 4 (1966): 203–210.

19. Albert J. Lott, Bernice E. Lott, Thomas Reed, and Terry Crow, "Personality-trait Descriptions of Differentially Liked Persons," *Journal of Personality and Social Psychology*, 16 (1970): 284–290.

20. Robert Bales, "Task Roles and Social Roles in Problem Solving Groups," in *Readings in Social Psychology*, ed. E. E. Maccoby, T. M. Newcomb, and E. L. Hartley (3rd ed.; New York: Holt, 1958), pp. 437–447. Robert Bales and Philip Slater, "Role Differentiation in Small Decision-making Groups," in *The Family, Socialization, and Interaction Process*, ed. T. Parsons and R. F. Bales (Glencoe, Ill.: Free Press, 1955).

21. Elliot Aronson, Ben Willerman, and Joanne Floyd, "The Effect of a Pratfall on Increasing Interpersonal Attractiveness," *Psychonomic Science*, 4 (1966): 227–228.

22. Kay Deaux, "To Err is Humanizing: But Sex Makes a Difference," *Representative Research in Social Psychology*, 3 (1972): 20–28.

23. Elliot Aronson, Robert Helmreich, and James LeFan, "To Err Is Humanizing—Sometimes: Effects of Self-esteem, Competence, and a Pratfall on Interpersonal Attraction," *Journal of Personality and Social Psychology*, 16 (1970): 259–264.

24. Walster, Aronson, Abrahams, and Rottman, *op. cit.*

25. Karen Dion, Ellen Berscheid, and Elaine Walster, "What is Beautiful is Good," *Journal of Personality and Social Psychology*, 24 (1972): 285–290.

26. Karen Dion and Ellen Berscheid, "Physical Attractiveness and Sociometric Choice in Nursery School Children" (mimeographed research report, 1971).

27. Karen Dion, "Physical Attractiveness and Evaluations of Children's Transgressions," *Journal of Personality and Social Psychology*, 24 (1972): 207–213.

28. Harold Sigall and Elliot Aronson, "Liking for an Evaluator as a Function of Her Physical Attractiveness and Nature of the Evaluations," *Journal of Experimental Social Psychology*, 5 (1969): 93–100.

29. Harold Sigall and Nancy Ostrove, "Beautiful but Dangerous: Effects of Offender Attractiveness and Nature of the Crime on Juridic Judgment," *Journal of Personality and Social Psychology*, 31 (1975): 410–414.

30. Byrne, *op. cit.*

31. Harold Sigall, "The Effects of Competence and Consensual Validation on a Communicator's Liking for the Audience." *Journal of Personality and Social Psychology*, 16 (1970): 251–258.

32. Paul Secord and Carl Backman, "Interpersonal Congruency, Perceived Similarity, and Friendship," *Sociometry*, 27 (1964): 115–127.

33. Elaine Walster, "The Effect of Self-esteem on Romantic Liking," *Journal of Experimental Social Psychology*, 1 (1965): 184–197.

34. Sara B. Kiesler and Roberta L. Baral, "The Search for a Romantic Partner: The Effects of Self-esteem and Physical Attractiveness on

Romantic Behavior," in *Personality and Social Behavior*, ed. Kenneth J. Gergen and David Marlowe (Reading, Mass.: Addison-Wesley, 1970).

35. Edward Jones, Linda Bell, and Elliot Aronson, "The Reciprocation of Attraction from Similar and Dissimilar Others: A Study in Person Perception and Evaluation," in *Experimental Social Psychology*, ed. C. G. McClintock (New York: Holt, Rinehart and Winston, 1971), pp. 142–183.

36. Robert Winch, *Mate-Selection: A Study of Complementary Needs* (New York: Harper & Row, 1958).

37. Elliot Aronson and Darwyn Linder, "Gain and Loss of Esteem as Determinants of Interpersonal Attractiveness," *Journal of Experimental Social Psychology*, 1 (1965): 156–171. See also: Harold Gerard and Charles W. Greenbaum, "Attitudes Toward an Agent of Uncertainty Reduction," *Journal of Personality*, 30 (1962): 485–495; David Mettee, Shelley E. Taylor, and H. Friedman, "Affect Conversion and the Gain–Loss Like Effect," *Sociometry*, 36 (1973): 505–519; Elliot Aronson and David R. Mettee, "Affective Reactions to Appraisal from Others," *Foundations of Interpersonal Attraction* (New York: Academic Press, 1974); Gerald L. Clore, Nancy H. Wiggins, and Stuart Itkin, "Gain and Loss in Attraction: Attributions from Nonverbal Behavior," *Journal of Personality and Social Psychology*, 31 (1975): 706–712.

38. *Ibid.*

39. Benedictus de Spinoza, "The Ethics," in *Spinoza's Ethics and 'De Intellectus Emendatione,'* tr. Andrew Boyle (New York: Dutton, 1910).

40. David R. Mettee, Shelley E. Taylor, and H. Friedman, "Affect Conversion and the Gain–Loss Like Effect," *Sociometry*, 36 (1973): 505–519.

41. David R. Mettee and Elliot Aronson, "Affective Reactions to Appraisal From Others," *Foundations of Interpersonal Attraction* (New York: Academic Press, 1974).

42. O. J. Harvey, "Personality Factors in Resolution of Conceptual Incongruities," *Sociometry*, 25 (1962): 336–352.

43. Harold Stevenson, Rachael Keen, and Robert Knights, "Parents and Strangers as Reinforcing Agents for Children's Performance," *Journal of Abnormal and Social Psychology*, 67 (1963): 183–185.

44. Joanne Floyd, *Effects of Amount of Reward and Friendship Status of the Other on the Frequency of Sharing in Children* (unpublished doctoral dissertation, University of Minnesota, 1964).

Chapter 8.   Communication in Sensitivity-Training Groups

1. Sigmund Koch, "Stimulus/Response—'Psychology Cannot Be a Coherent Science.'" *Psychology Today*, September 1969, p. 68.

2. Michael Kahn, *Sensitivity Training at Kresge College* (unpublished, 1971).

3. Carl Rogers, "The Group Comes of Age," *Psychology Today*, December 1969, p. 58.

4. Nancy E. Adler and Daniel Goleman, "Goal Setting, T-group Participation, and Self-rated Change: An Experimental Study," *The Journal of Applied Behavioral Science*, 11 (1975): 197–209.

5. Matthew Miles, "Changes During and Following Laboratory Training: A Clinical Experimental Study," *Journal of Applied Behavioral Science*, 1 (1965): 215–242. Douglas Bunker, "Individual Applications of Laboratory Training," *Journal of Applied Behavioral Science*, 1 (1965): 131–148. I. M. Valiquet, *Contribution to the Evaluation of a Management Development Program* (unpublished master's thesis, Massachusetts Institute of Technology, 1964).

6. Marvin Dunnette and John Campbell, "Effectiveness of T-group Experiences in Managerial Training and Development," *Psychological Bulletin*, 70 (1968): 73–104.

7. Irwin Rubin, "The Reduction of Prejudice Through Laboratory Training," *Journal of Applied Behavioral Science*, 3 (1967): 29–50.

8. Charles Tart, "Increases in Hypnotizability Resulting from a Prolonged Program for Enhancing Personal Growth," *Journal of Abnormal Psychology*, 75 (1970): 260–266. Jerrold Shapiro and Michael Diamond, "Increases in Hypnotizability as a Function of Encounter Group Training: Some Confirming Evidence," *Journal of Abnormal Psychology*, 79 (1972): 112–115.

9. Marvin D. Dunnette, "People Feeling: Joy, More Joy, and the 'Slough of Despond.'" *Journal of Applied Behavioral Science*, 5 (1969): 25–44.

10. *Ibid.*, p. 42.

11. Ralph Cranshaw, "How Sensitive is Sensitivity Training?" *American Journal of Psychiatry*, 126 (1969): 868–873.

12. James Cadden, Frederic Flach, Sara Blakeslee and Randolph Charton, "Growth in Medical Students Through Group Process," *American Journal of Psychiatry*, 126 (1969): 862–868.

13. Charles Seashore, "What is Sensitivity Training?" *NTL Institute News and Reports*, April 1968.

14. Kahn, *op. cit.*

15. Morton Lieberman, Irvin Yalom, and Matthew B. Miles, *Encounter Groups: First Facts* (New York: Basic Books, 1973).

Chapter 9.   Social Psychology as a Science

1. Elliot Aronson and Judson Mills, "The Effect of Severity of Initiation on Liking for a Group," *Journal of Abnormal and Social Psychology*, 59 (1959): 177–181.

2. Robert Liebert and Robert Baron, "Some Immediate Effects of Televised Violence on Children's Behavior," *Developmental Psychology*, 6 (1972): 469–475.

3. Elliot Aronson and J. Merrill Carlsmith, "Experimentation in Social Psychology," in *Handbook of Social Psychology*, Vol. 2, ed. G. Lindzey and E. Aronson (2nd ed.; Reading, Mass.: Addison-Wesley, 1969), pp. 1–79.

4. Stanley Milgram, "Behavioral Study of Obedience," *Journal of Abnormal and Social Psychology*, 67 (1963): 371–378.

5. *Ibid.*, p. 377.

6. Elliot Aronson, Harold Sigall, and Thomas Van Hoose, "The Cooperative Subject: Myth or Reality?" *Journal of Experimental Social Psychology*, 6 (1970): 1–10.

7. Solomon Asch, "Effects of Group Pressure Upon the Modification and Distortion of Judgment," in *Groups, Leadership and Men*, ed. M. H. Kuetzkow (Pittsburgh: Carnegie, 1951), pp. 117–190. Solomon Asch, "Studies of Independence and Conformity: A Minority of One Against a Unanimous Majority," *Psychological Monographs*, 70 (1956): No. 9, Whole No. 416.

8. Elliot Aronson, "Avoidance of Inter-subject Communication," *Psychological Reports*, 19 (1966): 238.

Name Index

Abrahams, Darcy, 60, 307, 321, 323
Adler, 270, 325
Adorno, Theodor, 191–192, 319
Ali Muhammad, 59
Allen, Vernon, 320
Allport, Gordon, 179–180, 305, 318
Argyle, Michael, 304
Aristotle, x, 1, 56–57, 60, 164, 306, 316
Arkoff, Samuel, 162
Aronson, Elliot, 8, 60, 74–76, 111,
    118–119, 128–129, 165–166, 206–210,
    216, 224, 228–229, 234, 237–240, 271,
    283, 285–286, 291–292, 307, 310, 311,
    312, 314, 321, 322, 323, 324, 326
Aronson, Vera, v, 321, 323
Asch, Solomon, 16–20, 22, 31, 194, 247,
    293–294, 304, 326
Asher, Steven, 320
Ashley Montagu, M. F., 152, 314
Aston, Nancy, v

Backman, Carl, 323
Bales, Robert, 322
Bandura, Albert, 150, 159–160, 314, 316
Baral, Roberta, 233, 323
Barker, Roger, 148, 313
Baron, Robert, 41, 159–160, 169, 306, 315,
    317, 326
Barton, Paul, 318
Baumrind, Diana, 316
Becker, Wesley, 316
Bell, Linda, 234, 324
Bem, Daryl, 51, 135–138, 182, 306, 312,
    318
Bem, Sandra, 182–183, 318
Beria, Laventri P., 122–123
Berkowitz, Leonard, v, 141, 146–147, 151,
    155, 307, 310, 313, 314, 315, 317, 321
Berscheid, Ellen, v, 8, 124, 127, 227, 303,
    311, 320, 323
Bettelheim, Bruno, 318

Blake, Robert, 304
Blakeslee, Sara, 326
Blanda, George, 59
Blaney, Nancy, 321, 322
Boone, Daniel, 12
Boye, David, 311
Bradford, David, v, 247
Bradley, Eleanor, 36
Brehm, Jack, 98, 102, 126, 131, 220, 309, 311, 312, 320, 325
Bridgeman, Diane, vi
Brown, George S., 180
Brown, Paul, 168, 174, 317
Bruce, Lenny, 93, 308
Buckholt, David, 316
Bugelski, Richard, 190, 319
Bunker, Douglas, 325
Burrus, Bernie, 318
Bushell, Donald, 316
Buss, Arnold H., 315
Byrne, Donn, 231, 321, 323

Cadden, James, 275, 326
Calley, William, 34–35, 124–125, 300
Campbell, Donald, 70, 307
Campbell, John, 274, 325
Camus, Albert, 88
Canon, Lance, 80, 308
Cantril, Hadley, 93, 308
Carlsmith, J. Merrill, vi, 74, 107, 109–110, 115, 165, 281, 291, 307, 309, 310, 312, 316, 326
Carnegie, Dale, 214–215, 217, 220, 233, 244, 321
Castro, Fidel, 107
Charton, Randolph, 326
Chase, Thomas, 312
Chesler, Phyllis, 318
Chiang Kai-shek, 106
Clark, Kenneth, 3, 174, 202, 303, 316, 317, 320
Clark, Mamie, 3, 174, 303, 317
Clore, Gerald L., 324
Cohen, Arthur R., 108, 134, 136–137, 309, 312
Cole, Ann, 220, 322
Collins, Mary Ellen, 198, 320
Cook, Stuart, 320
Cooper, Joel, 312
Cranshaw, Ralph, 275, 326

Cronkite, Walter, 141
Crow, Terry, 322

Darley, John, v, vi, 36, 38–41, 127, 304–306, 311, 320
Darwin, Charles, 152, 214, 321
Davis, Keith, 123, 156, 311, 315, 317
Davitz, Joel, 169, 317
Dean, John, 14
Deaux, Kay, 178, 226, 318, 323
DeCharms, Richard, 315
Deci, Edward, 113, 310
Dembo, Tamara, 148, 313
DeSalvo, James, 305
Deutsch, Morton, 20, 198, 204, 304, 320, 322
Devine, Dan, 154
DeVinney, Leland, 320
Diamond, Michael, 325
Dion, Karen, 227–228, 323
Dittes, James, 21, 305
Dollard, John, 186, 318, 319
Dominick, J. R., 316
Doob, Anthony N., 315
Dunnette, Marvin, 274, 325

Easterlin, Richard, v
Ebbeson, Ebbe, 53, 306
Ehrlich, Danuta, 97–98, 309
Eibl-Eibesfeldt, Irenäus, 145–146, 313
Eichmann, Adolf, 34–35
Einstein, Albert, 163
Eisley, Loren, 154, 163, 314
Eliot, T. S., 76, 299
Elliott, Rogers, 168, 317
Ellis, Desmond, 316
Ellisor, Lyn, vi
Emswiller, Tim, 178, 318
Eron, Leonard, 316

Feldman-Summers, Shirley, 178, 317
Ferritor, Daniel, 316
Feshbach, Norma, 171, 317
Feshbach, Seymour, 155, 170–171, 315, 317
Festinger, Leon, vi, 22, 61, 81, 88, 107, 109–110, 305, 307, 308, 309
Field, Peter, 181–182
Flach, Frederic, 326
Floyd, Joanne, 224, 243, 323, 325

Frager, R., 304
Frank, Jerome, 148
Franklin, Benjamin, 221
Fraser, Scott, 100, 309
Freedman, Jonathan, v, 78, 100, 116–117, 165, 308, 309, 310, 316
Freel, James, v
Frenkel-Brunswik, Else, 319
Freud, Sigmund, 144–145, 154, 313
Friedman, H., 324
Funt, Allen, 37

Galbraith, John Kenneth, 50
Gallup, George, 223, 282
Genovese, Kitty, 36, 38–41, 282
Gerard, Harold, 20, 119, 304, 311, 320, 324
Gerbner, George, 160
Gibbons, Euell, 52
Gibson, Faye, vi
Ginsberg, Allen, 55–56
Glass, David, 123, 156, 311, 315
Goldberg, Philip, 174, 317
Goldberg, Solomon, 304
Golden, Burton, 58–60, 307
Goldwater, Barry, 107
Goleman, Daniel, 270, 325
Gottlieb, Pilar, vi
Gray, Susan W., 318
Greeley, Andrew, 319
Green, James, 315
Greenbaum, Charles W., 324
Greenberg, B. S., 316
Greene, David, 113, 310
Grey, Patrick, 14
Guttman, Isaiah, 309

Hamblin, Robert, 165, 316
Hamburg, David, 151, 314
Hammond, P., 312
Harris, Jonathan, 303
Hartley, Ruth, 183, 318
Hartmann, Donald, 315
Hartmann, George W., 64, 307, 315
Harvey, O. J., 72, 75, 242, 307, 319, 320, 321, 324
Hastorf, Albert, 93, 308
Heller, Joseph, 36
Helmreich, Robert, v, 111, 310, 312, 323
Hilton, Judy, vi

Hindenberg, Paul von, 181
Hitler, Adolf, 14
Hoffman, L. W., 316
Hoffman, M. L., 316
Homans, George, 321
Hood, William, 319, 320, 321
Hovland, Carl, x, 56–57, 72, 75, 189, 306, 307, 319
Hruska, Roman, 226
Hutchins, D. E., 59

Ickes, William, vi
Inkster, James, 101, 309
Iscoe, Ira, 48, 306
Itkin, Stuart, 324

James, William, 24–25, 305
Janis, Irving, 181–182, 308, 309
Janowitz, Morris, 318
Jecker, Jon 221, 322
Jennings, Helen Hall, 219, 322
Johnson, Lyndon, 153, 313
Johnson, Warren, 155, 315
Jones, Edward E., 95–96, 123, 126, 156, 218–219, 234, 309, 311, 312, 315, 317, 322, 324
Jones, Russell, 136, 312

Kahn, Michael, v, 157–158, 247, 277–278, 315, 325, 326
Kaplan, John, v
Kaye, Donald, 308
Kazmaier, Dick, 92–93
Keen, Rachael, 324
Kelley, Harold, 21, 305, 317
Kelman, Herbert, 305
Kennedy, J. C., 320
Kennedy, John F., 13, 93, 223–224, 282
Kepner, C. Richard, 169, 317
Khrushchev, Nikita, 122–123, 311
Kiesler, Charles, 31, 305, 312
Kiesler, Sara, 178, 233, 317, 323
Kirschner, Paul, 308
Klapper, Joseph 315
Knights, Robert, 324
Knox, Robert, 101, 309
Koch, Sigmund, 256–257, 325
Kohler, Rika, 95–96, 309
Kramer, Bernard, 320
Kropotkin, Peter, 153, 314

Kuetner, Carolin, 305
Kuo, Zing Yang, 145–146, 313

Landry, Jack, 91–92, 300
Landy, David, 221, 322
Latané, Bibb, 36–41, 305, 306
Lazarsfeld, Paul, 197, 319
LeBoeuf, Burney, 152, 314
LeFan, James, 323
Lefkowitz, Monroe, 316
Lemann, Thomas, 321
LePage, Anthony, 314
Lepper, Mark, 113, 310
Lerner, Melvin, 180, 222, 318, 322
Lester, Julius, 320
Leventhal, Howard, 65–67, 307
Levin, Harry, 316
Levinson, Daniel, 319
Levitas, Mitchel, 319
Lewin, Kurt, x, 148, 313
Lichtenstein, Edward, 305
Lieberman, Morton, 277, 326
Liebert, Robert, 159–160, 315, 326
Linder, Darwyn, 134–135, 238, 312, 324
Lindzey, G., 326
Lipman-Blumen, Jean, 183, 318
Loewenton, E. P., 312
Lombardi, Vince, 154
Lorenz, Konrad, 146, 151, 313, 314, 315
Lott, Albert, 219, 322
Lott, Bernice, 219, 322
Lubin, Ardie, 304
Lucker, William, 321
Lumsdain, Arthur, 307

MacArthur, Douglas, 230
Macaulay, Jacqueline, 315
McCandless, Boyd, 150, 314
McCarthy, Joseph, 79
McCauley, C., 312
Maccoby, Eleanor, 316
Maccoby, Nathan, 81, 308, 309
MacCrone, Ian, 319
McGinniss, Joe, 49, 306
McGuire, William, 78–79, 308, 310
Machiavelli, Nichola, 104
McIntyre, J. J., 316
McKay, Joan T., 174
McKay, John T., 174
McNamara, Robert, 100
Magruder, Jeb Stuart, 14
Malenkov, G., 122

Mallick, Shabaz, 150, 314
Mann, Philip, 48, 306
Mao Tse-tung, 105–107
Marlowe, Christopher, 194–195
Mathewson, Grover, 119, 311
Mausner, Bernard, 304
Mees, Hayden, 305
Menninger, William, 155, 314, 315
Mettee, David, 128, 241, 311, 312, 324
Michener, James, 8, 122, 170, 303, 311, 317
Miles, Matthew, 325, 326
Milgram, Stanley, 33–35, 291–296, 304, 305, 326
Miller, Neal, 190, 319
Miller, Norman, 70, 307, 320
Mills, Judson, v, 62, 103, 109, 118–119, 133, 216, 271, 283, 285–286, 292, 307, 309, 310, 311, 322, 326
Moul, M., 318
Mouton, Jane, 304

Nader, Ralph, 82–83
Namath, Joe, 59, 62
Napolitano, Joe, 60, 299
Nel, Elizabeth, 111, 310, 312
Nicholls, John G., 178, 318
Nisbett, Richard, 126, 311
Nissen, Henry, 314
Nixon, Richard, 14, 49–50, 53, 93–94, 226
Nowlis, Vincent, 310

Occonner, John J., 306
Olmstead, Joseph, 307
Oppenheimer, J. Robert, 56–57, 299
Ostrove, Nancy, 229, 323

Pallak, Michael, 137, 313
Papageorgis, Dimitri, 78, 308
Pearson, Karl, 181, 318
Pettigrew, Thomas, 193–194, 201, 210–211, 319, 320, 321
Piliavin, Irving, 40, 306, 312
Piliavin, Jane, 136, 306, 312
Pittman, Thane, 137, 313
Porter, Herbert, 14
Poussaint, Alvin, 173, 317
Prasad, Jamuna, 87–88, 121, 308
Pulitzer, Joseph, 207–209

Radler, D. H., 321
Reed, Thomas, 322

Remmers, H. H., 321
Rice, Grantland, 153
Rodin, Judith, 37, 305, 306
Rogers, Carl, 270–271, 325
Roosevelt, Franklin Delano, 133
Rosenberg, Milton, 134, 312
Rosenfield, David, 321
Ross, Dorothea, 314, 316
Ross, Sheila, 314, 316
Rottman, Leon, 321, 323
Rousseau, Jean-Jacques, 144, 313
Rubin, Irwin, 273, 325
Ruhnke, Ronald, 312
Russell, Bill, 59

Sanford, R. Nevitt, 319
Schachter, Stanley, 13, 24–25, 86–87, 304, 305
Schmidt, Grace, vi
Schneider, Frank W., 305
Schönbach, Peter, 309
Scott, John Paul, 146, 313
Sears, David, 78, 308
Sears, Pauline, 310
Sears, Robert, 189, 310, 316, 319
Seashore, Charles, 276, 326
Secord, Paul, 323
Semonov, Pavel, 281
Shakespeare, William, 194–195, 197
Shipiro, Jerrold, 325
Shaw, George Bernard, 126, 311
Sheatsley, Paul, 319
Sheffield, Frederick, 307
Sherif, Carolyn, 319, 320, 321
Sherif, Muzafer, 72, 75, 188, 204, 215, 319, 320, 321
Sigall, Harold, 228–229, 231, 323, 326
Sikes, Jev, v, 321, 322
Simmons, Carolyn, 222, 322
Singer, Jerry, 86–87, 305
Sinha, Durganand, 88, 121, 308
Slater, Philip, 322
Snapp, Matthew, 321, 322
Solomon, Leonard, 322
Solomon, Richard, 321
Speer, Albert, 14, 304, 319
Spinoza, Benedictus de; 241, 324
Spitz, Mark, 59
Stalin, Joseph, 122
Star, Shirley, 320
Stephan, Cookie, 321, 322

Stephan, Walter, 320, 321
Stevenson, Harold, 324
Storr, Anthony, 145, 313
Stouffer, Samuel, 320
Suchman, Edward 320
Sumner, William Graham, 196

Tart, Charles, 325
Taylor, Shelley E., 324
Teevan, J. J., 316
Thomas, Edward, 315
Thurber, James, 11–12, 22, 304
Triplett, N., x
Tumin, Melvin, 317
Turner, Judith, 74, 307

Valiquet, I.M., 325
VanHoose, Thomas, 326

Walder, Leopold, 316
Walkley, Rosabelle, 320
Wallace, George, 107
Walster, Elaine, 60–61, 227, 232, 307, 311, 321, 323
Walters Richard, 315
Warren, Earl, 196
Washburn, Sherwood, 151, 314
Watson, Jeanne, 194, 319
Weatherley, Donald, 190, 319
Weiss, Walter, 56–57, 306
White, B. Jack, 319, 320, 321
White, Ralph, 99, 311
Whiting, John, 310
Wiesel, Elie, 309
Wiggins, Nancy H., 324
Wilde, Oscar, 162
Wilkins, Edward J., 315
Willerman, Ben, 224, 323
Williams, Robin, Jr., 320
Wilner, Daniel, 320
Winch, Robert, 234, 324
Winder, Alvin, 320
Wizan, Joe, 162
Wood, Larraine, 158, 315

Yalom, Irvin, 326

Zajonc, Robert, 52, 306
Zanna, Mark, 305, 312
Zimbardo, Philip, 9, 53, 72, 130–131, 303, 306, 307, 311

Subject Index

Aggression, 141–171
  catharsis in, 154–162
  cognitive dissonance and, 113–117,
    164–166
  and conformity, 169–170
  definition of, 142–144
  displaced, 186–191
  fantasy in, 155–156
  frustration and, 147–149, 165
  "hydraulic" theory of, 144–145
  instinct and, 144–147
  instrumental, 143–144
  in the mass media, 159–162
  model effects on, 159–160, 167–168,
    169–170
  motives for, 151–163
  punishment and, 164–169
  reduction of, 163–171
  social learning and, 149–151
  territorial behavior and, 146

Attitude
  vs. opinion, 82–83
  See also Persuasion
Attitude change. *See* Persuasion
Attraction, 213–245
  and attribution, 218–220, 231–232
  cognitive dissonance and, 113–117,
    221–222
  complementarity and, 234–236
  consensual validation and, 231
  cooperation and, 203–210, 215–216
  "gain–loss" theory of, 236–245
  ingratiation and, 218–221
  insecurity and, 232–233
  liking as a cause of, 232–236
  personal attributes and, 222–230
    and blunders and competence,
      223–226
    and physical attractiveness, 226–230
  praise and favors and, 217–222

proximity and, 216
reward theory of, 215–222
and self-esteem, 232–233
similarity and, 233–234
Attractiveness
and attraction, 226–230
of a communicator, 61–62
and identification, 30
and the self-concept, 229–230
Attribution
in aggression, 149–150
in attraction, 217–220, 230
in prejudice, 125–126, 174–181
and sex roles, 178
and stereotyping, 176–181
theory of, 177–178
Authentic relationship, 244–245, 257–264
Authoritarian personality, 191–193

Beauty. *See* Attractiveness
Behavior modification, 32
Brainwashing, 79
Bystander intervention, 36–42

Catharsis
and aggression, 154–162
and public policy, 159–162
Cognitive dissonance, 85–139
and aggression, 113–117, 164–166
alternative modes of reduction, 120
application in education, 111–113
and attitude change, 103–111
and attraction, 113–117, 221–222
and counterattitudinal advocacy,
    106–111
critique of, 131–139
and cruelty, 120–126
decision-making and, 96–103
and distortion, 92–94
effort and, 117–120, 271, 283
and escalation, 99–101
historical examples of, 98–101, 121–126
and immoral behavior, 101–104
inevitability and, 126–127, 128–129
and intrinsic motivation, 112–113
physiological and motivational effects of,
    129–131
and rational behavior, 94–96
and rumor transmission, 87–88
and self-attribution, 135–138

and the self-concept, 110–111, 123–124,
    127–129, 138–139
theory of, defined, 88, 131–139
Commitment, 89–94, 129–131
Communication, 45–83
and distraction, 81–82
logical vs. emotional appeals, 63–67
the nature of, 63–76
overheard, 61
and selective exposure to information, 80,
    89
in the sensitivity-training group,
    247–279
source of, 55–62
See also Persuasion
Competence
and attraction, 223–226
of sensitivity-group trainers, 276
Competition, 153–154
and prejudice, 186–189, 203–210
Compliance, 26–27
distinguished from identification and
    internalization, 26–32
forced, 105–109
motives for, 26–27
and persuasion, 106–109
power and, 30
Conflict about decisions, 96–104
Conformity, 11–43
and aggression, 169–170
adaptive and maladaptive forms of, 13–15
definition of, 15
examples of, 1–2, 11
factors influencing, 19–22
group pressure and, 16–19
and individualism, 12–14
and liking, 13
motives for, 18–19, 22
and prejudice, 193–196
social status, 20–21
types of, 26
Consensual validation and attraction, 231
Cooperation
and attraction, 203–210, 215–216
and the reduction of aggression, 168–169
and the reduction of prejudice, 203–210
survival value of, 152–153
Counterattitudinal advocacy, 106–111
Credibility, 22–24
of communicator, 55–61

Credibility (*continued*)
  and internalization, 30–31
Cruelty and cognitive dissonance, 120–126

Debriefing in sociopsychological research,
    296–299
Deception in sociopsychological research,
    292–299
Decision-making and cognitive dissonance,
    96–103
Dehumanization, 9, 124–126, 170–171,
    173–174
Dependent variable, definition of, 284
Deprivation
  vs. frustration, 148–149
  relative, 149
Desegregation, 199–202
Deviance, 13, 21–22
Dissonance. *See* Cognitive dissonance
Distortion
  cognitive dissonance and, 92–94
  prejudice and, 178–181

Education
  and cognitive dissonance, 111–113
  and propaganda, 53–55
Effort and cognitive dissonance, 117–120,
    271, 283
Empathy
  in bystander intervention, 41–42
  and the reduction of aggression, 170–171
  in the sensitivity-training group, 270,
    273–274, 278–279
Encounter group. *See* Sensitivity-training
    group
Ethics in experimentation, 42–43, 111,
    271–272, 292–301
Experiential learning in the sensitivity-
    training group, 251–252
Experimental control, 283–289
  vs. impact, 290–292
Experimental realism, 291–292
Experimentation
  and causal inference, 286–289
  debriefing in, 296–299
  deception in, 292–299
  ethical problems with, 42–43, 111,
    271–272, 292–301
  in the sensitivity-training group,
    271–274
  in social psychology, 281–301

Expertise of communicator, 55–61

Fantasy in aggression, 155–156
Favors and attraction, 217–222
Fear arousal
  and persuasion, 64–67
  and self-justification, 87–88
Feedback in the sensitivity-training group,
    257–264
Feelings
  vs. evaluations, 258–263
  and intentions, 264
Frustration
  and aggression, 147–149, 163–165
  vs. deprivation, 148–149
  and prejudice, 189–191

"Gain–loss" theory of interpersonal attrac-
    tion, 236–245

"Hydraulic" theory of aggression, 144–145

Identification, 27
  attractiveness and, 30
  and persuasion, 62
  and prejudice, 192
Immoral behavior, cognitive dissonance
    and, 101–104, 128–129
Independent variable, definition of,
    283–284
Inevitability, 126–127, 199–202
Ingratiation, 218–221
Inoculation, 78–79
Insecurity
  and attraction, 232–233
  and authoritarianism, 191–192
  and conformity to the group, 20–21
Interdependence, 203–210
  See also Cooperation
Internalization, 27–28
  credibility and, 30–31
Irrevocability in decision-making, 101

Justification
  of effort, 117–120
  external vs. internal, 104–109
  inadequate, 104–117, 129–131
  See also Self-justification

Leadership role in the sensitivity-training
    group, 265–267, 276–277

Liking
   of communicator, 61–62
   See also Attraction

Male chauvinism as a form of prejudice,
   181–184
Mass media
   aggression in, 159–162
   persuasion and, 45–53

Nonconformity, 12–14
   See also Conformity, Deviance
Non-conscious ideology, 182

Obedience,
   as a form of compliance, 32–36
   insecurity and, 191–192
Openness in the sensitivity-training group,
   255–257, 268–269
Opinion vs. attitude, 82–83
Opinion change. *See* Persuasion
Order of presentation of arguments, 68–71

Persuasion, 45–83
   attractiveness of the communicator and,
      61–62
   audience characteristics and, 68, 77–79,
      181–182
   cognitive dissonance and, 103–111
   distraction and, 81
   fear and, 64–67
   forewarning and, 77–78
   immunization against, 78–79
   logical vs. emotional appeals and, 63–67
   one-sided vs. two-sided arguments and,
      67–68
   order of presentation of arguments
      and, 68–71
   overheard communication and, 61
   and propaganda, 45–55
   self-esteem and, 65–67, 77
   size of the discrepancy and, 71–76
Power of the influencing agent, 30
Praise and attraction, 217–222
Prejudice, 173–211
   and attribution, 174–181
   causes of, 184–196
      cognitive dissonance, 184, 197,
         199–203
      conformity, 193–196

economic and political competition,
      186–189
   frustration and displaced aggression,
      189–191
   personality, 191–193
   self-justification, 184–185
   socialization, 192–196
   social status, 184–189
definition of, 174–181
and distortion, 178–181
male chauvinism as a form of, 181–184
non-conscious ideology and, 182
reduction of, 196–211
   by equal-status contact, 198–199
   by information campaigns, 196–197
   by mutual interdependence, 203–210
   by vicarious effects of desegregation,
      199–202
toward foods, 179
and self-esteem, 173–174, 202–203
"well-deserved reputation" phenomenon
      and, 180
Primacy effect in persuasion, 68–71
Propaganda, 45–55
   in advertising, 50–53
   in education, 53–55
   in the mass media, 45–53
   in news reports, 46–48
   in presidential campaigns, 48–50
   See also Persuasion
Proximity and attraction, 216
Punishment
   and authoritarianism, 192
   as frustration, 164–165
   insufficient, 113–117
   as a means of reducing aggression,
      164–169

Random assignment in experimentation,
      286–289
Recency effect in persuasion, 68–71
Reward. *See* Justification
Reward theory of attraction, 215–222
Rumors, 87–88

"Scapegoating," 189–191
Scientific method, 72–76, 281–301.
Selective exposure, 80–81, 89–91
   See also Distortion
Self-concept
   attractiveness and, 229–230

Self-concept, (*continued*)
  See also Self-esteem
Self-esteem
  and attraction, 232–233
  and cognitive dissonance, 110–111,
    123–124, 127–129, 138–139
  and conformity, 20–21
  and persuasion, 65–67, 77
  prejudice and, 173–174, 202–203
Self-fulfilling prophecy, 126, 152–153,
  229–230
Self-justification, 85–139
  fear and, 87–88
  prejudice and, 184–185
  See also Cognitive dissonance
Sensitivity-training group, 247–279
  application of, 268–269
  attribution in, 254–255
  characteristics of effective feedback in,
    257–264
  dangers of, 256–257, 275–278
  definition of, 249–253
  emphasis on here and now in, 255–256
  experiential learning in, 251–252
  goals of, 250–251
  openness vs. privacy in, 255–257
  research on, 269–274
  role of group leader in, 265–267,
    276–277
  types of, 277–278
Sexism, 174, 178, 181–184, 195–196
Similarity
  and attraction, 233–234
  vs. complementarity, 234–236

Social comparison
  and emotion, 24–26
  examples of, 22–24
  social reality, 22–24
Social influence
  examples of, 1–4
  See also Compliance, Identification, In-
    ternalization
Social learning and aggression, 149–151
  See also Behavior modification
Social psychology as a science, 7–8,
  281–301
  definition of, 4–6
Social status
  and conformity, 20–21
  and prejudice, 184–189
Socialization in authoritarianism and prejudice, role of, 192–196
Stereotype, 174–181, 186–188, 194–195,
  198, 230
  and attribution, 176–181

Territorial behavior, 146
T-group. *See* Sensitivity-training group
Trustworthiness of communicator, 55–61
  See also Credibility

Violence
  factors in the reduction of, 163–171
  See also Aggression

Watergate affair
  as conformity, 14–15
  and dissonance reduction, 94